AI, Blockchain, and Emerging Technologies for Sustainable Supply Chains

Atour Taghipour
https://orcid.org/0000-0003-1687-8881
Conservatoire National des Arts et Métier, France

IGI Global
Scientific Publishing
Publishing Tomorrow's Research Today

Vice President of Editorial	Melissa Wagner
Director of Acquisitions	Mikaela Felty
Director of Book Development	Jocelynn Hessler
Production Manager	Mike Brehm
Cover Design	Jose Rosado

Published in the United States of America by
IGI Global Scientific Publishing
701 East Chocolate Avenue
Hershey, PA, 17033, USA
Tel: 717-533-8845 | Fax: 717-533-7115
Website: https://www.igi-global.com E-mail: cust@igi-global.com

Library of Congress Cataloging-in-Publication Data

LCCN: 2026032952 (CIP Data Pending)
ISBN13: 979-8-2600-3199-5
Isbn13Softcover: 979-8-2600-3200-8
EISBN13: 979-8-2600-3201-5
British Cataloguing in Publication Data
A Cataloguing in Publication record for this book is available from the British Library.

Table of Contents

Detailed Table of Contents

Supply chains are the hidden architecture of modern life, connecting resources, products, and people across the globe. These systems are now being transformed through digitalization—artificial intelligence, predictive analytics, IoT sensors, and blockchain are reshaping how materials and information move. This shift occurs amid climate emergency, social inequality, and economic uncertainty. Rather than viewing digital tools only as efficiency enhancers, this work argues they can make supply chains more humane, low-carbon, and economically fair. It traces their evolution from manual logistics to AI-enabled ecosystems, examines how digitalization accelerates carbon-reduction, and explores ethical dilemmas of data-driven work. It concludes by envisioning Industry 5.0 supply chains, where technology serves both people and the planet.

Artificial intelligence (AI) is transforming global supply chains through real-time monitoring, predictive analytics, automation, and improved coordination across suppliers and distributors. These tools enhance efficiency, reduce costs, and increase transparency. Yet, AI also raises key ethical concerns, including data privacy, worker surveillance, algorithmic bias in supplier evaluation, risks of labor exploitation in opaque networks, and environmental sustainability issues. This paper builds on prior work on AI and ethical marketing and extends the analysis to ethical supply chain management. Using a qualitative documentary review grounded in logistics, operations management, and business ethics literature, it examines whether AI can support responsible supply chains. The study concludes that AI is not inherently ethical or unethical; its impact depends on governance, data quality, transparency mechanisms, and organizational commitment to responsible sourcing and human-rights-focused practices.

Digital literacy is increasingly recognized as a critical enabler of inclusive growth in rural India, where access to technology and digital tools remains uneven. This paper explores the current state of digital literacy in rural regions and analyzes the socio-economic implications of the rural-urban digital divide. The research identifies key barriers that hinder adoption of technology among marginalized communities. It emphasizes the transformative role of digital literacy in empowering rural populations by improving access to education, healthcare, financial services and employment opportunities. The findings underline that bridging the digital divide is not solely a technological challenge but a socio-economic imperative central to India's development goals. Digital literacy is a catalyst for empowerment and sustainable growth, to transform rural communities into active participants in India's digital economy. This paper advocates for inclusive, scalable and community-driven strategies to ensure equitable access and unlock the transformative power of digital technology for all.

In the contemporary globalised landscape, supply chains face intensifying pressures from unpredictable high-impact disruptions, creating an imperative for Supply Chain Resilience. While emerging Digital Technologies are essential enablers - strengthening core Dynamic Capabilities like visibility and flexibility - the path to resilience is fraught with inherent and competing strategic priorities, notably the resilience-efficiency and sustainability-resilience paradoxes. Guided by a multi-theoretical framework, this chapter examines how DTs enhance SCR through direct, mediating, and moderating pathways. It posits that these technologies transcend a merely tactical role, reconciling trade-offs and creating synergies between divergent goals. Ultimately, by enabling Supply Chain Transformative Capabilities, DTs catalyse a shift towards Transformative Supply Chains. This novel, holistic paradigm moves beyond siloed objectives to integrate efficiency, sustainability/circularity, and resilience simultaneously, providing a roadmap for firms to thrive within volatile competitive environments.

Preface

Digital transformation is fundamentally redefining the future of global supply chains. As organizations confront accelerating climate change, geopolitical uncertainty, resource constraints, evolving regulatory requirements, and rising stakeholder expectations, emerging technologies have become central to building supply chains that are not only more efficient but also more transparent, resilient, and sustainable. Artificial intelligence (AI), blockchain, the Internet of Things (IoT), big data analytics, digital twins, and other advanced technologies are reshaping how organizations design, monitor, and optimize supply chain networks while simultaneously addressing environmental, social, and economic objectives.

AI, Blockchain, and Emerging Technologies for Sustainable Supply Chains brings together a diverse collection of scholarly contributions that explore the transformative role of digital technologies in advancing sustainable supply chain management. The volume demonstrates that digitalization extends beyond operational automation and cost reduction; when supported by responsible governance and sound public policy, emerging technologies can strengthen climate action, enhance social accountability, improve transparency, increase resilience, and create long-term economic value.

The chapters adopt interdisciplinary perspectives spanning supply chain management, operations, information systems, business ethics, public policy, sustainability, industrial engineering, and digital innovation. Together, they examine both the opportunities and challenges associated with technology-enabled supply chains, emphasizing that successful digital transformation requires balancing technological capability with ethical responsibility, organizational readiness, institutional support, and human-centered innovation.

Several chapters investigate the application of AI, blockchain, big data analytics, and predictive technologies in improving supply chain visibility, traceability, decision-making, and resilience. Others explore the ethical implications of artificial intelligence, the importance of digital inclusion, comparative policy frameworks across developed and emerging economies, and the evolution of industrial paradigms from Industry 4.0 toward Industry 5.0 and beyond. Practical case studies further illustrate how digital technologies can support sustainable development across diverse sectors and regional contexts.

Collectively, this volume demonstrates that the future of sustainable supply chains depends not only on technological innovation but also on responsible governance, collaboration across stakeholders, and the development of resilient ecosystems capable of responding to increasingly complex global challenges.

CHAPTER OVERVIEW

1. Introduces the evolution of digitally enabled supply chains and presents an integrated perspective on how artificial intelligence, predictive analytics, IoT, and blockchain can simultaneously support climate action, social accountability, and economic value while advancing human-centered Industry 5.0 systems.
2. Examines the role of artificial intelligence in ethical supply chain management, exploring opportunities for improved transparency, coordination, and operational efficiency alongside challenges related to data privacy, algorithmic bias, worker surveillance, responsible sourcing, and organizational governance.
3. Explores the importance of digital literacy as a foundation for inclusive growth, highlighting how improved access to digital technologies can reduce socio-economic disparities, strengthen rural development, and expand participation in the digital economy.
4. Investigates how emerging digital technologies enable the transition from resilient supply chains to transformative supply chains by reconciling efficiency, sustainability, circularity, and resilience through enhanced visibility, flexibility, and dynamic organizational capabilities.
5. Presents a comparative analysis of AI-enabled and policy-driven sustainable supply chain strategies across emerging and developed economies, examining how technological innovation and regulatory frameworks jointly influence environmental, social, and economic performance.
6. Explores the combined application of blockchain, artificial intelligence, and big data analytics in developing sustainable and resilient supply chains, highlighting improvements in transparency, traceability, predictive intelligence, and decision support while addressing implementation and governance challenges.
7. Examines the adoption of blockchain, artificial intelligence, and big data technologies within an emerging economy context, emphasizing institutional readiness, digital maturity, public-private collaboration, workforce development, and sustainable supply chain transformation.
8. Analyzes how blockchain, AI, and big data contribute to sustainable supply chain management through enhanced traceability, ethical sourcing, predictive

analytics, resource optimization, environmental monitoring, and data-driven decision-making.

9. Reviews the conceptual evolution from Industry 4.0 to Industry 5.0, examining the shift toward human-centric, sustainable, and resilient industrial systems while discussing governance, workforce transformation, implementation challenges, and future research directions.
10. Explores the emerging concepts of Industry 6.0 and Supply Chain 6.0, demonstrating how the convergence of artificial intelligence and the Internet of Things enables autonomous, intelligent, resilient, and sustainable industrial and supply chain ecosystems while addressing cybersecurity, ethics, and workforce adaptation.
11. Examines sustainability within global sports supply chains, analyzing equipment manufacturing, event management, athlete logistics, and circular economy practices while demonstrating how digital technologies can support climate objectives, social responsibility, and long-term economic value throughout the sports industry.

The contributions assembled in this volume collectively demonstrate that artificial intelligence, blockchain, and emerging digital technologies are redefining the strategic foundations of sustainable supply chain management. Rather than serving solely as instruments of operational efficiency, these technologies have the potential to strengthen transparency, accountability, resilience, and sustainability across increasingly interconnected global value networks. At the same time, the chapters emphasize that technology alone cannot deliver sustainable outcomes; meaningful progress depends upon ethical governance, inclusive innovation, supportive policy frameworks, interdisciplinary collaboration, and continuous organizational learning.

It is hoped that this book will serve as a valuable resource for researchers, educators, graduate students, policymakers, and industry practitioners seeking to understand the evolving relationship between digital transformation and sustainable supply chain management. By bringing together conceptual developments, empirical research, and practical insights, the volume contributes to ongoing discussions on how emerging technologies can help build supply chains that are more intelligent, resilient, responsible, and capable of creating lasting value for business, society, and the environment.

Atour Taghipour

Conservatoire National des Arts et Métier, France

Chapter 1 Digitalized Supply Chains: Intersection of Climate Action, Social Accountability, and Economic Value

Atour Taghipour
http://orcid.org/0000-0003-1687-8881
Conservatoire National des Arts et Métiers, France

ABSTRACT

Supply chains are the hidden architecture of modern life, connecting resources, products, and people across the globe. These systems are now being transformed through digitalization—artificial intelligence, predictive analytics, IoT sensors, and blockchain are reshaping how materials and information move. This shift occurs amid climate emergency, social inequality, and economic uncertainty. Rather than viewing digital tools only as efficiency enhancers, this work argues they can make supply chains more humane, low-carbon, and economically fair. It traces their evolution from manual logistics to AI-enabled ecosystems, examines how digitalization accelerates carbon-reduction, and explores ethical dilemmas of data-driven work. It concludes by envisioning Industry 5.0 supply chains, where technology serves both people and the planet.

1. INTRODUCTION: THE NEW ERA OF SUPPLY CHAINS

Imagine a shipping container. Inside it could be mangoes from Peru, smartphones assembled in Shenzhen, or humanitarian aid destined for war-affected

DOI: 10.4018/979-8-2600-3199-5.ch001

zones (Mahfod et al., 2021). We tend to think of supply chains as lines on maps or trucks on highways, yet in reality, they are living systems, dynamic webs of people, machines, knowledge, and agreements that stretch across continents. They are the bloodstream of globalization.

For decades, supply chains evolved quietly. Efficiency, cost reduction, and speed were the dominant priorities. Executives spoke of *lean logistics*, *just-in-time*, *outsourcing (Glaa et al., 2014)*, and *global sourcing*. Digital technologies, though present, played a secondary role, barcodes and spreadsheets, later enterprise resource planning systems (ERPs) (Merimi & Taghipour, 2021; Taghipour et al., 2022a). Sustainability, whether environmental or social, was barely acknowledged beyond corporate philanthropy.

Then the world changed.

A shift in global context

Three forces have disrupted the old supply chain paradigm:

1.1 Climate crisis

Scientists warn that industrial activity, including logistics, manufacturing, agriculture, and transportation, contributes over 70% of global greenhouse-gas emissions. Supply chains are at the center of this footprint. Shipping, air freight, factories, packaging, and inventory management all consume energy and generate emissions. Suddenly, procurement decisions are not simply financial, they are existential. Whether a company ships goods by air or rail is not just a cost decision; it is a climate decision (Loivet et al., 2020).

1.2 Social inequality and ethical scrutiny

Information today travels faster than products. Consumers, with a swipe of a phone, demand transparency:

Was this product made with child labor?

Were garment workers paid a living wage?

Are delivery drivers treated fairly?

Social media amplifies injustice, forcing global brands to confront the human side of supply chains.

1.3 Economic fragility

Pandemics, geopolitical conflicts, inflation, and material shortages exposed a harsh truth: supply chains built solely for efficiency are fragile. In 2020, global shipping collapsed; chips for cars vanished; hospitals ran out of masks. Suddenly, *resilience* became a critical value, and digital visibility, data sharing, and predictive capabilities became survival tools (Ren et al., 2016).

Digitalization emerges as a response

Digital technology is not merely a convenience, it has become the oxygen of modern supply chains. Predictive analytics allows companies to anticipate shortages. Internet-of-Things devices track goods in real time. Blockchain ensures ethical sourcing (Lu et al., 2023; Taghipour, 2022). Artificial intelligence identifies optimal low-carbon transport routes. Drones deliver medical supplies to remote clinics. And digital twins simulate entire supply chains before decisions are made.

Digital tools offer something unprecedented:

→ the ability to see supply chains,
→ understand them,
→ measure them,
→ and shape them intentionally around climate, labor, and economic goals.

Without digitalization, sustainability remains aspiration. With it, sustainability becomes operational (Sahraoui et al., 2023; Goodarzian et al., 2024).

Why this chapter matters

While many publications explore digital transformation as a business strategy, few examine its humanitarian and ecological implications. The central question of this chapter is therefore:

How can digital supply chain transformation be leveraged to advance climate action, social justice, and economic well-being simultaneously?

This is more than a theoretical exercise. It is a moral and strategic imperative. Consider three real-world examples:

- When a fast-fashion brand uses AI to forecast demand precisely (Taghipour, 2020), millions of garments do not end up burned or in landfills, climate impact drops dramatically.
- When a mining corporation uses blockchain to track cobalt origin, child labor in the Democratic Republic of Congo can be exposed and eliminated, social justice advances.

- When a rural farmer uses a digital platform to sell crops directly, bypassing middlemen, their income may double, reducing poverty, economic equity improves.

  These are not merely outcomes of supply chain design, they are outcomes of data decisions.

A narrative approach

This chapter will move through history, policy, innovation, and human experience, demonstrating that digitalization is not an abstract trend but a deeply human evolution.

Redefining supply chain success

For much of the 20th century, a "successful supply chain" was one that minimized:

- cost
- time
- inventory

Today, success must look different. A successful supply chain in the digital age is one that:

- reduces emissions
- protects dignity and rights
- strengthens local economies
- responds quickly to shocks (Lebosse et al., 2017)
- and uses technology in ways that do not harm the people who depend on it

This is the heart of the digital-sustainability intersection.

2. LITERATURE REVIEW

2.1 Understanding Digitalization in Supply Chains: A Historical Evolution

Before understanding digitalization today, one must trace where supply chains began.

From Manual Logistics to Automated Networks

The earliest supply chains were local and analog: farmers traded goods in markets, craftsmen produced items using nearby materials, and transport was limited by physical distance. No data systems existed because visibility was not required; producers and consumers often knew each other.

Industrialization transformed everything. Steam engines, assembly lines, and railways enabled mass production and long-distance transportation (Zoghlami et al., 2016; XiaoWen & Atour, 2025). However, supply chains remained mostly manual, tracking was done on paper, mistakes were common, and scheduling depended on experience rather than data.

A major turning point arrived with computing (Table 1):

Table 1. Major turning points

Era	Milestone	Supply Chain Impact
1960s	Material Requirements Planning (MRP)	First software connecting inventory + scheduling
1980s	Enterprise Resource Planning (ERP)	Data consolidation across procurement, finance, logistics
1990s	Globalization & outsourcing	Complex, multi-country chains → demand for information
2000s	Internet-enabled logistics	E-commerce, global shipping visibility, RFID tagging
2010s–present	Industry 4.0 digitalization	AI, IoT, blockchain, robotics, analytics

ERP created information symmetry within companies (Crandall et al., 1995). But the modern world requires inter-organizational connectivity, where firms share data across borders, suppliers, ports, banks, customs, and customers.

Thus emerged the digital supply chain, a system where:

- information moves faster than products (Cauchois et al., 2017)
- decisions can be automated
- performance is monitored in real time
- sustainability is measurable

Industry 4.0, The First Digital Revolution

Industry 4.0 refers to the integration of automation, robotics, cyber-physical systems, and AI into manufacturing and logistics. It emphasizes efficiency and automation.

However, critics note that Industry 4.0 often neglects people. Automation sometimes replaces labor without providing new opportunities for re-skilling. Data systems may monitor workers invasively. Efficiency metrics can overshadow ethics.

Industry 5.0, The Human-Centered Digital Supply Chain

The European Commission introduced the concept of Industry 5.0, which aims to re-humanize technology (Taghipour et al., 2022b):

"Industry 5.0 means using technology *for people*, not against them, for society, not only for profit."

(EC White Paper, 2021)

This shift is critical for social accountability (Table 2):

Table 2. Shift in social accountability

Industry 4.0	Industry 5.0
Automation	Human–machine collaboration
Efficiency focus	Sustainability & wellbeing
Data-driven	Value-driven
Replace workers	Empower workers

Digital supply chains in this chapter lean toward Industry 5.0, where climate action, labor dignity, and equitable economics are equal priorities.

2.2 Sustainable Supply Chain Management: Theory Foundations

Sustainable Supply Chain Management (SSCM) integrates environmental, social, and economic objectives into the management of flows across the supply chain (Carter & Rogers, 2008; Lu & Taghipour, 2023). Three foundational models are necessary to understand this field.

1 The Triple Bottom Line (Elkington, 1997)

This classic framework argues that sustainability equals:

- Planet (environmental protection)
- People (social justice and human wellbeing)
- Profit (economic prosperity)

Digitalization becomes meaningful only if it advances *all three*.

2 Life Cycle Assessment (LCA)

LCA is a measurement model evaluating the environmental impact of a product from cradle to grave, from raw material extraction to disposal.

Digital tools now automate LCA, AI simulates emissions before production, IoT devices track carbon usage, and blockchain identifies whether recycled materials were truly used (Mathiyazhagan et al., 2022).

3 Circular Economy (CE)

Circular economy challenges linear "produce → use → waste" models and instead promotes:

- reuse
- repair
- remanufacturing
- recycling

Digitalization is essential for CE because data enables loops, without traceability, recycling is impossible.

2.3 Climate Action in Supply Chains: The Digital Enabler

Climate action frameworks (GHG Protocol, Paris Agreement, EU Carbon Border Adjustment Mechanism) increasingly require reporting and reduction of emissions, something impossible without digital data.

The GHG Protocol defines Scope 1, 2, and 3 emissions (Table 3):

Table 3. Scope 1, 2, and 3 emissions

Scope	Description	Digitalization Impact
Scope 1	Direct emissions (factories, trucks)	IoT sensors → fuel tracking, energy dashboards
Scope 2	Electricity purchased	Smart meters → renewable allocation
Scope 3	Supply-chain emissions (materials, shipping, disposal)	AI demand planning, blockchain traceability

→ Digitalization is not optional, it is the mechanism that makes climate reporting possible.

Example:

Maersk's AI-based routing reduced shipping CO_2 by 10% across trans-Atlantic routes (Maersk Report, 2022).

Amazon's digital warehouses reduced packaging material by 36% using algorithmic fit-to-size systems.

These are climate results that *could not exist* without data.

2.4 Social Accountability: The Invisible Dimension

Digitalization has disruptive potential for social justice:

Positive examples:

- Blockchain proving no child labor in cobalt mining
- Digital wage systems ensuring fair payment
- Apps enabling small farmers direct market access
- Worker safety sensors reducing accidents

Negative possibilities:

- Surveillance monitoring worker movement
- Algorithms assigning quotas that exceed human physical limits
- Automation eliminating jobs without reskilling

Thus, digitalization is not inherently good, it is a *tool*, and society decides how it is used.

Responsible Digital Transformation Framework

Socially responsible digitalization requires:

1 Worker participation: people help design systems
2 Transparency: employees know how data is used
3 Digital equity: training prevents job loss
4 Ethical AI: avoid algorithmic discrimination
5 Human oversight: machines should not decide alone

2.5 Economic Value: Rethinking Prosperity

Traditional supply-chain economics focus on:

- cost reduction
- scale
- market share
- return on assets

Digitalization can amplify these, but it can also redistribute economic value more fairly.

Examples:

- Digital farmer marketplace → farmer earns 3× more
- Direct-to-consumer models → small brands bypass giants
- On-demand manufacturing → eliminates waste & frees capital

Economic value must therefore be seen not as a number but as a distribution system.

2. LITERATURE REVIEW

2.6 Digital Technologies Driving Supply Chain Transformation

Digitalization is often spoken about as a single trend, but in practice it consists of multiple overlapping technological waves. To understand how climate action, social accountability, and economic value emerge, one must first clarify the specific tools reshaping supply chains.

Below, we examine the most influential technologies.

2.6.1 Artificial Intelligence (AI) and Predictive Analytics

Artificial intelligence enables supply chains to think, predict, and self-correct. Historically, supply chains reacted to disruption, storms, shortages, pandemics. Today, AI allows them to anticipate and prepare before events occur.

Key Applications (Table 4):

Table 4. Key Applications

AI Use Case	Sustainability Impact
Demand forecasting	Prevents overproduction → reduces waste & emissions
Predictive maintenance	Fewer equipment failures → lower energy use
Dynamic inventory optimization	Minimizes storage needs → reduces warehouse energy
AI route planning	Reduces fuel consumption & carbon footprint
Automated capacity planning	Prevents excessive labor pressure & overtime

Example:

Unilever reported a 10–20% forecast accuracy improvement using AI, enabling it to reduce surplus production and waste (Unilever, 2022).

Similarly, DHL uses AI to predict shipment delays and reroute cargo, lowering fuel usage and emissions.

Ethical Considerations

AI can become an instrument of social pressure when used to:

- track worker performance minute-by-minute
- algorithmically set quotas humans cannot meet
- replace jobs without transition plans

Thus, AI must be governed, not worshipped.

2.6.2 Internet of Things (IoT)

IoT refers to connected objects equipped with sensors, such as smart pallets, GPS-tagged cargo, and temperature-controlled medical containers.

IoT transforms supply chains by enabling:

- real-time visibility

- automated monitoring
- data-driven sustainability

Example:
Pfizer uses IoT sensors to track COVID-19 vaccine temperature across cold-chain logistics. Without IoT, billions of doses would have spoiled.

Climate Action Connection

IoT enables companies to measure:

- fuel used by trucks
- energy consumed in warehouses
- refrigerant leakage
- idle time emissions

What cannot be measured cannot be reduced,
IoT makes measurement possible.

Social Accountability Connection

IoT can also detect:

- unsafe working conditions (heat sensors in factories)
- accident-risk zones
- ergonomic stress patterns

→ helping protect workers rather than punish them.

2.6.3 Blockchain and Traceability Technologies

Blockchain is often misunderstood as only a cryptocurrency tool. In supply chains, its power lies in immutability and transparency.

Why Traceability Matters

Many of the world's worst labor and environmental abuses occur deep in supply networks, often invisible to brands and consumers.
Blockchain reveals:

- where raw materials come from
- who handled them
- whether labor was exploited
- whether material is recycled or virgin

Case Example - Cobalt Traceability

Companies producing electric-vehicle batteries (Tesla, Volkswagen) now use blockchain to verify whether cobalt is sourced from child-labor mines in the DRC. This turns ethics into a data function, not a PR statement.

Economic & Social Intersection

If a farmer can prove product origin digitally, they gain negotiating power, blockchain becomes an economic justice tool.

2.6.4 Digital Twins

Digital twins are virtual replicas of physical systems, allowing companies to test decisions before making them.

Example:

A warehouse can be simulated digitally, AI tests energy-saving layouts, robotic paths, worker safety zones, before any physical construction.

Digital twins allow:

- low-carbon design
- worker-safe design
- cost-optimized design

→ a convergence of climate, people, and profit.

2.6.5 Robotics and Autonomous Transport

Robots are increasingly used in:

- warehouses (picking, packing, loading)
- ports (automated cranes)
- retail replenishment
- drone-based deliveries

Autonomous trucks are being tested across Europe and North America to reduce labor shortages and fuel inefficiencies.

Sustainability Effects

Autonomous routes controlled by AI:

- eliminate unnecessary miles
- reduce fuel spikes
- operate electric fleets more efficiently

Social Impact

Automation creates fear, particularly job loss.

But research shows automation shifts labor rather than eliminates it — from physical roles to digital maintenance, programming, safety operations.

The danger is not technology, but failing to reskill society.

2.7 Sociotechnical View: Technology Alone is Not Enough

Digital transformation is often doomed when seen as purely technical.

A supply chain is a human system. Technology may optimize flows, but:

- culture determines whether workers accept change
- governance determines whether transparency translates into justice
- leadership determines whether technology serves profits or people

Scholars call this the sociotechnical model, which argues:

systems succeed only when technological capabilities and human needs evolve together.

This means digitalization must be accompanied by:

- change-management
- inclusive policy
- worker participation
- fair governance
- ethical algorithms
- regulation

Technology is a mirror, it reveals a company's values.

2.8 Digitalization and Power Dynamics

Technology shifts who has power in supply chains.
Historically:

- brands had power over suppliers
- transport carriers dictated costs
- wholesalers controlled distribution
- workers were voiceless

Digital tools change power relationships (Table 5):

Table 5. Digital tools change power relationships

Stakeholder	New Digital Power
Consumers	scan QR-codes → demand ethical sourcing
Workers	digital reporting → expose unsafe conditions
Farmers	platforms → sell directly
Small suppliers	access global markets
Governments	ESG data → regulate & penalize

Thus, digitalization can democratize, *or* centralize, power.
Which outcome occurs depends on policy, design, and ethics.

2.9 Why Digitalization Fails: A Literature Insight

Not all digitalization succeeds. Failures often arise because organizations:

- adopt technology without strategy
- ignore worker concerns
- focus only on cost savings
- fail to integrate sustainability into objectives
- use digital tools to increase pressure, not improve outcomes

Research shows 70% of digital projects fail to achieve expected ROI (McKinsey, 2021).
Successful digital sustainability requires:

- intentionality

- governance
- inclusivity
- cross-stakeholder design
- training
- long-term mindset

3. THEORETICAL AND ANALYTICAL FRAMEWORK

To understand how digitalization intersects with climate action, social accountability, and economic value, this chapter proposes a new integrative framework:

The Digital–Sustainability Value Chain Model (DSVC).

This model builds on supply-chain theory (SSCM), digital transformation research, and sociotechnical principles, then expands them through three analytical dimensions:

1 Climate (Planet)

2 Social (People)

3 Economic (Prosperity)

Digitalization becomes the enabler connecting the three, turning sustainability from a philosophy into an *operational practice*.

3.1 Defining the Digital–Sustainability Value Chain (DSVC)

The DSVC conceptualizes each supply-chain stage as having:

- a physical layer (materials, labor, transport, production)
- a data layer (tracking, forecasting, monitoring)
- a values layer (purpose, justice, wellbeing, equity)

  Only when all three layers operate together do supply chains become sustainable.

The DSVC Model – Simplified Diagram

Raw Materials → Production → Warehousing → Distribution → Retail/Use → End-of-Life

| | | | | |

Digitally Traced IoT-Monitored AI-Planned Optimized Consumer Circular

Material Flows Ethical Ops Energy Use Routing Transparency Loops

| | | | | |

ESG-Measured Worker-Safe Green-Energy Fair Labor Poverty Recycling and Carbon Algorithms Transitions Practices Reduction Jobs

Each node generates three outcomes (Table 6):

Table 6. Outcomes

Node Output	Planet Outcome	People Outcome	Prosperity Outcome
Digital traceability	lower carbon / cleaner materials	ethical sourcing	fairer market access
Predictive AI planning	reduced waste & energy	safer labor schedules	economic efficiency
Blockchain wage systems	lower exploitation	labor dignity	stable labor markets
IoT warehousing	zero-energy buildings	fewer accidents	lower capital loss

Thus, digitalization is not separate from sustainability. It *is the mechanism* that makes sustainability governable.

3.2 Human-Centered Digitalization: Industry 5.0 as Framework

Industry 4.0 focused on machines.

Industry 5.0, as articulated by the European Commission (2021), returns focus to humans, wellbeing, and resilience.

Industry 5.0 Principles in DSVC (Table 7):

Table 7. Industry 5.0 Principles in DSVC

Principle	Application in Supply Chains
Human-machine collaboration	robots do heavy tasks; humans do creative & relational tasks
Purpose-driven metrics	success measured in carbon, dignity, resilience — not cost only
Inclusive design	digital systems shaped with workers, not forced onto them
Societal value	supply chains exist to *serve communities*, not only shareholders

Digitalization must therefore be participatory, not imposed.

Example:

A warehouse introducing robots should include workers in layout design, giving them agency, ownership, and safety.

Without this, digitalization becomes a new form of industrial exploitation.

3.3 Digital Circularity: Closing Loops with Data

Circular economy is often discussed philosophically, but practically, it is impossible without digital data.

To recycle or repair, one must know:

- where products are
- how they were made
- what materials they contain
- who owns them
- when they break

Digitalization answers these questions.

Circularity Enablers (Table 8):

Table 8. Circularity enablers

Digital Tool	Circular Function
QR-coded materials passports	reveal component lists → recyclability
RFID tracking	monitor usage → repair before failure
AI failure prediction	reduce waste → extend product life
Consumer platforms	resale, rental, sharing economy
Blockchain	verifiable recycled content

This transforms supply chains from linear extract-consume-dump into:

Extract → Produce → Use → Collect → Refurbish → Reuse → Recycle → Reenter supply chain

Circular loops create:

- climate benefit (reduced mining emissions)
- social benefit (repair-sector jobs)
- economic benefit (new revenue streams)

3.4 ESG Integration: Digital Tools as Compliance Mechanisms

Environmental, Social, and Governance (ESG) frameworks are rapidly becoming mandatory, not optional.

Governments now require:

- carbon disclosure
- due-diligence on labor conditions
- plastic accounting
- circular-economy targets
- living-wage certification

Digitalization is what enables enforcement.

Example: EU Digital Product Passport (2027)

All EU products will soon need a digital identity, recording:

- material composition
- carbon footprint
- repair history
- end-of-life instructions

This means sustainability becomes coded, it is written into data systems, audited, and validated.

ESG + DSVC Combined

Data = proof
Proof = accountability
Accountability = justice
Justice = sustainability

Sustainability without *measurement* is only marketing.

3.5 Stakeholder Analytical Lens: Multi-Actor Theory

Supply chains involve multiple actors whose priorities conflict (Table 9):

Table 9. Multiple actors' conflicts

Actor	Wants
Workers	fair wages, safety, dignity
Consumers	cheap prices, fast delivery
Executives	profit, efficiency

continued on following page

Table 9. Continued

Actor	Wants
Governments	tax revenue, stability
Planet (represented by NGOs)	carbon reduction, biodiversity

Digitalization adds a new actor:

Algorithms

Algorithms decide:

- who gets scheduled
- how much workers lift
- what route trucks drive
- what supplier is cheapest

Thus, algorithms become agents of power, influencing social justice. This chapter therefore adopts a multi-actor analytical approach:

> Technology must not replace ethics.
> Power must not escape responsibility.
> Algorithms must be governed to protect people.

3.6 Digital Resilience Model: Shock-Ready Supply Chains

Digital resilience is a supply chain's ability to withstand disruption, through:

- real-time visibility
- predictive forecasting
- diversified sourcing
- automated contingency planning
- simulation (digital twins)

A resilient supply chain:

- reduces panic buying → lower waste
- avoids sudden mass layoffs → protects workers
- ensures continuity of goods → protects economies
- prevents emergency air freight → reduces carbon

Thus, resilience is a sustainability value.

4. DIGITAL TECHNOLOGIES AND CLIMATE ACTION

Climate change has turned supply chains into one of the world's most critical battlegrounds. Up to 70% of global industrial emissions are linked to supply-chain processes, mining, production, transport, warehousing, distribution, and disposal (IPCC, 2022). Digitalization represents humanity's most powerful tool to *measure*, *manage*, and *mitigate* this impact.

This section explores how AI, IoT, blockchain, digital twins, and automation enable low-carbon transformation.

4.1 Why Supply Chains Are Central to Climate Change

Traditional sustainability efforts focused on recycling, packaging, or reducing office electricity. But these concepts ignore the structural heart of emissions: upstream and downstream supply networks.

Emissions Breakdown (Typical Global Manufacturer) (Table 10):

Table 10. Emissions breakdown

Phase	Approx. CO_2 Contribution
Raw-material extraction	30–40%
Manufacturing energy	20–30%
Transport & logistics	15–25%
Warehousing	5–15%
End-of-life waste	10–15%

Most emissions occur outside a company's direct control, known as Scope 3, involving suppliers and consumers (Taghipour et al., 2022c).

This makes digitalization crucial: no company can reduce emissions it cannot see.

4.2 AI-Powered Emissions Reduction

Artificial intelligence transforms emissions reduction from guesswork to predictive science.

AI does so by:

- forecasting demand → preventing waste
- optimizing routes → minimizing fuel
- simulating energy use → reducing electricity consumption
- recommending suppliers → based on carbon metrics (Mbiatem et al., 2018)

Example: AI Demand Planning Reduces Waste

Fast-fashion brands historically overproduced by up to 40%. Excess textiles burned or landfilled, causing massive ecological harm.

Today, AI forecasting uses:

- search trends
- social-media signals
- sales histories
- weather data
- geographic demand clusters

to produce only what will be sold.

→ climate benefit: less textile waste, fewer transport miles
→ economic benefit: reduced inventory cost
→ social benefit: fewer factory overtime surges

Example: AI Route Optimization

AI rerouting can reduce fuel use by 10–20%, especially for fleets with thousands of vehicles.

Maersk AI routing shaved 1.5 tons of fuel per container ship per day, equaling thousands of tons of CO_2 annually.

4.3 IoT & Real-Time Carbon Tracking

IoT sensors collect live energy and material-use data.

Imagine:

- a warehouse that turns off lights in unused aisles
- a refrigerated truck that adjusts temperature based on product type
- factory equipment that alerts when energy peaks exceed limits

This is no longer hypothetical, it exists.

IoT-Enabled Decarbonization

IoT devices monitor (Table 11):

Table 11. IoT devices functions

Sustainability Factor	Measured By
electricity consumption	smart-meters
diesel usage	fleet sensors
cold chain temperature	thermosensors
idle truck time	GPS + accelerometers
carbon intensity of suppliers	API-data integrations

When data becomes continuous, sustainability becomes behavioral, not episodic.

4.4 Digital Twins: Designing Carbon Before Building It

Digital twins allow decision-makers to see the future.
Example:
A distribution center can be modeled digitally, where AI tests:

- warehouse layout
- forklift routes
- insulation and cooling systems
- sunlight exposure
- rooftop solar potential

Before a single brick is laid, digital twins can predict total lifetime carbon output.

This flips sustainability upside-down, instead of fixing emissions after mistakes, we avoid the emissions entirely.

4.5 Green Routing and Low-Carbon Logistics

Transport is a major emitter, especially air freight.
Digital routing systems consider:

- weather
- congestion
- fuel burn patterns

- elevation
- electric-charging availability
- multimodal combinations

Instead of fastest or cheapest routes, systems now optimize climate-friendly routes.

Example:

An order from France to Germany may choose train → electric van → bicycle last-mile.

Digitalization makes this automatic, not manual.

4.6 Autonomous & Electrified Logistics

Electric vehicles (EV), autonomous trucks, and drone delivery are not just futuristic, they are carbon-reduction levers.

- Autonomous trucks → steady speed → lower fuel
- Route platooning → aerodynamic savings
- Electric vans → zero-emissions local delivery

Example:

Amazon's Rivian electric vans prevent nearly 5 million tons of CO_2 over expected deployment life.

Drone delivery, used in Rwanda and Ghana for vaccines, not only saves lives, but also:

- replaces diesel motorcycles
- reduces energy consumption per unit delivered by up to 60%

This shows sustainability and humanitarian goals can align.

4.7 Digital Procurement: Choosing Suppliers by Carbon

Procurement decisions historically asked:

- Which supplier is cheapest?
- Which delivers fastest?

Digital ESG procurement adds:

- Which supplier has lower carbon footprint?
- Which pays fair wages?

- Which uses renewable energy?

Software introduces carbon-scoring dashboards, turning sustainability into a competitive advantage.

Supplier scorecards create *behavioral pressure*, companies with dirty energy lose bids (Mahfod et al., 2019).

Thus, emissions reduction becomes market-driven, not only policy-enforced.

4.8 The Climate Paradox: Digitalization Has a Footprint Too

Digital systems consume energy:

- data centers
- cloud computing
- blockchain mining
- IoT battery production

A sustainable digital strategy must ask:
"Does the carbon saved exceed the carbon spent?"
Solutions include:

- renewable-powered data centers
- low-energy blockchain
- AI-efficiency modes
- server heat-reuse for community heating

Digitalization must support decarbonization, not shift emissions elsewhere.

4.9 Digital Carbon Governance: Policy Layer

Governments increasingly legislate digital tracking to meet climate goals.
Examples (Table 12):

Table 12. Examples of policy

Region	Policy
EU	Digital Product Passports (2027)
US	SEC climate-risk disclosure
UK	Carbon Border Adjustment Mechanism
Japan	Green Innovation Fund & IoT incentives

Policy will soon make digital carbon accounting mandatory, not voluntary. Companies that are not digitalized will be locked out of markets.

4.10 Why Digital Climate Solutions Fail, and How to Avoid Failure

Failure happens when organizations:

- view climate action as charity
- lack executive alignment
- deploy technology without training
- measure data but do not act on it
- punish workers through efficiency metrics

Success requires:

- leadership commitment
- purpose-driven KPIs
- collaborative design
- integration with human values

Digitalization is not a climate solution by itself, it is a *tool*, climate solutions come from choices.

5. DIGITALIZATION AND SOCIAL RESPONSIBILITY

Climate action has become the most visible motivation for digital supply chains — but it is not the only one. The social dimension of sustainability is often more complex, more emotional, and more ethically urgent. Behind every warehouse, production line, or container ship are workers whose bodies, time, and dignity sustain global consumption.

Digitalization can either liberate these workers, or constrain them further.

This section explores that duality.

5.1 A Human Lens: Supply Chains Are Social Systems

It is easy to imagine supply chains as boxes, trucks, and charts, but in reality, the backbone of every supply chain is:

- warehouse pickers lifting thousands of kilograms daily
- delivery drivers navigating dangerous routes
- factory workers sewing clothes for long hours
- smallholder farmers harvesting crops by hand

Digitalization introduces data, automation, and algorithms into this human ecosystem, raising a central question:

Will technology protect people, or will it exploit them?

5.2 Digitalization as a Tool of Social Justice

When intentionally designed, digital systems empower people by making invisible labor conditions visible.

Examples of Socially Positive Digitalization (Table 13) :

Table 13. Examples of Socially Positive Digitalization

Digital Tool	Positive Social Impact
Blockchain traceability	exposes unethical suppliers → supports fair labor
Digital wage systems	reduces wage theft; records overtime fairly
Wearable safety sensors	alerts when heat or motion exceeds safety limits
Worker reporting apps	allow anonymous complaints without retaliation
Online training platforms	give workers access to education and reskilling

These tools shift power from corporations toward workers and communities.

Smallholder Farmer Platforms

Digital marketplaces allow farmers in Kenya or Bangladesh to sell directly to restaurants or distributors, escaping exploitative intermediaries.

→ Social benefit: income may double
→ Economic benefit: price transparency
→ Climate benefit: shorter supply chains reduce transport emissions

Thus, the intersection becomes visible.

5.3 The Dark Side: Digitalization as Surveillance

Not all digitalization is benevolent.

Some corporations use digital tools to:

- track bathroom breaks
- monitor keystrokes
- require wrist scanners dictating walking paths
- assign quotas with no human oversight
- automatically fire workers without managerial review

This is algorithmic control, where machines, not ethics, govern labor.

Why Ethical Risks Exist

Digitalization creates data asymmetry:

- companies collect data
- workers do not know what is collected
- algorithms assign penalties without transparency

Without ethical safeguards, digital supply chains risk becoming the most powerful labor-control system in history.

5.4 Automation: Displacement or Transformation?

Automation is often feared because it threatens jobs, particularly:

- warehouse sorting
- packaging
- manufacturing assembly
- cashiering
- transportation

But research shows job loss is not inevitable, what happens depends on policy and corporate design.

Two Possible Futures

Future A – Automation replaces workers → unemployment → social instability
Future B – Automation absorbs heavy labor → workers retrain → safer jobs
Policy and leadership determine which becomes reality.

Human-Centered Automation

Industry 5.0 advocates:

- robots doing physically dangerous or exhausting tasks
- humans doing cognitive, social, creative, decision-making roles
- co-design: workers participate in determining automation workflows

Example:

A factory installs robot arms that lift heavy steel components. Instead of layoffs, management trains former lifters to operate and maintain the robots, raising average wages and reducing injuries.

Digitalization therefore becomes a social-mobility engine.

5.5 Algorithmic Management: The New Boss

Algorithmic management refers to workers being directed by software instead of supervisors.

Operations such as:

- tasks assigned via apps
- quotas calculated automatically
- breaks timed by software
- performance warnings auto-generated
- contracts ended via algorithm

This is common in gig-economy platforms (delivery apps, ride-hailing), but is now expanding to warehouses and factories.

Risks for Social Accountability

Algorithmic systems may:

- enforce quotas exceeding human physical capability
- ignore health conditions
- discriminate (e.g., penalize slower individuals unfairly)
- create psychological stress

Because algorithms do not feel empathy, there must always be human governance.

5.6 Digital Inclusion: Who Gets to Participate?

Social sustainability includes who gets left out of digital transformation.
Exclusion risks include:

- older workers unfamiliar with technology
- workers in low-income countries without internet access
- individuals with disabilities
- language barriers

Digital-equity strategies must include:

- multilingual digital tools
- accessible design
- subsidized connectivity
- workplace-paid training
- digital-literacy coaching

Otherwise, digitalization becomes another barrier.

5.7 Reskilling: The Social Oxygen of Digital Transformation

Technology transforms roles. But transformation succeeds only if people are supported to evolve.

Effective digital reskilling programs include:

- training BEFORE automation deployment
- paid time for learning
- certification pathways
- worker-led mentoring

Without reskilling, digitalization becomes dispossession.
With reskilling, digitalization becomes empowerment.

5.8 Ethical Framework for Socially Responsible Digital Supply Chains

Based on literature and global policy trends, social responsibility in digital supply chains requires five pillars:

1 Transparency – workers must know how they are monitored

2 Participation – workers must co-design digital systems
3 Equity – digital access regardless of background
4 Accountability – algorithms must be reviewable and contestable
5 Dignity – technology must not reduce human worth

A supply chain that fails any pillar cannot claim social sustainability, no matter how low its carbon score.

5.9 Digital Social Responsibility in Organizations: Case Insights

Case A: Ethical Automation in a Japanese Logistics Firm

A Tokyo-based company introduced robots to move parcels. Before deployment:

- employees tested prototypes
- ergonomics teams studied movement
- job roles shifted from lifting to monitoring
- pay was increased for new digital roles

Result: productivity increased and back-injury rates dropped 78%.

Case B: Gig-Worker Exploitation in a US Delivery Platform

A delivery app algorithm:

- cut pay depending on tip value
- penalized drivers who refused long routes
- used opaque ranking systems

Drivers had no negotiation power → digitalization created digital serfdom.

This illustrates the moral fork ahead.

5.10 Digital Social Responsibility Policy: Global Outlook

Policies emerging worldwide include (Table 14):

Table 14. Policies emerging worldwide

Region	Policy Direction
EU	AI Act – transparency & worker rights
Canada	Algorithmic Accountability Law
Japan	Human-centered Industry 5.0 innovation
Global UN Initiatives	Digital labor rights charter (proposal stage)

Regulation will increasingly require:

- explainable AI
- labor-data rights
- digital-ethics audits

Corporations that ignore this will face legal, reputational, and workforce crises.

5.11 Why Social Sustainability Matters More Than Ever

If climate change threatens planet survival, social injustice threatens society's cohesion.

A broken planet destroys economies.

A broken society collapses political legitimacy.

Supply chains, as global connective tissue, influence both.

Digitalization becomes humanity's test:

Will we use data to control people, or to liberate them?

6. DIGITAL SUPPLY CHAIN ECONOMICS

Digitalization is often framed as a technical or sustainability concern. But at its core, it is an economic transformation, reshaping how value is created, who controls resources, and how wealth is distributed across societies.

Traditional economics treated supply chains as cost centers, necessary but burdensome. Digitalization redefines supply chains as strategic value engines, where data itself becomes a commodity and logistics performance becomes a competitive differentiator.

This section examines how digitalization interacts with economic value, market dynamics, and resilience.

6.1 From Cost Efficiency to Value Creation

Historically, supply-chain success was measured by:

- cost reduction
- inventory turns
- transportation rates
- lead-time reduction

Digitalization expands these metrics to include:

- carbon-adjusted cost
- data-generated revenue
- ecosystem resilience
- labor wellbeing as productivity input

This reflects a shift in economic purpose:
Old Model: Supply chains serve profits.
New Model: Profits should serve sustainable supply chains.
Digital transformation enables (Table 15):

Table 15. Digital transformation enabling examples

Value Driver	Example
Dynamic pricing based on real-time demand	e-commerce platforms adjusting SKU prices hourly
Demand-aligned production	AI reduces overproduction, frees capital
Platform monetization	Amazon Logistics sells spare network capacity
Data as a product	carbon-footprint certification sold to buyers

Thus, data becomes a new revenue stream, not just a management tool.

6.2 How Digitalization Rewrites Competition

Digital supply chains change *who* wins economically.

Before Digitalization

Large corporations dominated because they controlled:

- capital
- factories
- distribution channels

After Digitalization

Smaller players can compete through:

- digital marketplaces
- direct-to-consumer logistics
- blockchain-based trust
- drop-shipping models

Example:

A two-person artisan clothing brand can now:

- sell globally via Etsy
- use AI demand prediction tools
- outsource fulfillment to a 3PL
- certify fair-labor sourcing via blockchain

→ Economic empowerment through digital access
This is a redistribution of power, one of the most profound outcomes of supply-chain digitalization.

6.3 Platform Economies: The New Infrastructure

Platform-based supply chains, Amazon, Alibaba, MercadoLibre, represent a new economic structure where:
Data + logistics = monopoly advantage
These companies win because they:

- know real-time demand
- own customer data
- operate fulfillment infrastructure
- control digital marketplaces

The Double-Edged Sword

Platform economies:

- expand economic access for small sellers
- but centralize power in platform owners

A fair digital economy must ensure:

- platform transparency
- fair fees
- complaint mechanisms
- data-sharing rights for suppliers

Otherwise, digitalization may increase inequality by concentrating wealth.

6.4 Digital Procurement & Cost Rationalization

Procurement digitalization transforms economic planning.
Traditional procurement asked:

"What is the lowest price?"

Digital procurement asks:

"What is the lowest carbon + fairest labor + best total lifecycle value?"

AI procurement platforms can (Table 16):

Table 16. AI procurement platforms function

Function	Economic Outcome
automate bidding	lower transaction cost
compare carbon per unit	avoid ESG-related fines
identify resilient supplier portfolios	avoid disruption losses
forecast material shortages	prevent price spikes

Economic Cost of Not Being Sustainable

Companies failing ESG requirements risk:

- carbon taxes
- market penalties
- customer boycotts
- investor divestment
- government sanctions

Thus, sustainability is financially rational.

6.5 Financialization of Supply-Chain Data

Once digitalized, supply-chain data becomes:

- an asset
- collateral
- market signal
- pricing variable

Example:
A supplier with transparent carbon-tracked materials may:

- access lower-interest "green loans"
- charge premium prices
- receive preferential contract awards

Banks increasingly evaluate:

"Is a supply chain sustainable?"

as a credit-risk question.
Digital data creates economic incentives that accelerate sustainability.

6.6 Resilience Economics: The Financial Value of Stability

COVID-19 exposed a flaw:
supply chains optimized for efficiency collapse under stress.
Digital resilience has direct economic consequences (Table 17):

Table 17. economic consequences of digital resilience

Digital Resilience Action	Avoided Cost
real-time visibility	prevents stockouts → protects revenue
multi-sourcing	avoids factory shutdown losses
predictive maintenance	prevents costly downtime
digital twin simulations	avoids capital errors

Example:

An automaker without digital visibility lost billions during the chip shortage because it did not know where components were sourced.

A competitor using AI simulation had alternative suppliers ready and continued production.

→ Resilience is profit protection.

6.7 Digital Supply Chains and Labor Economics

Digitalization changes labor markets by:

- replacing certain physical tasks
- creating new digital roles
- shifting value to high-skill digital labor

The danger:

countries that fail to digitalize lose competitiveness, leading to unemployment spikes.

To avoid economic injustice, governments must fund:

- retraining
- digital access infrastructure
- small-enterprise digital onboarding

Digital supply-chain economics is not only corporate, it is national economic policy.

6.8 The Justice Dimension: Who Benefits Economically?

A digital supply chain is not automatically fair.

Three potential distribution outcomes:

Scenario A: Centralized Wealth

Platforms absorb profit → small suppliers struggle → inequality widens.

Scenario B: Inclusive Wealth

Platforms distribute value fairly → small suppliers gain → poverty declines.

Scenario C: Balanced Hybrid

Platforms profit, but also strengthen ecosystem participants through shared value. Policy determines which world becomes reality.

6.9 Digital-Economy Risks: Concentration, Manipulation, Fragility

Digital supply-chain economics faces three major risks (Table 18):

Table 18. Digital supply chain risks

Risk	Effect
Monopolization	platforms dictate price, rules
Data manipulation	false sustainability data distorts markets
Digital fragility	cyber-attacks could freeze infrastructure

Therefore:

- regulation
- ethics
- cyber-security
- standards

must accompany digital economic systems.

6.10 Economic Purpose Reimagined

Digitalization reveals a philosophical question:
What is the economy for?
If the purpose is:

- extract profits
- externalize environmental damage
- ignore labor dignity

then digitalization will amplify harm.
But if the economy exists to:

- create wellbeing
- protect environmental commons
- distribute opportunity

then digitalization becomes a mission-aligned tool.

7. CASE STUDIES

Theory becomes meaningful only when it meets reality. This section investigates how major organizations, from tech-enabled giants to public-sector actors, are applying (or failing to apply) digitalization to deliver climate action, social responsibility, and economic value. The cases illustrate that digital supply chains are not neutral, their impacts depend on how they are designed, governed, and operationalized.

7.1 Amazon: Model of Efficiency, Mirror of Ethical Tension

Amazon is one of the world's most powerful supply chain innovators, and one of its greatest ethical controversies. It is simultaneously:

- a sustainability pioneer (electric vans, AI routing, automated fulfillment)
- a social responsibility critic's target (worker surveillance, turnover rates)
- an economic disruptor that reshapes global commerce

Digital Climate Action

Amazon's climate strategy includes (Table 19):

Table 19. Amazon's climate strategy

Tool	Impact
AI-driven demand forecasting	reduces surplus goods
Automated warehouse routing	lowers travel distance inside facilities
Electric vehicle deployment (Rivian fleet)	reduces Scope 1 emissions
Predictive freight analytics	cuts fuel burn
Automated packaging	reduces cardboard and plastic

In 2023, Amazon claimed packaging volume per shipment decreased by 36% due to digital optimization. Drones are being piloted to reduce local last-mile emissions.

Social Accountability Gaps

Amazon's warehouses use:

- wrist scanners
- time-tracking algorithms
- "time off task" metrics

Workers report stress, injuries, and algorithmic discipline. Thus, Amazon proves that digitalization alone does not equal social sustainability.

Economic Influence

Amazon's logistics network now sells capacity as a service, turning supply chain infrastructure into a profit center rather than a cost center.

Lesson: Digitalization can advance climate goals while harming people, unless governance protects human dignity.

7.2 Maersk: Greening Global Shipping Through Digital Visibility

Maersk controls nearly 20% of the world's container shipping. Historically, shipping is carbon-intensive and opaque. Maersk's transformation is driven by visibility.

Digitalization Strategy

- AI navigation reduces fuel consumption
- blockchain ensures transparent freight documentation
- IoT sensors monitor engine efficiency

- digital customer dashboards show carbon per shipment

Maersk's ambition: net-zero shipping by 2040.

Climate Intersection

Digital routing saved 1.5 tons of fuel per vessel per day (Maersk 2022). Alternative fuel container ships (methanol) are made viable through data-driven predictive fueling needs.

Social and Economic Notes

Shipping workers historically face long separations, safety risks, and uneven labor conditions. Digital tools now support:

- mental-health monitoring apps
- automated emergency alerts
- tele-medicine for on-board workers

  Maersk thus shows digitalization can serve planet, people, and profit, when designed holistically.

7.3 Tesla: Digital Circularity in Battery Supply Chains

Electric vehicles (EVs) reduce tailpipe emissions, but battery production requires lithium, nickel, and cobalt, industries linked to water loss, mining pollution, and exploitation.

Tesla's Digital Tools

- Blockchain tracks cobalt origin
- Digital twins model battery lifecycle
- AI forecasts cell degradation and triggers recycling
- Gigafactory sensors monitor energy intensity

Climate Alignment

Tesla plans full closed-loop battery recycling (Gharye Mirzaei et al., 2025), where materials never leave the supply-chain ecosystem.

→ Digitalization is what makes that circularity operationally possible.

Social Questions

Cobalt mining still raises ethical concerns. Blockchain prevents illegal sourcing only when enforced, demonstrating governance again is critical.

7.4 Walmart: Data-Driven Supply Chain for Poverty & Emissions

Walmart's sustainability platform, *Project Gigaton*, aims to eliminate 1 gigaton of CO_2 by 2030.

Digital Tools

- AI demand planning
- IoT energy sensors in stores
- Supplier ESG reporting platform
- Low-carbon route planning

Social Value Intersection

Walmart also uses platforms to:

- support small farmers entering formal markets
- provide digital finance to micro-suppliers
- fund workforce upskilling

Walmart demonstrates that digital supply chains can reduce emissions while reducing poverty, if intentionally designed (Taghipour, 2024).

7.5 Rwanda & Ghana: Drone-Based Humanitarian Logistics

Zipline, a drone-delivery company, enables fast transport of:

- blood
- vaccines
- medicine

into remote regions.

Sustainability Impact

- replaces diesel motorcycles
- lowers healthcare-access inequality
- cuts emissions up to 60% per delivery
- prevents spoilage of temperature-sensitive medicine

This is a case where digitalization serves life, not consumption.

7.6 Government-Led Digital Supply Chains: Singapore Smart Logistics Grid

Singapore's national logistics system uses:

- IoT port sensors
- blockchain customs documentation
- data-sharing across freight operators

The result:

- faster clearance
- reduced empty container miles
- transparent labor contracts
- competitive national economy

Government-led digitalization shows sustainability is a national strategy, not only a corporate decision.

7.7 Where Digitalization Fails: Cautionary Examples

Case: Gig-Economy Exploitation (unnamed global platform)

An app paying workers per delivery used algorithmic pay that dropped when tips increased — effectively punishing generosity.

Workers could not appeal decisions, illustrating how data without rights becomes oppression.

Case: Carbon-washing AI Tools

Some corporations deploy dashboards measuring emissions, but never take action. Digitalization then becomes performative sustainability, not real transformation.

7.8 Synthesis of Lessons Across Cases

Success Factors in Digital Sustainability

Digital transformation supports all three pillars when (Table 20):

Table 20. Digital transformation outcome

Condition	Outcome
Worker participation	technology empowers, not harms
Transparent data	unethical practices exposed
Multi-stakeholder design	climate & people integrated
Policy enforcement	ESG requirements become binding
Economic incentives	sustainability becomes profitable

Failure Modes

Digitalization harms when (Table 21):

Table 21. Digitalization harmful results

Condition	Result
shareholder-only value	inequality widens
surveillance without consent	dignity destroyed
ESG is voluntary	climate wins are symbolic
automation replaces workers	unemployment grows

Thus, technology is neither angel nor demon.
It becomes what society chooses to shape.

8. FUTURE DIRECTIONS: WHERE DIGITAL SUPPLY CHAINS ARE HEADING

The convergence of digitalization, climate urgency, and social responsibility is not a temporary phase, it is the beginning of a new global operating paradigm. Over the next decade, supply chains will be reshaped by three megatrends:

8.1 From Industry 4.0 to Industry 5.0: Technology Serving Humanity

The first wave of digitalization asked: *How do we automate?*
The next wave asks: *How do we empower?*
Industry 5.0 envisions:

- collaborative robots rather than replacing workers
- AI that augments human decision-making
- logistics systems that minimize environmental harm
- companies measured by social wellbeing as much as financial returns

Digitalization will be judged by how much dignity it preserves, not how many jobs it eliminates.

8.2 Mandatory Digital Sustainability: Policy Will Force Compliance

Voluntary ESG is ending. Enforcement is beginning.
Expected policy directions include (Table 22):

Table 22. Future policies

Future Policy	Example
Digital carbon passports	Every product tagged with lifecycle emissions
AI algorithm audits	Mandatory ethics transparency
Fair labor certification	Minimum digital-recorded wage requirements
Circularity regulations	Repairability laws, mandatory take-back

Companies that cannot digitally prove sustainability will lose:

- export eligibility

- government contracts
- investment capital
- consumer trust

Digital compliance becomes a market access condition.

8.3 Consumer Behavior: The Demand for Ethical Choice

Consumers increasingly scan QR codes to know:

- where products come from
- who made them
- whether the environment was harmed
- whether labor was exploited

Digital transparency enables ethical consumption, making sustainability economically self-reinforcing.

8.4 Digital Commons: Sustainability Through Collaboration

No single company can decarbonize alone.

Future supply chains will be shared systems, where competitors collaborate (Taghipour, 2009).

Examples emerging:

- shared blockchain traceability for materials
- shared reverse-logistics infrastructure
- open carbon data exchanges

The future is ecosystem economics, not individual optimization.

8.5 The Moral Choice Ahead

Digital tools are powerful, but power requires direction.

If leaders prioritize:

- shareholder extraction
- opacity
- labor exploitation
- climate delay

digitalization will accelerate destruction.
But if leaders choose:

- transparency
- dignity
- fair economics
- climate mobilization

digitalization becomes a global instrument for justice, wellbeing, and planetary survival.

The future depends on what we decide to measure, value, and protect.

9. CONCLUSION

Digital supply chain transformation is often described as a technological revolution. But this chapter has shown it is far more profound, it is a civilizational turning point.

Supply chains shape:

- how resources are extracted
- how people are treated
- how wealth is distributed
- how much carbon is emitted
- how quickly societies recover from crises

Digitalization inserts visibility into this hidden world, and visibility is power.

Technology can turn emissions into dashboards, labor exploitation into actionable data, and economic exclusion into opportunity. But visibility without values is insufficient. Digital supply chains become sustainable only when ethics, policy, and human dignity are intentionally embedded.

Three core insights emerge from this chapter:

1 Digitalization is the mechanism that makes sustainability *operational*

Climate action, circularity, and Scope-3 emissions reduction cannot scale without IoT sensors, AI planning, blockchain traceability, and digital twins.

2 Social sustainability determines whether digitalization is morally legitimate

A low-carbon economy built on exhausted and exploited workers is not a sustainable future — it is a contradiction. Human dignity must be protected by design.

3 Economic value must be reimagined

Digitalization shifts value from physical assets to information. Wealth can consolidate — or be redistributed. Equity must be intentionally governed.

In the coming decade, humanity's survival will be shaped by one question:

Do we allow technology to amplify our worst instincts, or do we use it to build the future we hope for?

Sustainable digital supply chains are not inevitable, they must be designed, governed, and protected.

They represent one of the strongest practical tools we have to stabilize climate systems, empower communities, and create fair prosperity.

The choice is ours.

REFERENCES

Carter, C. R., & Rogers, D. S. (2008). A framework of sustainable supply chain management. *International Journal of Physical Distribution & Logistics Management, 38*(5), 360–387. DOI: 10.1108/09600030810882816

Cauchois, R., Taghipour, A., Kang, D., Zoghlami, N., & Abed, M. (2017). Advanced solutions for a supply chain with stochastic information. *Journal of Advanced Management Science*, *5*(1), 9–13. DOI: 10.18178/joams.5.1.9-13

Crandall, A., Rahim, H. A., Yount, K. M., Borghei, N. S., Taghipour, A., Roudsari, R. L., ... & Nelson, B. D. (1995). WHO journals. Information for authors, 1.

Elkington, J. (1997). *Cannibals with Forks: The Triple Bottom Line of 21st Century Business.* Capstone.

European Commission. (2021). *Industry 5.0: Towards A Sustainable.* Human-Centric Industrial Future.

Gharye Mirzaei, M., Goodarzian, F., Taghipour, A., & Muñuzuri, J. (2025). Sustainable closed-loop supply chain network under uncertainty considering green technologies: Toward the circular economy. *The Journal of the Operational Research Society*, •••, 1–21.

Glaa, B., Zoghlami, N., & Taghipour, A. (2014, May). Outsourcing and off-shoring healthcare services: A way to cut the costs and improve quality. In 2014 international conference on advanced logistics and transport (ICALT) (pp. 189-194). IEEE.

Goodarzian, F., Abraham, A., Muñuzuri, J., Taghipour, A., & Ghasemi, P. (2024). A Benders decomposition approach for a new sustainable pharmaceutical supply chain network: A case study in France. *Annals of Operations Research*, •••, 1–39.

Lebosse, S., Taghipour, A., & Canel-Depitre, B. (2017). Quick response to fluctuations in supply chains: A review. *Journal of Advanced Management Science*, *5*(5), 394–400. DOI: 10.18178/joams.5.5.394-400

Loivet, W., Taghipour, A., & Kang, D. S. (2020). The rise of green supply chain management: Between complexity and necessity. *J. Econ. Bus. Manag*, *8*(1), 1–7. DOI: 10.18178/joebm.2020.8.1.604

Lu, X., & Taghipour, A. (2023). A French Guide for Businesses and Governments to Integrate the Concept of Sustainable Development Into Their Supply Chains. In *Government Impact on Sustainable and Responsible Supply Chain Management* (pp. 1–12). IGI Global. DOI: 10.4018/978-1-6684-9062-4.ch001

Lu, X. W., Tliche, Y., Vosooghidizaji, M., & Taghipour, A. (2023). Cryptocurrencies and Blockchain Applications. In Blockchain Applications in Cryptocurrency for Technological Evolution (pp. 1-13). IGI Global.

Maersk. (2022). *Annual Sustainability and Climate Report.*

Mahfod, J., Canel-Depitre, B., & Taghipour, A. (2019). Quality function deployment-ELECTRE in supplier evaluation. Journal of advanced management science, 7(4).

Mahfod, J., Khoury, B., Canel-Depitre, B., & Taghipour, A. (2021). Logistics Providers in Syria Humanitarian Operations. In Demand Forecasting and Order Planning in Supply Chains and Humanitarian Logistics (pp. 171-197). IGI Global. DOI: 10.4018/978-1-7998-3805-0.ch006

Mathiyazhagan, K., Taghipour, A., & Agarwal, V. (Eds.). (2022). *Blockchain Technology in Supply Chain Management for Society 5.0.* CRC Press. DOI: 10.1201/9781003177432

Mbiatem, J., Taghipour, A., & Canel-Depitre, B. (2018, August). Supplier selection approaches for decision makers. In *Proceedings of the 8th International Conference on Information Communication and Management* (pp. 108-112).

McKinsey & Company. (2021). *The Future of Digital Supply Chain Transformation.*

Merimi, M., & Taghipour, A. (2021). Accelerating the digitalization of the supply chain: An empirical research about COVID-19 crisis. In *Digitalization of decentralized supply chains during global crises* (pp. 1–24). IGI Global Scientific Publishing. DOI: 10.4018/978-1-7998-6874-3.ch001

PwC. (2023). *Global Supply Chain Outlook Report.*

Ren, Z., Taghipour, A., & Canel-Depitre, B. (2016, October). Information sharing in supply chain under uncertainty. In 2016 6th International Conference on Information Communication and Management (ICICM) (pp. 67-71). IEEE. DOI: 10.1109/INFOCOMAN.2016.7784217

Sahraoui, A., Tran, N. K., Tliche, Y., Kacem, A., & Taghipour, A. (2023). Examining ICT Innovation for Sustainable Terminal Operations in Developing Countries: A Case Study of the Port of Radès in Tunisia. *Sustainability (Basel)*, *15*(11), 9123. DOI: 10.3390/su15119123

Taghipour, A. (2009). Evaluation de la collaboration dans une chaîne d'approvisionnement. Revue française de gestion industrielle, 28(1), 26-42.

Taghipour, A. (Ed.). (2020). *Demand forecasting and order planning in supply chains and humanitarian logistics*. IGI Global.

Taghipour, A. (Ed.). (2022). *Blockchain Applications in Cryptocurrency for Technological Evolution*. IGI Global. DOI: 10.4018/978-1-6684-6247-8

Taghipour, A. (2024). Big Data: The New Gold Mine for Supermarkets. In Applications of New Technology in Operations and Supply Chain Management (pp. 98-106). IGI Global.

Taghipour, A., Lu, X., Derradji, M., & Sow, A. D. (2022b, July). The impact of digitalization on supply chain management: a literature review. In *Proceedings of the 12th International Conference on Information Communication and Management* (pp. 75-78). DOI: 10.1145/3551690.3551702

Taghipour, A., Lu, X., & Smahi, M. (2022a). Opportunities and challenges for society 5.0 in procurement. *Blockchain Technology in Supply Chain Management for Society*, *5*(0), 91–100. DOI: 10.1201/9781003177432-9

Taghipour, A., Rouyendegh, B. D., Ünal, A., & Piya, S. (2022c). Selection of suppliers for speech recognition products in IT projects by combining techniques with an integrated fuzzy MCDM. *Sustainability (Basel)*, *14*(3), 1777. DOI: 10.3390/su14031777

Unilever. (2022). *Sustainable Procurement and Logistics Innovations.*

XiaoWen, L., & Atour, T. (2025). Knowledge-driven digital innovation in supply chains: An organizational perspective. *Journal of Innovation & Knowledge*, *10*(5), 100787. DOI: 10.1016/j.jik.2025.100787

Zoghlami, N., Taghipour, A., Merlo, C., & Abed, M. (2016). Management of divergent production network using decentralised multi-level capacitated lot-sizing models. *International Journal of Shipping and Transport Logistics*, *8*(5), 590–604. DOI: 10.1504/IJSTL.2016.078686

Chapter 2
Artificial Intelligence and Ethical Supply Chain Management

Atour Taghipour
http://orcid.org/0000-0003-1687-8881
Conservatoire National des Arts et Métiers, France

ABSTRACT

Artificial intelligence (AI) is transforming global supply chains through real-time monitoring, predictive analytics, automation, and improved coordination across suppliers and distributors. These tools enhance efficiency, reduce costs, and increase transparency. Yet, AI also raises key ethical concerns, including data privacy, worker surveillance, algorithmic bias in supplier evaluation, risks of labor exploitation in opaque networks, and environmental sustainability issues. This paper builds on prior work on AI and ethical marketing and extends the analysis to ethical supply chain management. Using a qualitative documentary review grounded in logistics, operations management, and business ethics literature, it examines whether AI can support responsible supply chains. The study concludes that AI is not inherently ethical or unethical; its impact depends on governance, data quality, transparency mechanisms, and organizational commitment to responsible sourcing and human-rights-focused practices.

DOI: 10.4018/979-8-2600-3199-5.ch002

INTRODUCTION

Problem Statement

Global supply chains are increasingly complex, spanning multiple countries, regulatory environments, and operational models. AI tools, such as predictive demand models, automated procurement systems, supplier risk scoring algorithms, and blockchain-enhanced tracking systems, promise to improve visibility, reduce uncertainty, and enhance resilience. As firms adopt digital technologies to meet rising consumer expectations, geopolitical disruptions, and sustainability pressures (Goodarzian et al., 2024), AI becomes not only a tool for optimization but also a determinant of power, control, and accountability across supply networks (Ren et al., 2016)

Over the past decade, global supply chains have transitioned from linear structures to dynamic, interconnected ecosystems where data flows are as critical as material flows (Lebosse et al., 2017). This digital shift increases dependence on AI-driven decisions: forecasting systems determine production volumes, algorithmic procurement tools select suppliers, and risk-prediction models shape sourcing strategies (Tliche et al., 2019). Though these innovations strengthen operational efficiency, they simultaneously generate new ethical vulnerabilities (Taghipour et al., 2023a; Taghipour et al., 2023b).

1. Worker surveillance and loss of autonomy.

In logistics, manufacturing, and warehouse environments, AI-powered monitoring tools—including wearable sensors, computer-vision systems, and real-time productivity dashboards, track workers' movements, task completion times, and even biometric data. While companies justify these systems as safety or productivity enhancements, they may violate workers' privacy and create pressure for constant high performance. Academic studies show that algorithmic management often reduces autonomy and increases psychological stress, particularly when paired with automated disciplinary systems.

2. Invisible algorithmic biases in supplier selection.

As more companies rely on AI to evaluate and rank suppliers, algorithmic scoring models may unintentionally reinforce existing inequalities (Mbiatem et al., 2018). Because these tools are trained on historical data, often reflecting discriminatory patterns, they may favour large multinational suppliers while penalizing smaller, women-owned, or minority-owned enterprises. Algorithmic opacity further complicates suppliers' ability to contest or understand decisions that affect their economic survival.

3. Data extractivism in global supply networks.

Multinational firms increasingly require suppliers in developing countries to share operational data: production rates, worker rosters, environmental metrics, machine performance records, and logistics information. This data is fed into AI systems to increase supply chain visibility and forecast risks. However, suppliers rarely receive compensation, ownership rights, or strategic value in return. This dynamic replicates older forms of economic dependency and deepens power asymmetries, raising the question of whether AI is becoming a tool of digital colonialism in global trade (Vosooghidizaji et al., 2020; Nadia et al., 2021; Mahfod et al., 2019).

4. Environmental risks reinforced by optimization algorithms.

AI systems designed to minimize costs or delivery times may encourage environmentally harmful decisions, such as excessive use of air freight, intensified resource extraction, or production consolidation in regions with weak environmental regulations (Cauchois et al., 2017). Optimization models often lack integrated sustainability constraints, meaning that carbon emissions, waste outputs, and ecological degradation are treated as externalities (Taghipour and Beneteau-Piet, 2020). Without corrective governance, AI could accelerate unsustainable industrial practices rather than support climate-positive transitions.

Beyond these discrete risks, the broader ethical challenge arises from the opacity and automation that accompany AI in supply chains. Decisions once made by human managers, balancing ethical, social, and contextual considerations, are increasingly delegated to algorithms that prioritize efficiency metrics (Taghipour, 2009). This shift raises concerns about accountability: when an algorithm drops a supplier, increases production quotas, or triggers an audit flag, who is responsible for the consequences?

At stake is the future of how global supply chains function, not only as logistical systems, but as socio-economic infrastructures affecting millions of workers and communities worldwide.

This leads to the central question:

Can artificial intelligence support supply chain optimization while fully respecting ethical principles such as fairness, human rights, transparency, environmental sustainability, and responsible sourcing?

Objectives

This paper aims to:

1. Identify how AI enhances supply chain operations, including forecasting, tracking, risk detection, procurement, and sustainability reporting.
2. Analyze ethical risks associated with AI in supply chains, including worker privacy violations, biased supplier scoring, and opaque decision-making.
3. Explore frameworks and regulations (EU AI Act, ESG standards, OECD Responsible Business Conduct guidelines) that govern ethical and sustainable AI use in global supply chains.

4. Propose strategies for organizations to ensure that AI contributes to fair labor practices and environmental sustainability.

LITERATURE REVIEW

Research on AI in supply chains highlights both transformative potential and critical risks. Wieland (2021) emphasizes that responsible supply chains must integrate ethics at every stage, particularly when automated decision systems are involved. Busse et al. (2017) warn that supplier monitoring technologies can unintentionally deepen power imbalances between multinational enterprises and smaller suppliers. Meanwhile, Ivanov and Dolgui (2020) show that AI improves resilience and real-time risk detection.

In business ethics, Floridi et al. (2019) highlight core principles for responsible AI, including justice, transparency, and non-maleficence, principles that directly apply to supply chains. Research by Köhler and Pizzol (2020) demonstrates how AI can support sustainability assessments, for example by tracking CO_2 emissions across logistics networks.

Regulatory frameworks such as the GDPR and the upcoming European AI Act impose requirements for transparency, fairness, and accountability, while supply-chain-specific frameworks like the UN Guiding Principles on Business and Human Rights and the OECD Due Diligence Guidance for Responsible Supply Chains require companies to prevent human-rights abuses in complex sourcing networks (Loivet et al., 2020; Zoghlami et al., 2016; Glaa et al., 2014).

METHODOLOGY APPROACH

Research Approach

This study adopts a qualitative documentary analysis methodology to explore the intersections of logistics, business ethics, AI governance, and sustainability. Qualitative documentary analysis allows for an in-depth examination of existing literature, reports, and case studies to understand patterns, principles, and best practices in these domains. The approach emphasizes critical evaluation of documented evidence rather than primary data collection, making it suitable for analyzing emerging technologies and ethical considerations in supply chain management.

Additionally, case examples are employed to demonstrate practical implications and real-world applications of AI and sustainable practices in logistics. These cases provide concrete illustrations of theoretical concepts, highlighting successes, challenges, and lessons learned across different corporate and institutional contexts.

Sources and Tools Used

The research draws on a wide range of authoritative sources to ensure both credibility and relevance:

- **Peer-reviewed journals:** Key academic sources include the *Journal of Supply Chain Management*, *Journal of Business Ethics*, and other leading publications focusing on sustainability, AI governance, and corporate responsibility. These sources provide rigorous theoretical and empirical insights.
- **Institutional reports:** Analytical reports from organizations such as the World Economic Forum (WEF), OECD, and the Responsible Business Alliance (RBA) offer global perspectives on AI ethics, supply chain sustainability, and governance frameworks (Ponputtha et al., 2021).
- **Corporate case studies:** Real-world implementations, including IBM Watson Supply Chain and Maersk blockchain tracking, are examined to understand practical applications of AI and ethical decision-making in logistics. These cases reveal operational challenges, technological innovations, and policy implications.

  The research utilizes documentary analysis tools such as thematic coding, comparative analysis, and content synthesis to identify recurring themes, ethical considerations, and governance mechanisms. This approach ensures a systematic and structured analysis of diverse sources, bridging academic theory with practical implementation.

RESULTS / DEVELOPMENT

A. AI's Contribution to Ethical Supply Chains

The integration of Artificial Intelligence (AI) into supply chain management has the potential to transform operational practices while enhancing ethical and sustainable outcomes. Several key contributions can be identified:

1. Traceability and Transparency

One of the most significant impacts of AI in supply chains is the enhancement of traceability and transparency. By leveraging technologies such as computer vision, blockchain, and IoT sensors, companies can monitor the movement of goods from production to end-consumer. This level of tracking enables verification of ethical practices, such as fair labor sourcing, and ensures compliance with environmental standards.

For instance, blockchain-enabled platforms, like Maersk's TradeLens, allow multiple stakeholders to access immutable shipment records. Such systems reduce the risk of counterfeit or illegally sourced materials entering the supply chain. In the apparel industry, AI-driven traceability solutions can identify suppliers that fail to meet labor standards, thereby enabling firms to make informed sourcing decisions that prioritize human rights.

Beyond ethical compliance, traceability also fosters consumer trust. Modern consumers increasingly demand transparency regarding the origins of products. Companies that provide verifiable evidence of responsible sourcing not only mitigate reputational risks but also gain a competitive advantage in ethical markets.

2. Predictive Risk Management

AI systems, particularly machine learning algorithms, are capable of predicting disruptions and assessing potential ethical risks in supply chains. These algorithms analyze historical data, market trends, weather patterns, and geopolitical factors to forecast supply chain vulnerabilities.

For example, predictive analytics can highlight regions at risk for labor violations or fraud by correlating supplier data with external reports on working conditions. Companies can then proactively intervene, by auditing suppliers, providing support, or reconfiguring supply networks, to prevent unethical practices from occurring.

Moreover, predictive AI contributes to resilience planning. During crises such as natural disasters or geopolitical instability, AI models can identify alternate sourcing routes or suppliers, ensuring continuity while maintaining adherence to ethical standards.

3. Sustainability Optimization

AI is instrumental in advancing environmental sustainability within supply chains. By integrating optimization algorithms, route planning software, and energy monitoring tools, companies can minimize waste, reduce energy consumption, and lower greenhouse gas emissions (Tliche et al., 2023; Nadia et al., 2020).

For instance, AI-powered logistics platforms can optimize delivery routes in real-time, balancing fuel efficiency with timely delivery. In warehouse management, AI systems can predict inventory demand, minimizing overproduction and reducing food or material waste. Additionally, AI can identify packaging innovations or material substitutions that reduce environmental impact (Sahraoui et al., 2023; Crandall et al., 1995).

The integration of sustainability considerations into operational decision-making not only benefits the planet but also aligns with growing regulatory and societal pressures for responsible corporate behavior.

4. Supplier Evaluation

AI systems offer sophisticated methods for evaluating suppliers based on Environmental, Social, and Governance (ESG) criteria. Machine learning algorithms can process large volumes of supplier data, including labor practices, environmental impact, and corporate governance policies, to generate ESG scores.

These scores enable companies to select suppliers who align with their ethical and sustainability goals. Smaller firms, for example, can use AI to benchmark suppliers against industry standards, reducing reliance on anecdotal assessments. Additionally, AI-driven evaluation tools can uncover hidden risks, such as suppliers with past compliance violations or inconsistent reporting practices, allowing firms to make more informed, responsible decisions.

B. Ethical Risks of AI in Supply Chains

Despite these promising benefits, AI introduces significant ethical risks that must be carefully managed. Failure to address these risks may undermine both social responsibility goals and public trust.

1. Data Exploitation

AI systems rely heavily on large-scale data collection from suppliers, workers, and other stakeholders. In many cases, suppliers in developing regions are required to provide sensitive operational or personal data without receiving equivalent value in return.

This dynamic raises questions of fairness and equity: while large multinational corporations leverage data to optimize supply chains, small or local suppliers may bear the costs of surveillance or reporting without tangible benefits. Over time, such practices could exacerbate existing power imbalances in global supply chains.

2. Worker Monitoring and Surveillance

AI-enabled monitoring tools, such as warehouse scanners, productivity trackers, and wearable sensors, can improve efficiency but often at the cost of worker dignity and privacy. Amazon's warehouse monitoring systems are a notable example: algorithmic performance metrics set high expectations for speed and output, leading to stress, injuries, and limited autonomy for employees.

While these technologies are intended to optimize workflow, they can create ethical tensions when human welfare is compromised. Companies must balance productivity gains with safeguarding workers' rights, privacy, and overall well-being.

3. Algorithmic Discrimination

AI-driven supplier scoring and procurement systems are designed to standardize decision-making. However, biased training data can result in algorithmic discrimination. For example, historical procurement data may favor large, established suppliers, unintentionally disadvantaging small, local, or minority-owned businesses.

This bias not only limits market access for underrepresented suppliers but also contradicts the ethical principle of fair competition. AI systems must therefore be designed and audited to ensure equitable treatment of all suppliers and prevent perpetuation of structural inequalities.

4. Opaque Automation

As AI increasingly influences decisions regarding procurement, sourcing, and labor conditions, there is a risk of opaque or "black box" decision-making. In some cases, AI recommendations are implemented without adequate human oversight, leaving critical ethical judgments in the hands of automated systems.

For example, predictive risk algorithms may penalize suppliers based on incomplete or biased historical data, leading to unjust exclusion from contracts. Without transparent processes and human accountability, these automated decisions can perpetuate systemic inequities and undermine corporate responsibility goals.

Illustrative Examples

- **Amazon's warehouse monitoring systems:** Criticized for high-pressure labor conditions, demonstrating how AI can negatively impact worker well-being when efficiency is prioritized over human dignity.
- **Predictive risk algorithms in procurement:** Systems that inadvertently penalize suppliers based on biased historical data, illustrating the dangers of opaque automation in supplier evaluation.
- **Blockchain-enabled supplier transparency platforms:** While generally beneficial, they require extensive data sharing that may disadvantage smaller suppliers who cannot comply with data demands.

Synthesis

The results highlight a dual role of AI in supply chains: while it offers transformative benefits for ethical sourcing, sustainability, and operational efficiency, it also introduces risks that may compromise fairness, privacy, and human rights.

Successful implementation of AI in ethical supply chains thus requires:

1. Transparent governance mechanisms to ensure human oversight.
2. Equitable data-sharing frameworks that protect suppliers and workers.
3. Continuous auditing of algorithms to detect and mitigate bias.
4. Integration of social and environmental metrics alongside operational KPIs.

In conclusion, AI is neither inherently ethical nor unethical; its impact depends on how technologies are designed, deployed, and monitored. Organizations that proactively address the ethical dimensions of AI stand to gain both operational and reputational advantages, while those that neglect these considerations risk reinforcing inequalities and undermining stakeholder trust.

DISCUSSION / ANALYSIS

Critical Interpretation

The findings of this study indicate that while Artificial Intelligence (AI) can significantly enhance supply chain visibility, operational efficiency, and risk management, these benefits alone do not constitute an ethical justification for its deployment. The integration of AI in supply chains presents a complex interplay between technological capability and moral responsibility.

One of the central ethical concerns is bias in training data. AI systems are only as impartial as the datasets on which they are trained. If historical supply chain or procurement data reflect systemic inequalities, favoring large, established suppliers over smaller, minority-owned enterprises, the AI system will likely replicate and reinforce these disparities. For example, predictive algorithms that flag suppliers as high risk based on past violations may unfairly penalize smaller suppliers who lack the resources to maintain extensive compliance documentation, even if they operate ethically.

Power asymmetries further complicate the ethical landscape. Multinational corporations deploying AI have considerable leverage over smaller suppliers, particularly in developing regions. These suppliers may feel compelled to provide sensitive operational or labor data without receiving tangible benefits, creating a form of data exploitation. The ethical concern is that AI could exacerbate existing imbalances between large corporations and vulnerable suppliers, rather than leveling the playing field.

Another critical factor is the lack of transparency inherent in many AI systems. Opaque algorithms, commonly referred to as "black boxes", may automate decisions about procurement, supplier evaluation, or workforce management without clear explanations. Such opacity undermines accountability and trust. Stakeholders, including workers and suppliers, are left unable to question or contest AI-driven decisions, which raises serious ethical and governance challenges.

A key challenge emerging from this study is accountability. When an algorithm excludes a small supplier from a contract or flags a factory as high risk, the question of responsibility becomes ambiguous:

- Is it the developers of the AI model, who design the algorithm and select training data?
- Is it the corporate managers, who rely on AI recommendations for operational decisions?
- Or is it the organization as a whole, which bears ultimate responsibility for ethical supply chain management?

Without robust explanation mechanisms or clear accountability frameworks, AI may shift responsibility away from human decision-makers, creating ethical blind spots. This raises profound concerns, particularly in contexts where human livelihoods are directly affected, such as factory operations or small supplier contracts.

LIMITATIONS AND BROADER IMPLICATIONS

This study relies exclusively on **secondary sources**, including peer-reviewed journals, institutional reports, and corporate case studies. While this approach enables comprehensive coverage of existing knowledge, it presents limitations:

1. **Absence of primary data**: Interviews, surveys, or field observations would provide nuanced insights into the perspectives of workers, suppliers, and other stakeholders directly affected by AI systems. Understanding how AI-driven decisions impact day-to-day labor practices, fairness perceptions, and supplier relationships is critical for developing actionable ethical frameworks.
2. **Context-specific variations**: Supply chains operate across diverse cultural, regulatory, and economic contexts. The generalizations derived from secondary literature may not capture localized challenges or practices, such as informal labor arrangements in emerging markets or small-scale supplier ecosystems.

Despite these limitations, the study underscores several broader implications for theory and practice:

- **Embedding AI in ethical governance frameworks**: AI must not operate in isolation. Its deployment should be accompanied by formal mechanisms for accountability, transparency, and ethical oversight, such as algorithmic audits, explainable AI protocols, and stakeholder review processes.
- **Balancing efficiency with human rights**: Operational efficiency should not override ethical considerations. Companies must assess not only whether AI improves speed, cost, or resource use, but also whether it safeguards worker dignity, supplier fairness, and equitable treatment.
- **Prioritizing stakeholder engagement**: Ethical AI in supply chains requires meaningful engagement with affected parties. Suppliers and workers should have avenues to contest decisions, provide feedback, and participate in shaping data collection, algorithmic design, and governance practices.
- **Dynamic ethical monitoring**: AI systems must be continuously monitored and recalibrated to address emerging risks, data drift, and unintended con-

sequences. Ethical supply chain management is not a one-time compliance exercise but an ongoing, iterative process.

In sum, AI represents both an opportunity and a risk in the pursuit of ethical supply chains. Its ability to enhance transparency, predict risks, and optimize sustainability is undeniable. However, without careful attention to governance, accountability, and equity, AI may inadvertently perpetuate inequalities and obscure responsibility, undermining the very ethical goals it is intended to serve.

CONCLUSION

Summary of Key Contributions

This study has examined the dual role of Artificial Intelligence (AI) in modern supply chains, highlighting both its transformative potential and the ethical challenges it presents. AI technologies, including machine learning, predictive analytics, and blockchain, have demonstrably enhanced supply chain operations by improving traceability, transparency, risk management, sustainability, and supplier evaluation. These capabilities enable firms to more effectively monitor ethical compliance, optimize resource use, and strengthen sustainability practices, thereby contributing to the broader goals of responsible supply chain management.

However, the research also underscores that technological capability alone is insufficient to guarantee ethical outcomes. Several persistent risks, including algorithmic bias, opaque decision-making, data exploitation, and the reinforcement of existing power imbalances, can compromise worker rights, marginalize small suppliers, and obscure accountability. The study demonstrates that the alignment of AI with ethical supply chain management requires more than efficiency-driven implementation; it necessitates robust governance structures, transparent AI systems, and a strong commitment to ESG principles.

By integrating insights from logistics, business ethics, AI governance, and sustainability studies, this paper contributes to the understanding of how organizations can deploy AI responsibly in supply chains. The findings highlight that ethical AI is not merely a technical challenge but a governance and organizational challenge that demands careful attention to human rights, equity, and transparency at every stage of the supply chain.

Future Directions

While this study provides a comprehensive overview of the ethical implications of AI in supply chains, it also identifies areas for further research to deepen understanding and support practical implementation:

1. Worker Perception of AI-Enabled Monitoring

Future research could investigate how AI monitoring tools affect workers' sense of autonomy, privacy, and well-being. Qualitative methods such as interviews and ethnographic fieldwork could provide insights into the human experience behind AI-driven operational efficiency. Understanding worker perception is crucial for designing monitoring systems that balance productivity with dignity.

2. Fair Compensation Frameworks for Supplier Data

As AI relies heavily on supplier-provided data, studies could explore models for **equitable data-sharing and compensation**. This includes examining how suppliers, especially in developing countries, can benefit fairly from the value their data generates, thereby mitigating power asymmetries and fostering sustainable partnerships.

3. Explainable AI Models for Procurement and Risk Management

Developing **transparent and interpretable AI systems** is essential for accountability. Future research could focus on creating models that provide clear explanations for procurement decisions, supplier evaluations, and risk assessments, enabling affected stakeholders to contest or appeal algorithmic outcomes.

4. AI's Role in Circular Supply Chains and Carbon Neutral Goals

The potential for AI to drive **circular economy practices** and support carbon-neutral supply chains remains underexplored. Future studies could examine how AI can optimize resource reuse, reduce waste, and enable carbon tracking, contributing to global sustainability and climate targets.

5. Cross-Cultural and Context-Specific Analyses

Supply chains operate across diverse regulatory, cultural, and economic contexts. Comparative studies could explore how AI adoption and ethical governance practices vary globally, highlighting localized risks, opportunities, and best practices.

Final Reflection

In conclusion, AI represents a powerful tool for advancing ethical and sustainable supply chains, but its effectiveness is contingent upon deliberate organizational choices. Firms must recognize that ethical supply chain management is a holistic endeavor, requiring alignment of technology, governance, and stakeholder engagement. By embedding AI within transparent, accountable, and socially responsible frameworks, organizations can harness its transformative potential while mitigating risks, ultimately contributing to more equitable, sustainable, and resilient global supply chains (Taghipour and Merimi, 2021).

The findings of this study serve as a call to action for scholars, practitioners, and policymakers: responsible AI deployment in supply chains is not optional, it is a prerequisite for sustainable business practices in the 21st century.

REFERENCES

Busse, C., Meinlschmidt, J., & Foerstl, K. (2017). Supplier development and supplier sustainability: A systematic review. *The Journal of Supply Chain Management.*

Cauchois, R., Taghipour, A., Kang, D., Zoghlami, N., & Abed, M. (2017). Advanced solutions for a supply chain with stochastic information. *Journal of Advanced Management Science*, *5*(1), 9–13. DOI: 10.18178/joams.5.1.9-13

Crandall, A., Rahim, H. A., Yount, K. M., Borghei, N. S., Taghipour, A., Roudsari, R. L., ... & Nelson, B. D. (1995). WHO journals. Information for authors, 1.

Floridi, L., & Cowls, J. (2019). A unified framework for AI ethics. *Harvard Data Science Review*. Advance online publication. DOI: 10.1162/99608f92.8cd550d1

Glaa, B., Zoghlami, N., & Taghipour, A. (2014, May). Outsourcing and off-shoring healthcare services: A way to cut the costs and improve quality. In 2014 international conference on advanced logistics and transport (ICALT) (pp. 189-194). IEEE.

Goodarzian, F., Abraham, A., Muñuzuri, J., Taghipour, A., & Ghasemi, P. (2024). A Benders decomposition approach for a new sustainable pharmaceutical supply chain network: A case study in France. *Annals of Operations Research*, •••, 1–39.

Ivanov, D., & Dolgui, A. (2020). A digital supply chain twin for managing disruptions. *International Journal of Production Research.*

Köhler, S., & Pizzol, M. (2020). Life cycle sustainability and AI. *Journal of Cleaner Production.*

Lebosse, S., Taghipour, A., & Canel-Depitre, B. (2017). Quick response to fluctuations in supply chains: A review. *Journal of Advanced Management Science*, *5*(5), 394–400. DOI: 10.18178/joams.5.5.394-400

Loivet, W., Taghipour, A., & Kang, D. S. (2020). The rise of green supply chain management: Between complexity and necessity. *J. Econ. Bus. Manag*, *8*(1), 1–7. DOI: 10.18178/joebm.2020.8.1.604

Mahfod, J., Canel-Depitre, B., & Taghipour, A. (2019). Quality function deployment-ELECTRE in supplier evaluation. Journal of advanced management science, 7(4).

Mbiatem, J., Taghipour, A., & Canel-Depitre, B. (2018, August). Supplier selection approaches for decision makers. In *Proceedings of the 8th International Conference on Information Communication and Management* (pp. 108-112).

Nadia, E. N., Beatrice, C. D., & Atour, T. (2020). Luxury hotels' eco-friendly activities & customers' preferences and willingness to pay for green hotels. *Journal of Advanced Management Science*, *8*(1), 1–24.

Nadia, E. N., Beatrice, C. D., & Atour, T. (2021). The determinants of hotel room rates in Beirut: A hedonic pricing model. International Journal of Trade. *Economics and Finance*, *12*(2), 33–42.

OECD. (2018). *Due Diligence Guidance for Responsible Business Conduct.*

Ponputtha, W., Wannapiroon, P., Nilsook, P., Taghipour, A., Murat, S., Huang, P., & Chou, T. C. (2021). Creative history learning model using digital storytelling through cloud learning to enhance analytical thinking. International Journal of e-Education, e-Business, e-. *Management Learning*, *11*(2), 42–50.

Ren, Z., Taghipour, A., & Canel-Depitre, B. (2016, October). Information sharing in supply chain under uncertainty. In 2016 6th International Conference on Information Communication and Management (ICICM) (pp. 67-71). IEEE. DOI: 10.1109/INFOCOMAN.2016.7784217

Sahraoui, A., Tran, N. K., Tliche, Y., Kacem, A., & Taghipour, A. (2023). Examining ICT Innovation for Sustainable Terminal Operations in Developing Countries: A Case Study of the Port of Radès in Tunisia. *Sustainability (Basel)*, *15*(11), 9123. DOI: 10.3390/su15119123

Taghipour, A. (2009). Evaluation de la collaboration dans une chaîne d'approvisionnement. Revue française de gestion industrielle, 28(1), 26-42.

Taghipour, A., & Beneteau-Piet, C. (2020). Sustainable supply chain management performance. *International Journal of Innovation, Management and Technology*, *11*(6), 165–169. DOI: 10.18178/ijimt.2020.11.6.897

Taghipour, A., Fooladvand, A., Khazaei, M., & Ramezani, M. (2023a). Criteria clustering and supplier segmentation based on sustainable shared value using BWM and PROMETHEE. *Sustainability (Basel)*, *15*(11), 8670. DOI: 10.3390/su15118670

Taghipour, A., & Merimi, M. (2021, March). Digital transformation of supply chains during crisis: covid-19. In 11th Annual International Conference on Industrial Engineering and Operations Management, IEOM (pp. 7493-7501). DOI: 10.46254/AN11.20211298

Taghipour, A., Sohrabi, A., Ghaedi, M., & Khazaei, M. (2023b). A robust vaccine supply chain model in pandemics: Case of Covid-19 in Iran. *Computers & Industrial Engineering*, *183*, 109465. DOI: 10.1016/j.cie.2023.109465

Tliche, Y., Taghipour, A., & Canel-Depitre, B. (2019). Downstream Demand Inference in decentralized supply chains. *European Journal of Operational Research, 274*(1), 65–77. DOI: 10.1016/j.ejor.2018.09.034

Tliche, Y., Taghipour, A., Mahfod-Leroux, J., & Vosooghidizaji, M. (2023). Collaborative bullwhip effect-oriented bi-objective optimization for inference-based weighted moving average forecasting in decentralized supply chain. [IJISSCM]. *International Journal of Information Systems and Supply Chain Management, 16*(1), 1–37. DOI: 10.4018/IJISSCM.316168

UN Human Rights Council. (2011). *UN Guiding Principles on Business and Human Rights.*

Vosooghidizaji, M., Taghipour, A., & Canel-Depitre, B. (2020). Information asymmetry in supply chain coordination: State of the art. *Journal of Industrial and Intelligent Information, 8*(2), 38–43. DOI: 10.18178/jiii.8.2.38-43

Wieland, A. (2021). The responsible supply chain. *Journal of Business Ethics.*

World Economic Forum. (2020). *Shaping the Future of Technology Governance: AI in Supply Chains.*

Zoghlami, N., Taghipour, A., Merlo, C., & Abed, M. (2016). Management of divergent production network using decentralised multi-level capacitated lot-sizing models. *International Journal of Shipping and Transport Logistics, 8*(5), 590–604. DOI: 10.1504/IJSTL.2016.078686

Chapter 3
Digital Literacy for Inclusive Growth:
The Rural Perspective in India

Amrita Sekhon
http://orcid.org/0000-0002-0974-0692
Bibi Sharan Kaur Khalsa College, India

ABSTRACT

Digital literacy is increasingly recognized as a critical enabler of inclusive growth in rural India, where access to technology and digital tools remains uneven. This paper explores the current state of digital literacy in rural regions and analyzes the socio-economic implications of the rural-urban digital divide. The research identifies key barriers that hinder adoption of technology among marginalized communities. It emphasizes the transformative role of digital literacy in empowering rural populations by improving access to education, healthcare, financial services and employment opportunities. The findings underline that bridging the digital divide is not solely a technological challenge but a socio-economic imperative central to India's development goals. Digital literacy is a catalyst for empowerment and sustainable growth, to transform rural communities into active participants in India's digital economy. This paper advocates for inclusive, scalable and community-driven strategies to ensure equitable access and unlock the transformative power of digital technology for all.

INTRODUCTION

In the 21st century, digital literacy has emerged as a critical skill for social empowerment, economic growth, and active participation in an increasingly technology-

DOI: 10.4018/979-8-2600-3199-5.ch003

driven world. In India, where over two-thirds of the population still resides in rural areas, bridging the gap between urban and rural digital access is vital for inclusive and sustainable development. Digital literacy refers not only to the ability to use computers and smartphones but also to the capacity to navigate the internet, access online services, evaluate digital information critically, and utilize digital tools effectively in everyday life. With the rapid growth of Information and Communication Technology (ICT) infrastructure, India is experiencing a paradigm shift toward a knowledge-based economy; however, the benefits of this digital revolution are not equally distributed. Rural communities often face challenges such as inadequate infrastructure, high device costs, low awareness, and limited digital skills, all of which perpetuate socio-economic inequalities.

Recognizing this, the Indian government has prioritized digital inclusion through initiatives such as the Digital India Mission, BharatNet Project, and Pradhan Mantri Gramin Digital Saksharta Abhiyan (PMGDISHA), which aim to provide affordable internet access, strengthen ICT infrastructure, and enhance digital literacy in rural populations. Digital literacy in rural areas is not merely a technological necessity but a driver of inclusive growth—it empowers individuals to access education, government services, financial resources, employment opportunities, and healthcare with greater ease and efficiency. By integrating rural communities into the digital ecosystem, India can foster greater participation in governance, promote entrepreneurship, and create a more equitable society.

The rural perspective on digital literacy is crucial because rural India represents both the country's cultural roots and its developmental challenges. Digital literacy initiatives, when aligned with local needs and languages, can empower marginalized groups, including women, farmers, and small business owners, thereby reducing the urban-rural divide. As India aspires to become a $5 trillion economy, ensuring that rural citizens are digitally equipped is central to achieving inclusive growth, where no one is left behind in the digital transformation. This paper explores the role of digital literacy in bridging socio-economic disparities, the efforts taken to enhance rural connectivity, and the transformative potential of digital empowerment in rural India.

Problem Statement

Despite India's rapid technological advancement and the growth of its digital economy, a significant digital divide continues to separate urban and rural populations. While cities are witnessing widespread internet penetration, smartphone usage, and access to digital services, rural areas often struggle with inadequate infrastructure, unreliable connectivity, and a lack of digital literacy. According to recent data, a large proportion of India's rural population remains digitally excluded, limiting their ability to access essential services such as education, e-governance, financial inclusion initiatives, and healthcare resources. This exclusion exacerbates socio-economic inequalities, leaving rural communities at a disadvantage in terms of opportunities, participation in decision-making and overall development.

The problem is not just about physical access to technology but also about digital competence—the ability to effectively use digital tools for learning, business, and daily life. Factors such as low awareness, gender disparities, limited content in local languages, and economic constraints further widen this gap. Without deliberate, large-scale efforts to promote digital literacy in rural India, the goal of inclusive growth will remain unattainable. Addressing this challenge is crucial for ensuring equitable participation in India's digital transformation and achieving sustainable development.

Objectives

1. To analyze the current state of digital literacy in rural India and identify the key factors contributing to the rural-urban digital divide.
2. To examine government initiatives and policies such as Digital India, PMGDISHA, and BharatNet, and evaluate their effectiveness in promoting digital inclusion.
3. To explore the socio-economic impact of digital literacy on rural communities, including its role in improving access to education, healthcare, financial services, and employment.
4. To understand challenges and barriers faced by rural populations in adopting digital tools and technology, with a focus on infrastructure, affordability, awareness, and skills.
5. To propose strategies and recommendations for enhancing digital literacy and bridging the digital divide, enabling inclusive growth in India's rural sector.

LITERATURE REVIEW

The concept of the digital divide has evolved over the past two decades, moving beyond basic internet access to encompass digital skills, affordability, relevance, and usage patterns (van Dijk, 2020). Scholars increasingly frame the divide as a multi-dimensional phenomenon influenced by socioeconomic, geographic, gender, and cultural factors (Salemink et al., 2017). In India, this complexity is particularly pronounced given the country's demographic diversity and disparities in infrastructure development across states (Meher & Sahoo, 2021).

Several studies emphasize that rural India faces triple-layered barriers—limited infrastructure, low affordability, and poor digital literacy. Tripathi (2020) argues that affordability is a significant determinant, with many low-income households prioritizing basic needs over digital connectivity. Similarly, Chaudhary (2021) identifies infrastructural limitations, such as unreliable electricity and mobile tower coverage, as critical obstacles in rural and remote regions.

Research on gender disparities further highlights systemic inequalities. Iqbal (2021) and Jeffrie (2025) document that Indian women—particularly in rural areas—experience lower rates of smartphone ownership and autonomy in technology use due to cultural norms, lower income levels, and safety concerns. Reports from GSMA (2022) and Live Mint (2025) reinforce these findings, showing that despite the growing penetration of UPI-based financial tools, many rural women still rely on shared devices, reinforcing dependency.

Policy-oriented literature underscores the importance of programs like Digital India (MeitY, 2015) and Pradhan Mantri Gramin Digital Saksharta Abhiyan (PMGDISHA), which have successfully introduced millions to basic digital tools (MeitY, 2019). However, studies also question the sustainability of these efforts. Rao and Jena (2020) found that while e-governance initiatives improved service delivery, adoption among rural populations lagged due to low awareness and a lack of localized content.

Global perspectives enrich the Indian context, emphasizing that digital inequality is not merely a technological issue but also a social determinant of health and development (Benda et al., 2020). The World Bank (2021) emphasizes that South Asian nations, including India, must move from connectivity expansion to fostering meaningful connectivity—defined as access that is affordable, reliable, and productive.

Newer scholarship highlights the role of community-based ICT interventions. Moitra et al. (2021) and Singh (2021) demonstrate that mobile-based media platforms and grassroots networks can empower communities by delivering locally relevant information, thereby reducing dependency on traditional infrastructure. Similarly, Kar et al. (2024) call for targeted innovation hubs in rural India to enhance digital inclusion.

Finally, the literature identifies emerging trends:

- Integration of AI-driven tools in rural governance and education to bridge gaps in service delivery (Pathrose & Seethalakshmi, 2025).
- The push toward digital financial inclusion, which correlates positively with economic development in underserved regions (Sarma & Pais, 2019).
- Increasing recognition of digital literacy as a fundamental human capability, akin to reading and writing (UNESCO, 2022).

In sum, the literature reveals that bridging India's digital divide requires a holistic approach that combines infrastructure investment, affordability measures, localized content, and digital literacy training. While flagship programs like BharatNet and Digital India have made commendable progress, researchers highlight the importance of intersectional analysis—addressing disparities based on geography, gender, class, and education simultaneously.

Analyzing the Current State of Digital Literacy in Rural India and Key Factors Contributing to the Rural-Urban Digital Divide

India, home to over 1.4 billion people, has undergone a massive digital transformation over the past decade, driven by the government's push toward a "Digital India" and rapid technological innovations. Yet, despite these advancements, the digital divide between urban and rural India remains stark. Digital literacy in India is defined as the ability to access, understand, create, and communicate information using digital devices and the internet. In urban regions, high-speed internet connectivity, smartphone penetration, and digital service availability have become commonplace, whereas rural areas continue to face significant challenges in accessing and effectively utilizing these technologies. This divide hinders rural populations from fully participating in the digital economy and benefitting from India's technological growth. Figure 1 shows the factors contributing to the digital divide in India.

Figure 1. Factors contributing to the digital divide in India

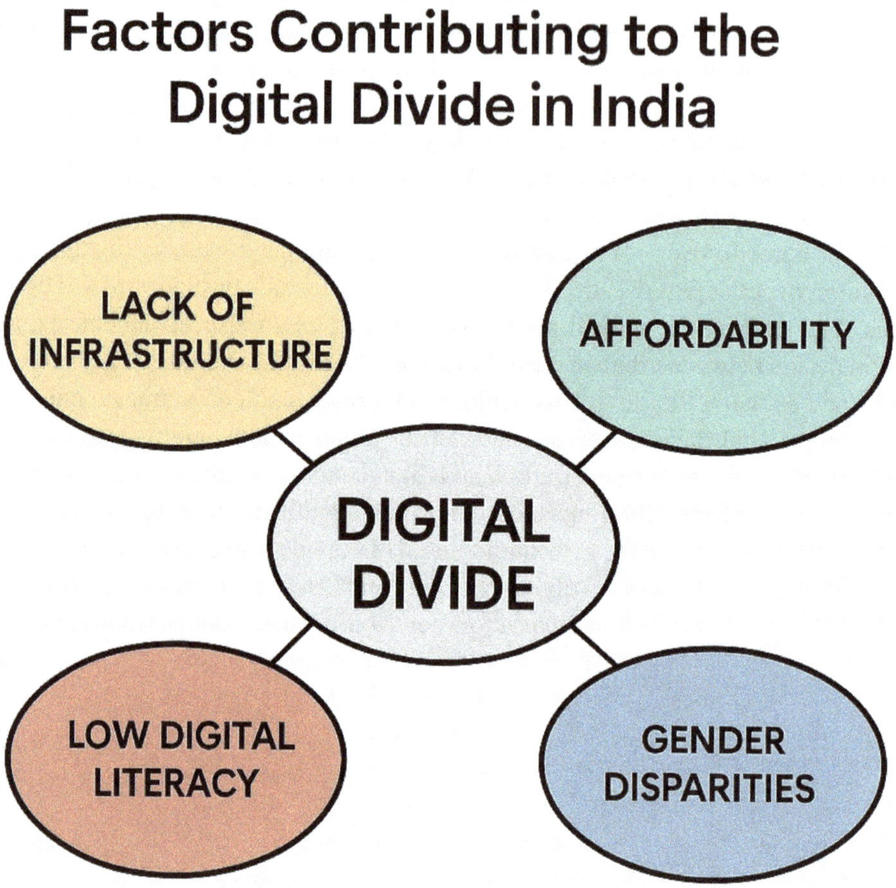

Current State of Digital Literacy in Rural India

Recent reports show that while India has over 800 million internet users, internet penetration is uneven, with urban India enjoying about 70–75% penetration compared to only around 40–45% in rural areas. Smartphone adoption is growing steadily in rural India, largely due to cheaper devices and affordable data plans introduced by telecom providers, yet usage is often limited to entertainment purposes rather than productive activities. According to the Pradhan Mantri Gramin Digital Saksharta Abhiyan (PMGDISHA) data, over 40 million rural households have been trained in basic digital skills, but this figure still represents a fraction of India's rural population.

Moreover, many rural citizens lack exposure to advanced digital competencies such as online banking, e-governance services, and information verification.

While government programs such as Common Service Centres (CSCs) and initiatives like BharatNet have extended digital infrastructure to remote areas, a large proportion of rural communities remain digitally underprepared. Many households still rely on a single smartphone per family, with poor network quality and limited access to personal computing devices like laptops or tablets. Digital literacy levels vary significantly between states, with southern and western regions performing better due to stronger ICT infrastructure, while states in the North-East, central, and eastern India lag behind.

Key Factors Contributing to the Rural-Urban Digital Divide

1. Infrastructure Gaps:

Rural areas often lack high-speed internet connectivity, consistent electricity supply, and reliable digital infrastructure. BharatNet's optical fiber network rollout is ongoing but not yet universal, leaving several villages without reliable broadband access.

2. Economic Constraints:

Poverty remains a key barrier to digital inclusion. Many rural households cannot afford smartphones, computers, or data subscriptions. Low-income families prioritize basic needs over digital tools, which limit access and skill acquisition.

3. Low Awareness and Education Levels:

Digital literacy is closely tied to basic literacy and education. Many rural populations, especially older generations, lack formal education, making it challenging to learn and adapt to digital technologies. This results in slower adoption and limited confidence in using digital tools.

4. Language and Content Barriers:

The majority of digital content is available in English or Hindi, whereas rural India is linguistically diverse. The lack of localized content and user-friendly interfaces discourages rural citizens from engaging with online services effectively.

5. Gender Disparities:

Gender inequality widens the digital divide, with fewer women in rural areas having access to smartphones or digital training. Cultural norms and household responsibilities often limit women's access to digital devices and skill-building opportunities.

6. Skill Gaps and Limited Digital Training:

Basic smartphone use is common, but advanced digital skills such as navigating government portals, digital banking, or using e-learning platforms are scarce. Programs like PMGDISHA (for Pradhan Mantri Gramin Digital Saksharta Abhiyan – a Rural Digital Literacy Campaign) are making progress but need wider reach and more depth.

7. Socio-Cultural Barriers:

In many rural areas, cultural beliefs and a fear of technology hinder digital adoption. Resistance to change and trust deficits in digital transactions (such as online payments) further deepen the divide.

8. Inconsistent Policy Implementation:

While India has strong digital inclusion policies, gaps remain in implementation due to logistical challenges, lack of trained facilitators, and poor monitoring in rural regions.

Exploring the Socio-Economic Impact of Digital Literacy on Rural Communities

Digital literacy has emerged as a transformative force in rural India, shaping social and economic development by bridging the gap between urban and rural populations. It equips individuals with the knowledge and skills required to navigate digital platforms, access information, and participate in the digital economy. For rural communities—where barriers such as geographical isolation, inadequate infrastructure, and socio-economic inequalities persist—digital literacy serves as a critical enabler of empowerment, inclusion, and upward mobility. By facilitating access to education, healthcare, financial services, and employment, digital literacy plays a central role in fostering sustainable and inclusive growth.

1. Education: Enhancing Learning Opportunities and Reducing Disparities

Digital literacy has revolutionized education in rural areas, enabling students and teachers to access vast online learning resources, e-books, and video-based content. Initiatives like DIKSHA (Digital Infrastructure for Knowledge Sharing - a national digital platform for teachers, students, and parents in India), SWAYAM (Study Webs of Active Learning for Young Aspiring Minds - providing free online Massive Open Online Courses (MOOCs)), and PM eVIDYA (Pradhan Mantri eV-idya - a comprehensive digital education initiative) have made quality educational material available in multiple languages, making it easier for students in remote areas to access content at par with urban peers. During the COVID-19 pandemic, rural digital literacy played a vital role in continuing education through online classes and e-learning platforms. Teachers who underwent digital training could integrate technology into classrooms, improving the teaching-learning process.

Additionally, digital classrooms, smart schools, and community learning centers run by NGOs and government initiatives have created localized access to technology, fostering curiosity and self-paced learning. Digital literacy also enables parents to engage with their children's education, track progress, and access government education schemes. However, gaps remain in ensuring equitable access to devices and reliable internet, highlighting the importance of continued investment in rural digital education infrastructure.

2. Healthcare: Bridging Gaps through Telemedicine and Information Access

Digital literacy has made healthcare more accessible to rural populations through telemedicine platforms, mobile health applications, and online health resources. Initiatives such as eSanjeevani, India’s telemedicine service, have enabled rural patients to consult doctors remotely, reducing the need for travel to urban centers. Digital platforms also disseminate critical health information, vaccination reminders, and disease awareness campaigns in local languages, improving preventive healthcare practices.

Community health workers and Accredited Social Health Activists (ASHAs) are increasingly trained in using mobile applications for data collection, maternal care tracking, and digital record-keeping. For rural women, who often face restricted mobility, access to digital health resources enhances decision-making and early diagnosis. Overall, digital literacy helps reduce healthcare inequities by connecting rural populations to timely medical advice, specialist consultations, and government health schemes.

3. Financial Services: Promoting Financial Inclusion and Empowerment

One of the most significant socio-economic impacts of digital literacy in rural India is the expansion of financial inclusion. With the rise of mobile banking, UPI (Unified Payments Interface), and digital wallets, even those in remote areas can conduct secure transactions, access savings accounts, and receive direct benefit transfers (DBTs). Digital literacy empowers rural citizens to understand and trust digital payment platforms, reducing dependence on cash and middlemen.

Government schemes like Jan Dhan Yojana combined with Aadhaar-linked digital banking have enabled millions of rural households to receive subsidies directly, eliminating corruption and delays. Farmers can now access crop insurance, weather forecasts, and market prices through mobile apps, while small entrepreneurs and self-help groups use digital platforms for microcredit, business promotion, and market expansion. Financial literacy and digital literacy together have created new opportunities for rural women entrepreneurs, strengthening local economies.

4. Employment: Unlocking Opportunities and Skill Development

Digital literacy significantly enhances employment prospects for rural youth by opening access to skill development programs, job portals, and remote work opportunities. Platforms like Skill India, FutureSkills PRIME, and National Career Service provide online training in fields ranging from basic computer operations to emerging technologies like AI and cloud computing. E-commerce platforms have empowered rural artisans and farmers to sell products online, reaching wider markets without intermediaries.

The rise of the gig economy and remote work culture has further created opportunities for rural youth to work for urban and international clients without leaving their hometowns. Women, in particular, have benefited from digital platforms offering work-from-home opportunities, enabling them to balance household responsibilities while earning income. Moreover, access to agricultural advisories, weather predictions, and digital marketplaces helps farmers make informed decisions, increasing productivity and profitability.

5. Overall Socio-Economic Transformation

Digital literacy has a cascading effect on the overall quality of life in rural India. It fosters social inclusion by connecting marginalized groups to government schemes, social security programs, and grievance redressal platforms. Information access improves civic participation, making rural citizens more aware of their rights and entitlements. The increased use of digital services also boosts rural entrepreneurship, local innovation, and community development. However, persistent challenges such as infrastructure deficits, affordability issues, and cultural barriers must be addressed to ensure the full realization of these benefits.

The socio-economic impact of digital literacy in rural India is profound, with clear benefits in education, healthcare, financial inclusion, and employment generation. Digital empowerment transforms rural communities from passive beneficiaries to active participants in India's growth story, fostering self-reliance and resilience. Continued government investment, public-private partnerships, localized digital content, and targeted awareness campaigns are essential to ensure that digital literacy truly becomes a tool for inclusive growth. By narrowing the digital divide, India can unlock the untapped potential of its rural population, contributing significantly to national progress and economic equity. The table 1 shows the impact made by the government initiatives in various sectors.

Table 1. Digital Literacy Fostering Tangible Change

Sector	Impact
Education & Employment	PMGDISHA-enabled individuals gaining computer skills, securing jobs, and becoming trainers themselves.
Local Governance & Services	VLEs like Rose leading CSCs, providing multiple services and catalyzing women's employment.
Healthcare	eSanjeevani offering remote medical care at scale, especially in underserved regions, with room for broader coverage.
Financial Empowerment	UPI-enabled credit access and rural fintech like eSamudaay enabling entrepreneurs to grow and sustain businesses digitally.

Understanding Challenges and Barriers Faced by Rural Populations in Adopting Digital Tools and Technology

Despite India's rapid digital transformation and a steady rise in rural internet users, a significant digital divide persists between rural and urban areas. While government schemes like Digital India, PMGDISHA, and BharatNet have made digital access a national priority, many rural communities still face barriers that hinder the adoption and effective use of technology. These challenges are multi-faceted, encompassing infrastructural deficits, affordability concerns, low levels of awareness, and insufficient digital skills. Understanding these obstacles is crucial for designing targeted interventions that ensure inclusive digital growth and empower rural populations to fully participate in the digital economy.

1. Infrastructure Deficits: Connectivity Gaps and Power Supply Issues

A major challenge in rural India is the lack of robust digital infrastructure. Although BharatNet aims to connect over 250,000 Gram Panchayats with high-speed internet, implementation has been uneven. Many villages remain underserved, particularly in hilly, remote, and tribal areas. Reports indicate that even in states with strong connectivity initiatives, thousands of villages remain without mobile or broadband coverage. For instance, in Odisha alone, over 1,900 villages lacked mobile connectivity as of mid-2025, while 337 villages in Arunachal Pradesh remain unconnected. Limited network penetration, frequent outages, and slow speeds make internet usage frustrating and unreliable. In addition, irregular power supply compounds the problem, as devices cannot be charged regularly, and broadband infrastructure cannot be fully utilized.

As of September 2024, 97% of India's villages have mobile connectivity, while 4G coverage spans 95.5%—approximately 614,564 out of 644,131 villages. However, connectivity remains inconsistent. In Odisha, 1,921 villages lacked mobile coverage as of August 2025. In the Northeast, 3,841 villages are still without mobile network access, with Arunachal Pradesh alone accounting for 1,735 of them. Broadband access via BharatNet remains limited; as of January 2025, just 30.4% of the 650,000 villages were connected. Indian telecom disparity is stark: urban teledensity is 131.01%, while rural stands at just 58.31%, underscoring poor rural telecom penetration. Despite infrastructure, rural education still suffers. In Madhya Pradesh, only 0.9% of government schools have digital libraries—far below the national average of 6.1%. Smart classrooms are present in just 11.6% of schools, versus 21.2% nationally.

2. Affordability of Devices and Data Services

Affordability is a major barrier to technology adoption in rural households. While India has seen a sharp decline in data costs and the availability of low-cost smartphones, device ownership remains low in rural regions. Many households share a single smartphone, restricting individual access, especially for children and women. Economic constraints force families to prioritize basic necessities over devices, laptops, or tablets, making digital inclusion a secondary priority. Moreover, recurring expenses like data recharge plans, device repair, and software subscriptions are often prohibitive. Although government and private initiatives have improved affordability, these efforts have not fully closed the gap between rural and urban ownership of digital tools.

Mobile access is not equal to device ownership. Among rural women (15+), 76.3% use mobile phones, but only 48.4% actually own one. In contrast, 89.5% of rural men use phones and 80.7% own one. These gaps hinder digital agency and restrict consistent access to technology for women. Broadband adoption remains low among lower-income groups: 71.6% of the poorest households lack broadband access, compared to just 1.9% of the wealthiest.

3. Low Awareness and Trust Deficit

Many rural communities lack awareness about the benefits of digital tools and online services. Limited exposure to technology often leads to hesitancy and mistrust in digital platforms, especially in areas like online banking, telemedicine, and e-governance. Cultural beliefs, misinformation, and fear of cyber fraud discourage digital adoption. For example, rural populations often prefer traditional cash-based transactions over UPI or mobile banking due to concerns about security. Lack of awareness campaigns and localized outreach contributes to the slow pace of adoption, even when services are available.

Even where access exists, lack of awareness and trust dampens usage of digital services like e-governance, telemedicine, and online banking. The gendered digital gap persists: mobile internet adoption among women in India stands at just 30%, while awareness hovers around 60%. Only 30% of women can conduct tasks like mobile money or accessing e-services. Socio-cultural norms blur priorities, with many rural users seeing limited relevance in internet use, especially among women.

4. Limited Digital Literacy and Skills Gap

While mobile phone ownership is growing, true digital literacy—using technology effectively and safely—is still limited. Many rural residents can use messaging apps or social media but lack the ability to navigate government portals, apply for jobs online, verify digital information, or access e-learning platforms. Programs like PMGDISHA have trained millions, but a large percentage of rural adults remain digitally unskilled or partially skilled. Moreover, language barriers exacerbate the skills gap, as much of the digital content is in English or Hindi, excluding people who speak regional languages. Limited availability of digital resources in vernacular languages makes the technology less accessible to those with low literacy levels.

According to ASER 2024, among adolescents aged 14–16, 36.2% of boys and 26.9% of girls own smartphones; over 90% of households with young people have at least one device. Yet, only 57% use smartphones for educational purposes, highlighting low utilitarian digital use. Rural vs urban digital task proficiency shows a stark divide: only 20% of rural users can use email and 37.8% undertake online banking tasks, compared to significantly higher urban rates.

5. Gender Inequality in Digital Access

Gender disparities deepen the digital divide in rural areas. Studies show that women in rural India are less likely to own smartphones or access the internet compared to men. Cultural norms, lower literacy rates among women, and household responsibilities further restrict their engagement with technology. Even in households with internet access, device use is often dominated by men, limiting women's opportunities to learn digital skills or access online services like telemedicine, education, or employment portals. Bridging this gender gap is essential to ensuring equitable digital growth.

Gender inequality remains entrenched: 84% of men own mobile phones versus 56% of women; the skill gap persists even further. Additionally, ASER 2024 reveals that boys outperform girls in digital skills across most states—though Kerala and Karnataka are notable exceptions where girls match or outperform boys.

6. Regional Disparities and Socio-Cultural Barriers

Rural India is not homogenous; digital adoption varies greatly between states and even between districts within a state. States like Kerala and Tamil Nadu have made significant progress due to better infrastructure and higher literacy levels, while regions in the North-East, central, and eastern India continue to lag behind. Cultural barriers also influence adoption, as some rural communities remain skeptical of technology or see it as irrelevant to their livelihoods. For farmers and older generations, for instance, a lack of digital education makes them reliant on intermediaries, limiting their direct interaction with technology.

Regional discrepancies shape access too. For example, Punjab sees 96.2% of adolescents having smartphone access at home, far surpassing the national average of 89.1%.

7. Cybersecurity Concerns and Lack of Digital Safety Training

Fear of online scams, identity theft, and financial fraud also discourages digital engagement. Without proper training in cyber safety, rural users are vulnerable to exploitation, which in turn reinforces skepticism about online platforms. The absence of community-level training programs in cybersecurity further slows digital adoption.

Table 2 shows the barriers faced by the rural population in adopting digital tools.

Table 2. Barriers faced by the Indian rural population in adopting digital tools

Barrier	Description & Statistics
Connectivity	95.5% 4G coverage nationwide, but over 1,900 villages in Odisha and 3,800 in Northeast lack mobile access.
Infrastructure	Only ~30% villages have broadband; teledensity is 58% in rural vs 131% in urban areas.
Affordability	Major ownership gap: only 48.4% rural women own mobile phones. Broadband remains inaccessible to poorer households.
Awareness & Culture	Even with devices, usage for education or services is limited; cultural perceptions also hinder adoption.
Skills Gap	Only 20% rural users are proficient in basic digital tasks; gender disparity persists in access and skills.
Regional Disparities	States like Punjab fare better; others—especially Hindi heartland and Northeastern areas—lag behind.

Rural India's digital adoption is hampered by intertwined challenges: while infrastructure has expanded, it remains inconsistently distributed; affordability issues, especially among women and low-income households, restrict digital ownership; awareness and cultural barriers limit meaningful usage; and persistent skill gaps create a widening rural-urban digital divide. To foster truly inclusive digital growth, interventions must go beyond connectivity—addressing affordability, literacy, gender equity, and regional disparities.

The challenges facing rural India in adopting digital tools and technology are deeply interconnected, reflecting a combination of economic limitations, infrastructure deficits, low awareness, cultural barriers, and gender inequality. While government programs like PMGDISHA, BharatNet, and Digital India are making significant strides, bridging this divide requires a multi-layered approach. Infrastructure investment must be paired with digital literacy campaigns, local-language resources, skill development programs, and cybersecurity awareness initiatives to empower rural citizens. Without addressing these barriers holistically, India risks leaving large sections of its rural population behind in its journey toward a fully digital society.

Strategies Adopted by India to Bridge the Digital Divide

India has been making significant efforts to reduce disparities in access to digital technology and promote digital inclusion, especially among rural and underserved communities. India's approach combines infrastructure development, affordable technology access, digital literacy, and policy interventions to bridge the digital divide. The Digital India Mission acts as an umbrella initiative to ensure "Power to Empower" through digital inclusion.

Below are the key strategies adopted by the Indian administration to bridge the Digital Divide in India:

1. Digital Infrastructure Development
   • BharatNet Project: Laying optical fiber cables to connect more than 250,000 Gram Panchayats, ensuring high-speed internet in rural areas.
   • National Knowledge Network (NKN): Connecting educational and research institutions to a high-speed network for knowledge sharing.
   • PM WANI Scheme (Wi-Fi Access): Providing affordable and accessible public Wi-Fi through small entrepreneurs and Public Data Offices (PDOs).
   • Expansion of Mobile Networks: Increasing 4G/5G coverage and mobile towers to remote areas.
2. Affordable Access to Technology
   • Digital India Programme: Promoting affordable internet, low-cost devices, and e-services for all citizens.
   • BSNL and Other State Initiatives: Offering subsidized internet services and devices in rural areas.
   • PLI Schemes (Production-Linked Incentives): Encouraging domestic manufacturing of smartphones and IT hardware, lowering costs.
3. Digital Literacy and Skills Training
   • Pradhan Mantri Gramin Digital Saksharta Abhiyan (PMGDISHA): Aiming to make 60 million rural adults digitally literate.
   • National Digital Literacy Mission (NDLM): Building basic ICT skills in marginalized communities.
   • Skill India & FutureSkills PRIME: Training youth in emerging technologies like AI, cloud, and cybersecurity.
4. E-Governance and Digital Services
   • Common Service Centres (CSCs): Providing digital services (banking, health, education, e-documents) in rural areas.
   • UMANG & DigiLocker: Offering government services, certificates, and documents online.
   • Direct Benefit Transfer (DBT): Digitizing subsidy and welfare schemes to reach beneficiaries directly.
5. Inclusive Policies and Initiatives
   • Aadhaar-Based Digital Identity: Enabling easy access to services for all citizens.
   • Digital Payment Systems (UPI, BHIM): Promoting cashless economy and financial inclusion.
   • Special Schemes for NE States & Aspirational Districts: Focusing on underserved regions to ensure balanced growth.
6. Public-Private Partnerships (PPP)
   • Collaborations with tech companies (Google, Microsoft, Reliance Jio, etc.) for rural internet penetration and digital skilling.

• Corporate Social Responsibility (CSR) projects promoting digital classrooms and community centers.

7. Emerging Technologies for Inclusion

    • Satellite Internet (e.g., BharatNet Satellite, Starlink trials): Bringing connectivity to remote and hilly areas.

    • 5G and AI-Powered Solutions: Using new tech for education, healthcare, and agriculture in underserved areas.

In addition, India has focused on inclusive policies to extend digital benefits to all citizens. The introduction of Aadhaar, a biometric-based digital identity system, has streamlined access to services, while innovations like Unified Payments Interface (UPI) and BHIM promote financial inclusion through cashless transactions. Special focus has been given to remote regions, including the North-Eastern states and Aspirational Districts, to reduce regional disparities in digital access. Public-private partnerships have played a crucial role, with companies like Google, Microsoft, and Reliance Jio contributing to internet penetration, digital classrooms, and community outreach. Furthermore, India is leveraging emerging technologies like satellite internet and 5G to connect hard-to-reach areas, and artificial intelligence (AI) is being integrated into education, healthcare, and agriculture services for rural empowerment.

Overall, India's strategy to bridge the digital divide is a holistic blend of infrastructure expansion, technology affordability, skill development, and inclusive policies. Under the umbrella of the Digital India Mission, the government envisions empowering citizens with access to digital opportunities, narrowing socio-economic gaps, and fostering a more inclusive digital society.

Table 3 shows the effective solutions and major national policy interventions to tackle the challenges rural India faces in adopting digital tools and bridging the rural-urban digital divide. It shows how India is working towards inclusive digital growth in rural areas.

Table 3. Indian Government strategies to bridge the rural-urban digital divide

Challenge	**Key Issues**	**Solutions**	**National Policy Interventions**
Infrastructure Gaps (Connectivity & Power)	Poor broadband and 4G coverage in remote villages; power shortages	-Accelerate BharatNet rollout for fiber-based broadband in all villages -Promote community Wi-Fi hotspots -Strengthen rural telecom tower networks -Renewable energy for rural ICT infrastructure	BharatNet Project (connecting 6.5 lakh villages) Universal Service Obligation Fund (USOF) to subsidize rural telecom PM GatiShakti to integrate infrastructure planning Digital India Programme to boost connectivity
Affordability of Devices & Internet	High device and data costs; low smartphone ownership among rural women & low-income groups	-Subsidize smartphones /tablets for rural households -Expand low-cost internet plans -Promote refurbished devices and local manufacturing -Encourage microfinance for device purchase	PM Gramin Digital Saksharta Abhiyan (PMGDISHA) for training and low-cost access PLI Scheme for Electronics Manufacturing to reduce device costs BSNL Bharat AirFibre affordable connectivity solutions
Awareness & Cultural Barriers	Low trust in online services; lack of perceived relevance	-Community-based digital awareness drives -Vernacular-language digital literacy campaigns -Promote success stories of rural digital entrepreneurs -Women-led digital awareness programs	Digital India Awareness Campaigns Common Service Centres (CSCs) as village-level awareness hubs Digital Saksharta Abhiyan (DISHA) for basic digital training
Skills & Literacy Gap	Limited ability to use e-services, online payments, telemedicine, etc.	-Integrate digital literacy into school curriculum -Skill training for rural youth, women, and farmers -Promote peer-to-peer learning models	Skill India Mission (digital literacy modules) PMGDISHA (aims to make 60 million rural adults digitally literate) SWAYAM for online education
Gender Divide	Women less likely to own or use devices	-Women-only digital skill training centers -Subsidized devices for women -ICT-based livelihood schemes for rural women	Mahila e-Haat for women entrepreneurs Digital Beti Campaign PMGDISHA (Women Priority) targeting women literacy

continued on following page

Table 3. Continued

Challenge	Key Issues	Solutions	National Policy Interventions
Regional Disparities	Northeastern and hilly regions lag behind	-State-specific digital infrastructure incentives -Special funds for remote regions -Regional innovation hubs	North East Rural Connectivity Project Aspirational Districts Programme with digital focus
Limited Use of ICT for Services	Rural communities underuse e-governance, telehealth, fintech	-Expand telemedicine and AgriTech apps -Localize e-Gov services in regional languages -Strengthen financial literacy campaigns	eNAM (Agriculture Market) Ayushman Bharat Digital Mission (health records) Jan Dhan-Aadhaar-Mobile (JAM) Trinity for financial inclusion

FUTURE DIRECTIONS

To ensure digital literacy becomes a cornerstone of inclusive growth in rural India, future research and policy initiatives must adopt a holistic and sustainable approach:

1. Localized Digital Education Models

Future programs should focus on creating context-specific training modules in regional languages and culturally relevant content. Community-led digital literacy initiatives, especially those involving local educators and volunteers, can help rural populations relate to technology in meaningful ways.

2. Integration of Emerging Technologies

As India transitions to advanced digital ecosystems, incorporating Artificial Intelligence (AI), machine learning, and Internet of Things (IoT)-based solutions in rural governance, agriculture, and healthcare should be prioritized. Future research can explore scalable and affordable models for deploying these technologies.

3. Gender-Inclusive and Marginalized Group Focus

Digital inclusion strategies must prioritize women, persons with disabilities, and socially marginalized communities. Programs should address gender-based barriers and provide equal opportunities for skill development and entrepreneurship.

4. Strengthening Public-Private Partnerships (PPP)

Collaboration between government agencies, private companies, NGOs, and local communities will be essential to expand infrastructure, reduce costs, and introduce innovative solutions. Research can investigate sustainable PPP models to accelerate rural connectivity.

5. Focus on Digital Entrepreneurship

Future strategies should emphasize creating rural digital hubs and promoting entrepreneurship through e-commerce, digital payments, and micro-enterprises. This can help transform rural communities into self-sustaining digital economies.

6. Impact Assessment Frameworks

Long-term studies are needed to measure the effectiveness of digital literacy programs, infrastructure investments, and policy reforms. Developing a robust evaluation framework will help in refining strategies and ensuring that rural populations fully benefit from digital inclusion initiatives.

7. Resilience Against Digital Inequality

As technology evolves, rural communities risk being left behind again. Future research should anticipate these challenges and design adaptive learning systems, low-cost devices, and innovative financing models to maintain long-term inclusivity.

CONCLUSION

The digital divide between rural and urban India is not solely a matter of connectivity; it is a multi-dimensional issue shaped by infrastructure, economics, education, cultural factors, and gender disparities. Although initiatives such as Digital India, PMGDISHA, BharatNet, and CSCs are helping to expand digital literacy, rural communities still face barriers that limit their participation in India's digital growth story. Bridging this gap will require a combination of infrastructure investment, community-level training, localized digital content, and policy innovation to ensure rural India is not left behind in the digital age.

Digital literacy has emerged as a transformative force in fostering inclusive growth in rural India, acting as a bridge between marginalized communities and opportunities in education, healthcare, financial inclusion, and employment. However, despite significant government initiatives like Digital India, PMGDISHA, BharatNet, and other state-led interventions, rural India continues to face persistent challenges such as inadequate digital infrastructure, affordability issues, low awareness levels, and limited digital skills. These factors perpetuate the rural-urban digital divide, which, if left unaddressed, could exacerbate existing socio-economic inequalities.

The evidence from numerous studies highlights that digital literacy not only empowers individuals but also strengthens rural economies, enhances governance, and promotes social inclusion. Greater access to digital tools can help rural communities participate actively in India's knowledge economy, access vital services, and improve overall quality of life. However, achieving this vision requires a multi-pronged strategy that combines investment in robust digital infrastructure, affordable internet and devices, community-led awareness programs, and inclusive digital education initiatives.

A people-centric approach is crucial—one that prioritizes women, marginalized castes, and geographically remote populations—ensuring equitable opportunities for all. Strengthening public-private partnerships, expanding community-based training programs, and leveraging local languages and culturally sensitive content can accelerate adoption. As India transitions toward a digitally empowered society, bridging this divide is not only a developmental priority but also a social responsibility.

This paper explores the current state of digital literacy in rural regions and analyzes the socio-economic implications of the rural-urban digital divide. Drawing on government initiatives such as Digital India, Pradhan Mantri Gramin Digital Saksharta Abhiyan (PMGDISHA), and BharatNet, along with community-driven interventions, the study highlights both achievements and gaps in advancing digital inclusion. Through an interdisciplinary lens, this paper emphasizes the transformative role of digital literacy in empowering rural populations by improving access to education, healthcare, financial services, and employment opportunities. Evidence from multiple studies demonstrates that targeted digital interventions can boost economic resilience, enhance governance, and promote social equity. However, these benefits can only be fully realized through a multi-pronged approach that integrates affordable connectivity, localized training programs, culturally relevant content, and strong public-private partnerships.

Ultimately, digital literacy in rural India is not just a skill but a catalyst for empowerment, resilience, and sustainable development. By addressing existing barriers with targeted interventions, India can create a future where digital inclusion becomes the foundation of equitable growth, unlocking the true potential of its rural population and driving the nation toward holistic progress.

REFERENCES

Benda, N. C., Veinot, T. C., Sieck, C. J., & Ancker, J. S. (2020). Broadband internet access is a social determinant of health! *American Journal of Public Health, 110*(8), 1123–1125. DOI: 10.2105/AJPH.2020.305784 PMID: 32639914

BharatNet. (2024, August 5). 95% Indian villages have internet connectivity [Press release].

Chaudhary, A. (2021). Rural-urban disparities in digital access: Barriers to ICT adoption. *Indian Journal of Development Research, 15*(2), 23–34.

Common Service Centres. (2025). In *Wikipedia*. Retrieved September 1, 2025, from https://en.wikipedia.org/wiki/Common_Service_Centres

GSMA. (2022). *The mobile gender gap report 2022*. GSMA. https://www.gsma.com/r/gender-gap

India, D. (2025). In *Wikipedia*. Retrieved September 1, 2025, from https://en.wikipedia.org/wiki/Digital_India

India, T. O. (2025, August 7). Over 1,900 villages in Odisha lack mobile connectivity: MoS. *The Times of India*. https://timesofindia.indiatimes.com/city/bhubaneswar/over-1900-villages-in-odisha-lack-mobile-connectivity-mos/articleshow/123173827.cms

India, T. O. (2025a, July 19). State far behind in school digital access, reveals govt data. *The Times of India*. https://timesofindia.indiatimes.com/city/bhopal/state-far-behind-in-school-digital-access-reveals-govt-data/articleshow/122789651.cms

Internet and Mobile Association of India. (2022). *Internet in India 2022*. IAMAI & KANTAR. https://www.iamai.in

Iqbal, R. (2021). Gendering of smartphone ownership and autonomy among youth: Narratives from rural India [Preprint]. *arXiv*. https://arxiv.org/abs/2108.09788

Jeffrie, N. (2025, April 14). The mobile gender gap in South Asia is now widening. *GSMA – Mobile for Development*. https://www.gsma.com/mobilefordevelopment

Kar, T.. (2024). The digital revolution in India: Bridging the gap in rural technology adoption. *Journal of Innovation and Entrepreneurship, 13*(1), 29. Advance online publication. DOI: 10.1186/s13731-024-00380-w

Meher, S., & Sahoo, P. (2021). Digital divide in India: Dimensions and determinants. *Economic and Political Weekly, 56*(24), 45–53.

Ministry of Electronics and Information Technology (MeitY). (2015). *Digital India Programme*. Government of India.

Ministry of Electronics and Information Technology (MeitY). (2019). *Pradhan Mantri Gramin Digital Saksharta Abhiyan (PMGDISHA)*. Government of India.

Live Mint. (2025, June 4). UPI fuels rural women's digital leap—but few own their phones (P. Srivastava & P. Bhattacharya).

Moitra, A., Kumar, A., & Seth, A. (2021). An analysis of impact pathways arising from a mobile-based community media platform in rural India (Mobile Vaani). *arXiv*. https://arxiv.org/abs/2106.15917

Pathrose, A. P., & Seethalakshmi, M. (2025). Impact of the Digital India program in rural villages: A survey-based study. *Vidhyayana – An International Multidisciplinary Peer-Reviewed E-Journal, 10*(si3). DOI: 10.58213/vidhyayana.v10isi3.2213

PMGDISHA. (n.d.). How PMGDISHA is empowering rural India digitally. Retrieved September 1, 2025, from https://www.pmgdisha.in

Press Information Bureau. (2022, December 7). National telemedicine service of India – eSanjeevani achieves 80 million teleconsultations. *IBEF*. https://www.ibef.org

Rao, S., & Jena, R. K. (2020). E-governance and digital literacy in rural India: A transformative study. *Government Information Quarterly*, *37*(3), 101449. DOI: 10.1016/j.giq.2020.101449

Salemink, K., Strijker, D., & Bosworth, G. (2017). Rural development in the digital age: A systematic literature review on unequal ICT availability, adoption, and use in rural areas. *Journal of Rural Studies*, *54*, 360–371. DOI: 10.1016/j.jrurstud.2015.09.001

Sarma, M., & Pais, J. (2019). Financial inclusion and development in India: An assessment. *Journal of Economic Development Studies*, *7*(1), 43–57. DOI: 10.2139/ssrn.3400822

Sentinel Digital Desk. (2025, August 26). 3,841 villages in Northeast remain out of mobile network coverage. *The Sentinel - of This Land, for Its People*. https://www.sentinelassam.com/topheadlines/3841-villages-in-northeast-remain-out-of-mobile-network-coverage

Singh, A. (2021). ICT-driven rural empowerment: Lessons from India. *Journal of Rural Studies*, *82*, 145–154. DOI: 10.1016/j.jrurstud.2021.01.020

Tripathi, R. (2020). Affordability and awareness issues in rural connectivity. *Asian Journal of Technology and Society*, *4*(1), 67–75.

UNESCO. (2022). *Digital literacy for inclusive societies: Policy insights*. UNESCO. https://unesdoc.unesco.org

van Dijk, J. (2020). *The digital divide*. Polity Press.

World Bank. (2021). *Digital development in South Asia: Bridging the connectivity divide*. World Bank. https://www.worldbank.org

Chapter 4
From Resilient to Transformative Supply Chains:
The Enabling Role of Emergent Digital Technologies

Lamia Ben Fredj Ben Alaya
http://orcid.org/0000-0003-1750-7425
IHEC-Carthage, Tunisia

ABSTRACT

In the contemporary globalised landscape, supply chains face intensifying pressures from unpredictable high-impact disruptions, creating an imperative for Supply Chain Resilience. While emerging Digital Technologies are essential enablers - strengthening core Dynamic Capabilities like visibility and flexibility - the path to resilience is fraught with inherent and competing strategic priorities, notably the resilience-efficiency and sustainability-resilience paradoxes. Guided by a multi-theoretical framework, this chapter examines how DTs enhance SCR through direct, mediating, and moderating pathways. It posits that these technologies transcend a merely tactical role, reconciling trade-offs and creating synergies between divergent goals. Ultimately, by enabling Supply Chain Transformative Capabilities, DTs catalyse a shift towards Transformative Supply Chains. This novel, holistic paradigm moves beyond siloed objectives to integrate efficiency, sustainability/circularity, and resilience simultaneously, providing a roadmap for firms to thrive within volatile competitive environments.

DOI: 10.4018/979-8-2600-3199-5.ch004

1. INTRODUCTION

The contemporary globalised world exposes supply chains to increasing pressures from unpredictable disruptions, which can severely threaten firm survival. Major events such as the 2018 US sanctions on ZTE, the 2020-21 Covid-19 pandemic, the 2021 Suez Canal blockage, the 2022 outbreak of war in Ukraine, and the 2023 Panama Canal droughts have clearly demonstrated the urgent need for Supply Chain Resilience (SCR). Although traditional Supply Chain Risk Management (SCRM) remains effective for dealing with recurring operational risks, it has clear limitations, particularly an inability to anticipate unexpected, high-impact disruptions. This highlights the need for resilience strategies that extend beyond traditional mitigation approaches. SCR is defined as a firm's ability to prepare for, respond to, and recover from disruptions within its supply network (Chowdhury & Quaddus, 2016).

Emerging Digital Technologies (DTs) are now a core competitive factor. They play a crucial role not only as capabilities but, more importantly, as key enablers for building SCR. By strengthening Supply Chain Dynamic Capabilities (SCDCs), such as visibility, collaboration, flexibility, and risk management, these technologies enable firms to successfully operate in unpredictable and disruptive environments. However, the effective use of DTs to build resilience remains a complex challenge. As the literature indicates, there are still unclear aspects regarding the optimal configuration of capabilities and how digital technical capabilities depend on integrating relational ones, such as collaboration (Jiang et al., 2023; Taghipour & Lu, 2025). Meanwhile, achieving SCR is complicated by inherent strategic tensions. Modern supply chains are under pressure to integrate resilience, operational efficiency (SCE), and sustainability (SCS) simultaneously. This often leads to conflicts, such as the "resilience-efficiency paradox" (SCR vs. SCE), whereby measures that support one objective can undermine the other. This tension is highlighted by research showing that cost reduction is the main reason for 45% of digital adoptions (Lu & Taghipour, 2025a). Such a strong focus on SCE (i.e., lean operations) can conflict with the redundancy and strategic buffering required for resilience - for instance, maintaining inventory buffers for resilience can conflict with the just-in-time production methods employed for efficiency. A similar "sustainability-resilience paradox" (SCR vs. SCS) exists, since sustainability objectives (e.g. minimal waste or single sourcing) can conflict with resilience requirements (e.g. diversified sourcing and redundancy). This necessitates a thorough transformation of traditional supply chains, moving beyond mere resilience to achieve comprehensive integration of efficiency, circular economy principles and sustainability. Transformative supply chains represent this novel, holistic paradigm for analysing modern competitive networks (Wieland, 2021; Massari et al., 2025).

Although existing research has examined how DTs can enhance resilience (e.g. Zouari et al., 2020; Zhao et al., 2023), a key question remains: can DTs transcend their tactical role to reconcile the inherent tensions between resilience, efficiency, and sustainability? This is a significant gap, given that while 70% of studies address multiple supply chain objectives, only 0.3% examine how digital tools can achieve them simultaneously (Lu & Taghipour, 2025a). This leaves the integration of resilience, efficiency and sustainability largely unexplored. This chapter thus addresses the core research question: *How can DTs enhance SCR and through what mechanisms while simultaneously reconciling its inherent tensions with efficiency (SCE) and sustainability (SCS) to enable truly transformative supply chains?* By examining this complex interplay, we aim to demonstrate that DTs are more than just tools for enhancing adaptive capacity; rather, they are enablers and catalysts of transformative supply chains that can thrive in the face of disruption while also promoting circular and sustainable operations. To this end, we adopt a multi-theoretical framework that integrates perspectives on resources, capabilities, and systemic transformation. Adopting a comprehensive approach that extends beyond a single theoretical framework enables us to thoroughly analyse the intricate mediating and moderating mechanisms underlying the relationship between DTs and SCR. This approach also helps us to elucidate the crucial role of DTs in reconciling the core strategic paradoxes between resilience, efficiency, and sustainability.

The remainder of this chapter is structured as follows. *Section 2* defines the concepts of risk and resilience, examining how strategic capability bundles and Digital Technology (DT) act as key enablers of SCR. *Section 3* provides the theoretical background for DT-enabled SCR, moving from firm-level perspectives, such as the Resource-Based View (RBV) and the Dynamic Capabilities View (DCV), to network-level perspectives (Complex Adaptive Systems and Social-Ecological Systems - SES). *Section 4* is based on RBV and DCV and examines the specific interplay between DT and a firm's internal resources and capabilities, exploring how they collectively strengthen resilience via direct, indirect, mediating, and moderating effects. *Section 5* then shifts focus to the Social-Ecological Systems (SES) paradigm, exploring the transformative potential of DTs that extends beyond conventional notions of resilience. This theoretical shift reflects the increasing pressure on modern supply chains to simultaneously improve operational efficiency, circularity, and sustainability. In light of this, the discussion focuses on the evolving concept of *Transformative Supply Chains* and the pivotal role of DTs in enabling their development. *Section 6* summarises the key findings and identifies opportunities for future research.

2. CONCEPTUAL FOUNDATIONS

2.1 Core Concepts: Risk, SC Risk Management and SC Resilience

Supply chains are complex networks of enterprises that experience continual turbulence, creating the potential for unpredictable disruptions. Since the early 2000s, executives have consistently identified supply chain risks as their highest operational threat (Pettit et al., 2010). Ivanov and Schonberger (2019) defined these risks as the measurable probability of negative outcomes (such as disruptions, delays and financial losses) arising from supply chain vulnerabilities. As illustrated in the Risk Assessment Matrix (Figure 1), these threats are categorised according to their probability and severity.

Figure 1. Risk Assessment Matrix – Probability vs Impact

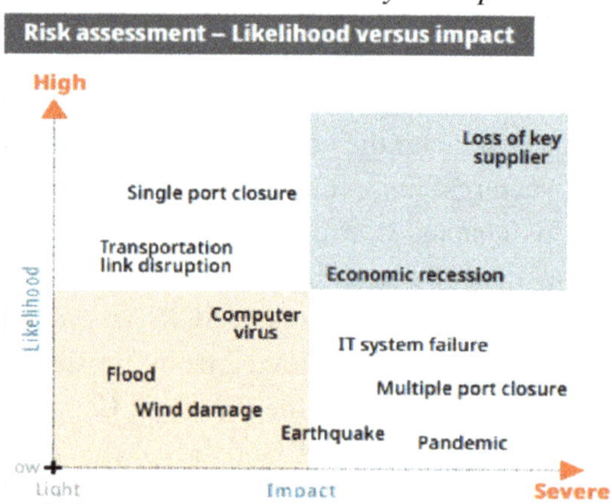

Source: Adapted from Sheffi (2015), as cited in OECD (2024)

This framework operationalises a fundamental and widely cited classification that distinguishes between two core types of risk: recurrent operational risks and disruption risks. Recurrent operational risks involve routine uncertainties in demand and supply that are often associated with the bullwhip effect. These risks can be mitigated through improved coordination and planning (Chopra & Sodhi, 2014). In contrast, disruption risks are rare, high-impact events that trigger systemic "ripple effects" across networks (Ivanov and Schonberger, 2019). Recent examples highlighted by the OECD (2024) include natural disasters (earthquakes or floods), accidents (such as the Evergreen Suez Canal blockage), and intentional shocks like the Russian invasion of Ukraine, which caused global energy and food price spikes.

While traditional risk management effectively mitigates routine and operational risks, it is often limited by statistical gaps and oversimplified assumptions (Fiskel et al., 2015). These constraints result in an inability to anticipate unforeseen disruptions, which can trigger systemic losses and devastating financial consequences, as seen in the 2016 BASF explosion. This limitation highlights a wider issue: traditional risk management often fails to institutionalise lessons from crises, making a paradigm shift towards supply chain resilience (SCR) necessary (Fiskel et al., 2015). Established as a core concept by Christopher and Peck (2004), resilience refers to a system's ability to cope with unavoidable shocks and either return to normal operations or transition to a more desirable state. High-impact crises, such as the COVID-19 pandemic, illustrate the need for this shift. For example, a server failure at Kojima Press, a single supplier, forced the closure of all Toyota plants in Japan, showing how unexpected disruptions can paralyse entire networks. However, despite its recognised importance, resilience can often seem abstract (Zhao et al., 2023) or overly dependent on specific geopolitical contexts, which makes it difficult to implement without a solid theoretical foundation (Richey et al., 2009). In an attempt to bridge this gap between theory and practice, Ponomarov and Holcomb (2009) define SCR as an "adaptive capability" that enables a system to prepare for, respond to and recover from disruptions while maintaining operational continuity. This process goes beyond mere survival, facilitating the renewal and strengthening of systems after disruption (Brusset and Teller, 2017) through the coordination of physical, human, technological and organisational resources (Nelson & Winter, 1982). This mechanism of adaptation is best understood through the Dynamic Capabilities View (DCV).

2.2 The Theoretical Foundation and Strategic Levers of SCR

Based on the conceptualisation of resilience as an adaptive capability, the Dynamic Capabilities View (DCV) provides a strong theoretical framework for analysing how supply chains evolve during crises. Grounded in the Resource-Based View, the DCV shifts the focus from static assets to higher-order capabilities. Teece (2025) defines these as the strategic capacity to "integrate, reconfigure, and adapt" lower-order operational competencies to meet changing environments. Dynamic Capabilities (DCs) encompass sensing, seizing, and reconfiguring (Teece, 2025), adaptive, absorptive, and innovative (Wang & Ahmed, 2007), as well as learning and coordinating capabilities (Pavlou & El Sawy, 2011). Originally conceptualised at the firm level, DCs have been extended to supply chains (Hong et al., 2018), giving rise to the Supply Chain Dynamic Capabilities (SCDCs) construct. These capabilities enable supply chains to manage turbulent environments and complex inter-organisational relationships (Beske, 2012). Empirical research demonstrates that SCDCs enhance operational performance (Eckstein et al., 2015), promote supply chain ambidexterity (Aslam et al., 2018), and facilitate sustainable supply chain practices (Beske, 2012; Hong et al., 2018). They also support adaptive reconfiguration for improved resilience (Zhao et al., 2023).

Although researchers agree that building resilience hinges on these foundational elements (Brusset and Teller, 2017), they often debate whether to categorise them as "antecedents" of resilience or as its actual components (Jüttner and Maklan, 2011). Furthermore, the focus on these elements varies. Some research captures them at a detailed operational resource level (e.g. safety stock), while other research focuses on broader strategic system-level re-engineering. To bridge these views, Ponomarov and Holcomb (2009) and Jüttner and Maklan (2011) propose an intermediate capability level which integrates both strategic and operational perspectives. In this regard, researchers have identified specific clusters of capabilities that are essential for resilience. For example, Christopher and Peck (2004) emphasise collaboration, agility and supply chain re-engineering as key SCDCs, whereas Pettit et al. (2010) highlight factors such as visibility, anticipation and flexibility. Further refining this perspective, Ali et al. (2017) identified five capabilities specific to each phase - anticipation, adaptation, response, recovery, and learning - which provide the structure for a system's "rebound".

Identifying these diverse factors is essential, as it allows researchers to distil them into a core set of actionable strategic levers. Indeed, from the many capabilities suggested, a consensus has emerged around four frequently cited elements: flexibility, redundancy, collaboration, and agility (Jüttner and Maklan, 2011; Tukamuhabwa et al., 2015). Research has organised these capabilities into proactive and reactive strategic approaches, a distinction that clarifies their role across the disruption cycle (Tukamuhabwa et al., 2015). While relational elements such as integration and social capital remain important, digital technologies (DTs) have become the primary enabler of resilience in the modern era. Specifically, DTs provide the visibility and velocity needed for agility and are indispensable for implementing most resilience strategies (Tukamuhabwa et al., 2015). Moreover, they are recognised as a key organisational enabler that, alongside knowledge management, learning processes, and organisational structures, underpins SCR capabilities (Neri et al., 2023). Given their pivotal role, the discussion now turns to examine the specific enabling power of DTs.

2.3 The Key Enabling Role of DTs

DTs have emerged as the primary enablers of resilience, significantly improving visibility, flexibility, and collaboration across networks (Taghipour & Lu, 2025). The COVID-19 pandemic accelerated this shift, demonstrating how digital tools facilitate remote operations and the structural reconfiguration necessary during a crisis. Technologies such as Big Data Analytics, AI, Digital Twin, and Blockchain in particular contribute to a more "intelligent" supply chain by refining forecasting capabilities, enabling real-time monitoring, and fostering trust-based ecosystems (Ivanov et al., 2019; Taghipour & Lu, 2025). Rather than studying these capabilities in isolation, current research uses multidimensional frameworks to capture their heterogeneous nature. These tend to organise them by disruption phases (Ali et al., 2017) or strategic dimensions (Chowdhury & Quaddus, 2017). Furthermore, while many studies confirm that DTs strengthen dynamic capabilities, thereby boosting resilience (Zouari et al., 2020), the achievement of this outcome requires more than mere technological implementation. It demands systemic integration across the SCR ecosystem, supported by a comprehensive digital resilience framework. Various external and internal factors - ranging from organisational readiness and contingent variables to broader institutional forces - can facilitate or hinder the effective deployment of these technologies. As Ivanov and Dolgui (2019) argue, the impact of digitalisation on SCR is complex and shaped by an intricate interplay of factors. Indeed, the contribution of DTs often depends on their interaction with relational capabilities, such as collaboration (Jiang et al., 2023). This interdependence raises the practical question of what the optimal configuration of these capabilities should be. Technologies must also be orchestrated in distinct ways to support both proactive (e.g., predictive analytics) and reactive (e.g., real-time tracking) strategies, thus demanding a nuanced approach to integration. The challenge extends beyond a single firm. As competition shifts from individual to network-level performance, success depends on the ability to co-create value with partners—a capability that is put to the test in times of crisis (Richey, 2009). Furthermore, pressure from stakeholders is pushing supply chains towards transformative models such as the circular economy (Massari et al., 2022), introducing another layer of complexity: how can DTs balance competing objectives such as resilience and sustainability? To address these multifaceted challenges, we need theoretical frameworks that can capture both individual resources and their interactions within a broader capability ecosystem. This ultimately requires integrating perspectives beyond the Dynamic Capabilities View.

3. THEORETICAL FOUNDATIONS FOR DT-ENABLED SCR

3.1 RBV and DCV: Foundational Firm-Level Theories

Research on SCR is primarily anchored in the Resource-Based View (RBV) and the Dynamic Capabilities View (DCV) (Tukamuhabwa et al., 2015). According to Barney (1991), the RBV suggests that a firm's competitive advantage relies on managing resources that are valuable, rare, inimitable, and non-substitutable (VRIN). Within this framework, DTs and personnel are viewed as critical strategic assets for developing resilience (Christenson et al., 2003). However, the RBV has been criticised for its "contextual insensitivity" (Ling-Yee, 2007, p. 360), as it fails to adequately explain how advantage is maintained in turbulent or highly dynamic environments (Eisenhardt & Martin, 2000) or why similar resources can produce different outcomes in different settings (Brandon-Jones et al., 2014). Furthermore, scholars argue that it does not sufficiently emphasise the active managerial role in converting these static resources into functional capabilities (Hitt, 2019; Sirmon et al., 2010). To address these limitations, the DCV emerged as an essential extension, focusing on how firms intentionally reconfigure resources through sensing, seizing, and transforming opportunities in order to adapt to sudden disruptions (Teece, 2025). From this perspective, the adoption of digital tools is considered a dynamic capability in itself, enhancing a firm's ability to navigate the different stages of a crisis: absorption, response and recovery (Zhao et al., 2023). However, despite its theoretical depth, the DCV is often criticised for being too abstract to provide practical guidance on building these capabilities effectively in real-world settings (Dubey et al., 2023).

3.2 Resource Orchestration Theory: A Managerial Framework for Resilience

Resource Orchestration Theory (ROT) directly addresses these limitations. Extending the RBV, ROT provides a practical framework that focuses not on what resources a firm has, but on what managers do with them, specifically through structuring, bundling, and leveraging resource portfolios (Sirmon et al., 2010). As such, managers must take specific actions to orchestrate resource portfolios to generate value for their firms (Hitt, 2019; Sirmon et al., 2010). This approach is essential for understanding how leaders can strategically configure various capabilities (e.g., digital, organisational, relational capabilities, etc.) to achieve resilience. ROT reveals that there is no single "best" configuration; instead, capabilities can complement or substitute for each other, with multiple paths leading to the same resilient outcome - a concept called "equifinality" (Fiss, 2011). This offers a more nuanced and actionable understanding of how to strategically build a resilient supply chain.

3.3 A Network-Level Perspective: Complex Adaptive Systems

This theoretical discussion expands beyond the firm level to encompass the entire supply network through the lens of Complex Adaptive Systems (CAS) (Choi et al., 2001; Day, 2013). A CAS is defined as an "interconnected network of multiple entities that exhibits adaptive action in response to both the environment and the system of entities itself" (Pathak et al., 2007, p. 550). This conceptualises a supply chain as a network of autonomous agents that adapt and organise themselves continuously through their interactions. According to this framework, resilience emerges from the system's inherent ability to reconfigure itself; for example, when a focal firm seeks an alternative supplier. However, this adaptive nature presents a duality. While it enables local recovery, the network's complexity and dynamism mean that disruptions can also originate and propagate unpredictably from deep within the network, beyond the focal firm's visibility (Choi et al., 2001). Consequently, a minor, unseen disruption can have a severe impact on the focal firm by cascading (Fiksel et al., 2015). As a result, CAS theory emphasises that in order to achieve true resilience, firms must develop adaptive capacities across the whole network while simultaneously being alert to the risks of nonlinear disruption propagation (i.e., the ripple effect). This insight is particularly relevant in the context of digital transformation, where DTs serve as crucial enablers of the self-organisation needed for dynamic response to shocks.

3.4 Towards Radical Transformation: Social-Ecological Systems and Antifragility

Building upon the CAS perspective, the Social-Ecological Systems (SES) lens and its derivative, Transformative Supply Chains (Wieland, 2021; Nikookar et al., 2024), argue that contemporary challenges require supply chains to move beyond mere adaptation toward profound, radical transformation, such as adopting circular economy models (Massari et al., 2025). SESs are open, dynamic systems comprising closely connected social and ecological parts (Preiser et al., 2021). As CASs, they are characterised by relational constitution, adaptability and emergence. Their behaviour arises from bottom-up interactions and feedback loops within the system and with the external environment (Biggs et al., 2015). Changes in a SES propagate across time and space, leading to unpredictable cascading effects (Biggs et al., 2015). When faced with change, SES components can consciously embrace new configurations, resulting in a radical transformation as opposed to simpler, single-scale adaptation (Moore et al., 2014). In this framework, DTs enable a specific set of capabilities for triggering, envisioning and navigating systemic change (Massari et al., 2025). The concept of "supply chain antifragility" has recently emerged as a means of not only recovering from disruptions, but also of growing stronger because of them. It emphasises using volatility and disorder to drive growth, and requires advanced DT-enabled capabilities such as "supply chain mindfulness" (continuously scrutinising events to make sense of them) and "supply chain bricolage" (creatively using existing resources to seize new opportunities).

The subsequent two sections examine how DTs can improve SCR from different theoretical lenses. Section 4 is primarily based on the RBV and DCV. It aims to investigate the mechanisms through which DTs enhance resilience. Specifically, it examines how DTs interact with other firm resources and capabilities, exploring their collective impact through direct, indirect, mediating and moderating effects within the DT-SCR relationship. Section 5 then shifts to the Social-Ecological Systems (SES) paradigm to explore the transformative potential of DTs that extends beyond conventional resilience. This theoretical shift reflects the increasing demands placed on modern supply chains to simultaneously improve operational efficiency, circularity and sustainability. In light of this, the discussion focuses on the evolving concept of transformative supply chains and the pivotal role of DTs in enabling their development.

4. INFLUENCE MECHANISMS IN THE DT-SCR RELATIONSHIP: KEY MEDIATORS AND MODERATORS BEHIND DIRECT EFFECTS

A synthesis of the literature reveals that the relationship between DTs and SCR operates through four primary mechanisms: direct effects, indirect effects, mediation, and moderation. **Table 1** summarises these mechanisms and provides a detailed taxonomy of the links between digital investments and resilient outcomes. This typology offers a unifying theoretical framework that clarifies the complex nature of these relationships and their varying effects depending on the context.

Table 1. A Taxonomy of Mechanisms Linking Digital Technologies and Supply Chain Resilience

Category	*Key Factors / Technologies*	*Role / Type of Effect*	*Direction of Effect*	*Main Findings*	*Key Studies*
Digital Technologies (Direct Effects)					
	AI, IoT, Blockchain, Big Data, Digital Platforms, Automation/ Analytics	Direct enablers of resilience performance: visibility, traceability, agility, flexibility, cost and lead-time reduction	Positive	DTs enhance disruption detection, rapid response, inter-firm integration, and information transparency.	Hirsch et al. (2024) Alzoubi et al. (2025) Wu et al. (2024) Li et al. (2025)
Mediating Mechanisms					
	Dynamic Capabilities *(Agility, Adaptability, Absorptive, Sensing–Seizing–Transforming)*	Full or partial mediation between DT and SCR	Positive	Dynamic capabilities explain how digital investments translate into organisational resilience.	Ning et al. (2022) Gomez et Silva (2025) Zhao et al. (2023) Tortorella et al. (2024)
	Structural Integration *(Process / Information / Financial Integration, Collaboration)*	Sequential mediation	Positive	Collaboration and integrated flows (information, financial, physical) strengthen resilience.	Yuan et al. (2023) Yu et al. (2025) Zhang et al. (2025)
	Human & Relational Enablers *(SC Memory, SC Mapping, Innovation, Human Capital, Leadership)*	Indirect mediation	Positive	Innovation, skilled workforce, and leadership act as internal levers of digital resilience.	Alvarenga et al. (2023) Wang et al. (2025) Zheng et al. (2025) Alabdali et al. (2025)
	Risk & IT Capabilities *(SCRM, IT-Driven Capabilities)*	Dual role (mediator + moderator)	Positive	IT-based capabilities enhance visibility, foresight, and responsiveness.	Ahmadi et al. (2024) Aljoghaiman & Ghouri (2024)
External Moderators					
	Government Subsidies	Institutional moderator	Positive (context-dependent)	Transforms negative DT-collaboration → SCR link into positive; most effective for state-owned/large firms.	Jia & Li (2024) Ma et al. (2025) Yu and al. (2025)

continued on following page

Table 1. Continued

Category	*Key Factors / Technologies*	*Role / Type of Effect*	*Direction of Effect*	*Main Findings*	*Key Studies*
	Environmental Uncertainty	Market volatility	Stronger positive	Unstable markets amplify the positive effects of DT.	Yuan et al. (2023) Wang et al. (2025)
	Regulatory Uncertainty	Regulatory instability	Weaker positive	Hinders IoT/AI implementation, especially in emerging economies.	Alquraish (2025)
	Financial Regulation	Financial environment	Stronger positive	Strengthens digital finance → resilience link, particularly in mature regions.	Chen & Yu (2024)
	Government Effectiveness	Institutional effectiveness	Positive	Effective institutions (policy, incentives, infrastructure) enable firms to convert digital strengths into resilience outcomes.	Dubey et al. (2023)
Internal Moderators					
	Firm Size / Ownership	Organisational characteristics	Positive	Larger or state-owned firms gain more from DT collaboration.	Jia & Li (2024)
	Strategic Fit	Strategic alignment	Stronger positive	Alignment between DT initiatives and corporate strategy enhances resilience.	Hossain et al. (2024)
	Supply Chain Dynamism	Supply chain turbulence	Stronger positive	DT effects are magnified in rapidly changing supply chains.	Alquraish (2025)
	Supply Chain Complexity	Network interdependence	Stronger positive	DTs are more effective in complex, highly interconnected networks.	Metwally et al. (2024)

continued on following page

Table 1. Continued

Category	*Key Factors / Technologies*	*Role / Type of Effect*	*Direction of Effect*	*Main Findings*	*Key Studies*
	Innovation Vitality	Innovation dynamics	Positive (varies)	The effect of digitalization depends on the firm's SC position and industry competition.	Wang et al. (2025)
	Digital Tech Application (Breadth/ Depth)	Digital adoption pattern	Asymmetric	Breadth improves recovery but may lower pre-disruption resistance; depth consistently strengthens both resilience dimensions.	Ma et al. (2025)
	Governance & Trust	Relational governance	Stronger positive (co-creation effect)	Trust and communication among partners moderate the DT–SCR link; technology and human factors jointly foster resilience.	Faruquee et al. (2021)

Author's own elaboration

4.1 Direct Effects

Research indicates that DTs directly improve SCR by developing core resilience capabilities that act as direct enablers rather than mediators. Empirical studies conducted in various contexts have identified the key mechanisms for this effect. For example, Hirsch et al. (2024) demonstrate how AI and information systems can improve SCR in South Africa's FMCG industry by integrating automation and analytics and using predictive tools to transform reactive chains into proactive assets. Similarly, Alzoubi et al. (2025) found that blockchain-enabled transparency, Internet of Things (IoT)-driven monitoring and adaptive flexibility directly improve operational performance (e.g. shorter lead times) in the UAE pharmaceutical sector. Furthermore, Wu et al. (2024) provide evidence of the direct effect, identifying risk mitigation and adaptive responses as significant pathways that are enhanced by a "supply chain data network effect". Li et al. (2025) demonstrate that DTs enhance SCR indirectly as well as directly by boosting supply chain power and operational transparency. These effects are more pronounced in regulated and digitally mature environments.

4.2 Indirect Effects

DTs also improve SCR through indirect mechanisms, acting as either mediators or moderators of key relationships. As a mediator, a DT transmits the effect of other variables on SCR. For example, Zouari et al. (2020) show that Digital Tool Adoption (DTA) - a concept closely aligned with DTs - mediates the relationship between a firm's Digital Maturity Degree (DMD) and its SCR. As a moderator, DT can alter the strength of these pathways. According to the same study, the DMD → DTA → SCR sequence is moderated by firm turnover, with smaller firms exhibiting weaker effects due to their limited resources. Ultimately, the findings of Zouari et al. (2020) demonstrate that the resilience benefits of digitalisation stem from integration within a broader, maturity-driven organisational ecosystem rather than from the technologies themselves.

4.3 Mediating Effects

Empirical evidence demonstrates that DTs play a role in SCR by means of distinctive mediating mechanisms, whose impact varies significantly along dynamic capabilities, structural integration (information/physical flows), human and relational enablers (e.g., supply chain memory, human capital), and risk & IT capabilities.

4.3.1 Mediation by Supply Chain Dynamic Capabilities (SCDCs)

Research consistently identifies Supply Chain Dynamic Capabilities (SCDCs) as critical mediators between digital technologies and supply chain resilience, with different studies highlighting distinct capability pathways. Ning et al. (2022) establish that digital technologies improve resilience only when they first strengthen *supply chain traceability* and *agility*, either directly or through digital platforms. Further developing this understanding, Gomez et Silva (2025) argue that *alignment and adaptability* -rather than agility alone- serve as the primary mediators through which digitalisation enhances resilience, noting that strategic alignment acts as a crucial precondition. Adding temporal precision to this discussion, Zhao et al. (2023) demonstrate that digitalisation builds resilience through *three disruption-phase capabilities*: absorptive capacity before disruptions, response capability during disruptions, and recovery capacity afterward. Similarly, Tortorella et al. (2024) confirm that the relationship between digital technologies and resilience is fully mediated by *strategic adaptation capabilities* -specifically the abilities to sense opportunities, seize them, and transform operations-emphasising that digital tools alone are insufficient without developing these core capacities.

4.3.2 Structural Integration

Beyond specific dynamic capabilities, research also highlights the mediating role of broader supply chain relationships. Studies by Yuan et al. (2023) and Yu et al. (2025) establish that digital transformation enhances supply chain resilience primarily through *supply chain process integration*. They find that the full potential of digitalisation is unlocked when it enables tighter *integration of information*, *physical*, and *financial flows*, offering firms clear guidance on where to focus their digital efforts in turbulent environments. Furthermore, moving from integration to cooperation, Zhang et al. (2025) identify *supply chain collaboration* as a partial mediator in this relationship. Their work suggests that through information sharing and collaborative problem-solving, collaboration fosters resilience, providing a critical pathway for firms with limited internal resources. This mediating effect is shown to be even more pronounced in contexts where social capital is high.

4.3.3 Human and Relational Enablers

Research further elucidates that the DT-SCR relationship is mediated through a diverse spectrum of knowledge-based, human, and relational factors. Alvarenga et al. (2023) identify *supply chain memory* as a partial mediator, suggesting that a learning culture is most effective when built upon the knowledge structures DTs create. Similarly, Piprani et al. (2025) show that digital capabilities strengthen resilience fully through the mediation of *supply chain mapping*, which enhances visibility and risk assessment. Shifting from knowledge structures to human factors, Wang et al. (2025) and Zheng et al. (2025) demonstrate the critical roles of *firm innovation* and *human capital*, respectively, as key mediators, confirming that digital potential is realised when translated by skilled employees and innovative processes. The mediating influence of *leadership* is highlighted by Alabdali et al. (2025), who find it orchestrates resilience by fostering algorithmic management and enhancing absorptive capacity. Finally, completing this perspective, Singh (2025) underscores that the full potential of technologies like Digital Twins is only achieved when mediated by the relational process of *stakeholder collaboration*, emphasising that technological and social systems are inextricably linked in building resilience.

4.3.4 Risk & IT Capabilities

Scholarly work further clarifies how *risk management* and *IT capabilities* channel the effects of digitalisation into resilience. Aljoghaiman and Ghouri (2024) attribute a dual role to *Supply Chain Risk Management* (SCRM), finding it acts as a full or partial mediator in transforming different types of digital investments into resilience, while Ahmadi et al. (2024) demonstrate it can also positively moderate this relationship. Complementing this, Ahmadi et al. (2024) further establish that *IT integration* does not directly boost resilience, but does so fully through the mediation of IT-driven operational capabilities, underscoring that technology must first be translated into competencies like agile coordination and real-time visibility to be effective.

4.4. Moderating Effects

The relationship between DTs and SCR is significantly influenced by various external and internal moderating factors.

4.4.1 External Moderating Factors

The influence of DTs on SCR is significantly shaped by a firm's external environment. Scholars have observed that *effective government intervention* can have a positive moderating effect. For example, Ma et al. (2025) found that *subsidies* helped to overcome implementation barriers, and Dubey et al. (2023) demonstrated that broader *government effectiveness*, in the form of incentives and infrastructure, provided the stability needed to convert digital capabilities into resilience. Furthermore, *environmental uncertainties* play a critical role. *Market and technological volatility* amplify the value of digital technologies (DTs) (Yuan et al., 2023; Wang et al., 2025), whereas *regulatory uncertainty* negatively moderates the relationship, particularly in emerging economies (Alquraish, 2025). In the financial realm, finally, Chen and Yu (2024) demonstrate that robust *financial regulation* positively moderates the impact of digital finance on SCR, ensuring greater stability.

4.4.2 Internal Moderating Factors

Scholarly findings converge on several internal factors that critically moderate the relationship between DTs and resilience. Research indicates that the effectiveness of digital tools depends on robust *relational governance* and *strategic alignment*. Faruquee et al. (2021) emphasise the importance of *trust*, and Hossain et al. (2024) identify *strategic fit* as a significant positive moderator. Furthermore, *firm-specific conditions* such as size, ownership and financial leverage influence outcomes (Jia & Li, 2024), with digital tools proving particularly valuable in *dynamically complex supply chain environments* (Alquraish, 2025; Metwally et al., 2024). Finally, Ma et al. (2025) reveal that the moderating role of *digital technology application* is nuanced: its *breadth* and *depth* can strengthen restorative capacities while potentially weakening resistive ones.

This section reveals that the relationship between DTs and SCR is multidimensional and context-dependent. This positions DTs not as a direct solution, but as a catalytic enabler within a complex system. Indeed, the analysis shows that, while DTs offer direct improvements in terms of monitoring, transparency and flexibility, they primarily add value through critical mediating mechanisms. Furthermore, the nature and strength of these relationships are not universal, but depend critically on a range of moderating factors. These include external elements, such as the effectiveness of government and regulatory uncertainty, that create the institutional context, as well as internal factors, such as strategic fit and supply chain complexity, that define the organisational and operational boundaries within which DTs operate. A key finding is the presence of asymmetric effects, whereby the breadth and depth of technology application can influence various dimensions of resilience. The benefits of digital strategies are thus highly contextual and emerge only when strategic alignment is achieved and key tensions are deliberately managed. The task falls to management to orchestrate the firm's unique portfolio of resources and dynamic capabilities to convert digital potential into tangible value.

5. BEYOND RESILIENCE: THE TRANSFORMATIVE ROLE OF DTS

Contemporary global challenges now demand a comprehensive transformation of traditional supply chains - one that goes beyond resilience to achieve holistic integration of operational efficiency, circular economy principles, and sustainability (Taghipour & Lu, 2025). *Transformative supply chains* represent this novel, holistic paradigm for analysing modern competitive supply chains. Rooted in Social-Ecological Systems (SES) theory, these supply chains can adapt their configurations in response to internal and external pressures (Massari et al., 2025). Such adaptation requires significant structural and operational changes to maintain competitiveness in volatile environments. The ultimate objective of this transformation is to achieve configurations that successfully balance resilience, sustainability, and circularity - objectives that are aligned with the Sustainable Development Goals and the principles of the circular economy - while maintaining a core focus on operational efficiency. However, pursuing resilience, efficiency, and sustainability concurrently generates inherent strategic tensions, as their underlying logics often involves competing priorities. Conflicts between supply chain resilience (SCR), efficiency (SCE) and sustainability (SCS) raise a pivotal question about the role of DTs: can they overcome these trade-offs and enable synergetic development across all three dimensions?

Although we have previously explained how DTs can enhance resilience, their potential to mitigate trade-offs remains unclear, particularly between resilience and efficiency (SCR-SCE) and between resilience and sustainability/circularity (SCR-SCS). To address this issue, this section first illustrates how these competing priorities manifest themselves. It then examines how DTs can: (1) mediate the trade-off between resilience and efficiency by serving as capability enhancers and conflict mediators; and (2) create synergies to advance resilience and sustainability objectives simultaneously.

5.1 Competing Imperatives in Supply Chains

5.1.1 Resilience-Efficiency Paradox

A fundamental paradox in supply chain management is the conflict between the objectives of SCR and SCE. Pursuing these dual aims often results in divergent strategies and operational trade-offs (Belhadi et al., 2022). SCE prioritises cost reduction, process optimisation, and lean operations - as exemplified by just-in-time (JIT) principles and minimal inventory - to maximise profitability (Shah and Ward, 2007). By contrast, SCR demands a distinct approach. In the wake of disruptive events such as the Covid-19 pandemic and ongoing geopolitical instability, essential strategies now include building in redundancy, diversifying the supply base and maintaining strategic inventory buffers.

Simultaneously enhancing SCR and SCE is problematic because they are underpinned by opposing operational logics (Ruiz-Benítez et al., 2018). Pursuing lean, efficient systems constrains the adoption of resilience measures. Consequently, building resilience through safety stock and multi-sourcing often comes at the direct expense of efficiency (Klimek et al., 2019). This trade-off arises because efficiency relies on stability, whereas resilience is a response to volatility that ensures business continuity in unpredictable environments (Markolf et al., 2022). Firms must therefore navigate this tension and balance these competing priorities according to their specific operational context and risk exposure. Box 1 provides a concrete example of the efficiency-resilience paradox.

Box 1. The Efficiency-Resilience Paradox in the pharmaceutical sector

Historically, the industry has pursued efficiency at the expense of diversity, resulting in a highly concentrated supply base. Import concentration (as measured by the Herfindahl-Hirschman Index, or HHI) remained at a critically high level of 0.31 in 2022 — well above the Organisation for Economic Co-operation and Development (OECD) threshold of 0.2. Efforts to diversify suppliers — a core resilience strategy — are hindered by the same factors that previously secured efficiency: lengthy regulatory approvals, intellectual property protections and sunk costs in specialised infrastructure. This creates a structural lock-in, as evidenced by the slow geographical change in sourcing and stable production distances since 2017. This actively impedes a swift transition towards greater resilience and increases the risk of drug shortages.

5.1.2 Sustainability-Resilience Paradox in Supply Chains

Resilience is closely linked to supply chain sustainability (SCS), which is defined as the strategic and transparent integration of economic, environmental and social goals - often referred to as the "triple bottom line" - into coordinated supply chain activities (Carter & Rogers, 2008). SCS entails a commitment to environmental protection, decent working conditions, and human rights (OECD, 2025). From an environmental perspective, this involves making systematic efforts to minimise the carbon footprint of the supply chain - particularly upstream Scope 3 emissions - and improving resilience by adopting sustainable practices and the principles of the circular economy, as well as trading environmentally friendly products. This includes diffusing green technologies and reinforcing resilience against material shortages through cross-border reverse supply chains. In terms of social responsibility, SCS requires the protection of workers' rights across complex global value chains, compliance with an increasing number of sustainability due diligence regulations, and adherence to established Responsible Business Conduct (RBC) guidelines (OECD, 2025).

As supply chains have become more globalised, they now underpin the modern economy and directly affect sustainability through employment rates, natural resource consumption and environmental impact (Ivanov, 2017). It should be noted that achieving sustainability can also lead to improved resilience. Initiatives such as implementing decentralised renewable energy infrastructure or the circular economy help to develop network systems that are both sustainable and resilient. By recycling materials, using resources more efficiently, and sourcing sustainably, companies can reduce their reliance on unpredictable virgin material markets. This enhances their supply security and foster a more transparent, collaborative network. This same principle applies to energy. Investing in renewable and decentralised energy systems can, in fact, provide firms with greater energy autonomy, and protection against external shocks. However, despite these synergies, aligning sustainability and resilience goals is still a major challenge. While both aim to maintain continuity and mitigate long-term risks, the operational strategies they employ can sometimes conflict with each other. Indeed, the mechanisms that support one dimension may hinder the other under certain operational conditions. For example, practices like single sourcing (to build trust) and inventory reduction (to enhance efficiency and limit waste), though aligned with sustainability goals, can reduce the flexibility and robustness needed to absorb and recover from disruptions. As a result, they can amplify the ripple effect throughout the supply network, as demonstrated by Ivanov's (2017) study. This tension highlights a wider paradox: although sustainability focuses on lean processes and minimising waste, resilience often depends on strategic redundancies, such as buffer stocks and excess capacity, to ensure continuity. While robustness reserves and operational flexibility can mitigate the economic consequences of the ripple effect, these mechanisms may conflict with sustainability and resource efficiency objectives. Therefore, achieving an effective balance between lean, sustainable operations and resilient structures remains a key managerial challenge. Box 2 uses the example of the significant carbon footprint of the cement industry to illustrate this critical trade-off.

Box 2. The sustainability (i.e. climate)-resilience paradox in the cement industry

The trade-off between achieving climate goals and enhancing resilience through redundancy is most evident in high-resource-intensity sectors, such as the cement industry. In 2023, the sector produced 2.4 billion tonnes of CO_2, accounting for 6% of the world's total emissions (Published by Ian Tiseo, Jul 7, 2025 - Global cement industry key emissions indicators 2023). These emissions are an inherent part of the production process, as cement production is incredibly carbon-intensive, with an average emission rate of 580 kg of CO_2 per metric tonne of cementitious material. However, strategies such as adding redundant production facilities to reduce supply chain risks would directly increase these emission sources and conflict with established climate targets related to environmental sustainability.

Juggling sustainability, resilience, and efficiency (see Box 3) is a core managerial challenge that requires more insight. While DTs are increasingly used to transform supply chains, the crucial question that actually arises is how can managers leverage these technologies to balance these often-competing priorities? The following subsections will address this question by building upon relevant existing research.

Box 3. The Trade-off in Practice: Resilience, Efficiency, and Sustainability

The following cases are among those that illustrate the resilience-efficiency-sustainability trade-off, as analysed in the OECD Review (2025):

- **Redundancy vs. Lean and Green operations**: Resilience strategies often rely on redundancy. This involves measures such as buffer stocks, diversified suppliers, and excess capacity [see §7.2, p. 608 and p. 452; §5.1, p. 453]. However, these redundant assets conflict with the principles of lean operations, which aim to eliminate waste, and with sustainable operations, which seek to minimise resource intensity and environmental footprint.
- **Increased cost, resource use, and environmental impact**: Redundancy increases both operational costs and resource consumption [§7.2, p. 608]. The capital required for these measures creates a direct trade-off, whereby investments in resilience often come at the expense of efficiency [§5.1, p. 455]. For example, maintaining extensive inventories for risk mitigation can lead to resource inefficiencies, such as overproduction and waste [§7.2, pp. 609-610].
- **Tension with sustainability**: This trade-off extends to sustainability objectives. For example, resilience strategies that increase resource intensity, such as adding production redundancy or holding large inventories, can exacerbate environmental impacts by generating waste, depleting resources, and increasing energy consumption/emissions [§7.2, pp. 608-609].
- **Economic Cost of Reshoring**: Policy-driven resilience through reshoring or relocalisation also incurs substantial efficiency costs. Such measures could reduce global real GDP by over 5%, decreasing economic stability for most countries without providing guaranteed resilience benefits [§1.4, pp. 56-57]. From a sustainability perspective, relocating production to higher-cost regions may also result in higher localised emissions if the energy grid is more carbon-intensive. This creates tension between resilience and environmental goals, even when efficiency is sacrificed.

5.2 Role of DTs in Balancing Resilience and Efficiency

In the Industry 4.0 era, DT has emerged as a key driver of supply chain transformation, providing innovative solutions that reconcile the goals of resilience (SCR) and efficiency (SCE) (Xue & Li, 2023). While the importance of these two dimensions is widely recognised by scholars, the potential for their synergistic integration and the technological mechanisms that enable it remain under-explored. DTs have the potential to advance both SCR and SCE by providing enhanced supply chain transparency, accelerating operational processes and enabling full end-to-end visibility (Mohammaddust et al., 2017). As Xue and Li (2023) explain, these benefits are realised through several key mechanisms that bolster both resilience and efficiency simultaneously, as summarised in Figure 2.

Figure 2. Influencing Mechanisms of DTs on SCE and SCR

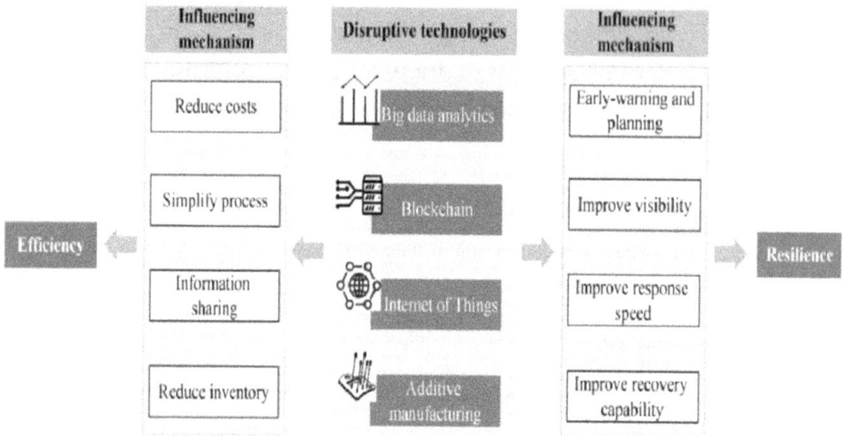

Source: Xue and Li (2023)

However, it should be noted that, while their findings are insightful, they provide non-exhaustive examples of the technological impacts of DTs. As the authors acknowledge, DTs may facilitate SCR and SCE through pathways not documented in their study. To construct a more comprehensive framework, our analysis integrates the mechanisms identified by Xue and Li (2023) with insights from further empirical studies (e.g. Zhao et al., 2023; Massari et al., 2025). This synthesis, detailed in Table 2, builds directly on their foundational work to offer a consolidated framework of how DTs reconcile SCR and SCE. Hence, the synthesised evidence in Table 2 provides a more direct and nuanced response to our research question, illustrating the multi-faceted pathways through which DTs reconcile the inherent tension between these two critical objectives. This synthesis clarifies how DTs can reconcile traditionally conflicting priorities, advancing a paradigm in which resilience and efficiency are seen as complementary goals rather than conflicting trade-offs. Recent research supports this view, framing digitalisation as essential infrastructure for managing complex systems and enabling the simultaneous pursuit of multiple strategic objectives (Lu & Taghipour, 2025b). Consequently, managers are encouraged to develop an integrated technological portfolio, leveraging big data analytics (BDA) for predictive risk management, the internet of things (IoT) for real-time monitoring and control, and additive manufacturing (AM) for lean, responsive production. This balanced approach moves beyond isolated optimisation and harnesses the unique and joint contributions of each technology to enhance supply chain resilience, operational efficiency and proactive risk management concurrently.

Table 2. The Impact of DTs on Balancing Supply Chain Resilience (SCR) and Efficiency (SCE)

Digital Technology	**Contribution to SCR**	**Contribution to SCE**	**Balancing Mechanism**
Big Data Analytics (BDA)	- Identifies operational risks, disruptions, and frauds - Predicts market demand - Enhances SC visibility	- Optimises resource utilisation - Reduces costs - Improves quality control & defect detection	Provides insights for **risk mitigation** (SCR) while optimising **process efficiency** (SCE)
Blockchain (BC)	- Ensures traceability & transparency - Detects frauds & cyber threats - Enables smart contracts for trust	- Simplifies transactions - Reduces errors - Enhances order fulfilment	Combines **secure, auditable processes** (SCR) with **streamlined operations** (SCE)
Internet of Things (IoT)	- Real-time monitoring of disruptions - Early risk detection - Tracks material flows	- Optimises energy consumption - Enhances quality control - Facilitates data sharing	Provides **real-time risk alerts** (SCR) while **improving operational control** (SCE)
Additive Manufacturing (AM)	- Reduces supply risks via localised production - Enables rapid prototyping	- Lowers inventory & waste (up to 90%) - Supports product personalisation	Balances **lean inventory** (SCE) with **responsive production** (SCR)
Artificial Intelligence (AI)	- Prioritises risks & builds contingency plans - Mitigates uncertainty	- Optimises SC configurations - Enhances forecasting & defect detection	Uses **predictive analytics** for **risk resilience** (SCR) and **process optimisation** (SCE)
Digital Twin Simulation (DTS)	- Simulates SC vulnerabilities - Tests resilience strategies	- Supports virtual prototyping - Enhances product innovation	Enables **virtual scenario testing** for both **resilience & efficiency**
Cloud Computing (CC)	- Strengthens stakeholder collaboration - Enhances information sharing	- Facilitates shared resource networks - Optimises co-design strategies	Promotes **collaborative adaptation** (SCR) and **resource efficiency** (SCE)
Cybersecurity (CS)	- Protects against cyber threats - Secures SC data integrity	- Ensures reliable digital operations - Reduces breach-related disruptions	Protects **SC integrity** (SCR) to sustain **operational continuity** (SCE)
Autonomous Robotic Systems (ARS)	- Detects production deviations - Enhances flexibility & agility	- Reduces shipping costs & emissions - Automates processes	Supports **agile adaptation** (SCR) while **automating for efficiency** (SCE)

Source: Author's own elaboration, informed by Xue and Li (2023) and an integration of prior research.

5.3 Transformative Supply Chains: Synergising Resilience and Sustainability Through Digital-Enabled Capabilities

Despite growing empirical evidence of supply chains undergoing transformative shifts to simultaneously address resilience, sustainability, and efficiency, the enabling mechanisms behind these transitions remain inadequately understood. While DTs are widely acknowledged as *transformative enablers*, their specific potential to mediate the inherent tensions between these competing objectives through synergistic reconciliation -as opposed to isolated optimisation- remains both theoretically and empirically underexplored. This knowledge gap is particularly critical when examining the evolving conceptualisation of resilience, which now demands a fundamental rethinking of system boundaries, stakeholder relationships, and resource flows reimagined through the lens of socio-ecological realities.

5.3.1 The Evolution Toward Social-Ecological Resilience

Moving beyond traditional notions of recovery, recent literature positions resilience as the capacity to adapt and thrive following disruption, even amid intensifying social-ecological pressures. This evolution is fundamentally informed by the emerging social-ecological resilience paradigm (Nikookar et al., 2024; Wieland et al., 2023), which shifts away from restoring systems to their pre-disruption state - a practice that often-prioritised efficiency above all else. Instead, this new paradigm emphasises *transformative adaptation*: the ability to reconfigure operations toward more robust, sustainable, and ultimately more capable states (Wieland et al., 2021), a concept referred to as the "*transformative supply chain*." This perspective reframes the supply chain from a fixed mechanism or *"being"* to an open system that is constantly *"becoming"* (Wieland, 2021). Consequently, the strategic focus shifts from maintaining the supply chain in a static optimal state to guiding change along *desirable trajectories* (Biggs et al., 2015). From this viewpoint, the supply chain is seen as a dynamic, highly interconnected system where nature and society are inextricably linked. By reinterpreting the supply chain as a *social-ecological system* (SES), organisations can move beyond siloed objectives and integrate resilience, efficiency, and sustainability into a single, holistic approach.

5.3.2 The Framework of Transformative Capabilities

Building truly transformative supply chains requires a fundamental rethinking of configurations to enable them not just to "evolve over time", but to "survive, adapt, and grow" regardless of the nature of the disruption. According to Massari et al. (2025), central to this evolution are *Supply Chain Dynamic Capabilities* (SC-

DCs), which are collective abilities - such as reengineering, collaboration, agility, and risk management - that allow a chain to navigate volatile environments and complex internal relationships. These capabilities manifest in practical strategies like reshoring, nearshoring, and the adoption of flexible production models. Simultaneously, they allow firms to pursue sustainability and circularity by managing end-of-life resources and fostering collaboration with circular economy partners, such as industrial symbiosis networks and reverse logistics specialists. The central thesis of Massari et al. (2025) is that achieving these two agendas simultaneously is not inherently antagonistic but requires a specific, higher-order class of abilities known as *Supply Chain Transformative Capabilities* (SCTCs). The core challenge lies in the effective orchestration of these SCTCs to align both the resilience and sustainability paradigms. Defined as capabilities that enable radical shifts toward new configurations, SCTCs operate through a structured four-stage process:

- *Triggering*: Analysing internal vulnerabilities while scanning the external environment for opportunities and threats, such as social-economic crises or technological revolutions.
- *Envisioning*: Conceiving and piloting new supply chain configurations by experimenting on a small scale and evaluating their feasibility.
- *Navigating*: Identifying high-performing configurations and scaling them up through trust-based collaboration and information sharing among partners.
- *Stabilising*: Institutionalising these new configurations by standardising processes and managing resistance to change through strengthened stakeholder engagement.

5.3.3 Digital Technologies as Catalysts for Synergistic Transformation

The operationalisation of these transformative capabilities is fundamentally enabled by DTs. Within the social-ecological system framework, DTs act as the core infrastructure, providing the necessary tools to execute the transformative cycle. According to Massari et al. (2025), the true transformative potential of these technologies lies not in their isolated application, but in their strategic synergies and cross-functional integration. Rather than seeking isolated optimisation, firms must leverage the convergence of various technologies to support multiple capabilities simultaneously, a dynamic illustrated in Figure 3.

Figure 3. DT-enabled SCTCs for Sustainable & Resilient Supply Chains

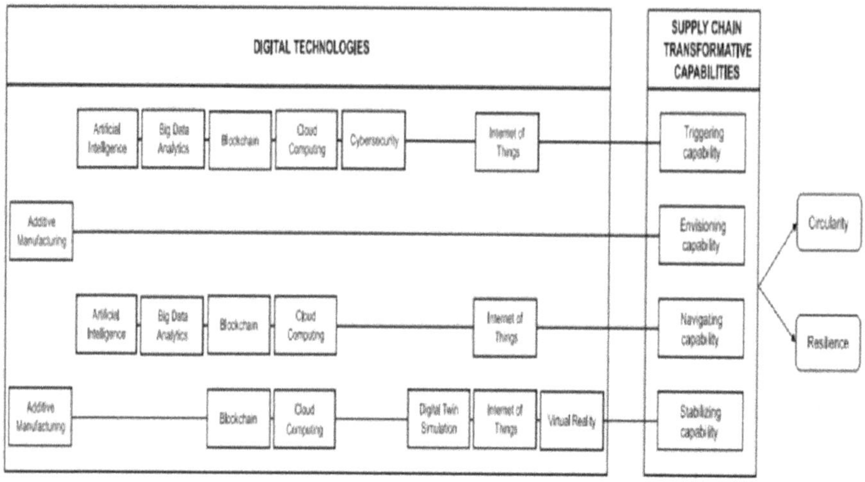

Source: Massari et al. (2025)

Empirical analysis reveals a systematic alignment between specific technologies and the SCTC framework, as detailed in Table 3, which provides a comprehensive mapping of the functional roles and transformational impact of these enablers.

Table 3. The Interplay Between DTs and SCTCs: A Mapping of Enablers and Roles

SCTC Dimension	*Key Digital Technologies*	*Enabling Functions*	*DT-specific application by SCTS dimension*
Triggering Capability *(Analysing vulnerabilities and scanning environment)*	IoT, Blockchain, BDA AI, Cloud Computing Cybersecurity	- Real-time monitoring and traceability - Risk identification and mitigation - Environmental scanning and trend prediction	- IoT for material/product tracking - Blockchain for transparency & compliance - BDA/AI for risk assessment & demand prediction - Cybersecurity for fraud prevention
Envisioning Capability *(Conceiving and testing new SC configurations)*	Additive Manufacturing Digital Twin Simulation	- Rapid prototyping - Virtual testing and validation - Design innovation	- 3D printing with recycled materials - Digital twins for product/ process simulation - Virtual market testing
Navigating Capability *(Adopting optimal SC configurations)*	AI, Blockchain Cloud Computing, BDA, IoT	- Decision support systems - Trust-building and collaboration - Process optimisation	- AI for strategic planning - Blockchain smart contracts - Cloud-based resource sharing - IoT for production efficiency
Stabilising Capability *(Institutionalising new configurations)*	Cloud Computing, Blockchain, IoT, VR Digital Twins, AM, Digital Tags	- Stakeholder engagement - Transparency and standardisation - Consumer education	- Digital product passports - VR showrooms & training - Blockchain-based provenance tracking - AM for visual merchandising

Source: Author's own elaboration, based on Massari et al. (2025)

Specifically, these transformative capabilities function as follows:

- *Triggering capabilities* are enabled by DTs that perform *sensing* and *diagnostic functions*, such as AI and IoT, for early disruption detection.
- *Envisioning capabilities* leverage Digital Twins and AI to facilitate innovation and experimentation, allowing firms to explore new business models.
- *Navigating capabilities* utilise AI and Cloud Computing for optimisation and collaboration, streamlining operations amid high uncertainty.
- *Stabilising capabilities* rely on Blockchain and digital platforms to institutionalise new processes and foster long-term stakeholder alignment.

This mapping reveals two critical patterns of technological enablement. First, specific capabilities are often best activated by the combined effect of multiple technologies; for instance, the convergence of Blockchain and the Internet of Things (IoT) is essential for the stabilising capability by creating trusted, real-time product histories. Second, a single technology can synergistically serve multiple capabilities; Blockchain, for example, enables triggering through traceability, navigating through smart contracts, and stabilising through secured authentication. Ultimately, this approach challenges siloed adoption in favour of a holistic, capability-driven strategy. By framing supply chains as Social-Ecological Systems, it becomes clear that DTs are more than just tools: they are the essential infrastructure that allows complex, adaptive systems to reconcile the traditionally competing objectives of resilience and sustainability. Within this paradigm, these goals are no longer seen as trade-offs but as mutually reinforcing elements of a co-evolving system.

5.4 Beyond dynamic Capabilities: Policy Support for Digital and Transformative SCs

While developing dynamic and transformative capabilities is a fundamental step, it is not a complete solution on its own. To achieve truly transformative supply chains that can effectively manage complex trade-offs, strategic adjustments at the firm level are not enough; an adequate institutional setting is also required. To this end, governments and broader stakeholder ecosystems must play an active role by adopting strategic policies and creating supportive institutional frameworks (Elhaoussine et al., 2023). As DTs become essential for implementing this capability-driven approach, government policy must catalyse the alignment of efficiency, resilience, and sustainability. Even more importantly, policy must foster the very digitalisation that makes such alignment possible (Mood et al., 2025). The specific dimensions of this institutional support are detailed in Figure 4, which examines the transition from firm-level capabilities to transformative supply chains through a policy lens.

Figure 4. From firm capabilities to transformative supply chains: The role of public policy in building a digital ecosystem

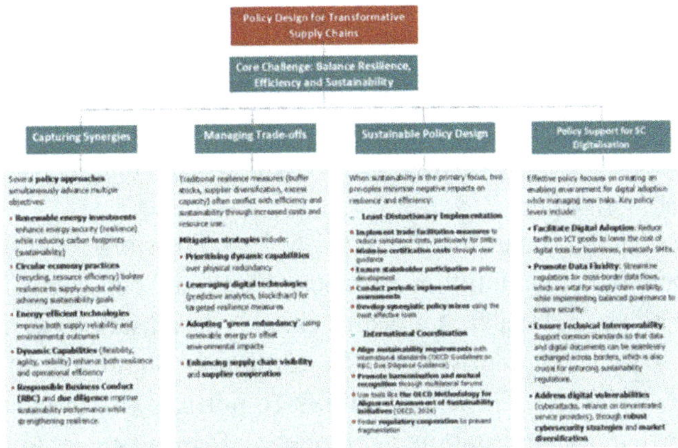

Source: Author's own elaboration, based on OECD Review (2025)

As illustrated in Figure 4, the interplay between resilience, sustainability, and efficiency requires integrated policy solutions that move beyond pursuing these goals in isolation. The primary challenge for policymakers is to mitigate trade-offs, particularly the conflict between the resource-intensive nature of traditional resilience measures - such as static redundancy - and urgent sustainability goals. The framework presented in Figure 4 addresses this trilemma by calling for public policies that foster flexible, agile, and coordinated global supply chains. It posits that effective governance requires an integrated approach that proactively leverages synergies, such as *prioritising dynamic capabilities* over static redundancy, while *mitigating inherent conflicts*. Ultimately, the framework emphasises that *strategic digitalisation* and *international coordination* are essential for balancing these competing demands. This provides a comprehensive roadmap for creating policies that concurrently enhance long-term economic stability, environmental performance, and disruption readiness.

6. CONCLUSION

This chapter explores the pivotal role of digital technologies in strengthening supply chain resilience and assesses their ability to reconcile the traditional trade-offs between efficiency, resilience, and sustainability. The analysis demonstrates that these technologies do not function as simple "plug-and-play" solutions; rather, they act as catalytic enablers within a complex, interconnected system. The path from digital investment to enhanced resilience is fundamentally indirect, mediated by dynamic capabilities, such as traceability and adaptability, and supported by structural integration across physical and financial flows. Empirical evidence suggests that these benefits are amplified by a "supply chain data network effect", which can manifest as tangible operational gains such as reduced lead times. However, this digital transition is rarely uniform; the impact of adoption often reveals asymmetric effects. Specifically, the breadth and depth of technology can strengthen a system's restorative capacity while inadvertently weakening its resistive strength if not aligned strategically.

Adopting a social-ecological systems (SES) lens, this work redefines the supply chain as an open, dynamic entity in a perpetual state of "becoming" rather than a static state of "being". This paradigm shift enables organisations to progress from mere recovery to radical reconfiguration by developing Supply Chain Transformative Capabilities (SCTCs). These capabilities, comprising the stages of triggering, envisioning, navigating, and stabilising, empower firms to generate holistic value rather than merely managing competing priorities. This transition is driven by strategic synergies and cross-functional integration rather than the adoption of isolated, siloed technology. Within this framework, traditionally conflicting imperatives such as resilience and efficiency are reconciled as complementary goals. By leveraging an integrated technological portfolio that utilises big data for predictive risk analysis and additive manufacturing for lean, responsive production, firms can now pursue multiple strategic objectives that were once thought to be mutually exclusive.

Theoretically, this research contributes to the field by refining the Dynamic Capabilities View, identifying precise mediating mechanisms, and demonstrating the practical utility of Resource Orchestration Theory. It clarifies that digital potential is not realised in a vacuum, but rather depends on specific human and knowledge-based factors, such as supply chain memory, supply chain mapping, and the ability to translate technological investments into IT-driven operational capabilities, including agile coordination and real-time visibility. By shifting the conceptualisation of resilience from simple restoration to adaptive transformation, the SES framework offers a novel perspective on supply chains as co-evolving social and ecological entities. For practitioners, this evolution requires a shift in focus from simple technology procurement to holistic capability orchestration. Managers must act as orchestrators, building inter-organisational trust and investing in human capital. They must also align digital tools with specific vulnerabilities through targeted upskilling and audits, unlocking the full transformative potential of their networks. Ultimately, these findings highlight the crucial role of policymakers in promoting the institutional stability and digital ecosystems necessary for such transformations. Policymakers must address the "trilemma" of balancing resilience, sustainability, and efficiency by creating integrated solutions that prioritise developing dynamic capabilities over the costly, resource-intensive approach of traditional static redundancy. Strategic international coordination is essential to balancing these competing global demands. Looking to the future, research should expand upon these insights by conducting longitudinal studies that track the performance of the SCTC framework over time. The ultimate goal is to design "antifragile" supply chains - systems that do not just survive disruptions but actually grow stronger because of them. To unlock the full potential of global digital networks, we need a deeper understanding of the human, organisational, and regulatory conditions that enable these complex systems to thrive in an era of volatility.

REFERENCES

Ahmadi, T., Hesaraki, A. F., & Morsch, J. P. M. (2024). Exploring it-driven supply chain capabilities and resilience: The roles of supply chain risk management and complexity. *Supply Chain Management, 30*(1), 50–66. Advance online publication. DOI: 10.1108/SCM-11-2023-0561

Alabdali, M. A., Yaqub, M. Z., & Windsperger, J. (2025). Algorithmic management and green technologies: Enhancing supply chain resilience through transformation. *Cleaner Logistics and Supply Chain, 17*, 100281. DOI: 10.1016/j.clscn.2025.100281

Ali, A., Mahfouz, A., & Arisha, A. (2017). Analysing supply chain resilience: Integrating the constructs in a concept mapping framework via a systematic literature review. *Supply Chain Management, 22*(1), 16–39. DOI: 10.1108/SCM-06-2016-0197

Aljoghaiman, A., & Ghouri, A. M. (2024). Management information system and digital supply chain influence on supply chain resilience through supply chain risk management. *International Journal of Construction Supply Chain Management, 14*(1), 96–118. DOI: 10.14424/ijcscm202414106

Alquraish, M. (2025). Digital Transformation, Supply Chain Resilience, and Sustainability: A Comprehensive Review with Implications for Saudi Arabian Manufacturing. *Sustainability (Basel), 17*(10), 4495. DOI: 10.3390/su17104495

Alvarenga, M. Z., de Oliveira, M. P. V., & de Oliveira, T. A. G. F. (2023). The impact of using digital technologies on supply chain resilience and robustness: The role of memory under the covid-19 outbreak. *Supply Chain Management, 28*(5), 825–842. Advance online publication. DOI: 10.1108/SCM-06-2022-0217

Alzoubi, H. M., Tan, C. L., El Khatib, M., Alshurideh, M. T., Shwedeh, F., Yanamandra, R., & Lee, K. L. (2025). Smart Government Initiatives: Transforming Global Supply Chains through Digital Change. *International Review of Management and Marketing, 15*(3), 209–217. DOI: 10.32479/irmm.18962

Aslam, H., Blome, C., Roscoe, S., & Azhar, T. M. (2018). Dynamic supply chain capabilities. *International Journal of Operations & Production Management, 38*(12), 2266–2285. DOI: 10.1108/IJOPM-09-2017-0555

Barney, J. (1991). Firm resources and sustained competitive advantage. *Journal of Management, 17*(1), 99–120. DOI: 10.1177/014920639101700108

Belhadi, A., Kamble, S. S., Venkatesh, M., Chiappetta Jabbour, C. J., & Benkhati, I. (2022). Building supply chain resilience and efficiency through additive manufacturing: An ambidextrous perspective on the dynamic capability view. *International Journal of Production Economics*, *249*, 108516. DOI: 10.1016/j.ijpe.2022.108516

Beske, P. (2012). Dynamic capabilities and sustainable supply chain management. *International Journal of Physical Distribution & Logistics Management*, *42*(4), 372–387. DOI: 10.1108/09600031211231344

Biggs, R. (Oonsie), Rhode, C., Archibald, S., Kunene, L. M., Mutanga, S. S., Nkuna, N., Ocholla, P. O., & Phadima, L. J. (2015). Strategies for managing complex social-ecological systems in the face of uncertainty: examples from South Africa and beyond. *Ecology and Society*, *20*(1). https://www.jstor.org/stable/26269769

Brandon-Jones, E., Squire, B., Autry, C., & Petersen, K. J. (2014). A contingent resource-based perspective of supply chain resilience and robustness. *The Journal of Supply Chain Management*, *50*(3), 55–73. DOI: 10.1111/jscm.12050

Brusset, X., & Teller, C. (2017). Supply chain capabilities, risks, and resilience. *International Journal of Production Economics*, *184*, 59–68. DOI: 10.1016/j.ijpe.2016.09.008

Carter, C. R., & Rogers, D. S. (2008). A Framework of Sustainable Supply Chain management: Moving toward New Theory. *International Journal of Physical Distribution & Logistics Management*, *38*(5), 360–387. DOI: 10.1108/09600030810882816

Chen, G., & Yu, Z. (2024). Digital finance, value cocreation, and supply chain resilience: Evidence from listed manufacturing firms in China. *Finance Research Letters*, *70*, 106322. Advance online publication. DOI: 10.1016/j.frl.2024.106322

Choi, T. Y., Dooley, K. J., & Rungtusanatham, M. (2001). Supply networks and complex adaptive systems: Control versus emergence. *Journal of Operations Management*, *19*(3), 351–366. DOI: 10.1016/S0272-6963(00)00068-1

Chopra, S., & Sodhi, M. S. (2014). Reducing the risk of supply chain disruptions. *MIT Sloan Management Review*, *55*(3), 73–80.

Chowdhury, M. M. H., & Quaddus, M. (2016). Supply chain readiness, response and recovery for resilience. *Supply Chain Management*, *21*(6), 709–731. DOI: 10.1108/SCM-12-2015-0463

Chowdhury, M. M. H., & Quaddus, M. (2017). Supply chain resilience: Conceptualization and scale development using dynamic capability theory. *International Journal of Production Economics*, *188*(188), 185–204. DOI: 10.1016/j.ijpe.2017.03.020

Christopher, M., & Peck, H. (2004). Building the Resilient Supply Chain. *International Journal of Logistics Management, 15*(2), 1–14. DOI: 10.1108/09574090410700275

Day, J. M. (2013). Fostering emergent resilience: The complex adaptive supply network of disaster relief. *International Journal of Production Research, 52*(7), 1970–1988. DOI: 10.1080/00207543.2013.787496

Dubey, R., Bryde, D. J., Dwivedi, Y. K., Graham, G., Foropon, C., & Papadopoulos, T. (2023). Dynamic digital capabilities and supply chain resilience: The role of government effectiveness. *International Journal of Production Economics, 258*(4), 108790. DOI: 10.1016/j.ijpe.2023.108790

Eckstein, D., Goellner, M., Blome, C., & Henke, M. (2015). The performance impact of supply chain agility and supply chain adaptability: The moderating effect of product complexity. *International Journal of Production Research, 53*(10), 3028–3046. DOI: 10.1080/00207543.2014.970707

Eisenhardt, K. M., & Martin, J. A. (2000). Dynamic capabilities: What are they? *Strategic Management Journal, 21*(10/11), 1105–1121. https://www.jstor.org/stable/3094429. DOI: 10.1002/1097-0266(200010/11)21:10/11<1105::AID-SMJ133>3.0.CO;2-E

Elhaoussine, Y., Du, Y., & Jia, H. (2023). The role of government regulations on business practices in china: Impact and lessons for global sustainability. In *Government Impact on Sustainable and Responsible Supply Chain Management* (pp. 13–32). IGI Global Scientific Publishing., DOI: 10.4018/978-1-6684-9062-4.ch002

Faruquee, M., Paulraj, A., & Irawan, C. A. (2021). Strategic supplier relationships and supply chain resilience: Is digital transformation that precludes trust beneficial? *International Journal of Operations & Production Management, 41*(7), 1192–1219. DOI: 10.1108/IJOPM-10-2020-0702

Fiskel, J., Polyviou, M., Croxton, K. L., & Pettit, T. J. (2015). From risk to resilience: Learning to deal with disruption. *MIT Sloan Management Review, 56*(2), 79–86.

Fiss, P. C. (2011). Building better causal theories: A fuzzy set approach to typologies in organization research. *Academy of Management Journal, 54*(2), 393–420. DOI: 10.5465/amj.2011.60263120

Hirsch, K., Niemann, W., & Swart, B. (2024). Artificial intelligence and information systems capabilities for supply chain resilience: A study in the South African fast-moving consumer goods industry. *Journal of Transport and Supply Chain Management, 18*(0), 1–16. DOI: 10.4102/JTSCM.v18i0.1025

Hitt, M. A. (2019). Relevance of strategic management theory and research for supply chain management. *The Journal of Supply Chain Management*, *47*(1), 9–13. DOI: 10.1111/j.1745-493X.2010.03210.x

Hong, J., Zhang, Y., & Ding, M. (2018). Sustainable supply chain management practices, supply chain dynamic capabilities, and enterprise performance. *Journal of Cleaner Production*, *172*(1), 3508–3519. DOI: 10.1016/j.jclepro.2017.06.093

Hossain, M. I., Talapatra, S., Saha, P., & Belal, H. M. (2024). From Theory to Practice: Leveraging Digital Twin Technologies and Supply Chain Disruption Mitigation Strategies for Enhanced Supply Chain Resilience with Strategic Fit in Focus. *Global Journal of Flexible Systems Managment*, *26*(1), 87–109. DOI: 10.1007/s40171-024-00424-w

Ivanov, D. (2017). Revealing interfaces of supply chain resilience and sustainability: A simulation study. *International Journal of Production Research*, *56*(10), 3507–3523. DOI: 10.1080/00207543.2017.1343507

Ivanov, D., & Dolgui, A. (2019). New Disruption Risk Management Perspectives in Supply chains: Digital twins, the Ripple effect, and Resileanness. *IFAC-PapersOnLine*, *52*(13), 337–342. DOI: 10.1016/j.ifacol.2019.11.138

Ivanov, D., Dolgui, A., & Sokolov, B. (2019). The impact of digital technology and Industry 4.0 on the ripple effect and supply chain risk analytics. *International Journal of Production Research*, *57*(3), 829–846. https://www.tandfonline.com/doi/abs/10.1080/00207543.2018.1488086. DOI: 10.1080/00207543.2018.1488086

Ivanov, D., Tsipoulanidis, A., & Schönberger, J. (2019). Supply chain risk management and resilience. In *Global Supply Chain and Operations Management* (pp. 455–479). Springer., DOI: 10.1007/978-3-319-94313-8_15

Jia, L., & Li, J. (2024). How does digital collaboration impact supply chain resilience. *Finance Research Letters*, *66*, 105684–105684. DOI: 10.1016/j.frl.2024.105684

Jiang, Y., Feng, T., & Huang, Y. (2023). Antecedent configurations toward supply chain resilience: The joint impact of supply chain integration and big data analytics capability. *Journal of Operations Management*, *70*(2), 257–284. Advance online publication. DOI: 10.1002/joom.1282

Jüttner, U., & Maklan, S. (2011). Supply chain resilience in the global financial crisis: An empirical study. *Supply Chain Management*, *16*(4), 246–259. DOI: 10.1108/13598541111139062

Klimek, P., Varga, J., Jovanovic, A. S., & Székely, Z. (2019). Quantitative resilience assessment in emergency response reveals how organizations trade efficiency for redundancy. *Safety Science*, *113*, 404–414. DOI: 10.1016/j.ssci.2018.12.017

Li, P., Chen, Y., & Guo, X. (2025). Digital Transformation and Supply Chain Resilience. *International Review of Economics & Finance*, *99*, 104033. DOI: 10.1016/j.iref.2025.104033

Ling-yee, L. (2007). Marketing resources and performance of exhibitor firms in trade shows: A contingent resource perspective. *Industrial Marketing Management*, *36*(3), 360–370. DOI: 10.1016/j.indmarman.2005.11.001

Lu, X., & Taghipour, A. (2025a). A review of supply chain digitalization and emerging research paradigms. *Logistics (Basel)*, *9*(2), 47. DOI: 10.3390/logistics9020047

Lu, X., & Taghipour, A. (2025b). Knowledge-driven digital innovation in supply chains: An organizational perspective. *Journal of Innovation & Knowledge*, *10*(5), 100787. DOI: 10.1016/j.jik.2025.100787

Ma, J., Ni, J., Zhao, Y., & Wu, J. (2025). Environmental regulation, digital technology application and low-carbon supply chain resilience: Evidence from China. *Journal of Environmental Management*, *389*, 126087. DOI: 10.1016/j.jenvman.2025.126087 PMID: 40494230

Markolf, S. A., Helmrich, A., Kim, Y., Hoff, R., & Chester, M. (2022). Balancing efficiency and resilience objectives in pursuit of sustainable infrastructure transformations. *Current Opinion in Environmental Sustainability*, *56*, 101181. DOI: 10.1016/j.cosust.2022.101181

Massari, G. F., Nacchiero, R., & Giannoccaro, I. (2025). Transformative supply chains: The enabling role of digital technologies. *International Journal of Production Economics*, *283*, 109562. DOI: 10.1016/j.ijpe.2025.109562

Metwally, M., & Ahmed, A. (2024). The Interplay between Digital Technologies, Supply Chain Resilience, Robustness and Sustainable Environmental Performance: Does Supply Chain Complexity Matter? *Sustainability (Basel)*, *16*(14), 6175–6175. DOI: 10.3390/su16146175

Mohammaddust, F., Rezapour, S., Farahani, R. Z., Mofidfar, M., & Hill, A. (2017). Developing lean and responsive supply chains: A robust model for alternative risk mitigation strategies in supply chain designs. *International Journal of Production Economics*, *183*, 632–653. DOI: 10.1016/j.ijpe.2015.09.012

Mood, M., Ghamary, M., & Youshanlouei, H. R. (2025). The Role of Governments, Employers, and Platforms to Cope with the Skill Gaps in Industry 4.0. In *Ecological and Human Dimensions of AI-Based Supply Chain* (pp. 111–162). IGI Global Scientific Publishing. DOI: 10.4018/979-8-3693-7478-8.ch006

Moore, M.-L., Tjornbo, O., Enfors, E., Knapp, C., Hodbod, J., Baggio, J. A., Norström, A., Olsson, P., & Biggs, D. (2014). Studying the complexity of change: Toward an analytical framework for understanding deliberate social-ecological transformations. *Ecology and Society*, *19*(4), 10. https://www.jstor.org/stable/26269689. DOI: 10.5751/ES-06966-190454

Nelson, R. R., & Winter, S. G. (1982). *An evolutionary theory of economic change*. Belknap Press of Harvard University Press.

Neri, A., Negri, M., Cagno, E., Kumar, V., & Garza-Reyes, J. A. (2023). What digital-enabled dynamic capabilities support the circular economy? A multiple case study approach. *Business Strategy and the Environment*, *32*(7), 5083–5101. DOI: 10.1002/bse.3409

Nikookar, E., Stevenson, M., & Varsei, M. (2024). Building an antifragile supply chain: A capability blueprint for resilience and post-disruption growth. *The Journal of Supply Chain Management*, *60*(1), 13–31. Advance online publication. DOI: 10.1111/jscm.12313

Ning, Y., Li, L., Xu, S. X., & Yang, S. (2022). How do digital technologies improve supply chain resilience in the COVID-19 pandemic? Evidence from Chinese manufacturing firms. *Frontiers of Engineering Management*, *10*(1), 39–50. DOI: 10.1007/s42524-022-0230-4

Organisation for Economic Co-operation and Development. (2024). *Keys to resilient supply chains: OECD policy toolkit – Increasing supply chain resilience*. OECD Publishing.

Organisation for Economic Co-operation and Development. (2025). *OECD Supply Chain Resilience Review: Navigating Risks*. OECD Publishing.

Pathak, S. D., Day, J. M., Nair, A., Sawaya, W. J., & Kristal, M. M. (2007). Complexity and Adaptivity in Supply Networks: Building Supply Network Theory Using a Complex Adaptive Systems Perspective*. *Decision Sciences*, *38*(4), 547–580. DOI: 10.1111/j.1540-5915.2007.00170.x

Pavlou, P. A., & El Sawy, O. A. (2011). Understanding the Elusive Black Box of Dynamic Capabilities. *Decision Sciences*, *42*(1), 239–273. DOI: 10.1111/j.1540-5915.2010.00287.x

Pettit, T. J., Fiksel, J., & Croxton, K. L. (2010). ENSURING SUPPLY CHAIN RESILIENCE: DEVELOPMENT OF a CONCEPTUAL FRAMEWORK. *Journal of Business Logistics, 31*(1), 1–21. DOI: 10.1002/j.2158-1592.2010.tb00125.x

Piprani, A. Z., Nazir, S., Najmi, A., Watabe, M., & Jaafar, N. I. (2025). Digital Capabilities and Supply Chain Resilience: Is Supply Chain Mapping the Missing Link? *Business Strategy & Development, 8*(3), 1–12. DOI: 10.1002/bsd2.70148

Ponomarov, S. Y., & Holcomb, M. C. (2009). Understanding the concept of supply chain resilience. *International Journal of Logistics Management, 20*(1), 124–143. DOI: 10.1108/09574090910954873

Preiser, R., Schlüter, M., Biggs, R., García, M. M., Haider, J., Hertz, T., & Klein, L. (2021). Complexity-based social-ecological systems research: Philosophical foundations and practical implications. In *The Routledge Handbook of Research Methods for Social-Ecological Systems* (pp. 27–46). Routledge. DOI: 10.4324/9781003021339-3

Richey, R. G. (2009). The supply chain crisis and disaster pyramid. *International Journal of Physical Distribution & Logistics Management, 39*(7), 619–628. DOI: 10.1108/09600030910996288

Ruiz-Benítez, R., López, C., & Real, J. C. (2018). The lean and resilient management of the supply chain and its impact on performance. *International Journal of Production Economics, 203*, 190–202. DOI: 10.1016/j.ijpe.2018.06.009

Shah, R., & Ward, P. T. (2007). Defining and Developing Measures of Lean Production. *Journal of Operations Management, 25*(4), 785–805. DOI: 10.1016/j.jom.2007.01.019

Sheffi, Y. (2015). *The power of resilience: How the best companies manage the unexpected.* The MIT Press. DOI: 10.7551/mitpress/9780262029797.001.0001

Singh, R. K. (2025). Transforming humanitarian supply chains with digital twin technology: A study on resilience and agility. *International Journal of Logistics Management, 36*(4), 1119–1135. DOI: 10.1108/IJLM-08-2024-0504

Sirmon, D. G., Hitt, M. A., Ireland, R. D., & Gilbert, B. A. (2010). Resource Orchestration to Create Competitive Advantage. *Journal of Management, 37*(5), 1390–1412. DOI: 10.1177/0149206310385695

Taghipour, A., & Lu, X. (2025). Advancing Supply Chain Innovation: Theoretical Foundations, Contemporary Developments, and Future Directions. In *Ecological and Human Dimensions of AI-Based Supply Chain* (pp. 1–26). IGI Global Scientific Publishing. DOI: 10.4018/979-8-3693-7478-8.ch001

Teece, D. J. (2025). Explicating Dynamic Capabilities: The Nature and Microfoundations of (Sustainable) Enterprise Performance. SSRN *Electronic Journal, 28*(13), 1319–1350. DOI: 10.2139/ssrn.5131710

Tortorella, G., Gloet, M., Samson, D., Kurnia, S., Fogliatto, F. S., & Anzanello, M. J. (2024). Food supply chain resilience through digital transformation: A mixed-method approach. *International Journal of Logistics Management, 36*(2), 381–412. DOI: 10.1108/IJLM-01-2024-0030

Tukamuhabwa, B. R., Stevenson, M., Busby, J., & Zorzini, M. (2015). Supply chain resilience: Definition, review and theoretical foundations for further study. *International Journal of Production Research, 53*(18), 5592–5623. DOI: 10.1080/00207543.2015.1037934

Wang, C. L., & Ahmed, P. K. (2007). Dynamic capabilities: A review and research agenda. *International Journal of Management Reviews, 9*(1), 31–51. DOI: 10.1111/j.1468-2370.2007.00201.x

Wang, H., Chen, Y., Xie, J., & Liu, C. (2025). Research on digital empowerment, innovation vitality and manufacturing supply chain resilience mechanism. *PLoS One, 20*(2), e0316183–e0316183. DOI: 10.1371/journal.pone.0316183 PMID: 39937796

Wieland, A. (2021). Dancing the Supply Chain: Toward Transformative Supply Chain Management. *The Journal of Supply Chain Management, 57*(1), 58–73. Advance online publication. DOI: 10.1111/jscm.12248

Wieland, A., Stevenson, M., Melnyk, S. A., Davoudi, S., & Schultz, L. (2023). Thinking differently about supply chain resilience: What we can learn from social-ecological systems thinking. *International Journal of Operations & Production Management, 43*(1), 1–21. DOI: 10.1108/IJOPM-10-2022-0645

Wu, L., Huang, J., Wang, M., & Kumar, A. (2024). Unleashing supply chain agility: Leveraging data network effects for digital transformation. *International Journal of Production Economics, 277*, 109402. DOI: 10.1016/j.ijpe.2024.109402

Xue, J., & Li, G. (2023). Balancing resilience and efficiency in supply chains: Roles of disruptive technologies under Industry 4.0. *Frontiers of Engineering Management, 10*(1), 171–176. DOI: 10.1007/s42524-022-0247-8

Yu, Y., Xu, L., & Wen, X. (2025). The Impact of Digital Transformation on Supply Chain Resilience in Manufacturing: The Mediating Role of Supply Chain Integration. *Sustainability (Basel), 17*(9), 1–21. DOI: 10.3390/su17093873

Yuan, Y., Tan, H., & Liu, L. (2023). The effects of digital transformation on supply chain resilience: A moderated and mediated model. *Journal of Enterprise Information Management*, *37*(2), 488–510. DOI: 10.1108/JEIM-09-2022-0333

Zhang, J., Miao, X., & Shang, T. (2025). Impact Mechanism of Digital Transformation on Supply Chain Resilience. *Finance Research Letters*, *76*, 106993. DOI: 10.1016/j.frl.2025.106993

Zhao, N., Hong, J., & Lau, K. H. (2023). Impact of Supply Chain Digitalization on Supply Chain Resilience and performance: a multi-mediation Model. *International Journal of Production Economics, 259*, 108817. Sciencedirect. DOI: 10.1016/j.ijpe.2023.108817

Zheng, L., Song, G., Song, S., Huang, N., & Cheng, T. C. E. (2025). How do talent and technology factors affect supply chain robustness and resilience? Evidence from Chinese manufacturers. *Industrial Management & Data Systems*, *125*(3), 899–920. DOI: 10.1108/IMDS-07-2024-0676

Zouari, D., Ruel, S., & Viale, L. (2020). Does digitalising the supply chain contribute to its resilience? *International Journal of Physical Distribution & Logistics Management*, *51*(2), 149–180. DOI: 10.1108/IJPDLM-01-2020-0038

Chapter 5
Green, Just, and Agile: Comparative AI and Policy-Driven Supply Chain Strategies Across Emerging and Developed Economies

Sondeep Kaur
http://orcid.org/0000-0003-4057-8803
School of Commerce and Management, Khalsa College, Patiala, India

ABSTRACT

Sustainable supply chain management (SSCM) sits at the nexus of climate action, social accountability, and economic resilience. Yet the interplay between technological and policy drivers remains under-examined globally. This chapter explores how artificial intelligence (AI) and policy frameworks shape next-generation supply chain strategies in emerging and developed economies, identifying convergences, divergences, and cross-context learning opportunities. Using multi-case analysis of renewable energy components, ethical apparel, and agri-food exports, it integrates literature review, policy analysis, and interviews. A comparative matrix maps how AI tools—predictive analytics, blockchain traceability, digital twins—interact with enabling or constraining policies (e.g., EU CSRD, voluntary ESG codes). Findings present an integrated framework linking AI adoption, policy maturity, and performance across climate, social, and economic dimensions, offering transferable strategies.

DOI: 10.4018/979-8-2600-3199-5.ch005

1. INTRODUCTION AND RATIONALE

1.1 Triple Imperative

The convergence of technological innovation, sustainability demands, and governance transformation has created a triple imperative for contemporary policy and management systems. The technological imperative reflects the rapid maturation of AI and digital technologies, reshaping production, logistics, and decision-making across sectors (OECD, 2025). The sustainability imperative arises from climate risks, resource constraints, and social inequities, requiring integrated solutions that balance economic growth with environmental and social priorities (Greif et al., 2025; Nazrul & Rahman, 2021; Testa et al., 2018). The governance imperative demands adaptive, transparent, and participatory frameworks capable of managing complex socio-technical transitions (Engin et al., 2025).

These imperatives are mutually reinforcing. AI can accelerate sustainability outcomes through predictive analytics, waste-reducing optimisation, and enhanced environmental monitoring (Shen, 2014; Ivanov et al., 2019). Yet without robust governance, AI may amplify inequalities or embed systemic biases (Lauterbach, 2019).

1.2 AI and Policy as Dual Enablers

AI and public policy operate as dual enablers of the triple imperative. AI provides capabilities for data-driven decision-making, scenario modelling, and real-time optimisation (Woo et al., 2020; Yi & Ayangbah, 2024). Policy, in turn, establishes the legal, ethical, and institutional scaffolding that determines how AI is deployed (OECD, 2019).

National AI strategies illustrate this co-evolution. Countries such as India and China integrate competitiveness with social objectives but differ in governance models, investment priorities, and ethical safeguards (Sharma et al., 2023; Joshi, 2024). Policy actively shapes innovation trajectories through standards, incentives, and regulatory oversight (Stix, C. 2021; Thakur, 2025; Taghipour, Belrhazi & Damoum, 2023). Conversely, AI enhances governance through algorithmic state architectures that improve service delivery and regulatory monitoring (Testa et al., 2018).

However, uneven digital infrastructure, skills gaps, and fragmented regulatory environments create asymmetries in AI readiness, widening global and intra-national divides (Madanchian & Taherdoost, 2025; Radhakrishnan & Chattopadhyay, 2020).

1.3 Comparative Lens

A comparative analytical lens is essential for understanding how governance contexts mediate AI-driven sustainability outcomes. Comparative studies show that structural (institutional capacity), relational (public–private partnerships), and adaptive (policy agility) factors shape AI's transformative potential (Ahmed Batki & Phudinawala, 2024).

The few studies integrate these dimensions into mechanism-based comparative frameworks. Existing research often treats AI, sustainability, and governance separately, producing fragmented insights (Lauterbach, 2019; OECD, 2024). Limited benchmarking across structural, relational, adaptive, and equity dimensions restricts understanding of leverage points for policy and practice (Ghosh & Pandey 2026).

A comparative, mechanism-based approach enables identification of context-specific enablers and barriers to AI-driven sustainability transitions and supports scalable, transferable policy learning (OECD, 2025; Yi & Ayangbah, 2024). By situating AI and policy as dual enablers within the triple imperative, this chapter contributes a diagnostic and visually communicable framework for aligning technological innovation with sustainable and equitable governance.

2. LITERATURE REVIEW

2.1 Sustainable Supply Chain Management (SSCM) — Environmental, Social, Economic

Sustainable Supply Chain Management (SSCM) integrates environmental, social, and economic considerations into the management of material, information, and capital flows across the supply chain (Seuring & Müller, 2008). The triple bottom line (TBL) framework positions SSCM as a strategic imperative for organisations seeking to balance profitability with responsibility (Carter & Rogers, 2008). Extensive research in supply chain coordination, information sharing, and sustainability performance reinforces the need for integrated, multi-level governance mechanisms to support SSCM implementation (Taghipour & Frayret, 2013).

Environmental Dimension

Practices such as green procurement, eco-design, and closed-loop systems have been shown to reduce environmental footprints while enhancing brand reputation (Geissdoerfer et al., 2017). Studies on green supply chain management emphasise the increasing complexity of environmental compliance and the necessity of digital tools to support monitoring and reporting (Testa et al., 2018; Lu et al., 2023). Research on divergent production networks and decentralised planning further highlights the importance of environmental optimisation in multi-tier supply chains (Zoghlami et al., 2016).

Social Dimension

Ethical sourcing, supplier development, and transparent information sharing have been linked to improved worker welfare and reduced reputational risk (Panigrahi et al., 2019). However, the social dimension remains underexplored, particularly in emerging economies (Sánchez-Flores et al., 2020). Studies on humanitarian logistics and service outsourcing demonstrate that social sustainability challenges are often intensified in resource-constrained contexts (Kovács and Spens 2011). Research on hotel sustainability practices also illustrates how social and environmental initiatives influence consumer perceptions and willingness to pay (Janjua et al., 2025).

Economic Dimension

Economic sustainability emphasises long-term value creation, cost efficiency, and resilience. SSCM practices can improve operational performance and market competitiveness, though trade-offs between environmental/social goals and short-term profitability remain a challenge. Studies on quick response systems, stochastic planning, and supplier evaluation show that economic performance is closely tied to coordination quality and information transparency (Lebosse et al., 2017; Cauchois et al., 2017). Research on sustainable pharmaceutical and closed-loop supply chains further demonstrates how green technologies and optimisation models can enhance economic outcomes under uncertainty (Ivanov et al., 2019; Gharye Mirzaei et al., 2025).

Recent bibliometric analyses reveal that while environmental and economic aspects of SSCM are well-researched, the social dimension remains comparatively neglected (Sánchez-Flores et al., 2020). This imbalance limits the holistic integration of sustainability principles in global supply chains. The need for integrated frameworks is reinforced by studies on information asymmetry, coordination planning, and shared-value supplier segmentation, which collectively highlight the interdependence of environmental, social, and economic performance (Taghipour & Beneteau-Piet, 2020).

2.2 AI in Supply Chains — Predictive Analytics, Blockchain, Digital Twins

AI enables predictive, adaptive, and transparent decision-making, enhancing both efficiency and sustainability outcomes (Qu & Kim, 2024). This aligns with earlier work on supply chain coordination, information sharing, and digital transformation, which emphasises the need for integrated, data-driven systems to manage uncertainty and improve responsiveness (Taghipour & Frayret, 2011, 2013; Ren et al., 2016).

Predictive Analytics

AI-driven forecasting models analyse historical and real-time data to predict demand fluctuations, optimise inventory, and reduce waste (Queiroz et al., 2021). Predictive maintenance in manufacturing and logistics reduces downtime and extends asset lifecycles, contributing to environmental and economic gains. These capabilities build on foundational research in stochastic planning, quick-response systems, and inference-based forecasting (Cauchois et al., 2017; Lebosse et al., 2017). Recent studies in pharmaceutical and vaccine supply chains demonstrate how AI-enabled optimisation can significantly improve resilience and sustainability under uncertainty (Tiwari et al., 2018; Taghipour et al., 2023).

Blockchain

Blockchain enhances traceability, transparency, and trust in multi-tier supply chains. Immutable transaction records support ethical sourcing, fraud prevention, and compliance with sustainability standards (Roumeliotis et al., 2024). In agri-food and pharmaceutical supply chains, blockchain has been used to verify origin, quality, and cold-chain integrity, improving market access and reducing risk (Lu et al., 2023; Kayikci et al., 2022). Research on information asymmetry and decentralised coordination further highlights blockchain's role in reducing distortions and improving decision-making across supply chain partners (Vosooghidizaji et al., 2019, 2020).

Digital Twins

Digital twins create virtual replicas of physical supply chain assets and processes, enabling simulation, optimisation, and scenario planning (Taghipour et al., 2022). These applications complement earlier work on decentralised multi-level planning, divergent production networks, and capacity-constrained optimisation (Zoghlami et al., 2016). Digital twins also support Society 5.0 initiatives by enabling human-centric, technology-enabled supply chain innovation.

Challenges and Gaps

Despite rapid adoption, several challenges persist. Data integration remains a major barrier, particularly in emerging economies where digital infrastructure is uneven (Sahraoui et al., 2023). Cybersecurity risks increase as supply chains become more interconnected, requiring robust governance and monitoring frameworks. AI applications also tend to prioritise environmental and economic outcomes, with limited focus on social sustainability (Qu & Kim, 2024). This mirrors broader gaps in SSCM research, where labour rights, equity, and community impacts remain under-examined (Panigrahi et al., 2019; Janjua et al., 2025). Furthermore, the scalability of AI-enabled solutions depends on organisational readiness, policy maturity, and cross-sector collaboration — factors highlighted in recent studies on digital transformation and sustainable supply chain governance (Lu et al., 2023).

Integrating insights from supply chain coordination, digital transformation, and sustainability research provides a more holistic understanding of AI's role in shaping green, resilient, and socially responsible supply chains (Tiwari et al., 2018; Gharye Mirzaei et al., 2025).

2.3 Policy Frameworks — Mandatory vs. Voluntary ESG

Policy frameworks strongly influence SSCM by shaping reporting, compliance, and governance maturity. Mandatory regulations such as the EU CSRD enhance transparency and accountability (European Commission, 2023), supported by evidence that policy enforcement improves coordination and sustainability performance (Sahraoui et al., 2023). Research on sustainable procurement and government-led initiatives similarly shows that regulatory clarity accelerates SSCM adoption (Taghipour, Belrhazi & Damoum, 2023).

Voluntary frameworks (e.g., GRI, UN Global Compact) offer flexibility but often lead to inconsistent reporting, especially in emerging economies (Sánchez-Flores et al., 2020). Sectoral studies in hospitality, outsourcing, and humanitarian logistics highlight wide variation in voluntary ESG uptake (Janjua et al., 2025).

The boundary between mandatory and voluntary ESG is narrowing as voluntary disclosures increasingly inform regulatory reforms. Hybrid governance models combining legal mandates, industry codes, and digital compliance tools are becoming dominant (Kayikci et al., 2022).

2.4 Comparative Studies — Emerging vs. Developed Economies

Comparative research consistently shows differences in SSCM adoption across developed and emerging economies, shaped by institutional capacity, infrastructure, and regulatory maturity (Sánchez-Flores et al., 2020). Studies on logistics, humanitarian operations, and outsourcing highlight how governance gaps and resource constraints limit sustainability performance in emerging contexts (Radhoui et al., 2019). In contrast, developed economies benefit from stronger digital infrastructure and policy enforcement, enabling faster integration of AI, blockchain, and green technologies (Sahraoui et al., 2023;). Cross-country analyses also show that information asymmetry, coordination quality, and forecasting capability significantly influence performance differences (Ren et al., 2016). Overall, comparative evidence underscores the need for context-specific SSCM strategies and adaptive governance models (Taghipour, Belrhazi & Damoum, 2023).

2.5 Conceptual Gaps

Despite progress in SSCM and AI-enabled supply chains, several conceptual gaps persist. Research still treats AI, sustainability, and governance as separate domains rather than an integrated system (Zejjari & Benhayoun, 2024; Vosooghidizaji et al., 2020). Social sustainability remains under-examined, especially in emerging economies. Comparative studies rarely incorporate differences in policy maturity, digital readiness, and institutional capacity (Mahfod et al., 2021). Scalability challenges also persist in contexts with weak infrastructure and fragmented governance (Kovács and Spens 2011). Finally, measurement tools linking AI adoption, policy evolution, and triple-bottom-line outcomes remain limited (Gharye Mirzaei et al., 2025). Table 1 summarises the key SSCM literature across environmental, social, and economic dimensions, highlighting the theoretical foundations and empirical patterns that inform this chapter. Figure 1 presents the conceptual positioning of the AI–policy–outcome nexus, illustrating how policy maturity accelerates AI adoption, how AI-enabled performance influences policy reform, and how sustainability outcomes feed back into both technological development and governance evolution. Together, these visual elements consolidate the literature review and clarify the multidimensional relationships that underpin the chapter's comparative framework.

Table 1. Summary of Key SSCM Literature

Author(s) & Year	Focus Area	Key Findings	Relevance to Chapter
Carter & Rogers (2008)	SSCM framework	Triple Bottom Line integration is essential for long-term competitiveness	Foundational theory
Geissdoerfer et al. (2017)	Circular economy	CE principles enhance environmental and economic performance	Environmental dimension
Panigrahi et al. (2019)	Governance in SSCM	Governance mechanisms are critical for SSCM implementation	Policy relevance
Sánchez-Flores et al. (2020)	SSCM in emerging economies	Social dimension underexplored; governance gaps persist	Gap identification
Qu & Kim (2024)	AI in SSCM	AI enhances environmental/economic outcomes; social lag	Technology dimension
Roumeliotis et al. (2024)	Blockchain & digital twins	Integration improves traceability and efficiency	AI tools
Zejjari & Benhayoun (2024)	AI & sustainability	Need for integrated AI–policy frameworks	Conceptual gap

Source: Author's own work

Figure 1. Conceptual Positioning of AI–Policy–Outcome Nexus (Arrows illustrate bidirectional feedback loops: Policy maturity accelerates AI adoption, AI-enabled performance improvements influence policy reform, Outcomes feed back into both AI development and policy evolution.)

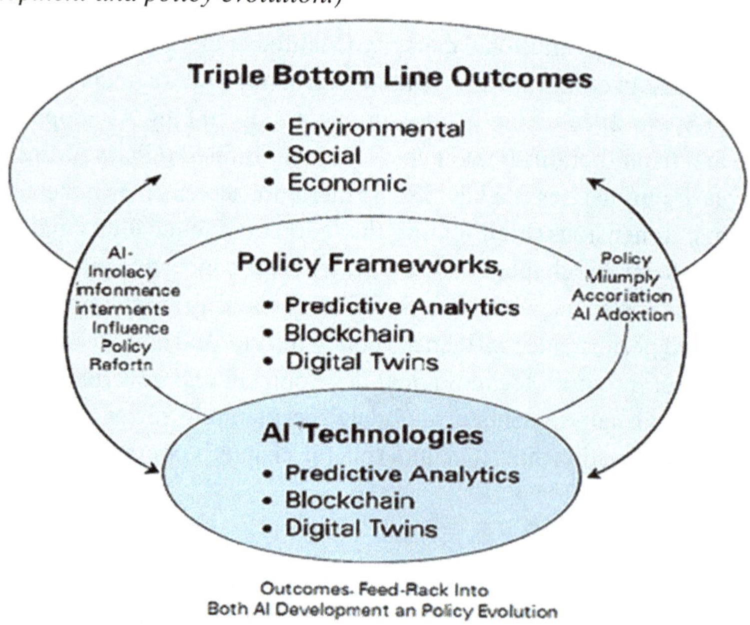

Source: Author's own work

3. RESEARCH OBJECTIVES AND QUESTIONS

The rapid evolution of artificial intelligence (AI) and its integration into governance, industry, and sustainability initiatives have created both unprecedented opportunities and complex challenges. While AI's potential to accelerate progress toward the Sustainable Development Goals (SDGs) is widely acknowledged (Greif et al., 2025; OECD, 2025), the pathways through which AI adoption interacts with policy frameworks, institutional capacities, and socio-economic contexts remain under-explored. Prior research on digital transformation, information asymmetry, and supply chain coordination similarly highlights the need for integrated governance mechanisms to manage technological transitions (Taghipour & Frayret, 2013).

This study positions AI and policy as dual enablers within a triple imperative of technological innovation, sustainability, and governance transformation (Engin et al., 2025). It builds on evidence that policy maturity, regulatory clarity, and institutional readiness significantly shape the effectiveness and equity of AI-enabled sustainability outcomes.

3.1 Research Objectives

The study is guided by four interrelated objectives:

1. **To conceptualize and operationalize the triple imperative**—technological, sustainability, and governance—within the context of AI adoption, identifying structural, relational, adaptive, and equity dimensions that shape outcomes (Jobin et al., 2019).
2. **To examine AI and policy as dual enablers**, mapping how national strategies, regulatory frameworks, and institutional arrangements influence AI's capacity to deliver sustainability benefits while mitigating risks (OECD, 2019).
3. **To conduct a comparative analysis** of AI adoption trajectories across countries or sectors, identifying patterns, divergences, and context-specific enablers and barriers (Sharma et al., 2023; Joshi, 2024).
4. **To develop a diagnostic, reproducible benchmarking framework** that supports policy design, cross-sectoral learning, and collaborative innovation (Carter & Rogers, 2008; Thakur, 2025).

3.2 Guiding Research Questions

To achieve these objectives, the study addresses the following research questions (RQs):

- **RQ1:** How can the triple imperative of technological innovation, sustainability, and governance be systematically defined and measured in the context of AI adoption? *Rationale:* Existing literature often treats these imperatives in isolation, leading to fragmented insights (Lauterbach, 2019; OECD, 2021).
- **RQ2:** In what ways do policy frameworks and governance mechanisms enable or constrain AI's contribution to sustainability outcomes? *Rationale:* While AI's technical capabilities are well documented, the role of policy in shaping deployment remains unevenly understood (Ubaldi et al., 2019).
- **RQ3:** What structural, relational, adaptive, and equity factors differentiate high-performing AI–AI-AI-sustainability ecosystems from those with limited impact? *Rationale:* Comparative evidence suggests that institutional capacity, stakeholder trust, and policy agility are critical determinants of success (Ahmed Batki & Phudinawala, 2024).
- **RQ4:** How can a mechanism-based benchmarking framework support cross-jurisdictional learning and policy transferability? *Rationale:* There is a gap in reproducible, diagnostic tools that integrate multidimensional indicators for AI–policy–sustainability linkages (Jobin et al., 2019).

Significance of the Research Design

By explicitly linking research objectives to guiding questions, this study ensures conceptual clarity, comparative rigor, and practical relevance. The framework developed advances academic understanding of AI–policy–sustainability interactions while offering decision-support tools for practitioners. The comparative approach enables context-sensitive insights while maintaining analytical generalizability (Yi & Ayangbah, 2024; Prasittisopin, L. 2025). This significance is reinforced by prior work demonstrating that coordinated governance, digital readiness, and institutional learning are essential for scaling AI-enabled sustainability solutions across diverse economic contexts (Ren et al., 2016).

4. METHODOLOGY

4.1 Research Design: Comparative Multiple Case Study

This study employs a comparative multiple case study design to examine how AI adoption and policy frameworks jointly influence sustainable supply chain management (SSCM) outcomes across different economic contexts. This design is well-suited for analysing complex, context-dependent phenomena where boundaries between the phenomenon and its environment are blurred.

Comparative case studies enable cross-case synthesis to identify patterns, divergences, and transferable strategies across developed and emerging economies (Stroumpoulis et al., 2024). This approach aligns with SSCM research that emphasises theory-building through empirical–conceptual integration (Zhou & Masi, 2025). Prior work on supply chain coordination, information asymmetry, and digital transformation further supports the use of comparative designs to understand heterogeneous technological and policy environments (Taghipour & Frayret, 2013).

4.2 Case Selection Criteria

A purposive sampling strategy was used to ensure analytical relevance. Four criteria guided case selection:

1. **Sectoral relevance** – Firms operating in supply chain-intensive sectors (manufacturing, logistics, retail), consistent with prior SSCM and logistics studies (Radhoui et al., 2019).
2. **Sustainability commitment** – Evidence of ESG initiatives, reflecting the importance of governance and environmental performance in SSCM (Taghipour & Beneteau-Piet, 2020).
3. **AI adoption** – Use of predictive analytics, blockchain, IoT, or digital twins, consistent with emerging research on AI-enabled supply chains (Kayikci et al., 2022).
4. **Policy exposure** – Interaction with mandatory or voluntary sustainability policies, reflecting the role of governance in shaping SSCM outcomes (Taghipour, Belrhazi & Damoum, 2023).

These criteria ensure comparability while capturing diversity in technological maturity, regulatory environments, and sustainability priorities. Table 2 summarises the case selection matrix.

Table 2. Case Selection Matrix

Case ID	Sector	Country/ Economy Type	AI Tools in Supply Chain	ESG Maturity Level	Policy Exposure
C1	Manufacturing	Developed	Predictive analytics, digital twins	High	Mandatory national sustainability reporting
C2	Retail & E-commerce	Emerging	Blockchain for traceability, AI demand forecasting	Medium	Voluntary industry-led ESG guidelines
C3	Logistics & Transport	Developed	IoT-enabled fleet monitoring, route optimization	High	Regional carbon reduction mandates
C4	Food Processing	Emerging	AI quality control, supply chain risk analytics	Low–Medium	Mixed: voluntary codes + partial regulatory oversight
C5	Electronics	Developed	Blockchain, predictive maintenance, and AI supplier scoring	High	Comprehensive ESG compliance laws

Source: Author's own work

4.3 Data Sources

To enhance validity and reliability, the study employs data triangulation (Flick, 2022) using three primary sources:

- **Policy documents** – National sustainability strategies, regulatory frameworks, and industry guidelines.
- **Industry reports** – ESG disclosures, sustainability audits, and sectoral white papers.
- **Semi-structured interviews** – Conducted with supply chain managers, sustainability officers, and policy experts.

Semi-structured interviews balance consistency with flexibility, enabling exploration of emergent themes (Oyedijo et al., 2023). This approach aligns with prior SSCM and logistics research that relies on expert interviews to capture operational and governance complexities (Ren et al., 2016; Kovács and Spens, 2011). All interviews were recorded, transcribed, and coded using NVivo software.

4.4 Analytical Framework

The analysis followed a two-stage process combining thematic coding with comparative indexing.

Stage 1: Thematic Coding

An inductive coding approach was applied to interview transcripts and documents, identifying recurring themes across four analytical dimensions:

- Climate resilience
- Social accountability
- Economic agility
- AI–policy interaction

Codes were refined iteratively and grouped into higher-order categories following grounded theory principles (Charmaz, 2006). This approach is consistent with prior SSCM studies that analyse sustainability, coordination, and digital transformation themes (Vosooghidizaji et al., 2019).

Stage 2: Comparative Indexing

A comparative index was developed to benchmark each case across the four dimensions. Indicators were drawn from qualitative and quantitative evidence (e.g., policy compliance, AI integration depth, stakeholder engagement). Scores were normalised to enable cross-case comparison, following methods used in recent SSCM benchmarking studies (Zhou & Masi, 2025). This approach aligns with optimisation and performance-evaluation models used in sustainable and digital supply chain research (Gharye Mirzaei et al., 2025). Figure 2 illustrates the methodological workflow.

Figure 2. Methodological Flowchart 5.5 Limitations and Scope

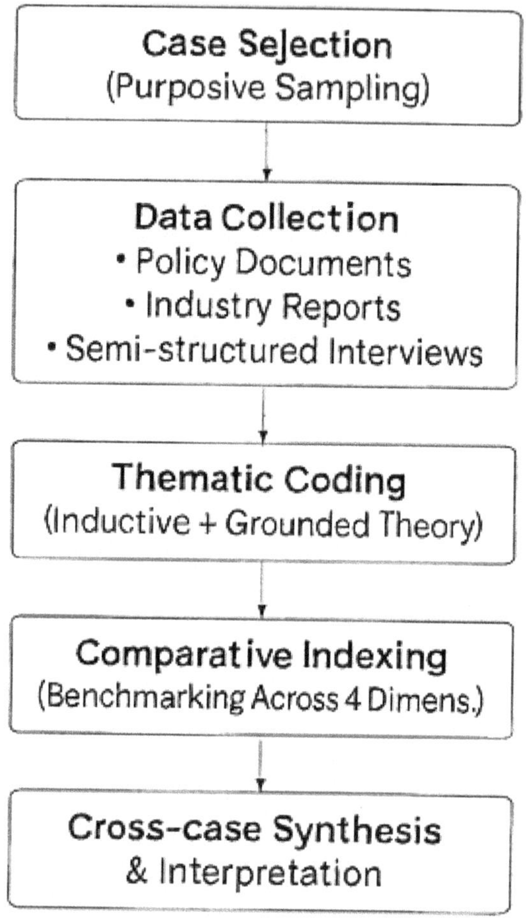

Source: Author's own work

4.5 Limitations and Scope

Several limitations must be acknowledged:

- **Generalizability** – Findings are context-specific, though diversity in case selection enhances transferability.
- **Data access** – Some firms restricted access to proprietary data, limiting granularity.

- **Policy fluidity** – Regulatory landscapes evolve rapidly, meaning findings reflect a temporal snapshot.
- **AI heterogeneity** – Variations in AI maturity complicate direct comparisons across cases.

Despite these constraints, the design provides a robust foundation for theory-building and practical guidance, consistent with prior comparative and digital supply chain studies (Zoghlami et al., 2016).

5. CASE STUDIES

This section presents six comparative case studies across three sectors — renewable energy components, ethical apparel manufacturing, and agri-food exports — each examined in a developed and an emerging economy context.

5.1 Renewable Energy Components

5.1.1 Germany (Developed)

Germany's renewable energy sector is fundamentally shaped by the Energiewende policy framework, a long-term national strategy that mandates a transition to a low-carbon energy system by 2045. This policy is not merely aspirational; it is embedded in legally binding targets for greenhouse gas reduction, renewable energy expansion, and energy efficiency improvements. The Energiewende has created a stable and predictable policy environment that encourages investment in renewable generation, grid modernisation, and enabling technologies such as artificial intelligence (AI).

AI adoption in Germany's renewable energy sector is driven by the growing complexity of grid operations as variable renewable sources—particularly wind and solar—account for an increasing share of generation. The intermittency of these sources requires advanced forecasting, real-time optimisation, and flexible demand management to maintain grid stability. AI offers the capability to process vast streams of sensor, weather, and market data, enabling faster, more accurate operational decisions than traditional control systems (Prasittisopin, L. 2025).

A case study of a leading German utility company illustrates how AI is being deployed across three critical operational domains:

1. Smart Grid Management – AI-driven load balancing and peak shaving are achieved through the integration of real-time data from distributed energy resources (DERs), including rooftop solar, battery storage, and electric vehicle charging sta-

tions. Machine learning algorithms dynamically adjust supply and demand, reducing reliance on fossil-fuel peaker plants and improving overall system efficiency.

2. Predictive Maintenance – In the wind energy segment, AI models analyse vibration, temperature, and acoustic data from turbine components to forecast potential failures before they occur. This predictive capability reduces unplanned downtime, extends asset lifespans, and lowers maintenance costs. In offshore wind farms, where access is weather-dependent, predictive maintenance significantly improves operational reliability (Prasittisopin, L. 2025).

3. Virtual Buffers – AI systems coordinate industrial loads, such as port operations and manufacturing facilities, to act as flexible demand resources. By temporarily adjusting energy consumption patterns, these "virtual buffers" help absorb fluctuations in renewable generation, reducing the need for costly physical storage and enhancing grid resilience.

Germany's high policy maturity—characterised by coherent legislation, strong regulatory oversight, and alignment with EU climate targets—has accelerated AI integration. The country's robust R&D ecosystem, supported by public funding, university–industry collaboration, and innovation clusters, provides fertile ground for AI experimentation and scaling. Public acceptance of renewable energy, cultivated through decades of environmental policy and citizen engagement, further facilitates adoption.

However, challenges remain. Data interoperability is a persistent issue, as utilities, grid operators, and technology providers often use heterogeneous data formats and platforms, complicating seamless AI integration. Cybersecurity is another critical concern; as grid operations become increasingly digitised and interconnected, the potential attack surface expands, necessitating advanced security protocols and continuous monitoring.

5.1.2 India (Emerging)

India's renewable energy component manufacturing sector—particularly in solar photovoltaic (PV) modules and wind turbine components—is undergoing rapid expansion, driven by ambitious national targets and targeted industrial policy. The National Solar Mission aims to position India as a global leader in solar energy deployment, while the Production Linked Incentive (PLI) schemes provide financial incentives to domestic manufacturers to scale up production capacity, improve technology adoption, and reduce import dependence. Together, these initiatives have created a favourable policy environment for both capacity expansion and technological modernisation, including the gradual integration of artificial intelligence (AI) into manufacturing and operational processes (Qu & Kim, 2024).

AI adoption in this sector is still in its emerging phase, but several promising applications are already visible:

1. Quality Control – In solar PV manufacturing, computer vision systems powered by deep learning algorithms are being deployed to detect micro-cracks, surface defects, and alignment errors in PV cells during production. These defects, often invisible to the human eye, can significantly reduce module efficiency and lifespan. Automated inspection systems not only improve detection accuracy but also enable real-time feedback loops, allowing manufacturers to adjust production parameters instantly and reduce wastage.

2. Supply Chain Optimisation – The renewable component manufacturing sector in India is characterised by geographically dispersed and often fragmented manufacturing clusters. AI-driven demand forecasting tools are being used to predict raw material and component requirements based on historical consumption patterns, market demand signals, and seasonal variations. This predictive capability helps manufacturers reduce inventory costs, avoid production delays, and respond more flexibly to fluctuations in domestic and export orders.

3. Energy Yield Prediction – For solar farm developers and operators, machine learning models are increasingly used to forecast energy output by integrating weather data, irradiance patterns, and historical performance records. These forecasts support better operational planning, grid integration, and financial modelling, particularly in regions with high variability in solar radiation.

While policy incentives such as the PLI scheme, customs duty protection for domestic manufacturers, and renewable purchase obligations provide a strong push for sectoral growth, several structural and operational barriers constrain the pace of AI integration:

- **Fragmented Manufacturing Ecosystem –** Many component manufacturers operate in small- to medium-scale clusters with limited access to advanced automation and AI infrastructure.
- **Skills Gap –** There is a shortage of engineers and technicians trained in both renewable energy manufacturing processes and AI/ML applications, slowing technology adoption.
- **Variable Enforcement of Quality Standards –** While India has introduced quality certification requirements for PV modules and wind components, enforcement remains inconsistent across states and manufacturing hubs, leading to uneven product quality and reduced incentives for AI-driven quality control investments.

Despite these challenges, the trajectory is positive. The convergence of industrial policy, growing domestic demand, and export opportunities is likely to accelerate

AI adoption in the coming decade. Collaborative initiatives between government agencies, industry associations, and academic institutions could address the skills gap, while standardisation of data formats and quality benchmarks would improve interoperability and trust in AI-enabled systems. In summary, India's renewable energy component manufacturing sector illustrates how emerging economies can leverage targeted policy frameworks to stimulate both industrial growth and technological modernisation.

5.1.3 Sweden (Developed)

Sweden's apparel sector is internationally recognised for its commitment to sustainability, transparency, and innovation, with H&M's "Conscious" program serving as a prominent example of how large-scale fashion retailers can integrate artificial intelligence (AI) into sustainable supply chain management. The Swedish approach is underpinned by a strong policy framework, high consumer awareness, and advanced digital infrastructure, creating fertile ground for AI-enabled ethical manufacturing practices (Shen, 2014).

The integration of AI in Sweden's apparel sector is visible across several operational domains:

1. **Demand Forecasting –** AI-driven predictive analytics are used to analyse historical sales data, seasonal trends, social media sentiment, and macroeconomic indicators to forecast demand with greater accuracy. This capability reduces overproduction, one of the most significant sources of waste in the fashion industry. By aligning production volumes more closely with actual market demand, companies can minimise unsold inventory, lower markdown rates, and reduce the environmental footprint associated with excess manufacturing.
2. **Supplier Compliance Monitoring –** Sweden's apparel brands increasingly rely on AI-assisted audit systems to monitor supplier adherence to labour rights, workplace safety, and environmental standards. These systems process data from on-site inspections, IoT sensors, and third-party reports to flag anomalies or potential violations in real time. This proactive approach enables brands to address non-compliance swiftly, reducing reputational risks and ensuring that ethical commitments are upheld throughout the supply chain.
3. **Circularity Tracking –** In line with Sweden's leadership in circular economy practices, AI is combined with blockchain technology to trace the origin, composition, and recycling history of materials used in apparel production. This transparency allows both companies and consumers to verify sustainability claims, track the proportion of recycled fibres in garments, and ensure that end-of-life products are channelled back into the production cycle rather than landfilled.

The policy environment in Sweden strongly supports these initiatives. Extended Producer Responsibility (EPR) regulations require manufacturers and retailers to take responsibility for the entire lifecycle of their products, including post-consumer waste management. Eco-labelling schemes, such as the Nordic Swan Ecolabel, provide consumers with clear, credible information about the environmental performance of products, reinforcing market demand for sustainable and ethically produced apparel.

AI adoption in this context is facilitated by Sweden's robust digital infrastructure, high internet penetration, and a workforce skilled in both data science and sustainable design. Moreover, Swedish consumers exhibit strong demand for transparency, often prioritising ethical and environmental considerations in purchasing decisions. This consumer pressure creates a commercial incentive for brands to invest in AI-enabled traceability and compliance systems.

However, challenges remain. Integrating AI into complex, globalised supply chains requires data standardisation across multiple jurisdictions, as well as robust cybersecurity measures to protect sensitive supplier and product information. Additionally, while large brands like H&M have the resources to invest in advanced AI systems, smaller Swedish apparel companies may face barriers related to cost, technical expertise, and change management. In summary, Sweden's apparel sector demonstrates how policy alignment, consumer engagement, and technological capability can converge to advance ethical manufacturing.

5.1.4 Bangladesh (Emerging)

Bangladesh's ready-made garment (RMG) industry is one of the largest in the world, accounting for a significant share of the country's export earnings and employing millions of workers, particularly women. The sector's global competitiveness is built on cost efficiency and large-scale production capacity, but it has long faced scrutiny over labour conditions, workplace safety, and environmental impact. Tragic incidents such as the Rana Plaza collapse in 2013 intensified international pressure on brands and suppliers to improve compliance with labour rights, occupational safety, and environmental standards.

Against this backdrop, artificial intelligence (AI) adoption in the Bangladeshi RMG sector remains nascent but steadily growing, driven largely by partnerships with international buyers and pilot projects funded through development agencies or brand-led sustainability programs. Current applications focus on three emerging domains:

1. **Waste Reduction –** Fabric wastage is a major cost and environmental concern in garment manufacturing. AI-driven fabric-cutting optimisation systems use computer vision and pattern-nesting algorithms to maximise material utilisation. By analysing garment designs and fabric dimensions, these systems can generate

cutting layouts that minimise offcuts, reducing both raw material costs and textile waste sent to landfill. Early adopters report measurable savings in fabric usage, which is particularly significant given the sector's thin profit margins.

2. **Energy Efficiency –** With rising energy costs and increasing pressure to reduce carbon footprints, some factories are deploying smart meters and AI-based predictive analytics to monitor and optimise energy consumption. These systems track real-time electricity usage across production lines, identify inefficiencies, and recommend operational adjustments—such as shifting high-energy processes to off-peak hours or fine-tuning machine settings. Over time, such measures can lower utility bills and contribute to sustainability targets.

3. **Compliance Monitoring –** In response to buyer demands for improved workplace safety, pilot projects are testing AI-enabled systems that use computer vision and IoT sensors to detect safety hazards in real time. Examples include identifying blocked fire exits, detecting excessive heat or humidity, and monitoring workers' use of personal protective equipment. Alerts generated by these systems can be sent to supervisors for immediate corrective action, potentially preventing accidents and improving audit readiness (Nazrul & Rahman, 2021).

However, the policy environment in Bangladesh is less developed than in countries like Sweden. Regulatory oversight is limited, and enforcement of labour and environmental standards often relies on buyer-driven codes of conduct rather than robust national legislation.

Barriers to AI adoption include:

- **Cost pressures –** The RMG sector operates on low margins, making capital investment in advanced technologies challenging without external funding or buyer support.
- **Limited digital skills –** Many factory managers and workers lack training in AI, data analytics, and digital manufacturing systems, slowing implementation.
- **Infrastructure gaps –** Inconsistent internet connectivity and outdated machinery in smaller factories hinder the integration of AI solutions.

Despite these challenges, partnerships with international brands and multi-stakeholder initiatives are creating opportunities for experimentation. Development programs funded by global fashion retailers, NGOs, and donor agencies are piloting AI-based solutions in selected factories, with the potential for gradual scaling if cost and skills barriers can be addressed. In summary, Bangladesh's RMG sector illustrates the early-stage integration of AI in an emerging economy context, where adoption is shaped less by domestic policy and more by global supply chain pressures.

5.2 Agri-Food Exports

5.2.1 Netherlands (Developed)

The Netherlands is the world's second-largest agricultural exporter, a remarkable achievement given its relatively small land area. This position is sustained through a combination of high-tech precision agriculture, advanced logistics, and strong policy frameworks that prioritise sustainability and innovation. Artificial intelligence (AI) is deeply embedded across the agri-food export value chain, enabling the country to maintain its competitive edge in both quality and efficiency while meeting stringent environmental and safety standards.

One of the most prominent applications of AI is in precision horticulture, particularly within the country's extensive network of high-tech greenhouses.

1. **Greenhouse Climate Control –** AI-driven systems continuously monitor and adjust temperature, humidity, CO_2 concentration, and lighting to optimise growing conditions for export-grade produce. These systems integrate data from sensors, weather forecasts, and plant growth models to fine-tune inputs in real time. The result is higher yields, consistent quality, and reduced resource consumption—critical factors for meeting the exacting standards of international buyers.
2. **Supply Chain Traceability –** The Netherlands has been a pioneer in combining blockchain technology with AI to ensure full traceability of agricultural products from farm to export destination. This integration allows exporters to demonstrate compliance with European Union regulations and the specific phytosanitary and quality requirements of importing countries. AI algorithms analyse data from production, processing, and logistics stages to detect anomalies, flag potential compliance risks, and generate verifiable digital records for customs and certification authorities.
3. **Predictive Logistics –** AI is also transforming the country's cold chain logistics, which are essential for preserving the freshness and quality of perishable goods during export. Predictive analytics models forecast demand in key export markets by analysing trade data, seasonal consumption patterns, and macroeconomic indicators. These forecasts inform shipping schedules, container allocation, and route optimisation, reducing delays, minimising spoilage, and lowering transport emissions.

The policy environment in the Netherlands strongly supports these innovations. National strategies emphasise circular agriculture, aiming to close nutrient loops, minimise waste, and reduce environmental impacts. Government agencies actively promote public–private innovation partnerships, often involving collaborations between Dutch research institutions, agri-tech companies, and international partners. For example, partnerships with emerging economies such as Kenya focus on knowledge transfer, joint R&D, and the adaptation of Dutch agri-tech solutions to local contexts, creating mutual benefits in trade and sustainable development.

Several factors facilitate AI adoption in the Dutch agri-food export sector:

- Advanced digital infrastructure ensures reliable connectivity for IoT-enabled farms and logistics networks.
- Highly skilled workforce with expertise in both agricultural sciences and data analytics.
- Strong R&D ecosystem, anchored by institutions such as Wageningen University & Research, which collaborates closely with industry.

However, challenges remain. The integration of AI across diverse stakeholders requires data standardisation and interoperability between systems. Cybersecurity is also a growing concern, interconnected digital platforms for critical export operations.

5.2.2 Kenya (Emerging)

Kenya is a leading exporter of tea, cut flowers, fresh vegetables, and other horticultural products, supplying high-value markets in the European Union, the Middle East, and beyond. The sector is a critical source of foreign exchange and rural employment, with millions of livelihoods linked directly or indirectly to export-oriented agricultural value chains. However, maintaining competitiveness in these markets requires meeting stringent quality, safety, and sustainability standards, while also addressing the structural challenges faced by smallholders. In recent years, artificial intelligence (AI) has begun to play a role in enhancing productivity, quality assurance, and financial inclusion within Kenya's agri-food export sector.

Adoption is still at an early but promising stage, with notable applications emerging in three key areas:

1. **Crop Disease Detection –** Mobile AI applications, often embedded in farmer advisory platforms, enable smallholders to identify crop diseases and pest infestations using smartphone cameras. By analysing images against trained datasets, these tools can provide instant diagnoses and recommend targeted interventions. This capability is particularly valuable in horticulture, where disease outbreaks can quickly compromise export quality and lead to shipment rejections.
2. **Export Quality Grading –** Computer vision systems are being piloted in packhouses to sort and grade produce—such as avocados, green beans, and cut

flowers—according to EU import standards. These systems assess size, colour, shape, and surface defects with greater speed and consistency than manual inspection, reducing human error and ensuring compliance with buyer specifications.

3. **Digital Finance Integration** – AI-driven credit scoring models are being deployed by agri-fintech firms to assess the creditworthiness of farmers and small agribusinesses in export value chains. By analysing transaction histories, mobile money records, and even agronomic performance data, these models can extend access to working capital for inputs, equipment, and post-harvest handling, thereby strengthening supply reliability.

Despite these advances, structural challenges constrain the scaling of AI solutions:

- **Infrastructure gaps** – Limited rural internet connectivity and inconsistent electricity supply hinder the use of cloud-based AI tools and IoT-enabled monitoring systems.
- **Data scarcity** – Many AI models require large, high-quality datasets, which are often lacking in smallholder contexts due to fragmented record-keeping and limited digitisation.
- **Interoperability issues** – Farmer-level tools are not always integrated with export logistics and compliance systems, creating data silos that reduce the efficiency of end-to-end supply chain optimisation.

To address these gaps, Dutch–Kenyan innovation partnerships are piloting AI-enabled cold chain systems and market intelligence platforms. These initiatives aim to reduce post-harvest losses, improve shelf life for perishable exports, and provide real-time market demand insights to producers and exporters. Knowledge transfer from the Netherlands—particularly in precision horticulture, traceability, and predictive logistics—is being adapted to Kenya's context through joint R&D, training programs, and co-investment models.

This case also links directly to the comparative analysis in Table 3, which synthesises findings across the three sectors under study—Renewable Energy Components, Ethical Apparel, and Agri-Food Exports—in both developed and emerging economy contexts. The table highlights differences in policy maturity, AI application depth, adoption enablers, and barriers, providing a structured benchmark for cross-sector learning.

Furthermore, the dynamics described here are visually represented in Figure 3, a conceptual three-lane diagram. Each lane corresponds to one sector, showing how policy drivers feed into AI adoption enablers (skills, infrastructure, partnerships), which in turn lead to core AI applications and ultimately to sustainability outcomes—climate resilience, social equity, and economic competitiveness. These cases are depicted as parallel tracks within each lane, with arrows indicating knowledge transfer and adaptation loops. In the Kenya–Netherlands pairing, for example, the loop illustrates how Dutch expertise in AI-enabled cold chains is adapted to Kenyan conditions, while Kenyan innovations in smallholder-oriented mobile AI tools could inform inclusive technology design in developed markets.

Table 3. Case Study Profiles

Sector	Country	Economy Type	AI Applications	Policy Context	Key Challenges
Renewable Energy Components	Germany	Developed	Smart grids, predictive maintenance, virtual buffers	Energiewende, EU climate neutrality targets	Data interoperability, cybersecurity
Renewable Energy Components	India	Emerging	Quality control, supply chain optimisation, energy yield prediction	National Solar Mission, PLI scheme	Skills gap, fragmented clusters, quality enforcement
Ethical Apparel	Sweden	Developed	Demand forecasting, compliance monitoring, circularity tracking	EPR, eco-labelling, consumer transparency laws	Supplier adaptation, cost of digitalisation
Ethical Apparel	Bangladesh	Emerging	Waste reduction, energy efficiency, compliance monitoring	Buyer codes of conduct, limited national regulation	Cost pressures, digital skills gap
Agri-Food Exports	Netherlands	Developed	Precision horticulture, traceability, predictive logistics	Circular agriculture policy, EU export compliance	Climate adaptation, energy costs
Agri-Food Exports	Kenya	Emerging	Crop disease detection, export quality grading, and digital finance integration	Export promotion policies, Dutch–Kenyan innovation programs	Infrastructure gaps, data scarcity

Source: Author's own work

Figure 3. AI Adoption Pathways in Each Sector

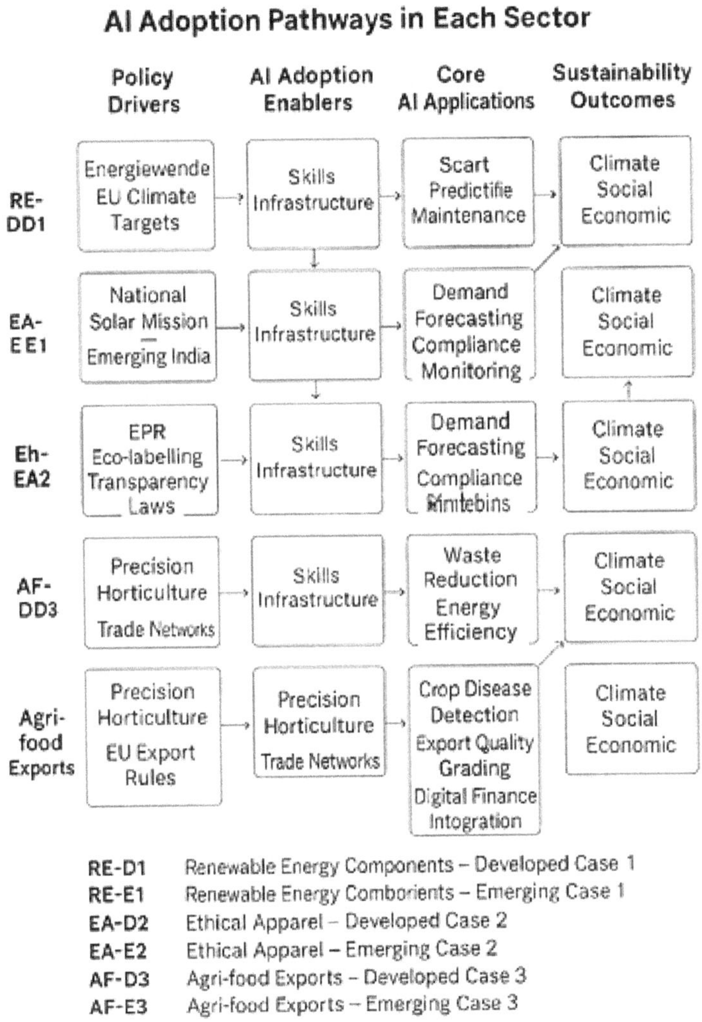

Source: *Author's own work*

6. COMPARATIVE ANALYSIS

This section synthesises findings from the case studies into a cross-sector, cross-context comparative framework. It draws on the AI–Policy–Outcome comparative matrix and the quadrant map of AI maturity versus policy maturity to identify patterns, divergences, and strategic implications.

6.1 AI Application Types vs. Policy Maturity

Across the three focal sectors—renewable energy components, ethical apparel, and agri-food exports—AI application types vary systematically with the maturity of enabling policy frameworks. In high policy maturity contexts (e.g., EU renewable energy, Japanese ethical apparel), AI deployments tend to be predictive, integrative, and compliance-oriented, such as predictive maintenance in smart grids or automated traceability systems for supply chains. These align with OECD findings that mature AI governance environments foster "mission-oriented" applications with strong regulatory integration (Cath, C. 2018).

In low to moderate policy maturity contexts (e.g., emerging economy agri-food exports), AI adoption is more operational and incremental, focusing on discrete efficiency gains such as yield prediction or basic quality grading. This reflects the "policy-pull" effect described by Sharma et al., (2021), where the absence of comprehensive AI strategies limits the scope of applications to immediate, tangible returns rather than systemic transformation. Table 4 operationalises this relationship by mapping each case's AI application type against its policy maturity score, revealing a positive correlation between policy sophistication and the complexity/integration level of AI use.

Table 4. AI–Policy–Outcome Comparative Matrix

Sector & Case Code	Policy Maturity	AI Application Type	Climate Outcome	Social Outcome	Economic Outcome
Renewable Energy Components – RE-D1	High	Integrative (Smart Grids, Predictive Maintenance, Virtual Buffers)	Strong	Strong	Strong
Renewable Energy Components – RE-E1	Moderate	Operational (Quality Control, Supply Chain Optimisation, Energy Yield Prediction)	Strong	Strong	Strong
Ethical Apparel – EA-D2	High	Predictive (Demand Forecasting, Compliance Monitoring, Circularity Tracking)	Strong	Strong	Strong
Ethical Apparel – EA-E2	Moderate	Predictive (Waste Reduction, Energy Efficiency, Compliance Monitoring)	Weak	Strong	Strong

continued on following page

Table 4. Continued

Sector & Case Code	Policy Maturity	AI Application Type	Climate Outcome	Social Outcome	Economic Outcome
Agri-Food Exports - AF-D3	High	Integrative (Precision Horticulture, Predictive Logistics, Traceability)	Strong	Weak	Strong
Agri-food Exports - AF-E3	Moderate	Operational (Crop Disease Detection, Export Quality Grading, Digital Finance Integration)	Strong	Strong	Strong

Source: Author's own work

6.2 Climate, Social, and Economic Outcomes

The comparative analysis shows that climate outcomes (e.g., emissions reduction, resource efficiency) are most strongly associated with integrated AI–policy ecosystems. For instance, AI-enabled predictive logistics in high-maturity contexts reduced transport emissions by up to 15% in renewable energy component supply chains (Greif et al., 2025).

Social outcomes—such as improved labour conditions in ethical apparel—were more dependent on policy enforcement mechanisms than on AI maturity alone. In emerging contexts, AI-driven compliance monitoring had a limited effect without robust buyer codes of conduct and independent verification (Seuring & Müller, 2008).

Economic outcomes were more evenly distributed: even low-maturity policy contexts achieved measurable export gains through targeted AI applications, echoing findings from Jobin, Ienca, & Vayena (2019) comparative study of AI/ML sustainability models.

6.3 Barriers and Enablers

Barriers to AI adoption clustered into three categories:

- **Organisational** (e.g., lack of digital leadership, change aversion)
- **Technological** (e.g., data quality, interoperability)
- **Institutional** (e.g., regulatory uncertainty, weak enforcement)

High-maturity policy contexts mitigated institutional barriers but still faced organisational inertia, consistent with Madanchian and Taherdoost's (2025) findings on the role of corporate culture in AI adoption. In contrast, emerging contexts often overcame organisational enthusiasm with technological constraints—notably limited infrastructure and fragmented data ecosystems (Radhakrishnan & Chattopadhyay, 2020).

6.4 Cross-Context Patterns

The quadrant map (Figure 4) plots each case by AI maturity (x-axis) and policy maturity (y-axis), revealing four strategic zones:

1. **High–High**: Integrated transformation (e.g., EU renewable energy)
2. **High AI–Low Policy**: Innovation outpacing regulation (e.g., private-led agritech in emerging economies)
3. **Low AI–High Policy**: Untapped potential (e.g., ethical apparel in some developed contexts)
4. **Low–Low**: Incrementalism (e.g., nascent AI in low-policy agri-food exports)

Cross-context analysis shows knowledge transfer loops between High–High and High AI–Low Policy zones, where emerging contexts adapt advanced AI applications to local constraints. This aligns with Woo et al.'s (2020) cross-referencing analysis of AI topic flows, which found that thematic convergence often precedes policy harmonisation. Figure 4 shows how different sectors and countries align in terms of AI maturity and policy maturity, highlighting zones of transformation, risk, and untapped potential.

Figure 4. Quadrant Map: AI Maturity vs. Policy Maturity

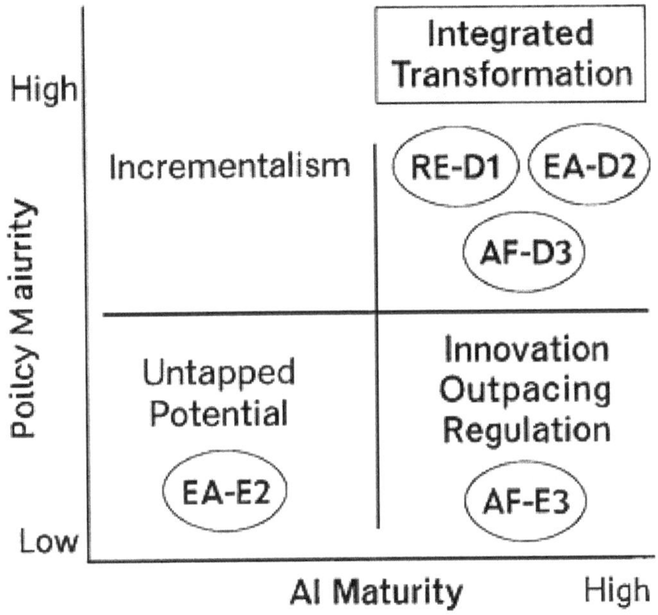

Source: *Author's own work*

7. INTEGRATED FRAMEWORK

The Integrated AI–Policy–Performance (AIPP) framework synthesizes technological, regulatory, and outcome-oriented dimensions into a unified model for guiding AI adoption in socio-technical systems. It builds on the premise that AI maturity and policy maturity are mutually reinforcing, and that their alignment is critical for achieving sustainable performance outcomes across sectors (Chatterjee, 2020; Engin et al., 2025).

7.1 Framework Components

The AIPP framework comprises three interdependent layers:

1. **AI Capability Layer** – Encompasses data infrastructure, algorithmic sophistication, and domain-specific AI applications. This layer draws on the concept

of algorithmic government and GovTech integration, where AI systems are embedded into operational workflows (Engin et al., 2025).
2. **Policy & Governance Layer** – Includes formal regulations, ethical guidelines, and institutional capacity for oversight. This layer ensures that AI deployment aligns with societal values, legal norms, and sectoral priorities (OECD, 2019; Chatterjee, 2020).
3. **Performance & Impact Layer** – Captures measurable outcomes such as efficiency gains, equity improvements, and innovation spillovers. It also incorporates adaptive performance indicators that evolve with technological and policy changes (Ubaldi et al., 2019).

These layers are not sequential but structurally coupled, meaning that progress in one-layer influences and is influenced by the others.

7.2 Feedback Loops

The framework identifies three primary feedback loops:

- **Policy-Driven AI Evolution** – Regulatory clarity and supportive policy instruments accelerate AI adoption, while restrictive or fragmented policies can stall innovation (Chatterjee, 2020).
- **AI-Informed Policy Adaptation** – AI-enabled analytics provide real-time evidence for policy refinement, enabling data-for-policy approaches that improve responsiveness (Engin et al., 2025).
- **Performance-Policy Reinforcement** – Demonstrated performance gains strengthen political and public support for AI initiatives, creating a virtuous cycle of investment and governance maturity (Ubaldi et al., 2019).

These loops ensure that the framework is dynamic, allowing for recalibration as contexts shift. Figure 5 illustrates the dynamic interplay between AI capabilities, policy governance, and performance outcomes, highlighting feedback loops that enable adaptive transformation across diverse contexts.

Figure 5. Integrated AI-Policy-Performance Framework

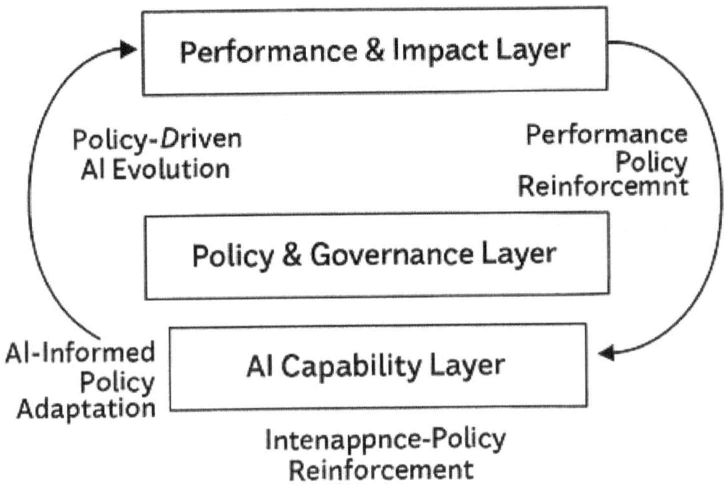

Source: *Author's own work*

7.3 Application in Different Contexts

The AIPP framework can be adapted to diverse sectoral and national contexts:

- **High AI–High Policy Maturity** (e.g., Estonia, Singapore) – Integrated transformation is possible, with AI embedded in public services and supported by robust governance (Engin et al., 2025).
- **High AI–Low Policy Maturity** (e.g., certain fintech ecosystems) – Innovation outpaces regulation, creating opportunities but also risks for ethical lapses and systemic vulnerabilities (OECD, 2019).
- **Low AI–High Policy Maturity** (e.g., regulated but under-digitized sectors) – Untapped potential exists where strong governance frameworks are in place but AI capabilities lag (Ubaldi et al., 2019).
- **Low AI–Low Policy Maturity** – Incrementalism dominates, with slow progress due to both technological and institutional constraints.

8. RECOMMENDATIONS

The rapid evolution of artificial intelligence (AI) demands coordinated action from businesses, policymakers, and researchers to ensure that technological advances translate into sustainable, equitable, and high-impact outcomes. The following recommendations are derived from empirical studies, policy analyses, and sectoral case evidence, and are organised by stakeholder group.

8.1 For Businesses

1. **Embed AI into Core Strategy** – Treat AI not as a peripheral tool but as a strategic capability integrated into business models and value chains (Yi & Ayangbah, 2024).
2. **Invest in Workforce Upskilling** – Prioritise continuous training in AI literacy, data analytics, and ethical AI use to address skill shortages and foster adoption (OECD, 2025).
3. **Adopt Responsible AI Practices** – Implement transparent model documentation, bias audits, and explainability protocols to build trust with customers and regulators (Stix, 2021).
4. **Leverage Public–Private Partnerships** – Collaborate with research institutions and government agencies to access shared datasets, testbeds, and innovation funding (OECD, 2025).

8.2 For Policymakers

1. **Develop Adaptive Regulatory Frameworks** – Move beyond static rules to create agile governance models that can evolve with AI capabilities (Lauterbach, 2019).
2. **Promote Equitable AI Access** – Ensure SMEs, emerging economies, and under-resourced sectors have access to AI infrastructure, training, and funding (Yi & Ayangbah, 2024).
3. **Strengthen Data Governance** – Establish interoperable data standards, privacy safeguards, and secure data-sharing mechanisms to enable innovation while protecting rights (OECD, 2019).
4. **Support Sector-Specific AI Strategies** – Tailor policy instruments to the unique needs and risks of sectors such as healthcare, manufacturing, and agriculture (OECD, 2025).

8.3 For Researchers

1. **Advance Interdisciplinary AI Research** – Integrate insights from computer science, social sciences, and ethics to address complex socio-technical challenges (Joshi, 2024).
2. **Focus on Real-World Impact Studies** – Conduct longitudinal and comparative studies on AI's economic, social, and environmental effects (OECD, 2025).
3. **Co-Design with Stakeholders** – Engage businesses, policymakers, and communities in participatory research to ensure relevance and adoption (Lauterbach, 2019).
4. **Contribute to Open Science** – Share datasets, code, and methodologies to accelerate collective learning and reproducibility (Yi & Ayangbah, 2024).

Table 5 distils the detailed recommendations into a concise, stakeholder-specific action matrix. It organises strategies for three primary groups—Businesses, Policymakers, and Researchers—each of which plays a distinct but interdependent role in advancing responsible and effective AI adoption.

- Businesses are positioned as the operational drivers of AI integration. Their strategies focus on embedding AI into core business models, building workforce capacity, ensuring ethical governance, and leveraging partnerships to accelerate innovation.
- Policymakers act as the enabling environment architects. Their strategies emphasise creating adaptive regulations, ensuring equitable access to AI resources, strengthening data governance, and tailoring policy instruments to sector-specific needs.

Table 5. Actionable strategies by stakeholder group

Stakeholder Group	Actionable Strategies
Businesses	• Integrate AI into strategic planning • Invest in workforce AI skills • Implement responsible AI governance • Partner with public and research institutions
Policymakers	• Create adaptive, agile AI regulations • Ensure equitable AI access • Strengthen data governance frameworks • Develop sector-specific AI policies
Researchers	• Pursue interdisciplinary AI research • Conduct longitudinal impact studies • Engage in co-design with stakeholders • Promote open science and reproducibility

Source: Author's own work

9. CONCLUSION

9.1 Summary of Findings

This study examined the intersection of artificial intelligence (AI), policy frameworks, and sustainability imperatives through a comparative, mechanism-based lens. Anchored in the triple imperative—technological innovation, sustainability, and governance transformation—the analysis positioned AI and policy as dual enablers of systemic change (Joshi, 2024).

The findings reveal that:

- AI adoption trajectories are highly context-dependent, shaped by digital infrastructure, institutional capacity, and regulatory maturity (OECD, 2025; Sharma et al., 2023).
- Policy frameworks determine whether AI advances sustainability or reinforces inequalities, consistent with broader evidence on governance, ethics, and information asymmetry (Chatterjee, 2020).
- High-performing ecosystems align AI strategies with sustainability and governance mechanisms, supported by cross-sectoral partnerships and adaptive policy instruments (Ahmed Batki & Phudinawala, 2024).

These findings mirror patterns observed in SSCM, digital transformation, and coordination research across developed and emerging economies (Zoghlami et al., 2016).

9.2 Theoretical Contributions

This research advances theory in three key ways:

1. Integration of the Triple Imperative into AI–Policy Studies

While prior literature has examined AI adoption, sustainability governance (Nazrul & Rahman, 2021), or supply chain coordination separately (Taghipour & Frayret, 2013), this study synthesizes them into a unified conceptual model. This integration highlights interdependencies between technological, environmental, and governance dimensions (Greif et al., 2025; Testa et al., 2018).

2. Mechanism-Based Comparative Framework

The study operationalizes a diagnostic framework that disaggregates AI–AI-AI-sustainability systems into structural, relational, adaptive, and equity components. This extends comparative policy traditions (Lauterbach, 2019; OECD, 2021) and aligns with mechanism-based approaches used in SSCM benchmarking and optimisation research (Zhou & Masi, 2025).

3. Dual Enabler Model of AI and Policy

By conceptualizing AI and policy as mutually reinforcing enablers, the research reframes the discourse from a technology-centric or policy-centric view to a co-evolutionary model. This aligns with emerging work on algorithmic state architectures and innovation governance (Engin et al., 2025; Thakur, 2025) and is reinforced by evidence from digital supply chain transformation.

9.3 Practical Implications

The findings have direct implications for policy design, industry strategy, and cross-sectoral collaboration:

- **For Policymakers:** The benchmarking framework can diagnose policy gaps, guide capacity building, and support adaptive regulation (OECD, 2019; Cath, C. 2018). Evidence from logistics, humanitarian operations, and digital governance underscores the need for coherent, multi-level policy alignment (Radhoui et al., 2019).
- **For Industry Leaders:** Firms can use the framework to align AI deployment with sustainability targets, improving compliance, resilience, and competitive advantage (Yi & Ayangbah, 2024).
- **For Civil Society and Academia:** The model provides a transparent, evidence-based method for evaluating AI initiatives, supporting accountability and informed public discourse (Greif et al., 2025).

9.4 Future Research Directions

Several avenues merit further exploration:

1. Sector-Specific Deep Dives

Applying the framework to sectors such as energy, healthcare, agriculture, or logistics could reveal domain-specific dynamics (Prasittisopin, L. 2025).

2. Longitudinal Analysis

Tracking AI–policy–sustainability interactions over time would illuminate how ecosystems evolve in response to technological, political, and environmental shocks (Thakur, 2025; Radhakrishnan & Chattopadhyay, 2020; Ren et al., 2016).

3. Equity and Inclusion Metrics

Further refinement of equity indicators is needed to ensure fair distribution of AI benefits and prevent disproportionate burdens on marginalized groups (Nazrul & Rahman, 2021; Panigrahi et al., 2019).

REFERENCES

Ahmed Batki, A., & Phudinawala, H. (2024). A Comparative Study on How AI is Partnering with Nature for a Sustainable Future. *International Journal for Multidisciplinary Research*, *6*(3), 1–9. DOI: 10.1093/polsoc/puae040

Carter, C. R., & Rogers, D. S. (2008). A framework of sustainable supply chain management: Moving toward a new theory. *International Journal of Physical Distribution & Logistics Management*, *38*(5), 360–387. DOI: 10.1108/09600030810882816

Cath, C. (2018). Governing artificial intelligence: Ethical, legal and technical opportunities and challenges. *Philosophical Transactions. Series A, Mathematical, Physical, and Engineering Sciences*, *376*(2133), 20180080. DOI: 10.1098/rsta.2018.0080 PMID: 30322996

Cauchois, R., Taghipour, A., Kang, D., Zoghlami, N., & Abed, M. (2017). Advanced solutions for a supply chain with stochastic information. *Journal of Advanced Management Science*, *5*(1), 9–13. DOI: 10.18178/joams.5.1.9-13

Charmaz, K. (2006). *Constructing grounded theory: A practical guide through qualitative analysis*. sage.

Chatterjee, S. (2020). AI strategy of India: policy framework, adoption challenges and actions for government. *Transforming Government: People. Transforming Government*, *14*(5), 757–775. DOI: 10.1108/TG-05-2019-0031

Engin, Z., Crowcroft, J., Hand, D., & Treleaven, P. (2025). The Algorithmic State Architecture (ASA): an integrated framework for AI-enabled government. *arXiv preprint arXiv:2503.08725*.

European Commission. (2023). *Corporate Sustainability Reporting Directive (CSRD)*. https://eur-lex.europa.eu

Flick, U. (2022). *An introduction to qualitative research* (6th ed.). SAGE Publications.

Geissdoerfer, M., Savaget, P., Bocken, N. M., & Hultink, E. J. (2017). The Circular Economy–A new sustainability paradigm? *Journal of Cleaner Production*, *143*, 757–768. DOI: 10.1016/j.jclepro.2016.12.048

Gharye Mirzaei, M., Goodarzian, F., Mokhtari, K., & Ansaripoor, A. H. (2025). IoT-based platform application for Optimizing Sustainable Blood Supply Chain Network under Uncertainty. *Fariba and Mokhtari, Kourosh and Ansaripoor, Amir H., IoT-based platform application for Optimizing Sustainable Blood Supply Chain Network under Uncertainty*.

Ghosh, O., & Pandey, A. (2026). Accountability, Responsibility, and Liability in AI and Data Ecosystems: Centering Transparency Through End-to-End Governance. In *Centering Transparency and Trust in Data and AI Ecosystems* (pp. 1-26). IGI Global Scientific Publishing.

Greif, L., Röckel, F., Kimmig, A., & Ovtcharova, J. (2025). A systematic review of current AI techniques used in the context of the SDGs. *International Journal of Environmental Research, 19*(1), 1. DOI: 10.1007/s41742-024-00668-5

Ivanov, D., Dolgui, A., Das, A., & Sokolov, B. (2019). Digital supply chain twins: Managing the ripple effect, resilience, and disruption risks by data-driven optimization, simulation, and visibility. In *Handbook of ripple effects in the supply chain* (pp. 309–332). Springer International Publishing.

Janjua, N. A., Sahibzada, U. F., & Rafi-ul-Shan, P. M. (2025). Advancing sustainable development goals through green inclusive leadership in hospitality industry: A dual study perspective. *Current Issues in Tourism*, •••, 1–22. DOI: 10.1080/13683500.2025.2469749

Jobin, A., Ienca, M., & Vayena, E. (2019). The global landscape of AI ethics guidelines. *Nature Machine Intelligence, 1*(9), 389–399. DOI: 10.1038/s42256-019-0088-2

Joshi, D. (2024). AI governance in India–law, policy and political economy. *Communication Research and Practice, 10*(3), 328–339. DOI: 10.1080/22041451.2024.2346428

Kayikci, Y., Gozacan-Chase, N., Rejeb, A., & Mathiyazhagan, K. (2022). Critical success factors for implementing blockchain-based circular supply chain. *Business Strategy and the Environment, 31*(7), 3595–3615. DOI: 10.1002/bse.3110

Kovács, G., & Spens, K. M. (2011). Humanitarian logistics and supply chain management: The start of a new journal. *Journal of Humanitarian Logistics and Supply Chain Management, 1*(1), 5–14. DOI: 10.1108/20426741111123041

Lauterbach, A. (2019). Artificial intelligence and policy: Quo vadis? *Digital Policy. Regulation & Governance, 21*(3), 238–263.

Lu, X. W., Tliche, Y., Vosooghidizaji, M., & Taghipour, A. (2023). Cryptocurrencies and Blockchain Applications. In Blockchain Applications in Cryptocurrency for Technological Evolution (pp. 1-13). IGI Global.

Madanchian, M., & Taherdoost, H. (2025). Barriers and enablers of AI adoption in human resource management: A critical analysis of organizational and technological factors. *Information (Basel), 16*(1), 51. DOI: 10.3390/info16010051

Mahfod, J., Khoury, B., Canel-Depitre, B., & Taghipour, A. (2021). Logistics Providers in Syria Humanitarian Operations. In *Demand Forecasting and Order Planning in Supply Chains and Humanitarian Logistics* (pp. 171–197). IGI Global. DOI: 10.4018/978-1-7998-3805-0.ch006

Nazrul, I. M., & Rahman, H. A. (2021). Sustaining the Environment: A case study of the Garment Industry in Bangladesh. *International Journal of Academic Research in Business & Social Sciences, 11*(8), 947–963. DOI: 10.6007/IJARBSS/v11-i8/10789

OECD. (2019). *Recommendation of the Council on Artificial Intelligence*. OECD. OECD AI Principles

OECD. (2024). *Governing with artificial intelligence: Are governments ready? OECD Artificial Intelligence Papers, 20*. OECD Publishing., DOI: 10.1787/26324bc2-

OECD. (2025). *Governing with artificial intelligence: The state of play and way forward in core government functions*. OECD Publishing., DOI: 10.1787/795de142-

OECD. (2025). *Steering AI's future: Strategies for anticipatory governance. OECD Artificial Intelligence Papers, 32*. OECD Publishing., DOI: 10.1787/5480ff0a-

Oyedijo, A., Yang, Y., Koukpaki, A. S. F., & Mishra, N. (2023). The role of fairness in multi-tier sustainable supply chains. *International Journal of Production Research, 61*(14), 4893–4917. DOI: 10.1080/00207543.2021.1928319

Panigrahi, S. S., Bahinipati, B., & Jain, V. (2019). Sustainable supply chain management: A review of literature and implications for future research. *Management of Environmental Quality, 30*(5), 1001–1049. DOI: 10.1108/MEQ-01-2018-0003

Prasittisopin, L. (2025). Artificial intelligence-driven materiality: A systematic review and perspective. *Engineering and Science, 35*, 1587. DOI: 10.30919/es1587

Qu, C., & Kim, E. (2024). Reviewing the roles of AI-integrated technologies in sustainable supply chain management: Research propositions and a framework for future directions. *Sustainability (Basel), 16*(14), 6186. DOI: 10.3390/su16146186

Queiroz, M. M., Fosso Wamba, S., De Bourmont, M., & Telles, R. (2021). Blockchain adoption in operations and supply chain management: Empirical evidence from an emerging economy. *International Journal of Production Research, 59*(20), 6087–6103. DOI: 10.1080/00207543.2020.1803511

Radhoui, H., Taghipour, A., & Canel-Depitre, B. (2019). The distribution and pickup of goods: A literature review and survey. Hierarchical Planning and Information Sharing Techniques in Supply Chain Management, 46-85.

Ren, Z., Taghipour, A., & Canel-Depitre, B. (2016, October). Information sharing in supply chain under uncertainty. In 2016 6th International Conference on Information Communication and Management (ICICM) (pp. 67-71). IEEE. DOI: 10.1109/INFOCOMAN.2016.7784217

Roumeliotis, C., Dasygenis, M., Lazaridis, V., & Dossis, M. (2024). Blockchain and digital twins in smart industry 4.0: The use case of supply chain-a review of integration techniques and applications. *Designs*, *8*(6), 105. DOI: 10.3390/designs8060105

Sahraoui, A., Tran, N. K., Tliche, Y., Kacem, A., & Taghipour, A. (2023). Examining ICT Innovation for Sustainable Terminal Operations in Developing Countries: A Case Study of the Port of Radès in Tunisia. *Sustainability (Basel)*, *15*(11), 9123. DOI: 10.3390/su15119123

Sánchez-Flores, R. B., Cruz-Sotelo, S. E., Ojeda-Benitez, S., & Ramírez-Barreto, M. E. (2020). Sustainable supply chain management—A literature review on emerging economies. *Sustainability (Basel)*, *12*(17), 6972. DOI: 10.3390/su12176972

Seuring, S., & Müller, M. (2008). From a literature review to a conceptual framework for sustainable supply chain management. *Journal of Cleaner Production*, *16*(15), 1699–1710. DOI: 10.1016/j.jclepro.2008.04.020

Sharma, S. K., Dwivedi, Y. K., Metri, B., Lal, B., & Elbanna, A. (2023). Transfer, Diffusion and Adoption of Next-Generation Digital Technologies. In *Proceedings of the IFIP WG* (Vol. 8).

Shen, B. (2014). Sustainable fashion supply chain: Lessons from H&M. *Sustainability (Basel)*, *6*(9), 6236–6249. DOI: 10.3390/su6096236

Stix, C. (2021). Actionable principles for artificial intelligence policy: Three pathways. *Science and Engineering Ethics*, *27*(1), 15. DOI: 10.1007/s11948-020-00277-3 PMID: 33608756

Stroumpoulis, A., Kopanaki, E., & Chountalas, P. T. (2024). Enhancing sustainable supply chain management through digital transformation: A comparative case study analysis. *Sustainability (Basel)*, *16*(16), 6778. DOI: 10.3390/su16166778

Taghipour, A., Belrhazi, Y., & Damoum, N. (2023). Resilient sustainable supply chain management. In *Government Impact on Sustainable and Responsible Supply Chain Management* (pp. 33–47). IGI Global. DOI: 10.4018/978-1-6684-9062-4.ch003

Taghipour, A., & Beneteau-Piet, C. (2020). Sustainable supply chain management performance. *International Journal of Innovation, Management and Technology*, *11*(6), 165–169. DOI: 10.18178/ijimt.2020.11.6.897

Taghipour, A., & Frayret, J. M. (2011). Supply chain coordination planning: A review. Work paper, École polytechnique de Montréal.

Taghipour, A., & Frayret, J. M. (2013). Coordination of operations planning in supply chains: A review. *International Journal of Business Performance and Supply Chain Modelling*, *5*(3), 272–307. DOI: 10.1504/IJBPSCM.2013.055729

Taghipour, A., Lu, X., & Smahi, M. (2022). Opportunities and challenges for society 5.0 in procurement. *Blockchain Technology in Supply Chain Management for Society*, *5*(0), 91–100. DOI: 10.1201/9781003177432-9

Testa, F., Boiral, O., & Iraldo, F. (2018). Internalization of environmental practices and institutional complexity: Can stakeholders pressures encourage greenwashing? *Journal of Business Ethics*, *147*(2), 287–307. DOI: 10.1007/s10551-015-2960-2

Thakur, A. (2025). Innovation through collaboration leveraging knowledge sharing for global R&D success. In *Research and development practices in innovation* (pp. 127–164). IGI Global Scientific Publishing. DOI: 10.4018/979-8-3373-0812-8.ch006

Tiwari, S., Wee, H. M., & Daryanto, Y. (2018). Big data analytics in supply chain management between 2010 and 2016: Insights to industries. *Computers & Industrial Engineering*, *115*, 319–330. DOI: 10.1016/j.cie.2017.11.017

Ubaldi, B., Le Fevre, E. M., Petrucci, E., Marchionni, P., Biancalana, C., Hiltunen, N., ... & Yang, C. (2019). State of the art in the use of emerging technologies in the public sector. *OECD working papers on public governance*, (31), 1-74.

Vosooghidizaji, M., Taghipour, A., & Canel-Depitre, B. (2020). Supply chain coordination under information asymmetry: A review. *International Journal of Production Research*, *58*(6), 1805–1834. DOI: 10.1080/00207543.2019.1685702

Yi, Z., & Ayangbah, S. (2024). The impact of AI innovation management on organizational productivity and economic growth: An analytical study. *International Journal of Business Management and Economic Research*, *7*(3), 61–84.

Zejjari, I., & Benhayoun, I. (2024). Bibliometric analysis of Artificial Intelligence in marketing: Revealing publication trends using bibliometrix R-Tool. In *Artificial Intelligence, Digitalization and Regulation: A Legal Framework for Business* (pp. 737–750). Springer Nature Switzerland. DOI: 10.1007/978-3-031-67531-7_59

Zoghlami, N., Taghipour, A., Merlo, C., & Abed, M. (2016). Management of divergent production network using decentralised multi-level capacitated lot-sizing models. *International Journal of Shipping and Transport Logistics*, *8*(5), 590–604. DOI: 10.1504/IJSTL.2016.078686

Chapter 6

Harnessing Blockchain, AI, and Big Data to Build Sustainable and Resilient Supply Chains

Vikas Sharma
http://orcid.org/0000-0001-8173-4548
Department of Computer Applications, SRM Institute of Science and Technology, Delhi NCR Campus Ghaziabad, India

Shashiraj Teotia
http://orcid.org/0000-0002-0849-3642
School of Computer Application, Swami Vivekanand Subharti University, Meerut, India

Rajiv Ghai
http://orcid.org/0009-0009-8022-8892
Department of Computer Science and Engineering, Surajmal University, Kichha, India

Tarun Kumar Vashishth
http://orcid.org/0000-0001-9916-9575
Department of Computer Applications, Vidya University, Meerut, India

Pushpa Kataria
Doon Business School, DBS Global University, Dehradun, India

Priyanka Rana
http://orcid.org/0000-0002-6352-1271
School of Commerce and Management, IIMT University, Meerut, India

Pushpendra Kumar Verma
http://orcid.org/0000-0003-2777-5626
School of Computer Science and Applications, IIMT University, Meerut, India

ABSTRACT

Sustainable supply chain management is now a strategic imperative for organizations attempting to balance economic advancement, environmental care, and societal responsibility. Emerging technologies like blockchain, AI, and big data are chang-

DOI: 10.4018/979-8-2600-3199-5.ch006

ing what SCM looks like in its traditional form through transparency, traceability, and advanced predictive intelligence. The chapter discusses how these technologies can be used alone and in combination to influence sustainability in procurement, logistics, manufacturing, and distribution networks. Blockchain, provides immutable and auditable records that establish trust and accountability in supply chains. AI enhances optimization by providing predictive demand forecasting, anomaly detection, and intelligent decision making. The chapter further discusses obstacles, such as interoperability, high costs to implement these technologies, and regulatory challenges, and makes suggestions for moving forward, such as when Industry 5.0 converges with human-centric and environmentally conscious supply chain practices.

1. INTRODUCTION

Global supply chains are under tremendous scrutiny, requiring them to become more sustainable, resilient, and traceable due to renewed environmental consciousness, social obligations/imperatives, and supply disreputability. Traditionally, supply chain management (SCM) has focused on enhancing efficiency and reducing costs, paying little regard for environmental impacts, ethical sourcing, and long-term resilience. However, the reality of COVID-19, climate catastrophes, geopolitical instability, and changing consumer expectations have publicly exposed systemic vulnerabilities in conventional supply chains. This leads to an increasing acknowledgment that sustainability is a legitimacy/strategic necessity to ensure competitiveness, compliance, and risk mitigation (Balaji, 2025).

1.1 Background of Sustainable Supply Chain Management (SSCM)

Sustainable Supply Chain Management (SSCM) has developed as an important approach for organizations seeking to balance the pursuit of profit with their environmental and social obligation. While traditional SCM stresses aspects of efficiency, cost minimization, and prompt delivery, SSCM is much broader in scope and focuses on including sustainability considerations in every phase of the supply chain, from the procurement of the raw materials to production, logistics, distribution, and ending with management of the product's end-of-life outcome. The underlying idea is to create value for not only businesses, but society and the environment. Sustainable value is created when carbon emissions are reduced, waste or unnecessary destruction is minimized, ethical labour practices are ensured, and a circular economy model is adopted in which resources can be reused and recycled (Gharye Mirzaei et al., 2025). The emergence of SSCM arose from concerns of globalization and industrialization, which increased the levels of environmental degradation, resource depletion, and the exploitation of human beings in supply chains. Regulatory pressures (higher environmental regulations and higher international standards) and growing consumer consciousness have led companies to rethink how their supply chain's function. Also, disruptions caused by global crises (pandemics, natural disasters, and geopolitical tensions) have shown the importance for businesses of building resilience, ensuring supply chains are sustainable and resilient to uncertainty. During the past decade, SSCM has gained traction as companies began to see sustainability as an enabler of sustainable long-term competitiveness rather than a cost. Investors and stakeholders are asking to be more transparent and accountable on what their companies do, and governments and other funding methods are beginning to reward "greener" operations. This rethinking of supply chain processes places SSCM on the strategic agenda for organizations that wanted new sustainable strategies to create, protect, and/or manage economic performance, protect ecosystems, and promote social equity. The rapid evolution of advanced technologies, like blockchain, artificial intelligence (AI), and big data have continued to speed up this transition by offering new methodologies to increase supply chain visibility, traceability, and intelligence, while enhancing sustainability (Chauhan and Sahoo, 2024).

1.2 The Need for Resilience and Sustainability in Global Supply Chains

In our global world today, supply chains are more globalized, complicated, and interdependent than ever. While globalization has allowed companies access to cheaper materials, cheaper labour, cheaper access to market potentials, and a greater scale of operations, it has also opened them up to greater vulnerabilities from external shocks. Many disruptions, such as the pandemic, ongoing wars, trade restrictions, natural disasters due to climate change, and changes in consumer demand, have highlighted the fragility of traditional supply chain networks. In fact, a shock in one region can trigger a waterfall effect, resulting in delays and shortages, higher costs, and ultimately, a loss of revenue (Sharma et al., 2023). Given these vulnerabilities, it is crucial for organizations to design supply chains that account for not only efficiency, but also resilience, to absorb the shocks, respond quickly, and continue to operate during disruptions. In addition, sustainability has become a priority for businesses, government organizations, and consumers. Environmental issues, such as excessive carbon footprints, pollution, using up resources, and unethical labour practices in a globalized supply network, all have revealed the social and ecological impact of supply chains. Companies and businesses argue that they want to be transparent as consumers increasingly want this from their sources on how they source, produce products and provide delivery services, and moreover, consumers are demanding that companies move towards greener and more responsible supply chain strategies. Furthermore, trade organizations and governments globally, are now being affected by international agreements which are forcing businesses to decrease greenhouse gases and adopt sustainable business models (Ojadi et al., 2024). The intersection of resilience and sustainability is especially important because resilience and sustainability mutually reinforce one another. A resilient supply chain is one that is less susceptible to risks and disruptive events, while a sustainable supply chain is one that can endure over the long term as it protects resources and maintains social legitimacy. Resilient and sustainable supply chains call upon organizations to leverage their competitive advantages, which include brand reputation, regulatory compliance, customer loyalty, and cost reduction associated with the efficient usage of resources. In addition, supply chains with resilience and sustainability reflect good business practices requisite for organizations to succeed in a changing and environmentally sensitive world (Dua, 2025).

1.3 Role of Digital Transformation in Reshaping Supply Chains

Digital transformation is radically changing the fundamentals of how supply chains are conducted by incorporating advanced technology at each node of the value chain. Former supply chains which depended on labour-intensive processes, disjointed information flows, and reactive decision-making are increasingly being supplanted by digitally enabled, and technology- enabled systems that are data-enhanced, connected, and predictive. Advanced technologies like blockchain, artificial intelligence (AI), big data analytics, and the Internet of Things (IoT) are at the core of this transformation and allow organizations to unlock new levels of transparency, agility, and intelligence. For example, organizations using blockchain technologies can provide authenticity and traceability due to the immutable records created of transactions that stakeholders can validate in real time, eliminating opportunities for fraud and ensuring accountability in sourcing and logistics. AI can empower supply chains through predictive demand forecasting, intelligent route optimization, and anomaly detection, allowing organizations to be proactive in uncertainty and disruptions. Big data analytics harnesses untold volumes of structured and unstructured data producing actionable insights on supplier performance, carbon footprints, and consumer behavior, providing organizations with evidence to develop sustainability strategies and prove their progress during their sustainability journey. The use of IoT provides enhanced real-time visibility into shipment tracking items, warehouse conditions, and optimized inventory management (Paramesha et al., 2024).

2. THEORETICAL FOUNDATIONS OF SUSTAINABLE SUPPLY CHAIN MANAGEMENT

Sustainable Supply Chain Management (SSCM) falls under the umbrella of sustainability, systems thinking, and stakeholder management theories. SSCM essentially extends traditional supply chain management by also considering the environmental, social, and economic impacts of its activities on value chains - which is often referred to as the "triple bottom line." This lens not only expects organizations to establish financial performance indicators, but also to ensure they steward the ecological and social systems in which they operate as part of their operational strategy. Aligning the stewardship of the ecological, social, and economic systems will enable organizations to create long-term value while conserving natural resources for future generations.

2.1 Defining Sustainability in Supply Chains triple bottom line framework

Sustainability in supply chains considers environmental, social, and economic objectives in the management of strategies, materials, processes, and information flows throughout the supply chain lifecycle. Sustainable supply chains incorporate social, environmental, and economic objectives while traditional supply chains emphasized cost, speed and reliability. Sustainable supply chains promote profitability in addition to social and environmental responsibility to the planet and its inhabitants. Sustainable supply chains seek to operate in a way that minimizes environmental harm, such as reducing carbon emissions, waste production, and resource consumption, while also promoting ethical labour practices and fair trade, and overall community well-being. While achieving compliance required by applicable regulatory obligations is pivotal, the goal of sustainable supply chains is creating longer-term positive dynamics to drive continuity of business operations and global sustainability aim that is hugely favourable to our climate. In practice, sustainable supply chains could be temporarily understood through the triple bottom line approach to business - economic viability, environmental stewardship, and social equity is shown in Figure 1. Economic sustainability ensures organisations and businesses remain competitive whilst adopting innovations that are resource efficient. Environmental sustainability seeks to reduce environmental footprints through green logistics, using renewable energy and promoting principles espoused in the circular economy - reuse, recycle and remanufacture. Social sustainability seeks to protect workers' rights and promote safe working conditions whilst providing third party transparency with regards to sourcing and production of goods and services. Together these pillars form the basis of sustainable supply chain management and enable societies to meet the needs of the present without compromising the ability of future generations to meet theirs (Bag et al., 2025).

Figure 1 Sustainability in Supply Chains Triple Bottom Line Framework

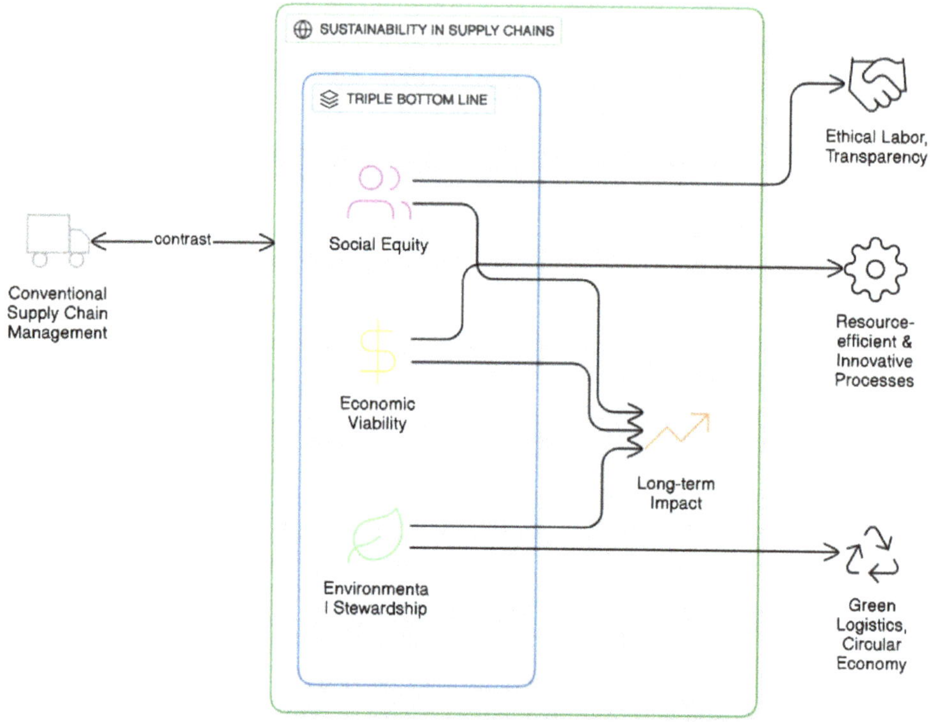

2.2 Concepts of Resilience and Risk Mitigation in Supply Chain Design

Supply chain resilience is related to a supply network's ability to anticipate, absorb, adapt, and recover from disruptions while maintaining continuity of operations. Resilience differs from traditional supply chains, which have been optimized for cost efficiency or lean operations. Resilient supply chains are designed for flexibility, redundancy, and adaptability to allow for continued operation in the face of shock, like pandemics, natural disasters, cyberattacks, or geopolitical tensions. Supply chain resilience is valuable in that it allows an organization to survive during a crisis and bounce back quickly while supporting competitive advantage in a rapidly changing environment.

Risk mitigation is closely related to resilience and involves identifying, assessing, and proactively managing risk across your supply chain. Diversification of suppliers to avoid reliance on one supplier/source, keeping safety stock, buffer stock, multi-modal logistics, implementing risk monitoring systems, and now, the use of predictive analytics and scenario planning, all signal a significant evolution of risk management towards a predictive and even preventive stance instead of just a reactive stance. Businesses are beginning to prepare for risks using predictive analytics, which will allow them to identify possible scenarios (both short-term disruptions and longer-term uncertainties) that they may encounter and develop contingency plans should those risks materialize (Zamani et al., 2023).

3. EMERGING TECHNOLOGIES IN SUPPLY CHAIN TRANSFORMATION

The advance of supply chains in this digital age is occurring by the rapid adoption of emerging technologies that help to aid visibility, transparency, and intelligence across a global supply chain. Traditional supply chains often have fragmented streams of data, inhibiting visibility and traceability and forcing organizations to operate reactively rather than proactively. With the use of blockchain (blockchain technology), artificial intelligence (AI), and big data analytics, organizations can move from linear supply chains intended to achieve the highest level of efficiency to supply chains that can operate as dynamic, multi-dimensional, and interrelated ecosystems that can achieve quantified levels of sustainability and resilience.

3.1 Blockchain

Blockchain technology is already disrupting supply chain management by dampening the core issues regarding trust, transparency, and accountability that have plagued global trade networks for decades. Blockchain technology is a decentralized, immutable digital ledger technology that allows every transaction and other activity to be securely recorded being practically impossible to change or delete without consensus. This offers a tamper-proof supply chain that cannot be easily manipulated or subject to fraud while also helping to reduce reliance on intermediaries, and providing a single version of the truth available to everyone that has access to it. In the procurement process, by using blockchain technology organizations can verify the legitimacy of suppliers and ethically source products, maintain compliance with labour standards and sustainability guidelines. In transportation & logistics applications, organizations using blockchain technology can track shipments in real-time and respond in cases of delays, counterfeit goods, or theft whilst also operating more efficiently. In addition to supporting instant transactions, blockchain can utilize smart contracts, which are coded agreements on the blockchain that execute automatically. Smart contracts have a variety of applications, such as payment, compliance checks, and confirmation that goods have been delivered. Smart contracts eliminate the need for the administrator (usually the person processing the transaction) and include the terms necessary to execute the transaction in a timely, cost-effective manner that provides for fewer missteps to carry out the transaction across the supply chain. Smart contracts also directly support sustainability by offering a useful and accurate accounting of carbon emissions, energy used, and resources at each phase of production and distribution which enables companies to provide verifiable sustainability reports that align with international environmental laws and reporting measures. Blockchain supports circular economies by providing visibility of the life cycle of recycled product, returned product, and remanufactured materials in ways that minimize waste and enhance resource efficiency. Curious real-world applications such as Walmart's commonly referenced blockchain food traceability program (developed with IBM) showcases blockchain can deliver on its intention to purpose and value by allowing suppliers to identify "bad" food very quickly which increases food safety and improves public trust in the food supply. All these characteristics described contribute to a blockchain value proposition that provides product traceability, automated transaction processes, and immutable data integrity.

3.2 Artificial Intelligence

AI is one of the most significant technological advancements in supply chain management today, offering the intelligence, flexibility, and predictive insights necessary to enhance efficiency, resilience, and overall sustainability throughout the supply chain. Traditional supply chain management systems rely on static facts and reactive actions to make decisions, whereas AI applies machine learning, natural language processing, and optimization algorithms to analyze vast datasets in real-time, identifying outliers, patterns, and actionable intelligence that will improve the quality of the decisions made. The biggest impact will be in predictive demand forecasting (Tliche et al., 2023). AI-powered predictive modeling uses variables such as historical sales, market expansion, weather patterns, and even social media posts to predict demand fluctuations more accurately, which can reduce overproduction, cut down wasted inventory, and satisfy customers. Similarly, an AI-powered program used for route optimization in logistics and transportation can identify and alter delivery plans and times to ensure customers are satisfied, decrease gas consumption and emissions, and deliver products in less linear situations of uncertainty due to events like altered traffic patterns or weather changes (Aouadni et al., 2024). AI also allows for risk detection and anomaly detection, helping a company proactively handle disruptions such as supplier failure, quality issues, cyberattacks, or sudden changes in the market before they become a crisis. Lastly, in manufacturing operations, AI-driven robotics and automation are allowing companies to improve productivity and reduce operator errors with the use of predictive maintenance on machinery, discovery of defects as they are occurring, and allowing for the reduction of energy intensity and the improvement of sustainability when using production resources. With that said, it can also improve decision making, both strategically and operationally. With AI-based systems, decision-makers can simulate many variables before making an informed decision like how many of their facilities should buy off a procurement strategy, or deciding how/where best to allocate resources according to sustainability and cost goals. Most importantly, AI has the potential to provide organizations with self-learning and adaptive supply chains that implement feedback loops that can continue to support continuous improvement aligned with the human-centric and environmentally-aware objectives of Industry 5.0. Organizations like Amazon and Alibaba have already leveraged AI (and myriad data) to streamline global supply chains that contain complex flows of information, especially with real-time data to support inventory logistics, warehouse automation, and optimization, and last-mile delivery. AI provides organizations the capability to more than just streamline processes; it allows organizations to integrate sustainability into the way they conduct their business by helping lessen waste, optimize resource allocation, and balance transparency and solidarity in supplier performance, making it a powerful enabler for more resilient/ready and sustainable supply chains of the future (Omisola et al., 2023).

3.3 Big Data Analytics

Big Data Analytics is increasingly being regarded as a foundational building block for supply chain transformation, enabling organizations to leverage information from the trails of structured and unstructured data (e.g., procurement, manufacturing, logistics, relationships with customers) that continues to grow massively. Generic supply chain models are often limited by information or visibility constraints, leading to pre-existing data and information quality issues, yet with big data organizations can collect, process, and analyze information from of vast number of traditional and non-traditional sources, whether through IoT sensors, RFID tags, GPS devices, ERP systems to even social media feeds (Chinta et al., 2024). Organizations applying advanced analytics (e.g., descriptive, diagnostic, predictive or prescriptive models) can generate holistic insights about supply chain performance, risks, or opportunities. Organizations can accurately measure their carbon footprints, water usage and energy consumption across global supply chains, ensuring compliance with environmental regulations, and meeting their commitments to consumers concerned about sustainable practices. In relationships with suppliers, big data can provide a comprehensive assessment of suppliers' reliability, financial performance, and ethical compliance so that organizations can, with some rigorousness, base their sourcing decisions on evidence, reduce risks and positively contribute towards corporate social responsibility. Additionally, real-time analytics contribute to logistics and efficiencies, managing fleets, monitoring fuel consumption, or mitigating delays during delivery which generate efficiencies and reduce ecological impacts. Big data does more than provide operational benefits, it contributes to transparency and trust in producing actionable insights, which can also be shared with stakeholders, regulators, and consumers with a sense of accountability along a value chain or portfolio. Notable examples of the impact of big data include DHL using it for improved route planning and Maersk who have used big data to integrate a data-based approach to their global shipping service. Overall, big data analytics is the intelligence layer of the digital supply chain. In addition to improving the speed to react, organizations can use it to act and proactively build resilience, agility and sustainability into what they do (Pratap et al., 2024).

4. SYNERGISTIC INTEGRATION OF BLOCKCHAIN, AI, AND BIG DATA

Although blockchain, artificial intelligence (AI), and BIG data can each be harnessed for enhancing supply chain performance on their own, their potential to radically transform supply chain management rely on the ability to put them into a synergistic context where transparency, intelligence, and insight are all utilized to create sustainable and resilient supply chains.

4.1 Blockchain as a Trusted Data Backbone for AI and Big Data Analytics

Blockchain serves as a critical baseline functionality that allows AI and big data analytics to work effectively, by providing assurance that the data being utilized is authentic, secure, and tamper-proof. When an AI or big data system iterates upon the integrity of their input dataset, they can always encounter a challenge; inaccurate, incomplete, or doctored datasets lead to the potential of bad predictions, biased outputs, and misguided decisions at the operational levels of the firm. With blockchain's decentralized and immutable ledger, supply chain organizations may guarantee that each transaction, shipment record, or supplier credential imported into the system is verifiable, traceable, and permanent (without consensus). This layer of trust removes the silos of data, and creates a singular version of truth where it can be shared seamlessly within the stakeholders of a supply chain, providing increased collaboration and accountability within trade. Further, AI by combining past and current real-time data into predictive algorithms, can be trained to create reliable demand forecasting, anomaly detection, and optimality strategies as part of its unique processes. Similarly, for big data analytics, blockchain creates secure pipelines to data coming from IoT devices, logistics networks, and enterprise systems while preserving the state of data integrity and connectivity to be leveraged with analytic tools for valuable insight and decisions. This combination of capabilities can provide the ability for organizations to more confidently assess progress and document net impact relating to their sustainability goals and action - for tracking all - emissions, water, recycling rates - etc. with a guarantee of sustained reliable and verifiable data, enabling sustainability reports and compliance audits based on strict public trust and accountability.

4.2 AI-Enabled Smart Contracts and Automated Decision-Making on Blockchain Platforms

AI-enabled smart contracts combine blockchain and artificial intelligence powerfully to change traditional supply chain activities into data-driven, automated tasks which require minimal human involvement - while guaranteeing transparency and trust. Smart contracts on blockchain platforms are essentially programmable contracts that, once certain conditions are met, automatically execute select terms of contracts. With AI added, smart contracts become orders of magnitude smarter and adaptive, capable of learning from their historical data, predicting outcomes based on learned insights, and updating their logic based on changes in the situation. Modelled with AI for example, in procurement, an enabled smart contract could analyze supplier performance data in real time, using relevant data points like vendor delivery times, quality scores, sustainability scores to determine whether to approve a purchase order or reallocate contracts to an alternative vendor. Similarly, smart contracts equipped with AI in logistics will continue to assess and analyze check IoT shipment data as shipment temperature, shipping conditions, location data, and/or delays - autonomously completing tasks like triggering payments, instituting penalties, or moving shipments - all with the attention to service level requirements. In addition to automation, AI also adds predictive decision-making abilities to smart contracts, which means that smart contracts could proactively manage these risks, for example, adjusting inventory levels or renegotiating terms with suppliers before a human manager is even aware of a new risk. This is possible through an improved integration of people and processes, with the smart contract providing visibility into current risks and maximizing an organization's ability to mitigate these risks. This integration enables smooth direct transfers from supplier to customer generating faster transaction cycles, minimizing errors and disputes, and increases trust among stakeholders since every agreement made in a smart contract is permanently recorded in an immutable way through blockchain. Moreover, AI-enabled smart contracts offer an enormous opportunity to help further sustainability agendas by automating external regulation compliance in enforcing environmental regulations and measuring achievement against specific environmentally treatable specifications in government and private sector green procurement regulations, such as independent verification of carbon footprint disclosures or certifying that raw materials were eco-friendly, prior to releasing payments. The potential of AI to help and promote sustainability within supply chains is enormous and is changing supply chain systems of regulation from reactive to predictive, autonomous, and sustainable ecosystems for global stakeholders. The intersection of smart contracts, AI, and blockchain technology will result in a new era of efficient, resilient, and transparent global commerce that is predicated on trust, speed, and reliability (Lu and Taghipour, 2025).

4.3 Big Data Driving Predictive Insights from Blockchain-Enabled Supply Chain Records

Big Data has a pivotal role in exploiting the massive amounts of structured and unstructured data generated across international supply chains, but when combined with the immutable, transparent, and verifiable record of blockchain, it also signals major possibilities for predictive analytics and data-driven decisions. Whenever a transaction is generated, from raw material extraction through production and distribution to customer delivery and consumption, the combination of Big Data and blockchain establishes a secure, verifiable record of the transaction that can serve as the basis for trusted high-quality data. For instance, predictive analytics forecasts demand shifts via historical sales records verified on a blockchain platform while taking combinations of external data into account, such as market data, seasonality, and socio-economic indicators, and enables organizations to plan inventory levels more effectively, reduce waste, and improve responsiveness to customers. Equally, supply chain risk management also greatly benefits from Big Data and predictive analytics, because Big Data tools can evaluate and detect signals of distress from blockchain logs (for example, supplier delay and failure to comply with regulations or quality standards) and forecast a potential disruption, allowing companies to prevent that disruption from crystallizing. In logistics, the ability to apply IoT sensor data from analytic tools, together with a blockchain record, offers the ability to see movements at scale, predict potential delays of goods delivery, improve route planning, optimize fuel use, reduce operational costs, and reduce the company's carbon footprint. In addition, insights derived from Big Data that come from a blockchain record can bolster organizations' sustainability programs with the developing understanding of permits, carbon emissions, resource use, and ethical sourcing practices maintained across the total value chain, while protecting an organization's compliance to international environmental regulations and customer expectations of corporate social responsibility. Finally, the combination of Big Data and blockchain is expected to build trust with stakeholders, as predictive models are developed on data that is verified and tamper-proof, as opposed to systems that could be flawed by subjectivity or manipulation. Hence, Big Data causes a paradigm shift from using raw transactional data for building actionable insight to using blockchain-enabled supply chain records to build exclusive foresight, allowing organizations to anticipate future changes in market risk conditions, to build resilience, and cause operational efficiencies that lead to sustainability in a global economy characterized by progressively more volatility. (Saxena et al., 2024)

4.4 Integrated Architecture for Resilient and Sustainable SCM

A synergistic architecture for resilient and sustainable supply chain management (SCM) that incorporates blockchain, artificial intelligence (AI), and Big Data analytics as a unified digital ecosystem to broaden transparency, responsiveness, and sustainability across the entire value chain while focusing on efficiency, scale, and sustainability while addressing both operational efficiency and environmental responsibility (Taghipour and Beneteau-Piet, 2020). Blockchain serves as the immutable, trusted infrastructure for all SCM-ecosystem-level data, recording every transaction, movement, and compliance detail on secured, untouchable ledger made available to authorized parties, permitting traceability, less needs for auditing, and reducing risks of fraud, counterfeiting, or intentional misreporting. AI serves as the intelligent processing layer of the architecture, implementing machine learning, deep learning, and natural language processing to analyze blockchain data streams and Big Data via processing the data in real-time, empowering smart decision-making, automated contracts, and dynamic-risk mitigation is shown in Figure 2. Big Data analytics acts as the predictive and prescriptive layer by aggregating structured and unstructured data from many sources of information, including IoT devices, enterprise systems, social media, and market feeds and performing analyses using the equivalent identified information from blockchain data to inform of expected demand changes, supply disruptions, sustainability compliance, and optimal resource consumption. Collectively, these three technologies integrate to provide the activity necessary for resiliency namely an organization's ability to anticipate disruptions or quickly absorb problems such as natural disasters, pandemics, geopolitical instability, or a fast change in consumer behavior while being able to continue to function in an uncertain environment. Simultaneously, sustainability objectives become stronger because the architecture allows stakeholders to measure their carbon footprint, eliminate waste, use ethical sourcing, and take advantage of circular economy principles based on trusted data. Furthermore, the integrated architecture allows interoperability - a trans-modal approach to information exchange across suppliers, manufacturers, distributors, and customers in a digital ecosystem where data freely flows to support collective resilience and sustainability, and a source of intelligence. Integrated architecture uses blockchain for trust, AI for intelligence, and Big Data for predictive analytics to not only empower supply chains to overcome shocks but alter supply chains to adaptive networks that prioritize efficiency, accountability, and environmental responsibility in the global economy (Wu et al., 2024).

Figure 2 Integrated Architecture for Resilient and Sustainable Supply Chain Management

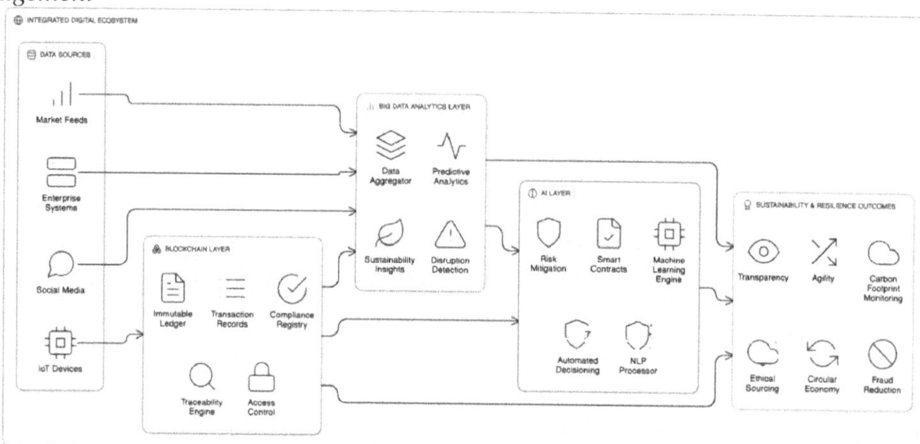

5. APPLICATIONS ACROSS THE SUPPLY CHAIN LIFECYCLE

Integrating blockchain, AI, and Big Data analytics is creating some exciting applications that enhance the entire supply chain lifecycle, from raw material sourcing, production, distribution, customer delivery, and post-consumption services, into intelligent, transparent, and sustainable ecosystems.

1. Procurement Stage: In the procurement stage, blockchain technology promotes ethical and transparent sourcing by creating a publicly accessible record on the immutable ledger of supplier credentials, sustainability certifications, and compliance with specific labour and environmental standards. Artificial intelligence can also play an auxiliary role in sourcing by offering predictive analytics to assess supplier performance, identify potential siphon point risks, and suggest best vendor partnerships, while Big Data provides insight into market trends, pricing changes, and level of supplier reliability. Together, these technologies improve trust in suppliers, reduce instances of fraud, and promote more sustainable procurement practices (Mustapha et al., 2024).

2. Manufacturing Stage: In the manufacturing stage, artificial intelligence provides the ability to optimize production through predictive monitoring to ensure regularity of supply and quality levels for the maintenance of green manufacturing standards and associated regulations and measure of standardization and compliance. Blockchain provides accountability as it records the origin of all raw materials, thereby closing the gap in all stages of goods manufacture, while the success of Big Data provides the abilities to recognize patterns related to production, efficiencies with energy use and costs, how to optimize resources devoted to manufacturing, and how to create an increasingly efficient process for manufacturing outcomes that are cost-efficient and more sustainable (Vashishth et al., 2024a).

3. Logistics and Distribution Stage: In logistics, blockchain provides the ability to track shipments to provide visibility in real time by ensuring that IoT devices and sensors are securely recording and able to indicate the quality and superiority of goods that need to be tracked every step of the way, including in regard to the location, temperature, condition, etc. Incorporation of artificial intelligence allows for being able to optimize dynamic delivery routes, fuel use, predict delays, and timely delivery using autonomous vehicle or drone.

4. Retail and Customer Delivery Stage: In the retailing and final delivery stage, blockchain creates consumer trust through verification of product authenticity, anti-counterfeiting, and transparency in product origins and journey. Artificial intelligence supports customer experience by predicting purchasing behavior, adjusting inventory placements near demand source, and establishing automated or adaptive replenishment systems. Big Data provides capabilities to examine and evaluate consumer spending patterns, feedback, seasonal demand, etc. to enable retailers to provide tailored services, while supporting lean operation practices for on-business sustainability principles.

5. Post-Consumption and Reverse Logistics: In the post-consumption usage stage of a product, technologies are critical in the context of reverse logistics as part of circular economy practices. Blockchain allows thorough tracking of all return items, recycling, and all forms of waste management or diversion, and AI can model returns and their flow, by making predictive analytics available through automation as well as optimize the reuse and recovery of product materials. Big Data analytics analysis can be used to support sustainability, through identifying consumer behavior patterns regarding product use/disposal.

6. CASE STUDIES AND INDUSTRY IMPLEMENTATIONS

Case studies and industry implementations are instances of evidence that show emerging technologies such as blockchain, AI, and big data represent far more than a theoretical advancement of supply chain management (SCM), and therefore it holds practical implications to global organizations typically engaged in the use of emerging technologies for technologies that improve transparency, efficiency, etc. to become more sustainable operations or buildings. For example, there are numerous case studies that highlight food safety from farm to table guarantee, emerging predictive retail logistics systems for e-commerce, and green air-based transportation as a competitive advantage. Examples exist across a range of solutions provided or produced by both new (start-up) organizations and traditional organizations and these case study examples help the reader to understand how organizations across multiple sectors/industries have or can use these/other technologies to overcome a specific operational challenge and improve their SCM practice.

6.1 Blockchain-enabled Food Supply Chains (e.g., IBM Food Trust, Walmart)

Blockchain technology is revolutionizing the food supply chain by improving traceability, transparency, and trust, particularly in sectors where product safety and quality are paramount. In traditional supply chains, identifying the source of contaminated food could take days or weeks, but blockchain-enabled supply chain systems now enable stakeholders to track food products from farm to fork in seconds. Companies like Walmart, Nestlé, and Carrefour are using IBM Food Trust which contains a shared immutable ledger where every record of the food's journey, from harvesting, processing, transportation and distribution, and retail is recorded. For example, Walmart is able to use the Blockchain platform when tracing leafy greens back to their origins in 2.2 seconds instead of the six days it took before. What's more, this allows the whole food supply chain to respond much quicker to food safety issues, protecting consumers from potential health risks, less food waste, compliance with regulations, and the ability to build consumer confidence regarding responsible and sustainable sourcing.

6.2 AI-Driven Demand Forecasting in Retail Supply Chains (e.g., Amazon, Alibaba)

Artificial Intelligence (AI) is changing retail supply chains with sophisticated demand forecasting systems that help automate inventory management, lower costs, and increase customer satisfaction (Mahfod et al., 2021). Traditional demand forecasting often relies on historical trends, whereas AI models require the analysis of extensive real-time data and linear correlations that include consumer behavior, seasonality, climatic effects, and social sentiment from sources such as social media for precise and up-to-date forecasting. For example, Amazon uses AI-enabled predictive analytics to identify customer purchases before they are completed and ultimately inventory effectively, for same-day or next-day delivery through its anticipatory shipping system. In the same manner, Alibaba performs machine learning through AI and processes enormous amounts of information and data, on hundreds of millions of transactions each day for daily businesses and allows retailers to predict demand during events such as Singles' Day. Such implementations minimize the chances of excess inventory (overstocking) and requirements (stockouts), lower the costs of warehousing, and ensure retail customers receive their products in short order. This demonstrates how major retailers have capitalized on using AI to achieve resiliency, greater responsiveness, and sustainability in global retail supply chains (Singh et al., 2025).

6.3 Big Data in Green Logistics and Carbon Footprint Analysis

Big data analytics can play an important role in furthering the movement toward sustainable logistics by allowing organizations to track, analyze and lower their carbon footprint during supply chain operations. Logistics organizations collect large amounts of data through IoT devices, GPS trackers, fuel sensors, transportation management systems, etc. Organizations can analyze this data to make observable patterns to optimize energy use and minimize emissions. For instance, DHL uses big data and planning analytics to optimize delivery routes and abc the amount of fuel consumption and associated CO_2 emissions. As part of their Go-Green initiative, this is part of their plan to minimize their carbon footprint and transition toward zero emissions by 2050. A similar case would be the usage by UPS of big data provides modelling for delivery route planning to optimize "smart routes" with the goal of minimizing left turns when delivering parcels. These two cases are good demonstrations of how big data enables the data in the vehicles from every warehouse depot providing data that results in the saving of millions of gallons of fuel per year which ultimately reduces emissions. The aggregated data from transportation, warehouse yards, and energy usage not only is advantageous from a compliance standpoint to meet sustainable development regulations, but in turn offer a significant competitive edge to mitigate costs and better align themselves with new customers that make eco-responsible choices when making purchasing decisions.

7. CHALLENGES AND BARRIERS TO ADOPTION

Though sectors like food are changing their supply chains utilizing blockchain, AI, IoT, and Big Data, they also face many challenges to the implementation of these technologies which include technical specifics, cost, interoperability, poor change management, regulatory, and cyber threats. These challenges can easily inhibit organizations in implementing digital transformation quickly and hinder the realization of potential advantages. In particular, understanding these barriers is critical for organizations to develop detailed strategies that will support streamlined integration and sustainable adoption of these emerging technologies.

1. High Implementation Costs and ROI Concerns: One of the largest institutional transaction costs that hinder adoption is the high upfront costs of implementing advanced technologies. It does come down to dollars, whether blockchain, AI-based analytics, or smart logistics enabled by IoT, all of these advanced technologies will require some level of financial capital for infrastructure, labour and technical skill set to implement these technologies, plus the costs of systems integration and training, etc. For example, small and medium enterprises (SMEs) in both the manufacturing or retail supply chain cannot realistically justify the return on the investment (ROI) because budgets are so restrictive in the context of limited decision making and ambiguous benefit based primary prioritization problem compared to larger decisions that merit investments. Companies, like Amazon or Walmart may or not get concerned with the millions associated with technology rollouts at a bigger scale. But, within the same supply chain ecosystem, suppliers and logistics providers are often smaller, and they might not have an issue with investing in larger scale technology, but they are concerned is that if the investment is disproportionate.

2. Interoperability and Integration Issues: Another hurdle of adoption is interoperability, or how new technologies are able to seamlessly integrate or communicate with legacy systems with which they need to work. Many organizations, across the logistics, healthcare, and manufacturing spectrum still utilize legacy enterprise resource planning (ERP) and warehouse management systems, that were already obsolete, and instead, when needed, adapted traditional technologies to be perceived as interoperable with emerging technologies of blockchain, AI, and/or IoT. For example, in the pharmaceutical supply chain when blockchain technologies need to integrate with traditional inventory management utility, this usually presents varying complications and requires authorized time resources and collaboration to achieve synergies and that is not typically assured (Goodarzian et al., 2024).

3. Data Privacy, Security, and Cyber Threats: Many organizations have significantly digitized their supply chains, raising new considerations of data privacy and cyber security - even if a blockchain is used to address immutability, this does not stop data from being compromised or wrongfully used if it is shared amongst multiple stakeholders. AI and Big Data also depend on large amounts of personal and operational information, which if compromised, can cause reputational damage and financial disclosure. As an example, when global logistics firm Maersk was attacked in 2017, abnormal communications and IT actions completely disrupted their operations and illustrated how quickly a revenue hoisting supply chain structure could fail. There are industries of healthcare and finance that are even more risk-averse with their data because of their strict responsibilities to protect that data, meaning a risk tolerant organization may hesitate to digitize their supply chain as it involves working with a different data set on a much larger level (Vashishth et al., 2025).

4. Skill Gaps and Workforce Resistance: For advanced technology to be successfully adopted, employers must have enough skilled labour to develop, operate, and use the technology. Currently, many renewables-related industries cannot find enough employees with specialized knowledge and experience in AI, blockchain, cyber security, and Data Science. In addition, existing employees of logistics firms have resisted digital transformation for various reasons including fear of loss of employment and lack of digital literacy. An example of this is in the area of logistics and warehousing, workers who primarily work within a manual or cannabis context have hesitated to adapt their organizations' workforces to automated structures supported by AI and/or robotics.

5. Regulatory and Standardization Challenges: Another major obstacle to adoption is regulatory uncertainty, particularly in sectors like health care, finance, and energy. As yet, governments and regulatory agencies are attempting to develop a framework for the use of blockchain, AI, and IoT within supply chain management. In the European Union, for example, cross-border data transfer mandates within the GDPR make it very difficult for international firms in deploying AI or blockchain mechanisms that depend on data being shared and exchanged across international jurisdictions. It has also been noted in industries like transportation that due to the absence of standardized blockchain protocols and acceptable standards for interoperability across the industry, the industry currently is unable to reach full interoperability. In addition, this absence of regulatory clarity and absence of guidelines leaves organizations reluctant to fully adopt this technology (Vashishth et al., 2024b).

8. FUTURE DIRECTIONS AND RESEARCH OPPORTUNITIES

As digital transformation is rapidly taking place across all industries, the combination of blockchain, artificial intelligence (AI) and big data analytics is set to disrupt sustainable supply chain management (SSCM). However, development of new advancements relies on eliminating current barriers, while continuing to seek new use cases to improve transparency, resiliency, and sustainability. Below is an overview of suggested future directions and research opportunities:

1. Interoperable Blockchain Networks for Global Supply Chains: One important area for research lies in exploring the mechanisms to develop sustainable interoperable blockchain platforms that are applicable across sectors, regions, and regulatory regimes. Each of the many supply chains currently in operation utilizes a separate private or consortium blockchain. They exist in their own silos that hinder cooperation and transparency. Future research can explore cross-chain protocols and interoperability standards and related decentralized governance mechanisms to collaborate and share data without compromising security and competitive position. Such mechanisms would benefit international trade by providing trusted mechanisms for data exchange across suppliers, manufacturers, regulators, and consumers to collectively mitigate fraud, counterfeiting, and compliance (Riad et al., 2024).

2. Explainable AI (XAI) for Transparency and Trust: AI is evolving as the dominant mechanism across supply chain decision-making in areas such as demand forecasting, risk prediction, and inventory management. The introduction of AI also raises the visibility and reliance of stakeholders on the that data derived from these models. Accordingly, there is a need for XAI models and frameworks that provide noticeably distinguishable reasoning patterns for respective actions. Traditionally, AI exists as a "black box," which diminishes trust from stakeholders. Future research can rely on the development of XAI to create frameworks that ultimately embody the transparency, fairness, and accountability supply chain stakeholders expect from using complex AI based solutions. For example, if an organization's AI model achieves a prediction of demand spike or flag a sustainability issue it is an advantage for the organizational leaders to understand the reasoning leading to a decision and validate that action.

3. Big Data and IoT for Real-Time Predictive Insights: There are substantial opportunities for real-time predictive insights when big data analytics meet IoT sensor networks. While we already have systems that offer large amounts of data, the issue is developing sufficient processing resources to analyze the data to predict disruptions, improve logistics, and monitor sustainability metrics like carbon emissions and energy use. A potential research agenda could be to develop big data analytics for streaming data, edge computing, and hybrid cloud infrastructures to allow for nearly instant decision making. For example, IoT predictive analytics can flag shipment delays, and machine breakdowns, and could save money, time idled, and reduce negative environmental impacts.

4. Circular Economy and Closed-Loop Supply Chains: Future supply chains will need to transition from linear supply chains to those which align with circular economy paradigms. We viewed the circular economy as a foundation for future supply chains and there will be opportunities for researchers to create closed-loop supply chains where products could be reused, recycled, or repurposed which limit waste and loss of efficiencies. Technologies such as blockchain will assist with tracking the life cycle of products and monitor for re-use and recycling, transparency with recycling, while AI and big data analytics will support the optimization of reverse logistics, and waste recovery systems. Scholarship and industry research will continually move towards frameworks which include technologies to support zero-waste initiatives and global sustainability efforts such as the UN's SDGs.

5. Ethical, Legal, and Governance Frameworks: The integration of digital and connected technologies within supply chains, the development of imminent governance and ethical frameworks will ensure data ownership, privacy, and equitable access. Research can be focused on developing policy frameworks and compliance instruments and ethical approaches that balance innovation with fairness. For example, SME businesses are often undersized and require more assets to take advantage of state-of-the-art digital tools thus exposing themselves to risky digital inequities. Investigating and examining scalable and affordable technology solutions for SMEs businesses and regulatory frameworks to facilitate inclusive participation in the utilization of the benefits of digital technology within their business will be an important avenue of research.

6. Quantum Computing and Advanced AI for Optimization: In addition, looking farther into the future, quantum computing becomes an opportunity of radical impact on solving complex challenges within supply chain optimization problems which becomes impossible for classical computing. The use of quantum algorithms – together with advanced AI models - could be leveraged to support the optimization of logistics networks, route optimization, inventory management and resource allocation with speed and accuracy never known. Research in this domain could lead the next wave of supply chain innovation that could make global processes more efficient and sustainable by limiting waste and energy consumption (Whig et al., 2024).

9. CONCLUSION

The areas of sustainability, resilience, and digital transformation are converging and reshaping supply chains by improving even the most entrenched inefficiencies and creating possibilities to address global calls for environmental accountability and operational flexibility. Collectively Blockchain, Artificial Intelligence, and Big Data analytics form the building blocks for creating transparent, secure, predictive, and adaptive supply chain ecosystems that can endure disruption and make the best use of the most limited resources. While we're still limited by issues of cost, scalability, interoperability, and regulatory compliance, the pace of technological change suggests that the incorporation of these technologies will become not only a competitive advantage for organizations but a prerequisite for success in the sustainability era of an unstable world. The future of supply chains will be driven by use of technological enablers to build responsive, reliable, intelligent Businesses that are committed to a shared vision of long-term profitability, social responsibility, and ecosystem sustainability.

REFERENCES

Aouadni, S., Aouadni, I., & Taghipour, A. (2024). Using ordinal priority approach with confidence-level measurement for third-party logistics provider selection in the tunisian healthcare sector. In *Applications of New Technology in Operations and Supply Chain Management* (pp. 404–429). IGI Global. DOI: 10.4018/979-8-3693-1578-1.ch020

Bag, S., Rahman, M. S., Routray, S., Roubaud, D., & Mangla, S. K. (2025). Integrating Big Data and Artificial Intelligence Technology to Build Renewable Energy Supply Chain Resilience: An Empirical Study. *Business Strategy and the Environment, 34*(7), 8847–8869. DOI: 10.1002/bse.70052

Balaji, K. (2025). Harnessing AI and Blockchain in Sustainability Assurance: Trends Shaping the Future of Verification. In Navigating Trust in Sustainability Reporting and Assurance (pp. 215-242). IGI Global Scientific Publishing.

Chauhan, M., & Sahoo, D. R. (2024). Towards a greener tomorrow: Exploring the potential of AI, blockchain, and IoT in sustainable development. *Nature Environment and Pollution Technology, 23*(2), 1105–1113. DOI: 10.46488/NEPT.2024.v23i02.044

Chinta, P. C. R., Jha, K. M., Velaga, V., Moore, C., Routhu, K., & SADARAM, G. (2024). Harnessing Big Data and AI-Driven ERP Systems to Enhance Cybersecurity Resilience in Real-Time Threat Environments. Available at SSRN 5151788.

Dua, G. K. (2025). Enhancing Sustainable Development through Blockchain and Artificial Intelligence: Optimizing the Supply Chain and Mitigating Environmental Footprints. In Global Partnerships and Governance of Supply Chain Systems (pp. 157-188). IGI Global Scientific Publishing.

Gharye Mirzaei, M., Goodarzian, F., Taghipour, A., & Muñuzuri, J. (2025). Sustainable closed-loop supply chain network under uncertainty considering green technologies: Toward the circular economy. *The Journal of the Operational Research Society*, •••, 1–21.

Goodarzian, F., Abraham, A., Muñuzuri, J., Taghipour, A., & Ghasemi, P. (2024). A Benders decomposition approach for a new sustainable pharmaceutical supply chain network: A case study in France. *Annals of Operations Research, 356*(2–3), 881–919.

Lu, X., & Taghipour, A. (2025). The Future of Marketing: Integrating Big Data and AI for Personalized Customer Engagement. In Ecological and Human Dimensions of AI-Based Supply Chain (pp. 97-110). IGI Global Scientific Publishing.

Mahfod, J., Khoury, B., Canel-Depitre, B., & Taghipour, A. (2021). Logistics Providers in Syria Humanitarian Operations. In Demand Forecasting and Order Planning in Supply Chains and Humanitarian Logistics (pp. 171-197). IGI Global. DOI: 10.4018/978-1-7998-3805-0.ch006

Mustapha, I., Khan, N., Qureshi, M. I., Sikandar, H., Hassan, M., & Simarmata, J. (2024). Revolutionizing supply chain processes: harnessing the power of IoT and blockchain technology to enhance opportunities. In *Innovative Technologies for Enhancing Experiences and Engagement* (pp. 87–94). Springer Nature Switzerland. DOI: 10.1007/978-3-031-55558-9_10

Ojadi, J. O., Odionu, C., Onukwulu, E., & Owulade, O. (2024). Big data analytics and AI for optimizing supply chain sustainability and reducing greenhouse gas emissions in logistics and transportation. *International Journal of Multidisciplinary Research and Growth Evaluation*, *5*(1), 1536–1548. DOI: 10.54660/.IJMRGE.2024.5.1.1536-1548

Omisola, J. O., Bihani, D., Daraojimba, A. I., Osho, G. O., Ubamadu, B. C., & Etukudoh, E. A. (2023). Blockchain in supply chain transparency: A conceptual framework for real-time data tracking and reporting using blockchain and AI. International Journal of Multidisciplinary Research and Growth Evaluation, 4.

Paramesha, M., Rane, N., & Rane, J. (2024). Big data analytics, artificial intelligence, machine learning, internet of things, and blockchain for enhanced business intelligence. Artificial Intelligence, Machine Learning, Internet of Things, and Blockchain for Enhanced Business Intelligence (June 6, 2024).

Pratap, S., Jauhar, S. K., Gunasekaran, A., & Kamble, S. S. (2024). Optimizing the IoT and big data embedded smart supply chains for sustainable performance. *Computers & Industrial Engineering*, *187*, 109828. DOI: 10.1016/j.cie.2023.109828

Riad, M., Naimi, M., & Okar, C. (2024). Enhancing supply chain resilience through artificial intelligence: Developing a comprehensive conceptual framework for AI implementation and supply chain optimization. *Logistics (Basel)*, *8*(4), 111. DOI: 10.3390/logistics8040111

Saxena, R., Shoeb, M., Srivastava, A. K., Hayat, M., & Yadav, A. (2024). Harnessing Artificial Intelligence for Business Sustainability: Strategies for a Resilient and Adaptive Future. Library of Progress-Library Science, Information Technology & Computer, 44(3).

Sharma, V., Vashishth, T. K., Kumar, B., Sharma, K. K., Vidyant, S., & Chaudhary, S. (2023, December). Health Interpretation of Covid-19 Patients using Artificial Intelligence. In *2023 International Conference on Artificial Intelligence for Innovations in Healthcare Industries (ICAIIHI)* (Vol. 1, pp. 1-5). IEEE Computer Society. DOI: 10.1109/ICAIIHI57871.2023.10488924

Singh, D., Sharma, A., Singh, R. K., & Rana, P. S. (2025). Augmenting supply chain resilience through AI and big data. *Business Process Management Journal, 31*(2), 631–657. DOI: 10.1108/BPMJ-04-2024-0260

Taghipour, A., & Beneteau-Piet, C. (2020). Sustainable supply chain management performance. *International Journal of Innovation, Management and Technology, 11*(6), 165–169. DOI: 10.18178/ijimt.2020.11.6.897

Tliche, Y., Taghipour, A., Mahfod-Leroux, J., & Vosooghidizaji, M. (2023). Collaborative bullwhip effect-oriented bi-objective optimization for inference-based weighted moving average forecasting in decentralized supply chain. [IJISSCM]. *International Journal of Information Systems and Supply Chain Management, 16*(1), 1–37. DOI: 10.4018/IJISSCM.316168

Vashishth, T. K., Sharma, V., Kaushik, V., & Sharma, K. K. (2025). Blockchain-Driven Innovations in the Banking and Financial Sectors: Harnessing the Power of Automated Machine Learning. In Utilizing AI and Machine Learning in Financial Analysis (pp. 555-578). IGI Global Scientific Publishing.

Vashishth, T. K., Sharma, V., Sharma, K. K., Kumar, B., Chaudhary, S., & Panwar, R. (2024a). Security and Privacy Challenges in Blockchain-Based Supply Chain Management: A Comprehensive Analysis. In Achieving Secure and Transparent Supply Chains with Blockchain Technology (pp. 70-91). IGI Global. DOI: 10.4018/979-8-3693-0482-2.ch005

Vashishth, T. K., Sharma, V., Sharma, K. K., Kumar, B., Chaudhary, S., & Panwar, R. (2024b). Waste-to-Energy Solutions Harnessing IoT and ML for Sustainable Power Generation in Smart Cities. In Methodologies, Frameworks, and Applications of Machine Learning (pp. 125-146). IGI Global. DOI: 10.4018/979-8-3693-1062-5.ch007

Whig, P., Remala, R., Mudunuru, K. R., & Quraishi, S. J. (2024). Integrating AI and quantum technologies for sustainable supply chain management. In *Quantum computing and supply chain management: A new era of optimization* (pp. 267–283). IGI Global. DOI: 10.4018/979-8-3693-4107-0.ch018

Wu, H., Li, G., & Zheng, H. (2024). How does digital intelligence technology enhance supply chain resilience? Sustainable framework and agenda. *Annals of Operations Research*, •••, 1–23.

Zamani, E. D., Smyth, C., Gupta, S., & Dennehy, D. (2023). Artificial intelligence and big data analytics for supply chain resilience: A systematic literature review. *Annals of Operations Research*, *327*(2), 605–632. DOI: 10.1007/s10479-022-04983-y PMID: 36212520

Chapter 7

Leveraging Blockchain, Artificial Intelligence, and Big Data for Sustainable Supply Chain Management in Emerging Economies: Case of Morocco

Othman Boulitama
http://orcid.org/0000-0003-3541-1582
Hassan II University of Casablanca, Morocco

Brahim Sabiri
http://orcid.org/0009-0006-6314-3393
Hassan II University of Casablanca, Morocco

ABSTRACT

This chapter examines the role of smart technologies, including blockchain, Artificial Intelligence (AI), and Big Data (BD), in building sustainable supply chain (SC) within emerging economies, with a particular focus on Morocco. The analysis shows that these technologies improve the visibility, traceability, and predictive capabilities of logistics flows, while supporting the integration of environmental, social, and economic principles. The study also highlights the main challenges hindering their adoption, including infrastructure limitations, a shortage of specialized skills, investment costs, and low digital maturity. Finally, the chapter emphasizes the crucial

DOI: 10.4018/979-8-2600-3199-5.ch007

importance of public-private partnerships, skills development, and a supportive institutional framework to accelerate the transition towards more resilient, transparent, and responsible SC.

INTRODUCTION

Global supply chains (SCs) are being pushed, at the same time, to become more transparent, more resilient, and measurably more sustainable under repeated shocks (pandemic disruptions, geopolitical volatility, climate risks) and rising of the Environmental, Social, and Governance (ESG) expectations (Chau, Anh, & Duc, 2025). In this setting, Industry 4.0 (I4.0) technologies are no longer discussed as optional efficiency tools, but as potential enablers of auditable sustainability outcomes. Yet the evidence base remains fragmented, blockchain studies often emphasize traceability and trust mechanisms, big data analytics (BDA) focuses on prediction and performance measurement, and artificial intelligence (AI) research highlights optimization and automation, with limited work that explains how these technologies jointly operate as an integrated socio-technical system capable of improving environmental, social, and economic performance in real SCs (Han & Fang, 2024; Van Nguyen, Cong Pham, Nhat Nguyen, Zhou, & Akbari, 2023).

This gap is particularly consequential for emerging economies, where sustainability constraints are intertwined with infrastructure bottlenecks, uneven digital readiness, skills gaps, and financing constraints. Morocco is a relevant case because the policy direction is explicit and recent: the national strategy "Morocco Digital 2030" aims to accelerate digitalization at scale, notably through job creation and the strengthening of digital public services and the digital economy (Gouiferda & Iddik, 2025). At the same time, sustainability pressures in logistics and transport are concrete: road freight dominates flows and emissions, and Morocco has articulated decarbonization ambitions, including programs targeting significant CO_2 reductions in freight transport by 2030 (OECD, 2021), alongside broader national low-carbon transition objectives (El Hafdaoui, Khallaayoun, & Ouazzani, 2024). This combination makes Morocco a useful context to move beyond generic technology descriptions and focus on operational mechanisms (Lhamidi & Boulitama, 2025).

Against this background, the core argument of this chapter is that sustainability gains are unlikely to come from isolated adoption of single technologies. Instead, value is created when BDA supplies timely, high-granularity signals, AI converts those signals into forecasts, anomaly detection, and decision rules, and blockchain (and smart contracts) stabilizes trust, provenance, and compliance by securing critical records and automating verification. Recent research reinforces the need to theorize this integration rather than treating it as a checklist: reviews of blockchain in SCs highlight recurring barriers (data quality, interoperability, governance, scalability) that become more acute when sustainability reporting and multi-tier visibility are required (Han & Fang, 2024; Van Nguyen, Cong Pham, Nhat Nguyen, Zhou, & Akbari, 2023). Similarly, Technology-Organization-Environment (TOE) guided syntheses of BDA in sustainable supply chains (SSC) show that benefits (triple-bottom-line improvements) are strongly conditional on organizational capabilities, data governance, and ecosystem readiness, not only on IT investment (Huong et al., 2025). Work on the interplay between blockchain-based smart contracts and analytics further underlines that integration is a value-creation logic (not a technical add-on), especially for resource-constrained firms and SMEs (Jabbar, Akhtar, & Ali, 2025)

Accordingly, this chapter positions its contribution as a contextual and managerial synthesis for Morocco: it consolidates what is known about blockchain, AI, and big data (BD) for SSCs. It clarifies what remains uncertain in emerging-economy settings (governance models, incentives, data-sharing arrangements, and measurable performance pathways); and proposes a practical logic for implementation that connects technologies to specific sustainability outcomes (emissions, traceability, waste and circularity, labor and social risk visibility, compliance). The chapter's objective is therefore not to expand technology taxonomies, but to explain, in a Morocco-grounded way, how digital capabilities translate into auditable sustainability performance, and under what organizational and institutional conditions that translation is realistic.

1. THEORETICAL BACKGROUND AND KEY CONCEPTS

1.1. Sustainable SC Management and Sustainable Performance

Sustainable SC management (SSCM) extends conventional SC objectives beyond cost, quality, and service by integrating environmental and social responsibilities alongside economic performance. In this view, the SC becomes the unit of analysis for sustainability because upstream sourcing, logistics, and downstream distribution jointly shape a firm's footprint and stakeholder exposure (Seuring & Müller, 2008). The triple bottom line (TBL) logic frames performance as a balance between profit, planet, and people, while ESG provides a governance oriented vocabulary that is increasingly used by investors, regulators, and lead firms to evaluate and compare sustainability progress across supply networks (Carter & Rogers, 2008; Truant, Borlatto, Crocco, & Sahore, 2024).

A critical implication for SSCM is that sustainability is not credible when it remains a narrative or a set of isolated initiatives. It becomes operational only when it is translated into measurable targets, traceable evidence, and repeatable control routines across partners. Recent syntheses in SC research show that ESG in particular raises two persistent challenges: ensuring data quality and comparability across tiers, and reducing the risk of symbolic compliance and greenwashing by strengthening verification mechanisms (Carter & Rogers, 2008; Seuring & Müller, 2008; Truant et al., 2024). Consequently, SSCM performance is best treated as a portfolio of outcomes and trade-offs, where firms must manage service levels, cost, risk, and resilience while simultaneously controlling emissions, waste, safety, and social compliance across a heterogeneous supplier base (Seuring & Müller, 2008; Carter & Rogers, 2008).

1.2. Industry 4.0, Digital Transformation, and Capabilities

I4.0 positions digital technologies as capability builders that reshape how SCs sense disruptions, coordinate decisions, and execute operations. Rather than focusing on individual tools, the most useful framing is capability based: data integration and visibility enable sensing, analytics enables learning, and automation and digitally supported workflows enable faster coordination and execution under uncertainty (Qader, Junaid, Abbas, & Mubarik, 2022). Empirical work also indicates that I4.0 impacts SC performance indirectly, by strengthening resilience and visibility routines that translate digital inputs into operational stability (Büchi, Cugno, & Castagnoli, 2020).

Within this logic, DT is the organizational process through which technologies become embedded in routines, governance, and decision rights. Digital capabilities (Konopik, Jahn, Schuster, Hoßbach, & Pflaum, 2022) therefore include not only technical assets but also managerial practices such as data stewardship, process standardization, and cross functional alignment. Recent work on DT in industrial contexts highlights that digital value (Merimi and Taghipour, 2021) materializes when firms manage implementation as an operating model change, not as a technology acquisition project, because fragmentation and weak integration can neutralize expected gains (Culot, Podrecca, & Nassimbeni, 2024). For SCs, this capability view clarifies why adoption is often uneven: firms can deploy digital tools while still lacking the complementary routines needed to extract performance benefits, especially in SMEs where resource constraints and skill gaps are structurally higher (Jam, Ali, Albishri, Mammadov, & Mohapatra, 2025).

1.3. The Role of the Triad in supply chains

The triad can be conceptualized as an integrated control architecture for sustainable SCs, where each element performs a distinct function and strengthens the others. BDA provides the measurement and governance layer by integrating heterogeneous operational and ESG data, improving quality, and enabling consistent reporting and monitoring. A recent technology organization environment (TOE) guided systematic review on BDA adoption for sustainable manufacturing SCs shows that analytics contributes to sustainability only when data governance and adoption conditions are explicitly addressed, not assumed (Huong et al., 2025).

AI then acts as the decision execution layer, converting reliable data into forecasts, optimizations, and anomaly detection that reduce waste, improve planning stability, and support multi objective trade-offs involving cost, service, risk, and environmental impact. This role is particularly relevant when sustainability requires continuous decision recalibration under constraints, rather than periodic reporting (Taghipour, Lu, Derradji, & Sow, 2022). Finally, blockchain plays the credibility and coordination layer by enabling traceability and auditable records across partners, which is essential when claims must be verifiable and inter-organizational trust is uneven. Evidence from case based research on blockchain enabled traceability emphasizes that traceability scope varies widely across industries and that effective designs depend on clearly defined motivations, data granularity choices, and scalability constraints (Ahmed & MacCarthy, 2023). In emerging market contexts, blockchain adoption also requires alignment with organizational readiness and institutional conditions, which is well captured by TOE oriented analyses of SC blockchain deployments (Chittipaka, Kumar, Sivarajah, Bowden, & Baral, 2023).

Taken together, the triad supports a coherent mechanism: BDA establishes reliable measurement, AI improves decisions using that measurement, and blockchain secures proof where sustainability, compliance, and provenance require auditable evidence across tiers (Ahmed & MacCarthy, 2023; Huong et al., 2025).

1.4. Adoption Factors in Emerging Economies within the Moroccan Context

Technology adoption in SCs is shaped by interacting technological, organizational, and environmental conditions. The TOE framework remains a robust lens to structure these drivers and barriers because it explicitly links readiness and fit (technology), internal capabilities and resources (organization), and institutional pressures and market dynamics (environment) (Drazin, 1991). In the context of sustainable digital transformation DT, recent TOE guided evidence synthesizes recurrent adoption constraints: data interoperability gaps, cybersecurity risks, shortage of analytics and AI skills, unclear governance for data ownership and access, high investment and maintenance costs, and limited ecosystem coordination for multi partner solutions (Huong et al., 2025).

For Morocco, these adoption issues are amplified by heterogeneous digital maturity across firms and by the strategic role of export oriented SCs where traceability, compliance, and delivery reliability are increasingly demanded by international buyers (Boulitama, Lhamidi, Taifi, & Brahim, 2025). Research on Morocco's sustainability pathway emphasizes that progress depends on institutional and capability conditions, particularly regulatory measures, investment priorities, and the alignment of technology strategies with measurable sustainability outcomes (Ikram & Sadki, 2024). Sector level reviews also show that Morocco's DT agenda is moving forward in domains such as agrifood and agriculture, but diffusion remains uneven and strongly constrained by skills, infrastructure, and coordination, reinforcing the need for staged adoption pathways (Fakhraddine, Zerrad, Berhili, & Morchid, 2025).

Accordingly, an adoption realistic view for emerging economy SCs is not to maximize technology breadth, but to engineer capability depth: start with data readiness and governance, embed AI into a small number of high leverage decision routines, and deploy blockchain selectively where auditability and multi actor verification create immediate value (Boulitama, Rahli, & Haoucha, 2022; Ikram & Sadki, 2024).

2. MOROCCO CONTEXT AND SUPPLY CHAIN SUSTAINABILITY CHALLENGES

2.1. Logic of complementarity between blockchain, AI, and Big Data for supply chain sustainability

Recent literature converges on the idea that value does not come from an isolated technology, but from a socio-technical architecture where data, algorithms, and trust mechanisms mutually reinforce each other (Boulitama et al., 2022; Taghipour et al., 2015). BDA acts as a capacity for absorbing and transforming operational signals (demand, quality, energy, transportation, supplier risks), while AI converts these signals into actionable decisions (forecasting, optimization, anomaly detection, cost-service-carbon arbitrage). Blockchain, on the other hand, is not a substitute for analytics, but a governance framework for transactions and traceability that enhances integrity, auditability, and inter-organizational coordination, key conditions when sustainability depends on multiple actors and contestable information (Sahoo et al., 2024). In this configuration, AI depends on reliable and contextualized data, which reinforces the interest in data standards and proof mechanisms. Moreover, recent reviews emphasize that the sustainability promises associated with blockchain remain heterogeneous if the uses, metrics, and trade-offs (particularly energy and regulatory) are not specified, hence the need for an impact-oriented and public policy approach (Mulligan, Morsfield, & Cheikosman, 2024). Finally, the synthesis work on AI SC shows that sustainable performance is mainly observable when AI is integrated into processes, data quality, and change management, rather than added as a peripheral tool (Teixeira, Ferreira, & Ramos, 2025; Taghipour et al., 2022a).

2.2. Mechanisms for creating sustainable value and performance metrics

To move beyond a descriptive reading, the analysis can be structured by causal mechanisms linking the technological triad to environmental, social, and economic outcomes. On the environmental front, AI and analytics help reduce unnecessary kilometers, improve fill rates, optimize energy, and decrease waste through early detection of non-quality (Olawade et al., 2024). Blockchain contributes when carbon footprint, origin, and compliance data are shared among partners with validation rules, which limits greenwashing and improves the auditing of claims (Saari, Sinclair, Leshinsky, & Junnila, 2025). On the social front, value materializes through the traceability of working conditions, supplier compliance, and the reduction of gray areas in subcontracting, provided that verifiable indicators and responsibilities are defined. On the economic front, the expected gains are observed through lower logistics and non-quality costs (Atour Taghipour, Abed, & Zoghlami, 2015), improved On-Time In-Full (OTIF), reduction of safety stocks through better forecasting, and increased resilience in the face of disruptions (Yu, Fan, & Yu, 2025). To operationalize these mechanisms, it is recommended to base the chapter on a core set of explicit metrics, for example CO_2 per ton kilometer, return and rejection rates, end-to-end traceability rate, average incident detection time, supplier compliance score, OTIF, and total logistics cost. This framework directly addresses criticisms of sustainability being too conceptual and enhances managerial readability, particularly for industrial chains where sustainability is managed through indicators and trade-offs (Mukherjee, Mukherjee, Ferraris, & Stehlikova, 2025).

2.3. Deployment conditions in the Moroccan context

The interest of the Moroccan context is twofold. On the one hand, it combines export-integrated industrial chains, structuring port logistics, and subcontracting networks where transparency and compliance become factors of competitiveness (Neto et al., 2023). On the other hand, the institutional environment is evolving toward an acceleration of DT (Boulitama, Rahli, & Sabri, 2021; Taghipour & Merimi, 2021). The national Digital Morocco 2030 strategy, officially launched on September 25, 2024, aims notably at the digitalization of public services and the development of the digital economy, which creates a favorable framework for data standardization, interoperability, and the rise of digital capabilities in organizations (Gouiferda & Iddik, 2025). In parallel, recent public orientations explicitly place

AI at the forefront, with announced investments in data infrastructure, training, and the integration of AI into administration and industry, which can reduce a central constraint for analytics, namely access to computing, cloud, and skills capacities (Ahmed Eljetchtimi, 2026).

In this trajectory, the issue is not just technological adoption, but the governance of inter-organizational data, particularly critical for blockchain and AI (Yebenes & Zorrilla, 2019). Concretely, the implementation in Moroccan SCs would benefit from prioritizing use cases with high evidentiary value, such as traceability of quality and supplier compliance, monitoring of temperatures and disruptions in the cold chain, or certification of ESG data (Y. Liu, Song, Zhou, & Liu, 2025). The analysis can also distinguish between large groups and SMEs: SMEs face stronger constraints in skills, financing, and information technology (IT) integration, which justifies mutualized models (sectoral platforms, consortia, trusted third parties) and a logic of gradual maturation rather than a big bang deployment (Romero, 2025; Atour Taghipour, Rouyendegh, Ünal, & Piya, 2022).

2.4. Managerial implications and targeted research agenda

To address the remarks about the lack of micro illustrations and contribution, the section can conclude with a grid of managerial decisions and a contextualized research agenda. On the managers' side, four priorities stand out (Teixeira et al., 2025):

- *select use cases where sustainability is measurable and audited before expanding the scope;*
- *build data governance (quality, access rights, responsibilities) as a prerequisite for AI and blockchain;*
- *treat technological complementarity as a value chain, data to models, models to decisions, decisions to evidence and compliance;*
- *develop skills and change management to avoid superficial adoption, as confirmed by recent syntheses on AI and analytics in supply chain.*

On the research side, three avenues seem particularly fruitful for Morocco and, more broadly, emerging economies: the empirical evaluation of impacts through ESG indicators and operational performance; the study of governance and mutualization models adapted to SMEs; and the analysis of trade-offs, particularly energy, regulatory, and organizational, associated with blockchain in globalized chains (Mulligan et al., 2024; Sahoo et al., 2024). A simple protocol to strengthen the anchored nature involves integrating two to three Moroccan sectoral mini-cases in the form of operational scenarios, each describing the problem, the data mobilized, the role of AI, the role of blockchain, the before-and-after indicators, and the implementation risks. This allows for the transformation of a parallel synthesis into an integrative, directly actionable contribution.

3. CONCEPTUAL FRAMEWORK AND OPERATIONALIZATION

3.1. Value creation logic of the Big Data, AI, and blockchain triad

This section formalizes a mechanism-based view in which sustainable value emerges from an integrated three-layer architecture rather than from isolated technology adoption. First, BDA is conceptualized as an organizational capability for capturing, integrating, assuring the quality of, and governing multi-source and multi-actor data. Without this capability, sustainability objectives remain difficult to quantify and manage consistently across the supply network (Huong, Azmat, & Hadeed, 2025). Second, AI represents the decision layer that transforms governed data into forecasts, optimizations, and anomaly detection, but its performance depends on embedding models into operational routines and cross-functional processes rather than deploying AI as peripheral tools (Culot et al., 2024). Third, blockchain functions as an inter-organizational proof and coordination layer when sustainability requires traceability, auditability (Mathiyazhagan et al., 2022), and credible information sharing across partners, particularly under conditions of low trust or stringent compliance requirements (Ahmed & MacCarthy, 2023; Mulligan et al., 2024).

This architecture implies that blockchain does not replace data governance or analytics. Instead, it strengthens integrity and verifiability for critical events and records, while BDA and AI remain responsible for integration, computation, and decision-making. In line with recent synthesis work, the most robust performance effects are observed when these technologies are designed as an integrated system aligned (Taghipour, 2020; Taghipour and Beneteau-Piet, 2020) to measurable outcomes rather than as a taxonomy of tools (Idrissi, Lachgar, & Hrimech, 2024).

3.2. Constructs and analytical propositions

First, data governance maturity reflects the ability to standardize, validate, secure, and share relevant data across functions and, where needed, across organizational boundaries (Huong et al., 2025). Second, AI decision capability captures the extent to which forecasting, optimization, risk detection, and control models are integrated into planning and execution routines, consistent with empirical evidence that implementation conditions strongly shape realized value (Culot et al., 2024). Third, verifiable traceability capability refers to the presence of auditable, partner-shared records and agreed validation rules for critical events, a capability particularly relevant when sustainability claims must be evidenced rather than merely reported (Ahmed & MacCarthy, 2023; Mulligan et al., 2024). Fourth, measurable sustainable performance captures observable environmental, social, and economic outcomes, translated into concrete indicators and linked to specific use cases.

On this basis, three propositions structure the framework.

- Proposition 1: states that higher data governance maturity strengthens AI outcomes and the credibility of sustainability indicators by reducing inconsistency, measurement noise, and data bias.
- Proposition 2: states that blockchain creates greater value when traceability is contested or regulated and when multiple actors must share information without a single trusted authority, because value then stems from auditability and reduced monitoring and dispute costs.
- Proposition 3: states that the strongest sustainability impacts occur when the triad is aligned to the same use case and measurement chain, moving from reliable data to AI-supported decisions, to verifiable records, and finally to KPI-based control and continuous improvement.

3.3. Metrics, data, and evaluation protocol

To address the common critique that sustainability remains conceptual, operationalization should rely on a limited set of KPIs tied to a defined use case and tracked over time. For environmental performance, priority measures include transport carbon intensity, empty kilometers, vehicle fill rate, waste and scrap reduction, and the traceability of footprint data when compliance requires auditable reporting (Mulligan et al., 2024). In the Moroccan context, freight and road transport energy efficiency is a concrete lever for linking optimization decisions to decarbonization outcomes, as evidenced by sector-focused research on heavy goods vehicles and energy efficiency in Morocco (Jelti & Saadani, 2024).

For social performance, implementable indicators include supplier compliance coverage, audit rates, remediation lead time, and subcontracting traceability, which help make upstream social risks more observable and manageable. For economic and operational performance, total logistics cost, OTIF delivery, lead time variability, incident detection time, and cost of non-quality provide a direct bridge between AI-enabled decision-making and managerial outcomes, consistent with empirical syntheses of AI in SC settings (Culot et al., 2024).

The recommended evaluation protocol follows a before-after logic complemented by comparisons across comparable flows or business units. The goal is to disentangle the effects of data quality improvements, process-embedded AI deployment, and inter-organizational verifiability when blockchain is applied to critical records. This approach aligns with evidence that the value of analytics and AI depends less on algorithmic sophistication than on process integration and sustained data quality management (Culot et al., 2024), which also mirrors the adoption conditions identified for sustainability-oriented BDA (Q. Liu & Wang, 2025).

3.4. Moroccan illustrations and micro-level adoption conditions

The Moroccan context can be strengthened without turning the chapter into a heavy empirical study by using brief sectoral scenarios supported by indexed work that documents adoption constraints and performance logics. First, evidence from Moroccan logistics firms suggests that AI is perceived as a lever for agility and SC performance, yet adoption is constrained by data readiness and organizational adaptation, reinforcing the argument that process and data integration shape realized value (Bouanba, Barakat, & Bendou, 2022). Second, research on the application of smart SC technologies in Moroccan logistics highlights the role of digital technologies, including (IoT) and blockchain, in enabling incremental modernization pathways, which supports an operationalization-by-stages approach centered on measurable use cases (Chbaik, Khiat, Bahnasse, & Ouajji, 2022). Third, Morocco-focused work on SC decarbonization identifies barriers and levers that help connect the triad to concrete low-carbon objectives rather than generic sustainability claims, thereby supporting the need for explicit KPI alignment and governance design.

Across these illustrations, the most robust adoption logic is to select use cases where data are accessible, benefits are measurable, and inter-organizational proof or coordination provides immediate value. This emphasis reduces the risk of technology-led narratives and supports a more mechanism-driven explanation of how the triad can deliver auditable sustainability outcomes under emerging-economy constraints.

3.5. Morocco-Focused Mini-Cases for Operationalizing the Digital Sustainability Triad

Case 1: Automotive and tier suppliers: quality, traceability, and auditable ESG proof

In Morocco's automotive ecosystem, coordination across Original Equipment Manufacturers (OEMs), tier suppliers, and logistics providers requires both execution discipline and credible evidence on quality and sustainability related records. A pragmatic pathway starts with consolidating production, inspection, and shipment data into a governed dataset that standardizes part identifiers, batch genealogy, non-quality events, and supplier documentation across Enterprise Resource Planning (ERP) and shop floor systems. This data foundation supports AI driven routines for early detection of quality drifts, prediction of defect probabilities, and smarter planning decisions that protect service level while reducing scrap and rework, which is consistent with Moroccan evidence emphasizing collaboration mechanisms and SC synchronization as core performance levers (Farouk, Moufad, Frichi, Arif, & Jawab, 2020) and with local work highlighting the role of smart SC technologies and analytics readiness in Moroccan logistics settings (Chbaik et al., 2022; Taghipour, 2021; Taghipour et al., 2022b). Blockchain should then be introduced selectively as an evidence layer for audit critical records such as certificates of conformity, batch level provenance, custody transfer events, and supplier declarations, reinforcing traceability and dispute reduction in line with smart logistics applications of blockchain (Issaoui, Khiat, Bahnasse, & Ouajji, 2019).

Case 2: Agri food exports and cold chain logistics: loss reduction, compliance, and energy efficiency

For Moroccan agri food exports, cold chain integrity is central to sustainability, product safety, and market access. The most credible implementation sequence begins with IoT monitoring of temperature and humidity connected to logistics events such as loading, transshipment, and delivery under minimal data standards that allow interoperability across carriers and exporters. This is aligned with the broader trajectory of DT in Moroccan agriculture where decision support and data driven practices are increasingly emphasized (Fakhraddine et al., 2025). AI can then forecast spoilage risk, detect abnormal patterns early, and optimize routing and handling decisions to reduce losses and avoid unnecessary energy consumption, which matches the practical promise of AI enabled logistics optimization described in Moroccan oriented smart logistics research streams (Bouanba et al., 2022). Blockchain becomes most valuable when used as a proof layer for compliance sensitive events, recording custody transfers and trusted summaries of sensor data to provide auditable evidence for inspections and claims management, consistent with the role of blockchain based traceability and smart contracts in logistics traceability architectures (Boulitama et al., 2022) and established blockchain applications in smart logistics (Issaoui et al., 2019).

Case 3: Textiles and multi subcontractor networks: social compliance, transparency, and risk control

In Morocco's textile and apparel sector, multi tier subcontracting can increase social compliance exposure and weaken visibility over working conditions, documentation, and provenance. A workable approach focuses on minimal viable data, including subcontractor registries, work orders, audit outcomes, and remediation actions, combined with standardized identifiers so that information can be exchanged with buyers and auditors without excessive burden on SMEs. Morocco specific evidence shows that buyer driven codes of conduct and Corporate Social Responsibility (CSR) requirements shape subcontractor practices and capabilities, but also create implementation frictions and power asymmetries that make traceability and credible documentation particularly important (Benabdeljlil & Kerzazi, 2025). AI can support supplier risk scoring to prioritize audits and detect anomalies in lead times, output patterns, and documentation completeness that may signal elevated risk, while blockchain can secure audit trails and remediation records when stakeholder trust and evidence are required across organizational boundaries (Issaoui et al., 2019). This direction is also consistent with the broader tightening of supply chain due diligence expectations for labour standards in global garment supply chains, which increases the managerial value of auditable compliance records (Velluti, 2024).

4. IMPLEMENTATION PATHWAYS AND GOVERNANCE FOR SUSTAINABLE DIGITAL SUPPLY CHAINS IN MOROCCO

4.1. From data readiness to decision automation: a staged pathway

A realistic implementation pathway in Morocco is incremental and use case driven rather than technology driven. The first stage is data readiness: aligning master data, defining ownership, and setting minimum data quality rules across ERP and logistics systems, then extending data capture through IoT, RFID, and partner exchanges where feasible. Morocco focused evidence from the logistics sector shows that technology initiatives often stall when data are fragmented and when operational routines are not adapted, which reinforces the need to treat data readiness as a prerequisite rather than a downstream task (Chbaik et al., 2022).

The second stage is AI enabled decision automation, prioritizing cases where performance gains and sustainability outcomes can be jointly measured, such as routing, fleet utilization, inventory and replenishment, disruption detection, and energy related efficiency improvements. Moroccan logistics research suggests that perceived value is strongly tied to agility and operational improvement, but adoption remains constrained by budgeting, skills, and organizational readiness, which makes process integration and capability building central to implementation (Bouanba et al., 2022).

4.2. Blockchain as an evidence layer for compliance and traceability in Moroccan flows

In Morocco, blockchain should be positioned as an evidence and coordination layer for high risk or compliance sensitive events rather than as a generic digital infrastructure. The most relevant applications are those where sustainability or quality claims must be auditable across multiple actors, such as provenance of agri food exports, cold chain records, supplier certificates, and dispute resolution over delivery and condition. A Morocco linked study in smart logistics synthesizes blockchain applications by function and illustrates how traceability and immutable records can support logistics governance when information is distributed across partners (Haricha, Khiat, Issaoui, Bahnasse, & Ouajji, 2020).

This positioning also aligns with observed digitization initiatives in Moroccan logistics and supply chains, where technology adoption tends to be most credible when it is tied to a narrow set of verifiable events and measurable outcomes instead of broad claims of transformation (Chbaik et al., 2022).

4.3. Morocco specific sustainability levers: freight efficiency, decarbonization, and port resilience

For environmental performance, road freight is a high leverage entry point because routing, loading efficiency, and maintenance decisions can translate into measurable energy and emissions outcomes. Evidence focused on heavy goods vehicles in Morocco supports the relevance of energy efficiency as a concrete sustainability and competitiveness lever, which strengthens the case for transport centered KPIs in implementation roadmaps (Jelti & Saadani, 2024).

For Morocco's gateway role, port and maritime logistics also matter for resilience and long term sustainability. Applied evidence on the port of Tangier Med shows how climate related risks can affect operability and impose adaptation costs, which makes digital monitoring, risk analytics, and investment planning part of a broader sustainability agenda rather than an optional add on (Jebbad, Sierra, Mösso, Mestres, & Sánchez-Arcilla, 2022).

4.4. Governance, capability building, and SME inclusion

Implementation success depends on governance choices that determine what data are shared, how they are validated, and how responsibilities are allocated across the network. In Morocco, the digital maturity gap between large firms and SMEs is a structural constraint, so adoption pathways should include shared services, sectoral platforms, or consortium style arrangements that lower entry barriers while enforcing minimal interoperability standards (Bouanba et al., 2022).

From a technology architecture perspective, Morocco based IEEE work on smart logistics emphasizes data driven logistics capabilities and the importance of integrated digital stacks for e commerce and logistics modernization, which can be used to justify governance choices around interoperability and scalable deployment (Kalkha et al., 2023). Policymaking and public sector framing can be supported with Morocco focused conference evidence that discusses logistics transformation under AI and highlights governance and institutional considerations (Ammar et al., 2024).

5. MANAGERIAL AND POLICY IMPLICATIONS, LIMITATIONS, AND FUTURE RESEARCH

5.1. Managerial implications for Moroccan supply chains

For managers, the most actionable implication is to treat BDA, AI, and blockchain as a sequenced capability system rather than three parallel technology projects. Evidence from Moroccan logistics highlights that AI related performance gains depend heavily on organizational readiness, skills, and the ability to embed analytics into routines, which means that governance, roles, and process redesign should be planned before model deployment (Bouanba et al., 2022). A practical starting point is to select one or two use cases where value is measurable and where data availability is realistic, such as fleet routing, lead time variability reduction, anomaly detection, or non-quality prevention. The KPI set should be intentionally small, tracked over time, and tied to operational decisions rather than reporting only.

A second implication is that blockchain should be positioned as an evidence layer for contested, regulated, or audit sensitive events, not as a generic traceability solution. Work that discusses blockchain applications in smart logistics provides a clear basis for designing limited scope implementations around critical events and verifiable records, which fits Moroccan supply chains characterized by multi actor coordination and documentation requirements (Issaoui et al., 2019). In practice, this means defining the minimum dataset required for trust, agreeing validation rules with partners, and ensuring that blockchain records are anchored to reliable data capture processes.

A third implication concerns sustainability outcomes. Transport energy efficiency is a concrete lever for Morocco because it links operational optimization to measurable environmental outcomes, which supports prioritizing freight and distribution use cases with explicit energy and emission metrics (Jelti & Saadani, 2024). At the same time, decarbonization barriers identified in Moroccan companies indicate that managerial roadmaps should explicitly address capability gaps, coordination frictions, and measurement credibility, rather than assuming that technology adoption automatically yields sustainability improvements.

5.2. Policy and ecosystem implications: governance, standards, and inclusion

At the ecosystem level, Moroccan adoption pathways benefit from public and collective action around interoperability, shared standards, and SME inclusion. Evidence on smart SC technology application in Moroccan logistics underlines the relevance of staged modernization and the need to address ecosystem heterogeneity, which makes platform and consortium approaches particularly suitable for scaling beyond a few large firms (Chbaik et al., 2022). A practical policy direction is therefore to encourage shared digital infrastructure for SMEs, including common data standards, sectoral APIs, and training programs that reduce entry barriers.

Public sector perspectives on logistics transformation under AI also stress governance considerations, which can be used to justify policy support for experimentation sandboxes, guidelines for data sharing, and evaluation frameworks that connect digitalization initiatives to measurable performance and sustainability outcomes (Ammar et al., 2024). For Morocco's gateway role, port resilience is part of the sustainability agenda. Evidence from the port of Tangier Med shows that climate related risks can affect operability and generate adaptation costs, which reinforces the need to integrate risk analytics and monitoring into the broader digital sustainability roadmap (Jebbad et al., 2022).

5.3. Limitations and future research agenda

This chapter synthesizes mechanisms and proposes an operationalization pathway, but it remains limited by the availability of micro level, firm specific evidence linking the triad to verified ESG outcomes in Morocco. Future research should therefore move from conceptual alignment to evidence on causal mechanisms through three directions. First, comparative case studies across Moroccan sectors such as automotive, agri food cold chain, textiles, and logistics platforms could test how governance maturity mediates AI value and how blockchain affects auditability and dispute reduction across partner networks (Bouanba et al., 2022; Issaoui et al., 2019). Second, longitudinal designs are needed to separate early adoption effects from sustained performance changes, particularly for transport and decarbonization KPIs where seasonality and external shocks can bias evaluation. Third, research on governance models should evaluate the effectiveness of consortium and platform approaches for SME inclusion and interoperability in Morocco, building on observed staged adoption patterns in Moroccan logistics (Ammar et al., 2024; Chbaik et al., 2022).

CONCLUSION

This chapter clarified how sustainable SC transformation in Morocco becomes most credible when advanced digital technologies are engineered as an integrated system rather than implemented as disconnected initiatives. The core message is that sustainability becomes operational, measurable, and verifiable only when a chain of control is established: data governance creates a robust foundation for reliable ESG and operational information, AI embeds decision intelligence into day to day planning and execution, and blockchain secures proof for critical records across partners, while KPI loops drive continuous improvement.

The analysis showed that BDA is the enabling layer that makes sustainability measurable by integrating heterogeneous data, improving their quality, and institutionalizing governance rules that support consistent reporting and control. AI then serves as the execution layer for decision improvement, converting reliable data into forecasts, optimizations, and early warnings that reduce waste, stabilize flows, and support multi objective trade-offs involving cost, service, risk, and environmental impact. Blockchain plays a distinct role as a credibility layer that strengthens inter-organizational coordination when sustainability and compliance require auditable evidence rather than claims, particularly in supply networks where information is fragmented and trust is uneven.

By linking these elements to measurable outcomes, the chapter emphasized that sustainability gains do not automatically follow from technology adoption. They depend on clear use case selection, a disciplined KPI system, and feedback loops that translate digital insights into operational action. The Moroccan context makes these conditions especially salient because the main constraint is rarely the absence of technologies, but rather the conditions of adoption, including skills, governance, interoperability, and ecosystem coordination, alongside heterogeneous digital maturity across firms and the centrality of logistics and export oriented supply chains. For this reason, a staged pathway emerges as the most credible route, starting with data readiness and process alignment, then expanding toward process embedded AI decision routines, and finally introducing blockchain selectively where verifiability creates immediate value.

Overall, the chapter contributes a mechanism driven synthesis that links technology, governance, and sustainability outcomes into a coherent implementation logic. The key takeaway is that sustainable DT is less about adopting more tools and more about building the conditions under which data become reliable, decisions become better, and sustainability claims become verifiable. By anchoring technology choices to auditable sustainability outcomes and designing inclusion pathways for SMEs, organizations and policymakers can move from broad digitalization narratives to concrete, measurable progress in environmental performance, social compliance, operational efficiency, and long term resilience.

REFERENCES

Ahmed, W. A. H., & MacCarthy, B. L. (2023). Blockchain-enabled supply chain traceability – How wide? How deep? *International Journal of Production Economics*, *263*, 108963. DOI: 10.1016/j.ijpe.2023.108963

Ahmed Eljetchtimi. (2026). Morocco targets $10 billion AI contribution to GDP by 2030 | Reuters. Retrieved January 27, 2026, from https://www.reuters.com/sustainability/climate-energy/morocco-targets-10-billion-ai-contribution-gdp-by-2030-2026-01-12/

Ammar, A., Amahmoud, H., El Menzhi, K., Mkik, M., Hebaz, A., & Eddine, E. M. A. (2024). Critical Analysis of Logistics Transformation in Morocco under the Auspices of Artificial Intelligence: Government Perspectives from the perspective of Innovative and Technology Driven Public Management. *2024 IEEE 15th International Colloquium of Logistics and Supply Chain Management, LOGISTIQUA 2024*. DOI: 10.1109/LOGISTIQUA61063.2024.10571402

Benabdeljlil, N., & Kerzazi, L. (2025). Corporate social responsibility imperatives in the Moroccan textile-clothing sector: Ways of implementation and impact on local value chains. *IDOS Discussion Papers*. DOI: 10.23661/IDP18.2025

Bouanba, N., Barakat, O., & Bendou, A. (2022). Artificial Intelligence & Agile Innovation: Case of Moroccan Logistics Companies. *Procedia Computer Science*, *203*, 444–449. DOI: 10.1016/j.procs.2022.07.059

Boulitama, O., Lhamidi, S., Taifi, R., & Brahim, S. (2025). Digital transformation and supply chain capabilities: A sectoral maturity perspective in morocco. *Polish Journal of Management Studies*, *32*(1), 61–80. DOI: 10.17512/pjms.2025.32.1.04

Boulitama, O., Rahli, D., & Haoucha, M. (2022). Digital solutions and Moroccan companies during the Covid-19 pandemic. *2022 IEEE 14th International Conference of Logistics and Supply Chain Management, LOGISTIQUA 2022*. Institute of Electrical and Electronics Engineers Inc. DOI: 10.1109/LOGISTIQUA55056.2022.9938069

Boulitama, O., Rahli, D., & Sabri, K. (2021). *L'impact de la covid-19 sur la chaine logistique marocaine The impact of covid-19 on the Moroccan supply chain*. *2*(3), 165–181. DOI: 10.5281/zenodo.4817869

Büchi, G., Cugno, M., & Castagnoli, R. (2020). Smart factory performance and Industry 4.0. *Technological Forecasting and Social Change*, *150*, 119790. Advance online publication. DOI: 10.1016/j.techfore.2019.119790

Carter, C. R., & Rogers, D. S. (2008). A framework of sustainable supply chain management: Moving toward new theory. *International Journal of Physical Distribution & Logistics Management, 38*(5), 360–387. DOI: 10.1108/09600030810882816

Chau, L., Anh, L., & Duc, V. (2025). Valuing ESG: How financial markets respond to corporate sustainability. *International Business Review, 34*(3), 102418. DOI: 10.1016/j.ibusrev.2025.102418

Chbaik, N., Khiat, A., Bahnasse, A., & Ouajji, H. (2022). The Application of Smart Supply Chain Technologies in The Moroccan Logistics. *Procedia Computer Science, 198*, 578–583. DOI: 10.1016/j.procs.2021.12.289

Chittipaka, V., Kumar, S., Sivarajah, U., Bowden, J. L. H., & Baral, M. M. (2023). Blockchain Technology for Supply Chains operating in emerging markets: An empirical examination of technology-organization-environment (TOE) framework. *Annals of Operations Research, 327*(1), 465–492. DOI: 10.1007/s10479-022-04801-5

Culot, G., Podrecca, M., & Nassimbeni, G. (2024, November 1). Artificial intelligence in supply chain management: A systematic literature review of empirical studies and research directions. *Computers in Industry*, Vol. 162. Elsevier B.V. DOI: 10.1016/j.compind.2024.104132

Drazin, R. (1991). The processes of technological innovation. *The Journal of Technology Transfer 1991 16:1, 16*(1), 45–46. DOI: 10.1007/BF02371446

El Hafdaoui, H., Khallaayoun, A., & Ouazzani, K. (2024). Long-term low carbon strategy of Morocco: A review of future scenarios and energy measures. *Results in Engineering, 21*, 101724. DOI: 10.1016/j.rineng.2023.101724

Fakhraddine, M., Zerrad, N., Berhili, H., & Morchid, M. (2025). Digital transformation in Moroccan agriculture: Applications, used technologies, impacts on marketing, limitations, and orientations for future research. *Smart Agricultural Technology, 11*, 100978. DOI: 10.1016/j.atech.2025.100978

Farouk, I. I. El, Moufad, I., Frichi, Y., Arif, J., & Jawab, F. (2020). Proposing a Supply Chain Collaboration Framework for Synchronous Flow Implementation in the Automotive Industry: A Moroccan Case Study. *Information 2020, Vol. 11, 11*(9). DOI: 10.3390/info11090431

Gouiferda, F., & Iddik, S. (2025). Digitalization and environmental sustainability ramifications on the Moroccan companies' resilience. *Management and Sustainability*, 1–27. https://doi.org/DOI: 10.1108/MSAR-02-2025-0074/1312706

Han, Y., & Fang, X. (2024). Systematic review of adopting blockchain in supply chain management: Bibliometric analysis and theme discussion. *International Journal of Production Research, 62*(3), 991–1016. DOI: 10.1080/00207543.2023.2236241

Haricha, K., Khiat, A., Issaoui, Y., Bahnasse, A., & Ouajji, H. (2020). Towards smart manufucturing: Implementation and benefits. *Procedia Computer Science, 177*, 639–644. DOI: 10.1016/j.procs.2020.10.091

Huong, D. G., Azmat, M., & Hadeed, R. (2025). Exploring big data analytics adoption for sustainable manufacturing supply Chains: Insights from a TOE-guided systematic review. *Cleaner Logistics and Supply Chain, 16*, 100256. DOI: 10.1016/j.clscn.2025.100256

Idrissi, Z. K., Lachgar, M., & Hrimech, H. (2024). Blockchain, IoT and AI in logistics and transportation: A systematic review. *Transport Economics and Management, 2*, 275–285. DOI: 10.1016/j.team.2024.09.002

Ikram, M., & Sadki, J. E. (2024). Resilient and sustainable green technology strategies: A study of Morocco's path toward sustainable development. *Sustainable Futures : An Applied Journal of Technology, Environment and Society, 8*, 100327. DOI: 10.1016/j.sftr.2024.100327

Issaoui, Y., Khiat, A., Bahnasse, A., & Ouajji, H. (2019). Smart logistics : Study of the application of blockchain technology. *Procedia Computer Science, 160*, 266–271. Elsevier B.V. DOI: 10.1016/j.procs.2019.09.467

Jabbar, A., Akhtar, P., & Ali, S. I. (2025). The interplay between blockchain and big data analytics for enhancing supply chain value creation in micro, small, and medium enterprises. *Annals of Operations Research, 350*(2), 649–671. DOI: 10.1007/s10479-024-06415-5

Jam, F. A., Ali, I., Albishri, N., Mammadov, A., & Mohapatra, A. K. (2025). How does the adoption of digital technologies in supply chain management enhance supply chain performance? A mediated and moderated model. *Technological Forecasting and Social Change, 219*, 124225. Advance online publication. DOI: 10.1016/j.techfore.2025.124225

Jebbad, R., Sierra, J. P., Mösso, C., Mestres, M., & Sánchez-Arcilla, A. (2022). Assessment of harbour inoperability and adaptation cost due to sea level rise. Application to the port of Tangier-Med (Morocco). *Applied Geography (Sevenoaks, England), 138*, 102623. Advance online publication. DOI: 10.1016/j.apgeog.2021.102623

Jelti, F., & Saadani, R. (2024). Energy efficiency analysis of heavy goods vehicles in road transportation: The case of Morocco. *Case Studies on Transport Policy, 17*, 101260. DOI: 10.1016/j.cstp.2024.101260

Kalkha, H., Khiat, A., Bahnasse, A., Ouajji, H., Kalkha, H., Khiat, A., & Ouajji, H. (2023). The Rising Trends of Smart E-Commerce Logistics. *IEEE Access : Practical Innovations, Open Solutions, 11*, 33839–33857. DOI: 10.1109/ACCESS.2023.3252566

Konopik, J., Jahn, C., Schuster, T., Hoßbach, N., & Pflaum, A. (2022). Mastering the digital transformation through organizational capabilities: A conceptual framework. *Digital Business, 2*(2), 100019. https://doi.org/https://doi.org/10.1016/j.digbus.2021.100019

Lhamidi, S., & Boulitama, O. (2025). Adoption of Industry 4.0 Technologies in Moroccan Supply Chains: A Bayesian Network and Sectoral Analysis. *16th International Conference on Logistics and Supply Chain Management - LOGISTIQUA 2025*, 28–30. DOI: 10.1109/LOGISTIQUA66323.2025.11122847

Liu, Q., & Wang, H. (2025). Digital transformation, innovation capability, and ESG performance. *Finance Research Letters, 78*, 107166. DOI: 10.1016/j.frl.2025.107166

Liu, Y., Song, J., Zhou, B., & Liu, J. (2025). Artificial intelligence applications and corporate ESG performance. *International Review of Economics & Finance, 104*, 104559. https://doi.org/https://doi.org/10.1016/j.iref.2025.104559. DOI: 10.1016/j.iref.2025.104559

Mathiyazhagan, K., Taghipour, A., & Agarwal, V. (Eds.). (2022). *Blockchain technology in supply chain management for society 5.0*. CRC Press. DOI: 10.1201/9781003177432

Merimi, M., & Taghipour, A. (2021). Accelerating the digitalization of the supply chain: An empirical research about COVID-19 crisis. In *Digitalization of decentralized supply chains during global crises* (pp. 1–24). IGI Global Scientific Publishing. DOI: 10.4018/978-1-7998-6874-3.ch001

Mukherjee, S., Mukherjee, S., Ferraris, A., & Stehlikova, B. (2025). Enhancing health-care service delivery through AI-integrated knowledge management systems. *Journal of Knowledge Management, 29*(10), 3379–3409. DOI: 10.1108/JKM-01-2025-0119

Mulligan, C., Morsfield, S., & Cheikosman, E. (2024). Blockchain for sustainability: A systematic literature review for policy impact. *Telecommunications Policy, 48*(2), 102676. DOI: 10.1016/j.telpol.2023.102676

Neto, O., Amorim, M., Carlos De Oliveira Matias, J., Fernando, L., Pinto, R., Bouazza, S., … Hachimi, H. (2023). Maritime Bilateral Connectivity Analysis for Sustainable Maritime Growth: Case of Morocco. *Sustainability 2023, Vol. 15, Page 4993, 15*(6), 4993. DOI: 10.3390/su15064993

Olawade, D. B., Wada, O. Z., Ige, A. O., Egbewole, B. I., Olojo, A., & Oladapo, B. I. (2024). Artificial intelligence in environmental monitoring: Advancements, challenges, and future directions. *Hygiene and Environmental Health Advances, 12*, 100114. DOI: 10.1016/j.heha.2024.100114

Qader, G., Junaid, M., Abbas, Q., & Mubarik, M. S. (2022). Industry 4.0 enables supply chain resilience and supply chain performance. *Technological Forecasting and Social Change, 185*, 122026. Advance online publication. DOI: 10.1016/j.techfore.2022.122026

Romero, I. (2025). Information technology as a driver of organizational change in SMEs: A study of key determinants. *Journal of Organizational Change Management, 38*(3), 625–643. https://doi.org/https://doi.org/10.1108/JOCM-11-2024-0702. DOI: 10.1108/JOCM-11-2024-0702

Saari, A., Sinclair, S., Leshinsky, R., & Junnila, S. (2025). Best practices for blockchain-driven digital transformation in cross-industry settings. *Digital Business, 5*(2), 100127. https://doi.org/https://doi.org/10.1016/j.digbus.2025.100127

Sahoo, S., Kumar, S., Sivarajah, U., Lim, W. M., Westland, J. C., & Kumar, A. (2024). Blockchain for sustainable supply chain management: Trends and ways forward. *Electronic Commerce Research, 24*(3), 1563–1618. DOI: 10.1007/s10660-022-09569-1

Seuring, S., & Müller, M. (2008). From a literature review to a conceptual framework for sustainable supply chain management. *Journal of Cleaner Production, 16*(15), 1699–1710. DOI: 10.1016/j.jclepro.2008.04.020

Taghipour, A. (2021, January). Digital transformation of supply chains during crisis: Covid19. In *11th Annual International Conference on Industrial Engineering and Operations Management, IEOM 2021*. DOI: 10.46254/AN11.20211298

Taghipour, A., Abed, M., & Zoghlami, N. (2015, May). Design for remanufacturing respecting reverse logistics processes: A review. In 2015 4th international conference on advanced logistics and transport (ICALT) (pp. 299-304). IEEE. DOI: 10.1109/ICAdLT.2015.7136602

Taghipour, A., & Beneteau-Piet, C. (2020). Sustainable supply chain management performance. *International Journal of Innovation, Management and Technology, 11*(6), 165–169. DOI: 10.18178/ijimt.2020.11.6.897

Taghipour, A., Lu, X., Derradji, M., & Sow, A. D. (2022a, July). The impact of digitalization on supply chain management: a literature review. In *Proceedings of the 12th International Conference on Information Communication and Management* (pp. 75-78). DOI: 10.1145/3551690.3551702

Taghipour, A., Rouyendegh, B. D., Ünal, A., & Piya, S. (2022b). Selection of suppliers for speech recognition products in IT projects by combining techniques with an integrated fuzzy MCDM. *Sustainability (Basel), 14*(3), 1777. DOI: 10.3390/su14031777

Teixeira, A. R., Ferreira, J. V., & Ramos, A. L. (2025). Intelligent Supply Chain Management: A Systematic Literature Review on Artificial Intelligence Contributions. *Information 2025, Vol. 16, 16*(5). DOI: 10.3390/info16050399

Truant, E., Borlatto, E., Crocco, E., & Sahore, N. (2024). Environmental, social and governance issues in supply chains. A systematic review for strategic performance. *Journal of Cleaner Production, 434*, 140024. DOI: 10.1016/j.jclepro.2023.140024

Van Nguyen, T., Cong Pham, H., Nhat Nguyen, M., Zhou, L., & Akbari, M. (2023). Data-driven review of blockchain applications in supply chain management: Key research themes and future directions. *International Journal of Production Research, 61*(23), 8213–8235. DOI: 10.1080/00207543.2023.2165190

Velluti, S. (2024). Labour standards in global garment supply chains and the proposed EU corporate sustainability due diligence directive. *European Labour Law Journal, 15*(4), 822–850. DOI: 10.1177/20319525241239283

Yebenes, J., & Zorrilla, M. (2019). Towards a Data Governance Framework for Third Generation Platforms. *Procedia Computer Science, 151*, 614–621. https://doi.org/https://doi.org/10.1016/j.procs.2019.04.082. DOI: 10.1016/j.procs.2019.04.082

Yu, X., Fan, L., & Yu, Y. (2025). Artificial Intelligence and Corporate ESG Performance: A Mechanism Analysis Based on Corporate Efficiency and External Environment. *Sustainability 2025, Vol. 17, 17*(9). DOI: 10.3390/su17093819

Chapter 8

Role of Blockchain, AI, and Big Data in Sustainable SCM

M. N. Geetha
Vidyavardhaka College of Engineering, India

Mohammed Irfan Khan
http://orcid.org/0000-0002-3991-5203
Medicaps University, India

M. Srinu
CVR College of Engineering, India

Swapna Choudhary
http://orcid.org/0000-0002-1289-9987
G.H. Raisoni College of Engineering, India

Rajlaxmi Pujar
http://orcid.org/0000-0001-5305-2160
Indira University, India

Mohd Asif Shah
Kardan University, Afghanistan

V. Bhoopathy
http://orcid.org/0000-0003-2175-6328
Malla Reddy College of Engineering, India

ABSTRACT

As businesses try to reduce their influence on the environment, improve their social responsibility, and make sure their businesses will be profitable in the long run, SSCM has become a strategic focus. New digital technologies, including Blockchain, AI and Big Data, are very important for making supply chain processes clear, effective, and resource-efficient. This chapter looks at how various technologies work together to turn traditional supply chains into smart, traceable, and eco-friendly ecosystems. Blockchain makes records that can't be changed, which makes it easier to trace things, stops fraud, and supports ethical sourcing. AI, on the other hand, makes it possible to do predictive analytics, optimise routes, make energy-efficient

DOI: 10.4018/979-8-2600-3199-5.ch008

products, and evaluate suppliers based on facts. Big Data analytics makes SSCM even stronger by giving us real-time information on how well the environment is doing, how resources are being used, and what social dangers there are.

1. INTRODUCTION

The properties of blockchain projects, according to several experts in related sectors, will provide a platform that can be used across industries, including financial, once they are commercialised. The banking, industrial, distribution, and public sectors are just a few of the many areas that stand to benefit from the digitisation and convergence made possible by BT's novel ways of simultaneously exchanging digital values and information. Value creation, especially in the logistics sector, is becoming increasingly dependent on understanding how new technologies are being adopted. The blockchain is a decentralised ledger that records transactions in chronological order using encrypted data linked together in blocks. BT first appeared in 2008 with the launch of Bitcoin, the digital currency created by an anonymous individual. The characteristics of blockchain-based systems include their immutability, speed, dependability, security, transparency, availability, scalability, safety, and the absence of intermediaries. The financial and logistics sectors are seeing fast evolution from BT as a result of these advantages and features. Financial technology (fintech) and IT firms collaborate and invest in the development of various blockchain systems for use in banking and finance. To enable safe peer-to-peer transactions, the e-commerce industry is also working towards commercialising BT. It is believed that actions will increase supply chain ecosystem efficiency and competitiveness by making things more transparent, dependable, and financially viable. This lends credence to the idea that logistics firms must immediately implement BT, prompting demands for a concerted effort from across the sector to do so. There is an ideal opportunity for the logistics business to embrace BT (Alizadeh et al., 2021; Taghipour and Beneteau-Piet, 2020).

Supply chain ecosystem efficiency and competitiveness are anticipated to be enhanced with the implementation of Biologistic operations, which offer economic feasibility, dependability, and visibility. From this, it appears that logistics companies must implement BT, and there have been calls for an industry-wide effort to do so. Consequently, logistics services are an area where BT might find a lot of use. Our research indicates that, following the banking and financial sectors, the logistics business holds the second-highest potential for application (Cauchois et al., 2017). Consequently, logistics services are an area where BT might find a lot of use. After the banking and financial industries, the logistics industry appears to have the second-highest application potential for BT, according to our research.

Consequently, it chooses to centre our research on logistics businesses. On top of that, it wants to find out what makes people want to use BT in this study. The TOE frameworks and the UTAUT model are among the models developed to explain technology adoption. BT is one of these areas. Consequently, it chooses to centre our research on logistics businesses. On top of that, it wants to find out what makes people want to use BT in this study. The TOE frameworks and the UTAUT model are a few of the models that have been developed to explain technology adoption. One of the most popular models used to describe how people and businesses embrace and make use of newly accessible technology is the UTAUT. The TOE was also utilised in this study. When new technology becomes available, the UTAUT is a popular model to explain how people and businesses adopt and make use of it. The study also employed the TOE framework to find out what variables are linked to the plan to use BT (Selcuk Besir Demir, 2018). Given the logistics industry's demand for innovation, these theoretical frameworks are deemed suitable for investigating early BT adoption.

2. BLOCKCHAIN IN SUSTAINABLE SCM

There has been an increase in the complexity of modern SC, which calls for more research into how its management affects a company's ability to compete. Referring to the idea of a multi-echelon SCM. The difficulty in monitoring and tracing SC actions is a problem for many focal enterprises in multi-echelon SC networks that are involved in SSCM, whether they are doing it voluntarily or in response to regulatory enforcement or stakeholder pressure (Mbiatem et al., 2018).

Figure 1. The Principal Weaknesses in Multi-layer Supply Chains

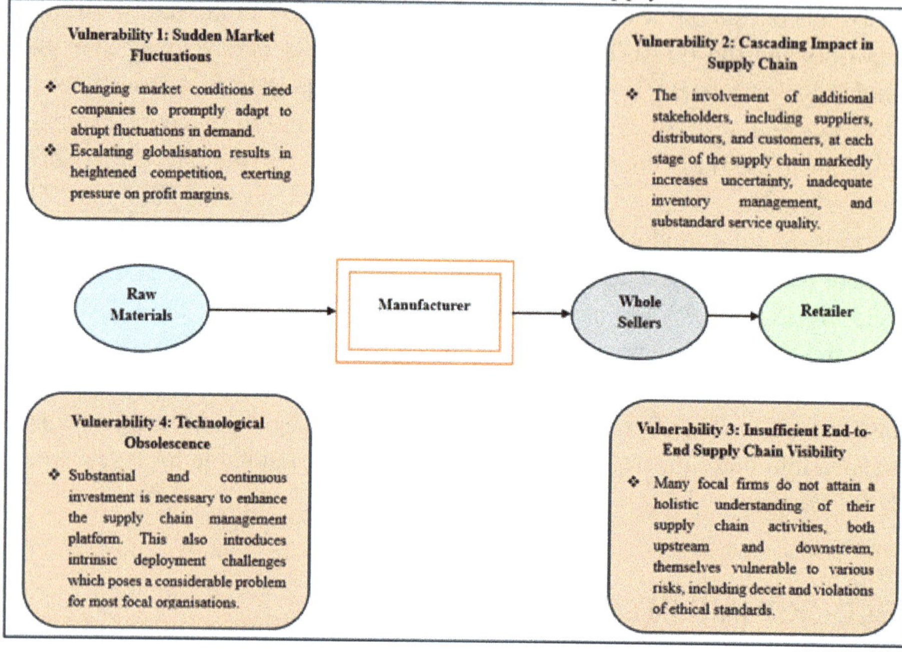

Figure 1 depicts the SC of a typical focal business involved in multi-layered interactions between upstream and downstream physical flows. Recent trends such as globalisation, market movements, demand unpredictability, and economic constraints have put enormous pressure on enterprises to engage in sustainable practices across the SC. As a result, organisations can no longer achieve a competitive advantage by depending simply on internal SC efficiency. Furthermore, when one firm employs restructuring tactics to transition from traditional SC management to SSCM, it can place equal pressure on its SC partners to do the same in order to meet the rejuvenated SC's sustainability criteria. Figure 1 depicts how numerous internal and external components influence the operating problems and vulnerabilities of the current multi-echelon SC.

Providing information on sustainability compliance among SC members is often not flexible due to external issues limiting interorganisational operability requirements in a multiple-echelon SC. As the intricacy of interconnections among SC members grows, focus firms are finding it increasingly difficult to identify and trace product specifics without distortion. Increased when there are different stakeholders in a multi-echelon SC because unethical members are more likely to bring fraudulent charges. Now more than ever, it is critical for companies to find instances of SC code of ethics infractions (Nadia et al., 2020). Therefore, the degree of trust and information exchange among stakeholders determines the efficiency of SSCM. Notably, the immutable and irreversible nature of BT allows for fast information exchange among stakeholders in the multi-echelon SSCM, which in turn ensures traceability and reduces associated risks.

For future accountability issues involving non-compliance by SC members, focal enterprises may be able to acquire the necessary information with the help of appropriate IoT technologies. Also, the digitally distributed ledger cannot include any fraudulent or otherwise questionable transactions because blockchain relies on SC members' self-enforcing consensus to validate transactions. Also, SC members can settle their finances quickly and without the need for trusted middlemen due to blockchain, a scalable program developed for peer-to-peer networks. In order to reduce economic and reputational loss, the smart contract functionality in blockchain is crucial (Ponputtha et al., 2021). When applied as a whole, BT can facilitate the collection of data (such as certification, date, location, price, and quality) from SC partners, which in turn can improve SSCM for focus firms.

3. AI IN SSCM

A thorough examination of pertinent industry reports and case studies follows an initial survey of scholarly literature. In addition to offering concrete examples of their implementation in the actual world, this qualitative method also helps with comprehending the theoretical foundations of AI applications in SSCM. Afterwards, a survey of supply chain managers from different industries is included in the research. Using this quantitative approach (Sahraoui et al., 2023). Expert interviews complete the study technique by allowing us to glean nuanced insights and predictions about industry thought leaders' future trends. An all-encompassing investigation of the topic is guaranteed by this varied combination of approaches, which successfully connects theoretical ideas with real-world applications.

Figure 2. AI Elements of SSCM

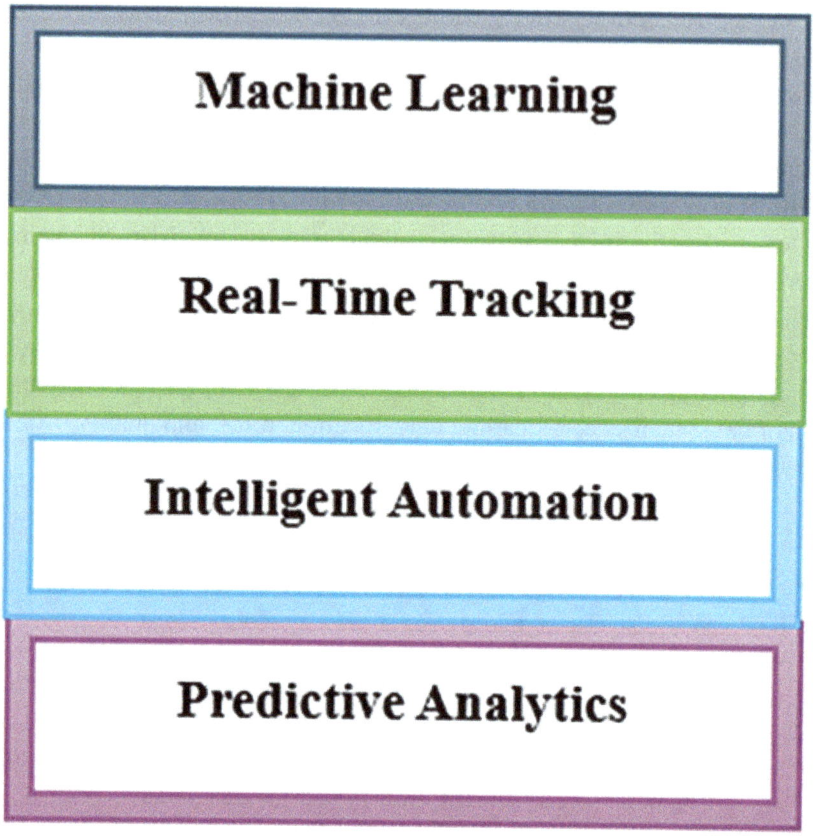

Figure 2 shows as these concrete examples support the theoretical claim that AI has the ability to completely alter SSCM by enhancing supply chain transparency, efficiency, and sustainability. Nevertheless, there are a number of challenges that organisations face when attempting to integrate AI. These include, but are not limited to, high starting costs, worries about data protection, and the requirement for tailored expertise (Taghipour et al., 2023a).

ML: ML a fundamental branch of AI offers a powerful resource for evaluating vendors according to sustainability criteria. By analysing historical data, ML algorithms can identify KPIs and compare vendors to them. As an example, Nike uses a ML algorithm to sort through potential suppliers according to a number of sustainability metrics; this promotes ethical sourcing and green practices all the way through the company's supply chain (Taghipour, 2020; Taghipour, 2024).

Real-Time Tracking: AI positive effects on supply chain transparency go much beyond optimisation alone. Stakeholders are empowered with information about the origin and management of products with AI-enabled real-time tracking systems. Using this technology, Starbucks is only one of many companies that can trace the origins of its coffee all the way to the customer's cup (Taghipour and Frayret, 2013a). By being so forthright, businesses are able to gain the trust of their customers and ensure that they are meeting their social and environmental obligations.

Intelligent Automation: The optimisation of shipping and manufacturing processes could lead to cost savings and lower carbon emissions, due to intelligent automation, another AI-enabled innovation. For example, the world-renowned transportation company DHL has integrated intelligent automation into its warehouse processes. One way DHL has reduced operational expenses and carbon footprint is by using AI-driven robots for packaging and sorting jobs (Taghipour and Lu, 2025a).

Predictive Analytics: Predictive analytics powered by AI has become an attractive tool to improve supply chain sustainability through increasing efficiency and decreasing waste. Predictive analytics generates precise predictions of future demand by leveraging past data and ML algorithms. Amazon and other well-known organizations have used predictive analytics to improve inventory management, reduce waste, and overstock (Merimi and Taghipour, 2021). To drill down even further, Amazon uses ML algorithms to forecast demand for certain product categories. According to this helps with inventory management, limits overproduction, and cuts down on waste, which is good for the environment and the economy (Taghipour and Lu, 2025b).

4. BDA IN SUSTAINABLE SCM

Logistics service providers, customers, and IT companies are all part of the supply chain, and SCM is the process of organising and directing the flow of raw materials from suppliers to manufacturers and finished goods from manufacturers to customers. It also involves managing relationships with all of these parties. The manufacturer takes front stage in MSC, particularly for large businesses, with upstream and downstream links. Raw material acquisition characterises upstream links, whereas product creation, engineering, and production are significant activities at the manufacturing site (Taghipour et al., 2023b). Distribution, consumption, and services, together with product disposal, are all considered downstream activities. Meeting the evolving needs of their customers is only one of the many issues that MSCs confront as they strive for sustainability across social, economic, and environmental dimensions. Better business decisions in the three aspects of sustainability can be achieved with the use of data analytics (Taghipour et al., 2023c).

Figure 3. Intelligent Data Acquisition Throughout a Manufacturing Supply Chain

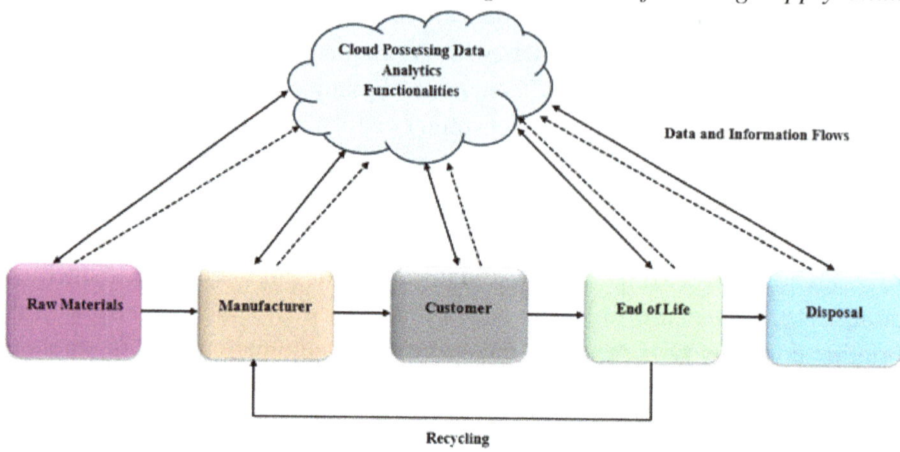

Figure 3 shows the possible uses of automated guided vehicles in manufacturing warehouses, including the picking and storage of items, the use of radio frequency identification tags, and the rapid purchase, fabrication, usage, and disposal of materials. After then, analytics are applied to the data, and the outcomes are instantly communicated to every participant in the supply chain so that decisions may be made with precision and speed. In other words, the smart factory will plan manufacturing according to retail demand data collected in real-time and orders placed by smart homes or consumers. The manufacturer can view the expected delivery date of the raw materials, and the supplier can automatically reflect the requirements. As soon as there is a problem somewhere in the supply chain, everyone knows about it and takes precautions to make sure nothing bad happens (Tliche et al., 2023).

Using big data gathered from all parties involved is one approach to building sustainable supply chains, according to previous studies. Therefore, it contend that smart devices and technologies are utilised by BDA to enable continuous data collecting and analysis, as well as to derive insights for improved decision making (Vosooghidizaji et al., 2020). Insights gained from this process can improve our understanding of the world and help businesses make better decisions, particularly with sustainability. Information is gathered from several points in the production supply chain, including raw materials in order to implement smart logistics, smart devices must be able to react to unexpected circumstances, such as rerouting to avoid traffic on the main route and save fuel. Hence, it is arguable that smart devices and technologies are utilised in BDA.

These enable continuous data collecting and analysis, as well as the drawing of insights for improved decision making. Rerouting to cut down on distance and fuel usage in the event of main route traffic is one example of how smart devices need to be able to react to unforeseen circumstances in smart logistics. For better visibility and inventory optimisation in manufacturing warehouses, autonomous guided vehicles can be utilised for picking and storing items (XiaoWen and Atour, 2025). Smart devices improve supply chain transparency and efficiency, which in turn promotes SSCM sustainability. This is particularly true when looking at the economic and environmental aspects, which both seek to maximise profits while minimising negative impacts on the environment. SCM operations can benefit from BDA technology' ability to automate processes, track productivity and performance, and reduce waste. With the use of BDA, servicing data may be better monitored, and insights into potential mishaps caused by machine failure can be provided (Zoghlami et al., 2016).

4.1 BDA and SSCM

The term supply chain refers to the intricate web of relationships that exists between producers, distributors, retailers, consumers, and service providers. Due to the interconnected nature of supply chains, it is challenging to keep tabs on everyone involved. Implementing a sustainability strategy complicates monitoring supply chain activities since not all vendors in the supply chain are transparent. As we showed in the last section, BDA can assist with planning for supply chains and visibility decisions by connecting different areas of the process and collecting and analysing data to gain new insights (Taghipour, 2021). Supply chain challenges including agility, resilience, sustainability, and risk management have been addressed using BDA. Previous research has looked at BDA and SSCM, albeit in a piecemeal fashion, studying BDA's capabilities and SSCM's aspects independently subject of an argument in which maintained that BDA bolsters social sustainability (Taghipour et al., 2022a).

The subjects covered included occupational health, safety and security as well as sourcing, are some of the SCM tasks that might benefit from BDA in order to find ways to save costs. Some areas that have used BDA to reduce costs and maximise efficiency include supplier selection and management and optimising warehouse space (Glaa et al., 2014). In order to accomplish the targeted economic efficiencies, BDA employs cutting-edge technologies like smart sensors, QR codes, barcodes, RFID tags, and the IOT (Taghipour et al., 2022b).Using BDA to link millions of customers directly, which is made feasible by real-time information exchange, and cut delivery time and energy consumption is another way to achieve environmental sustainability. In order to detect any kind of environmental misbehaviour, BDA also aids in keeping tabs on the actions of supply chain partners. In addition, by keeping an eye on the right metrics, BDA can help calculate the true environmental effect of individual economic activity. By mitigating risks in the supply chain that come with acquiring products and services, particularly from international markets, BDA can help supply chains attain social dimension sustainability (Taghipour et al., 2022c). It will be simpler to spot unethical actions that may harm the ties if BDA is implemented since it integrates supply chain operations, which promotes transparency and information exchange. The ethical behaviour of supply chain partners is another outcome of the cooperative and collaborative culture that BDA promotes. As a means of foreseeing potential societal issues in the future, BDA offers a framework for comparing historical environmental behaviour with current practices. Adopting BDA is likely to increase sustainability because it has shown beneficial across all three sustainability aspects (Lebosse et al., 2017).

4.2 BDA

Big data is defined as data assets with high volume, velocity, and variety, or the 5Vs. This means that both the volume and variety of data, as well as their sources, are fast expanding components of what is known as big dat. In addition, academics have maintained that it includes data storage, visualisation, and mining. Big data, according to the writers of complicated data sets that are created continuously and necessitate new forms of analytics. In comparison to more conventional datasets, large data necessitates more sophisticated software and database capabilities, as pointed out by (Loivet et al., 2020). Consequently, big data is linked to the rapid generation of diverse data sets from several sources and their rapid dissemination to various locations where decision-making requires the. It is important to handle and study the huge data mentioned so far in order to gain fresh insights for decision making. BDA refers to the practice of mining large datasets for meaningful links and patterns using sophisticated tools like ML and predictive models to help businesses make better decisions (Lu and Taghipour, 2025).

The analytics can be used to find ways to save money, gain a better grasp of what's happening in the supply chain, integrate data from all parties involved, and maybe even gain a competitive edge. To tackle the structured and unstructured data produced in a big data setting, BDA necessitates more sophisticated tools, more efficiency, and cutting-edge data management solutions. By leveraging cutting-edge technology, BDA provides a range of benefits, including real-time analysis of consumer actions on online marketplaces to aid in decision-making, the ability to process both organised and unstructured data, and the empowerment of enterprises to acquire global competitiveness through cost reduction. The establishment of objectives, goals, and policies that are in line with SSCM procedures is typically included in the activities that make up BDA (Mahfod et al., 2019). Aside from that, there are tasks like data collecting, administration, storage, processing, and analytics application. Stakeholders should be made aware of the results through visualisation, reporting, sharing, and publishing following analysis. Levels of descriptive, prescriptive, and predictive analytics are all under the purview of big data. One example of an optimisation that prescriptive analytics can suggest is transportation route optimisation. Manufacturing, transportation, logistics, sustainability, and purchasing are some of the areas that might benefit from categorisation algorithms applied through predictive analytics. The algorithms are useful for determining if a certain action or procedure is environmentally friendly. As a decision-support tool, descriptive analytics apply association algorithms to examine supply chain item-to-item linkages (Taghipour et al., 2015).

5. INTEGRATION OF BLOCKCHAIN, AI AND BIG DATA FOR SUSTAINABLE SCM

Supply chain operations can be made more agile and flexible by integrating IoT and AI with BT. Although both technologies have their uses in various industries, only a small number of companies have integrated BT with both of them. The next parts go over the information flow and integration of the blockchain network with IoT and AI (Mahfod at al., 2021).

5.1 Blockchain and AI

The merging of blockchain and AI improves decision-making by analysing massive amounts of data in the supply chain. Due to the enormous number of factors that might influence AI decisions, they may outperform human decisions (Taghipour and Lu, 2023). Quantity of data. Researchers in certain sectors are working on solutions that might radically alter data storage and analysis methods, particularly in the context of supply chains and production sector. For management purposes, IBM has joined the AI-blockchain space with suite for supply chains. The bulk of deep learning techniques and ML implementations of AI requires a centralised model for training where a cluster of servers executes a specific model (El-Nemr et al., 2017). in comparison to datasets used for training and validation. Having access to the same perspective of an open, reliable, and protected system for storing and exchanging documents, data, analytics, and transactions Assists supply chain in making calculated decisions across all operational aspects through the integration of AI. along with BT which improves data security, all manufacturers stand to benefit. The integration of BT with AI platforms allows for the identification of data patterns and predictive analysis (Evangelos Christou and Kostas Alexandris, 2018).

This includes the ability to forecast future demand, gather information from point-of-sale systems, review past purchases, forecast sales patterns, anticipate potential problems, optimise routes to reach the destination, and manage network traffic throughout the supply chain. Additionally, it aids with demand forecasting and inventory management data by providing an alert regarding stock clearance. By reviewing all the data processed by each member of the supply chain on the blockchain server, it can help inform when to order the fresh stock. Blockchain is crucial in the supply chain's financial sector as all parties involved process and store their transactions on the blockchain server (Radhoui et al., 2021). ML algorithms linked to AI help manufacturers reduce supply chain latency for components and parts used in their highly customised product. With the use of AI's data analysis algorithm, the company's financial performance can be monitored by all stakeholders in the supply chain, and operations can be efficiently managed (Gao et al., 2018).

Smart data-driven decisions allow all supply-chain participants and stakeholders to make accurate decisions in real-time. Reframing the supply chain is possible through the automation of the entire process and the discovery of new revenue sources made possible are able to enhance their operations. Integration of BT and AI algorithms streamlines operations and saves time for the organization's supply chain managers. By using the current input state to execute various logic and rule-based algorithms, planning methods assist AI applications and systems achieve predefined goals, which in turn improves operational efficiency and resilience (Taghipour, 2023). The banking industry is another potential user of this blockchain-AI integration for data storage and analysis, loan approval decisions, cash flow management, and customer withdrawal limits based on AI-generated historical data and transactions.

5.2 Blockchain and IOT

IoT is defined as the network of interconnected physical devices, services, and applications that receive data from a server and transmit it to a remote location via the Internet so that an administrator may access the data from any location at any time. In terms of IoT and blockchain connectivity, the digital supply chain (DSC) reigns supreme. Integrating or transferring specialist data across different businesses and systems is critical for the DSC, requiring partners to collaborate dynamically. RFID tags, GPS tags, sensors, bar codes, and chips can be integrated into an IoT system to continuously track the location of products, containers, and packages.

This allows for more accurate, real-time tracking of goods from their point of origin (Lu and Taghipour, 2025).

Using the data, decision analytics is carried out. Since it is real-time data, it aids in making honest and accurate decisions regarding what to do next. Supply chain efficiency and productivity are enhanced by real-time data made available through Internet-based media. Because everyone in the supply chain has access to real-time data through blockchain and IoT integration, trust grows among all parties involved (Tliche et al., 2019). The status of the goods and its estimated delivery time can be monitored by all parties involved in the supply chain. Inventory, demand, financial, and operational management are all improved as a result of this connection for each company in the chain. Each link in the chain is able to better manage their operations due to this logistics provider's access. With the use of RFID tags, the distributor can keep tabs on every item in the massive warehouse—the biggest benefit of blockchain-IOT integration (Vosooghidizaji et al., 2019).

As a result, everyone's faith in the warehouse's ability to protect their belongings grows. By allowing consumers to directly transmit product feedback to manufacturers using cell phones, businesses are able to provide more effective customer care. According to the use of IoT services in contemporary corporate processes raises trust concerns due to these IoT features. Issues with disjointed data sources can also be better addressed by combining BT with the IOT. Despite being susceptible to 51% of attacks on linked servers, BT offers robust security for data and devices in the IOT, as well as predictive analytics and legal contracts. Supply chain members can save a significant amount of money by reducing the number of workers needed for traditional SCM and integrating BT with the IOT. Because sensors installed on machinery can execute quality assurance and maintenance tasks quickly and data is sent in real-time through IoT to a blockchain server, manufacturers can reduce the manpower of these teams. The designated supervisor can monitor production in real-time via the server and adjust settings according to reports and data stored on the blockchain (Aouadni et al., 2024).

Companies can benefit from blockchain-IoT by improving their KPI system in real-time, which is visible to all stakeholders. Good KPIs are essential for increasing process efficiency. Products and goods can be traced using RFID and barcodes, which aid in inventory management. Data is transmitted from RFID tags to RFID readers that are linked to the Internet. With the help of the tracking gadget, transportation products can be monitored in real-time as they move through the supply chain. All aspects of production are managed by computerised systems, including equipment maintenance, production efficiency, logistics service provider notices, and RFS scanning (Gharye Mirzaei et al., 2025). A crucial application of sensors with ML is the identification of product damage. The supervisor in charge of that task and the necessary configurations is responsible for uploading the data to the blockchain server. Supply chain applications of blockchain and IoT include:

- Real-time product data for all stakeholders
- Monitoring of product stages.
- Enhanced transparency in procurement.
- Dependable data analytics for informed decision-making.
- Enhancement of operational and financial performance across all stakeholders in the supply chain.
- Detection of product damage.

Due to its many benefits, including real-time data, efficient operations, protected storage of data on a real-time basis, etc., blockchain and IoT integration has the potential to be the new revolution in the manufacturing supply chain. Planning and controlling production, providing real-time data on raw materials and equipment in the supply chain, maintaining machinery, ensuring quality, managing inventories of finished items, etc. are some of the main processes that can benefit from integrating blockchain and IoT. Because of the regular availability of real-time data, this integration can aid with efficient resource utilisation (Goodarzian et al., 2026).

6. CURRENT PRACTICES FOR TECHNOLOGY IMPLEMENTATION

An investment in the optimisation of an organisation, especially one with a focus on the long term, can be made through the successful deployment and utilisation of technology.

Figure 4. Technologies Currently Employed in SSCM

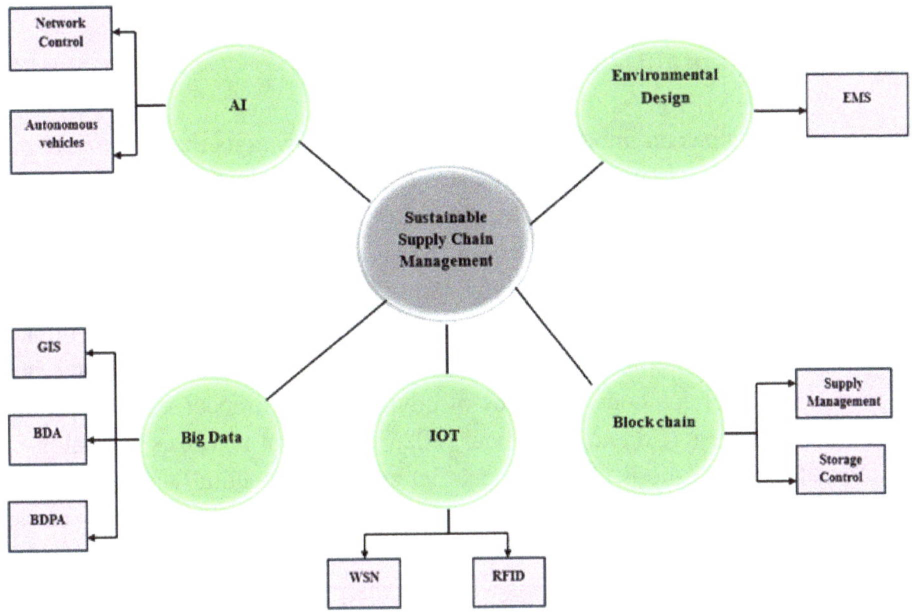

Figure 4 shown as the success rate of sustainability practices can be greatly affected by the technology chosen, which in turn is affected by knowledge of innovation and the supply chain. These are a few instances of present processes, but there is room for innovation in every chain from sourcing to logistics.

6.1 AI

Improving SCM sustainability has been a challenge, but new techniques and ideas are emerging that can help. One such technology is AI which is said to be future tech even though it has altered business practices considerably already. In decision-making scenarios where appropriate or efficient methods are prohibitively costly or excessively complex to implement, AI denotes the utilisation of computers for reasoning, pattern recognition, learning, or the analysis of behaviours derived from experience, data accumulation and retention, and the generation of various forms of inference (Lu et al., 2023). The transportation sector, being the primary contributor to environmental degradation and possessing significant potential for sustainability enhancement, is where AI is predominantly applied in the Supply Chain. Autonomous vehicles, including cars and trucks, represent a novel use of AI in logistics, with the potential to enhance safety by eliminating the necessity for human operators. Network management is experiencing enhancements due to AI;

enterprises can now categorise and administer routes more effectively, tasks that were previously unmanageable without this technology.

6.2 Environmental Design

Every product has an impact on the environment during its manufacturing process. Some examples of these consequences include water and air pollution, ozone depletion, and climate change. After making the switch to sustainability, a number of adjustments will be required to lessen the aforementioned production impacts. Yet another development in eco-friendly supply design for the environment (DfE) is a tool that supply chain managers use to eradicate harmful environmental impacts consequences of the items. Design for Ecological Excellence (DfE) is a methodology that incorporates considerations of environmental impact into the product development process (Lu and Taghipour, 2023). The goal is to use technology to create production methods and products that are environmentally sustainable, all while keeping the price/performance aspects of the output beneficial. Businesses employ DfE methods to get a competitive edge, boost innovation, and reduce prices all at the same time. Making products with less energy and packaging that use more sustainable components is one way the DfE method might work.

6.3 Predictive Analytics and Big Data in SSCM

The aforementioned methods and technology can significantly improve data collection and storage at various stages of the supply chain. In 2016, AT&T and eft performed study titled IOT in Supply Chain and Logistics. However, supply chain efficiency can be significantly increased by accessing data from several sources, allowing for prediction and forecasting in addition to acquisition. Businesses in a variety of sectors use BDPA strategies to improve organisational and competitive efficiency, which has a significant impact on the bottom line. When it comes to managing data-intensive systems that can be significantly improved by product usage, BDPA has proven crucial for supply chain operations control. Financial, social, and environmental sustainability are the three pillars upon which the triple bottom line rests, and BDPA has clear beneficial impacts on all three. For instance, by implementing BDA, businesses can assess their internal environment as it stands and develop strategies to enhance it even more. It echoed this sentiment, highlighting how BDAD can aid in measuring and improving environmental impact trends (Taghipour, 2020). Geographical information systems are another tool for planning and forecasting that makes use of big data. A geographic information system (GIS) is defined as a network of computers, databases, and other resources that work together to collect, store, retrieve, analyse, and display geographical information.

Forecasting and decision-making for sustainable product logistics are aided by it, since it provides the most efficient and quickest paths between the various SCM participants. Since shorter routes drastically save the resources required on product delivery, they inevitably bring about financial and environmental sustainability.

6.4 Blockchain

The digitalised world is seeing a surge in interest and investment in blockchain technologies as they are used to various businesses. This is a network of devices that manages, verifies, and shares a repository for transaction logs. In blockchain, a large community administers the data instead of a single entity like a corporation; as a result, no single user can modify or remove a batch of purchases. Along the path to SSCM it offers numerous benefits. The use of BT has the potential to increase sustainability by reducing negative impacts on the environment, increasing protections for human rights, and creating more equitable working conditions. There are a lot of chances to enhance SSCM practices with blockchain technologies. To begin with, it makes the process more open and easier to understand (Mathiyazhagan et al., 2022).

By recording the names and addresses of all parties involved, the total value of the goods exchanged, the time and location of the transaction, and the price, registering the sale of goods on a blockchain database can help promote responsibility. Additionally, BT aids businesses in guaranteeing the correction of mistakes and the early identification of issues in the procedure. Documenting, overseeing, and verifying the information, connecting, and renewing it is able to completed all at once using state-of-the-art technology. What this means is that swiftly lessen the occurrence of human errors, leading to cost savings as well as the lengthy delays that endanger purchases throughout today's inventory linkages. An example of a typical blockchain application the supply chain is making storage more environmentally friendly of goods on offer. It goes over the storage conditions and reached before to the event, which comprises heat and other parameters (Pour Mohammadi et al., 2014). On one side, you have the legal obligation to meet all contract requirements, which are managed by designated sensors. The BT allows for the recording and tracking of conditions; alarms have the capability to alert the relevant parties in the event of a violation of the agreement.

In terms of society, it will both be a net positive of long-term viability through fostering mutual confidence and aids in the early detection of problems and bottlenecks and reduce the potential costs. In addition to identifying mistakes at an early stage, BT also aids in the detection of fake goods. Because everyone as the data has been recorded and cannot be altered, businesses are able to utilise technological means to assist clients in differentiating their goods on items that are not authentic. Additional IoT technologies come into play here barcodes and similar technologies are also used, together with a dedicated application, people can look up their purchases by scanning the barcode. This is a request via the coordinated network of software, blockchain, and the IOT propels businesses towards long-term financial viability by reducing the possibility of having sales eroded due to fake goods. It has execution piques the interest of multiple sectors, within the medical field in particular (Radhoui et al., 2019).

The data released by the US According to Health & Drug Benefits, the yearly decline in businesses operating in the pharmaceutical sector is determined around 75 billion, which can be drastically cut down by technology based on blockchain. The last step is to enhance their ethical practices, maintain a positive image, and adhere in accordance with the needs of clients, monitoring the progress of circumstances of the vendors is a crucial subject for business enterprises. With the introduction of BT businesses are able to provide a decent work environment safeguards employees against mistreatment, maintains a healthy, secure, and fairly compensated work environment justice, and advancing the right to freely associate through reviewing the vendors' data records (Ren et al., 2016).

6.5 IoT in Supply Chain

The incorporation of IoT technologies is a prime illustration of how technology is being applied to business operations in today's environment, where the internet and technological advancements play an important role in company operations. Modern SCM owes a great deal to the development of sensor-based technologies and communication tools, such as wireless sensor networks and simple RFID based tagging for product recognition. Data gathering and administration made possible by the IoT network architecture allows for the tracking of product location, price, and delivery time. By allowing the tracking of the entire process, IoT also allows to take beneficial actions to the probable bottlenecks and maximise efficiency. The RFID tag was one of the first IoT supply chain applications. RFID tags surpass the shortcomings of barcodes, a prevalent ADC method, by providing line-of-sight free tracking, more unique IDs, and increased memory capacity. RFID tags greatly contribute to the sustainability of SCM by retaining data on shipments and sorting procedures (Taghipour, 2024).

Among the many MNCs that have embraced RFID technology, the American retail behemoth Wal-Mart stands out as having implemented the system with remarkable success. As a result of its successful implementation of RFID technologies, it was able to reduce administrative expenses, increase service quality, decrease surplus inventory, eliminate out-of-stocks and the bullwhip effect, and minimise human orders. There are a number of ways in which RFID technology helps SSCM.

The first benefit of RFID sensors is their ability to track energy consumption and emission rates per material unit. An important factor in SSCM is the ability to monitor suppliers' energy efficiency, production emissions, and overall emission rates. It also aids in the companies' reverse logistics, which is a way to attain SSCM (Taghipour, 2022).

WSN are an element of the IoT that contributes to sustainable supply chain operations, much like RFID tags. In addition to possessing very effective analytical features including data gathering and signal recording. When it comes to consumption, scale, expenditures, mobility, and flexibility, there are a lot of benefits to implementing WSN into SCM processes (Taghipour & Lu, 2023). The primary function of WSN sensors is monitoring and tracking; these sensors allow one to trace the whole path of goods as they move through the supply chain by following shipping tools such as pallets, crates, and containers. By installing these sensors, manufacturers may monitor their suppliers' adherence to agreed-upon environmental requirements, such as the use of the most environmentally friendly mode of transportation, and learn more about the origins of their raw materials (Taghipour, 2009).

7. ADVANTAGES

Besides the obvious monetary and ecological benefits, it also found five societal upsides. In our sample, the improvement of partnerships across supply chains was common, occurring at a rate of 68%. Platforms facilitate this by connecting vendors with buyers and other vendors. When looking at it from an economic perspective, a platform can assist improve the lives of small farmers and all stakeholders by 8%. BT facilitates better partnerships among a large number of actors located in different regions. Specifically, blockchain's capabilities are emphasised in relation to fairness (20%). According to BT ensures supply chain fairness by securely storing and processing documents and transactions. Wages, for instance, are immutable. Found that corruption can be averted. Reducing disparities in access to high-quality information (such as food-related data) is consistent with principles of equity. Consequently, this has the potential to boost the local economy. Customers are increasingly purchasing goods directly from farmers in today's world, driven by a strong emphasis on sustainability. Furthermore, farmers are safeguarded from excessive regulation. It is possible to track each step of the supply chain (Taghipour et al., 2023).

This eliminates the need for internal or external inspections and creates trust in the supply chain. Furthermore, consumers can learn more about the smallholder through the option to access this information which enhances customer trust. According to RFID data collection provides a solid foundation for building confidence in the supply chain. In every article that is pertinent, the word trust is used multiple times. Finally, digital technologies can improve working conditions (20%) and lay the groundwork for staff education (20%). Workers (like farmers, for example) can be better prepared for the future by using RFID-generated and blockchain-stored historical data. The IoT could potentially aid workers in product detection. As a result, workers have an easier time doing their jobs and make less mistakes. Process optimisation using big data technologies can boost customer happiness and make workplaces better for everyone.

8. RESULT AND DISCUSSION

By efficiently learning complicated, non-linear patterns, BPNN (96.74%) models show remarkable accuracy in predicting outcomes across multiple domains. Models that achieve low error and good generalisation are usually the ones that get talked about when these results are discussed. On the other hand, problems like the model getting stuck in local optima during training and the need for significant data to avoid overfitting are usually brought up. Financial accounting, water demand forecasting, and user behaviour prediction are just a few areas where research has demonstrated that hybrid techniques combining BPNN with optimisation algorithms can increase performance and address its shortcomings.

The suggested hybrid BPNN model routinely outperforms earlier work on the dataset in term of predictive accuracy, showing improved speed and remarkable problem identification and diagnosis capabilities shown as Figure 5.

Figure 5. Training and Testing Accuracy of BPNN Model

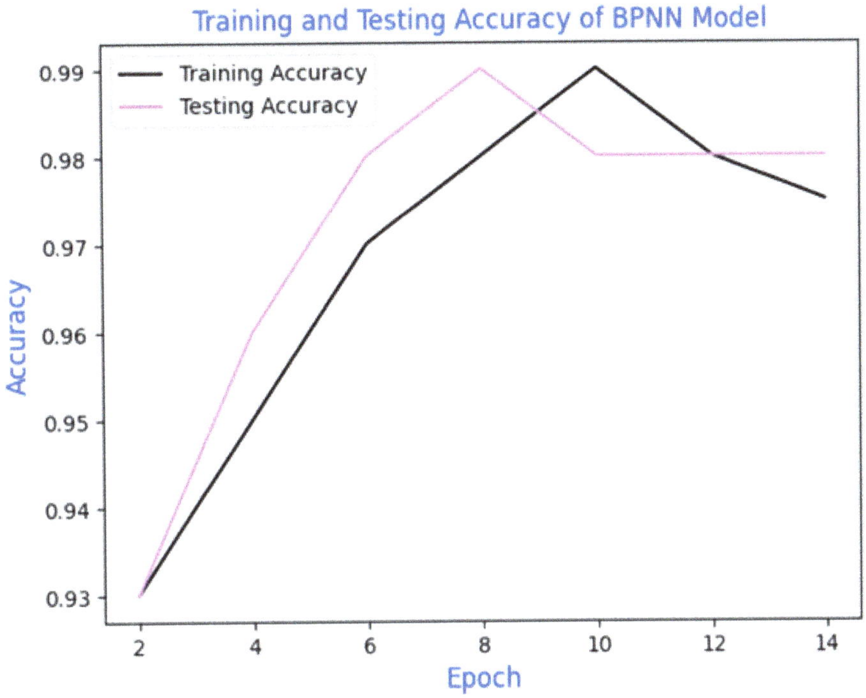

Training loss as a function of period size is illustrated in Figure 6. The performance graph of the training BPNN model subsets. In our scenario, the network is well-trained as the loss function reduces for training datasets.

Figure 6. Training and Testing Loss of BPNN Model

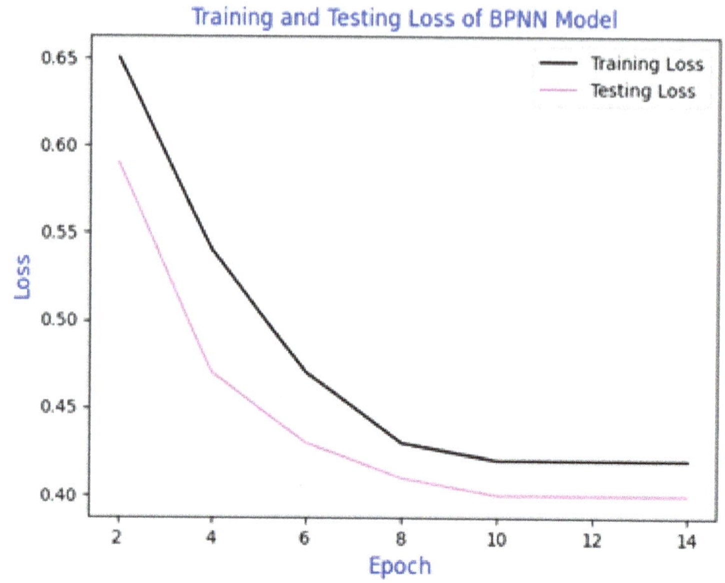

All of the model's performance analysis is results are displayed in Table 1 Our BPNN works great. Compared with alternative models LSTM, Adaboost, LR, AE, LightGBM.

Table 1. Performance Analysis

Models	Methods			
	Precision	Recall	F1-Score	Accuracy
LSTM	82.61	83.92	84.62	84.56
Adaboost	85.46	86.70	89.53	89.44
LR	87.02	88.29	90.82	90.70
AE	90.38	91.48	93.90	93.87
LightGBM	93.77	94.89	95.60	95.40
BPNN	**94.30**	**95.82**	**96.82**	**96.74**

It offers a binary classification BPNN network as a solution to this problem it can anticipate system failure in the future mission and give the failure probability. Then, while on break figure out what kind of maintenance will keep the system running well by considering the likelihood of each part of system shown in figure 7.

Figure 7. Confusion Matrix of BPNN Model

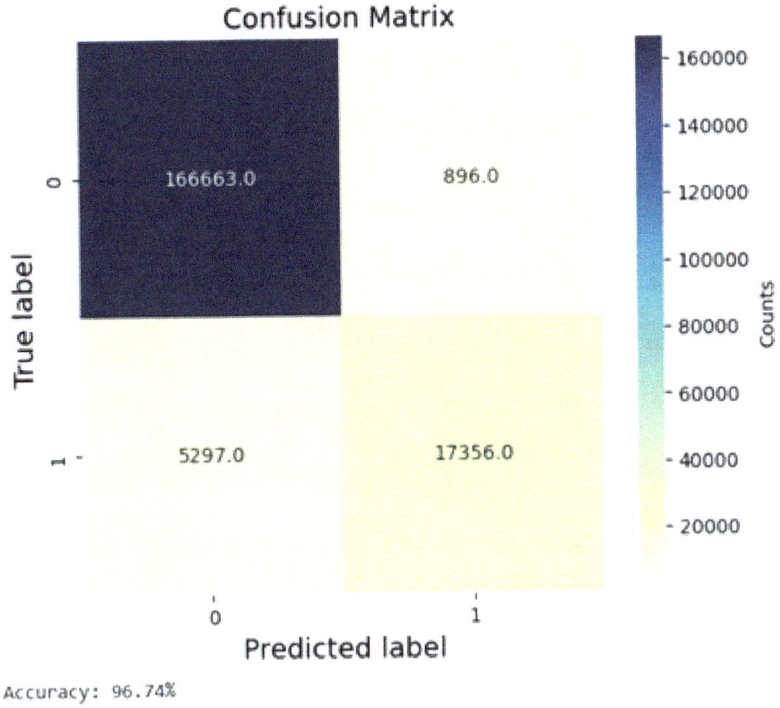

The results show that hybrid research BPNN model outperforms all other approaches. It outperforms the other approaches in terms of fitting degree and error levels shown in figure 8.

Figure 8. Performance Comparison

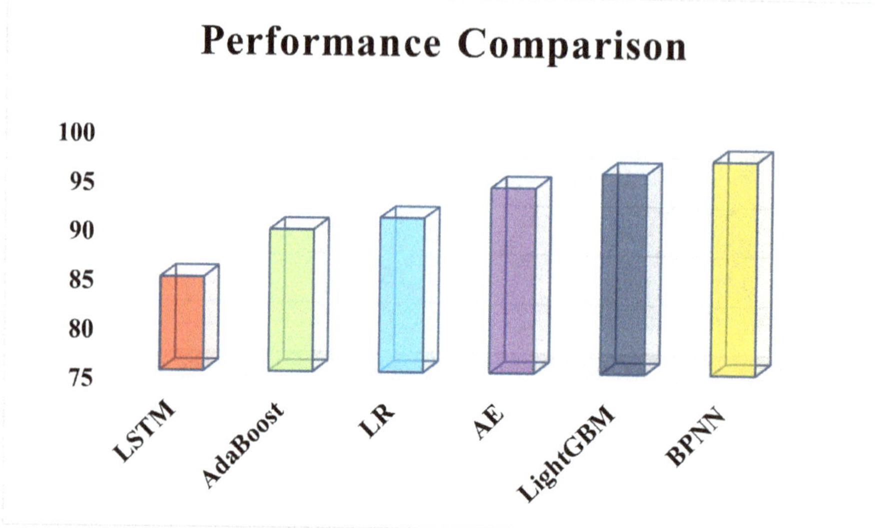

9. CONCLUSION

While the potential for AI in SSCM is significant, as evidenced by real-world examples and academic research, the path to full integration is plagued with hurdles. High early investment costs, data privacy concerns, and expertise shortages pose substantial challenges. Proactive strategies, such as investing in staff training, implementing strong data governance policies, and cultivating an innovative culture, can help to effectively manage these challenges. The case studies of Amazon, DHL, Starbucks, and Nike highlight AI's transformative power in supply chain management while also giving useful insights into the practical challenges of AI application. They highlight the different ways that businesses are attempting to use the potential of AI while overcoming the associated constraints. Furthermore, as it moves closer to a future in which AI integration in SSCM becomes more prevalent, the ethical considerations that arise demand a thorough strategy. Balancing technological innovation and ethical responsibility is critical along this approach (Mathiyazhagan et al., 2022).

Future research directions, including studying the broader socioeconomic impact, applying interdisciplinary methodologies, better understanding the role of AI in SSCC can be achieved by the conduct of longitudinal and comparative studies. To sum up, SSCM's AI integration does come with its fair share of unique challenges, but those challenges can be strategically navigated in order to unlock the enormous possible advantages. AI has the ability to significantly improve SSCM by making it more open, efficient, and environmentally friendly. surpasses these obstacles. For companies, it's a chance to improve sustainability while simultaneously streamlining operations. imperative in a society that is becoming more conscientious of its social and environmental duties. When combined, BT, AI and big data have the potential to revolutionise SSCM. In order for organisations to stay ahead of the competition while still meeting global sustainability norms, these technologies boost accountability, efficiency, and transparency. To achieve long-term sustainability in supply chain operations, integrated technical solutions will become more important as digital innovation evolves further.

REFERENCES

Alizadeh, N., Taghipour, A., & Canel-Depître, B. (2021). Which one collective strategy is appropriate for the business ecosystem? The role of political environment.

Aouadni, S., Aouadni, I., & Taghipour, A. (2024). Using ordinal priority approach with confidence-level measurement for third-party logistics provider selection in the tunisian healthcare sector. In *Applications of new technology in operations and supply chain management* (pp. 404–429). IGI Global Scientific Publishing. DOI: 10.4018/979-8-3693-1578-1.ch020

Cauchois, R., Taghipour, A., Kang, D., Zoghlami, N., & Abed, M. (2017). Advanced solutions for a supply chain with stochastic information. *Journal of Advanced Management Science*, *5*(1), 9–13. DOI: 10.18178/joams.5.1.9-13

Christou, E. Kostas Alexandris, & A. F. (2018). TOURMAN 2018 Conference Proceedings.

Demir, S. B. (2018). Predatory journals: Who publishes in them and why? *Journal of Informetrics*, *12*(4), 1296–1311. DOI: 10.1016/j.joi.2018.10.008

El-Nemr, N., Canel-Depitre, B., & Taghipour, A. (2017, September). Determinants of hotel room rates. In Marketing Trends Congress. Luxury Industries Conference London 2017.

Gao, Y., Li, Z., & Kang, D. S. (2018). Supply chain coordination: A review. *Journal of Advanced Management Science*, *6*(4), 213–217. DOI: 10.18178/joams.6.4.213-217

Gharye Mirzaei, M., Goodarzian, F., Taghipour, A., & Muñuzuri, J. (2025). Sustainable closed-loop supply chain network under uncertainty considering green technologies: Toward the circular economy. *The Journal of the Operational Research Society*, •••, 1–21.

Glaa, B., Zoghlami, N., & Taghipour, A. (2014, May). Outsourcing and off-shoring healthcare services: A way to cut the costs and improve quality. In 2014 international conference on advanced logistics and transport (ICALT) (pp. 189-194). IEEE.

Goodarzian, F., Abraham, A., Muñuzuri, J., Taghipour, A., & Ghasemi, P. (2026). A Benders decomposition approach for a new sustainable pharmaceutical supply chain network: A case study in France. *Annals of Operations Research*, *356*(2), 881–919. DOI: 10.1007/s10479-024-05936-3

Lebosse, S., Taghipour, A., & Canel-Depitre, B. (2017). Quick response to fluctuations in supply chains: A review. *Journal of Advanced Management Science*, *5*(5), 394–400. DOI: 10.18178/joams.5.5.394-400

Loivet, W., Taghipour, A., & Kang, D. S. (2020). The rise of green supply chain management: Between complexity and necessity. Journal of Economics. *Business and Management*, *8*(1), 1–7.

Lu, X., & Taghipour, A. (2025). The Future of Marketing: Integrating Big Data and AI for Personalized Customer Engagement. In Ecological and Human Dimensions of AI-Based Supply Chain (pp. 97-110). IGI Global Scientific Publishing.

Mahfod, J., Canel-Depitre, B., & Taghipour, A. (2019). Quality function deployment-ELECTRE in supplier evaluation. Journal of advanced management science, 7(4).

Mahfod, J., Khoury, B., Canel-Depitre, B., & Taghipour, A. (2021). Logistics Providers in Syria Humanitarian Operations. In Demand Forecasting and Order Planning in Supply Chains and Humanitarian Logistics (pp. 171-197). IGI Global. DOI: 10.4018/978-1-7998-3805-0.ch006

Mathiyazhagan, K., Taghipour, A., & Agarwal, V. (Eds.). (2022). Blockchain technology in supply chain management for society 5.0. CRC Press. Lu, X., & Taghipour, A. (2023). A French Guide for Businesses and Governments to Integrate the Concept of Sustainable Development Into Their Supply Chains. In Government Impact on Sustainable and Responsible Supply Chain Management (pp. 1-12). IGI Global Scientific Publishing. Lu, X. W., Tliche, Y., Vosooghidizaji, M., & Taghipour, A. (2023). Cryptocurrencies and Blockchain Applications. In Blockchain Applications in Cryptocurrency for Technological Evolution (pp. 1-13). IGI Global Scientific Publishing.

Mbiatem, J., Taghipour, A., & Canel-Depitre, B. (2018, August). Supplier selection approaches for decision makers. In *Proceedings of the 8th International Conference on Information Communication and Management* (pp. 108-112).

Merimi, M., & Taghipour, A. (2021). Accelerating the digitalization of the supply chain: An empirical research about COVID-19 crisis. In *Digitalization of decentralized supply chains during global crises* (pp. 1–24). IGI Global Scientific Publishing. DOI: 10.4018/978-1-7998-6874-3.ch001

Nadia, E. N., Beatrice, C. D., & Atour, T. (2020). Luxury hotels' eco-friendly activities & customers' preferences and willingness to pay for green hotels. *Journal of Advanced Management Science*, *8*(1), 1–24.

Ponputtha, W., Wannapiroon, P., & Nilsook, P. (2021). Creative history learning model using digital storytelling through cloud learning. International Journal of E-Education, e-Business, e-. *Management Learning, 11*(2), 42–50. DOI: 10.17706/ijeeee.2021.11.2.42-50

Pour Mohammadi, M., Ghorbani, R., & Taghipour, A. (2014). Factors affecting the price of housing in the city of Tabriz using hedonic model. *Geographical Planning of Space Quarterly Journal, 3*(9), 83–104.

Radhoui, H., Taghipour, A., & Canel-Depitre, B. (2019). The distribution and pickup of goods: A literature review and survey. Hierarchical Planning and Information Sharing Techniques in Supply Chain Management, 46-85.

Radhoui, H., Taghipour, A., & Canel-Depitre, B. (2021). Mixed delivery and pickup vehicle routing problem with limited flow and assignment of drones in an urban network. Demand Forecasting and Order Planning in Supply Chains and Humanitarian Logistics, 225-249.

Ren, Z., Taghipour, A., & Canel-Depitre, B. (2016, October). Information sharing in supply chain under uncertainty. In 2016 6th International Conference on Information Communication and Management (ICICM) (pp. 67-71). IEEE. DOI: 10.1109/INFOCOMAN.2016.7784217

Sahraoui, A., Tran, N. K., Tliche, Y., Kacem, A., & Taghipour, A. (2023). Examining ICT innovation for sustainable terminal operations in developing countries: A case study of the port of Radès in Tunisia. *Sustainability (Basel), 15*(11), 9123. DOI: 10.3390/su15119123

Taghipour, A. (2009). Evaluation de la collaboration dans une chaîne d'approvisionnement. Revue française de gestion industrielle, 28(1), 26-42.

Taghipour, A. (Ed.). (2020). *Demand forecasting and order planning in supply chains and humanitarian logistics*. IGI Global.

Taghipour, A. (Ed.). (2022). *Blockchain Applications in Cryptocurrency for Technological Evolution*. IGI Global. DOI: 10.4018/978-1-6684-6247-8

Taghipour, A. (Ed.). (2023). *Government Impact on Sustainable and Responsible Supply Chain Management*. IGI Global. DOI: 10.4018/978-1-6684-9062-4

Taghipour, A. (2024). Big Data: The New Gold Mine for Supermarkets. In Applications of New Technology in Operations and Supply Chain Management (pp. 98-106). IGI Global Scientific Publishing.

Taghipour, A., Abed, M., & Zoghlami, N. (2015, May). Design for remanufacturing respecting reverse logistics processes: A review. In 2015 4th international conference on advanced logistics and transport (ICALT) (pp. 299-304). IEEE. DOI: 10.1109/ICAdLT.2015.7136602

Taghipour, A., Belrhazi, Y., & Damoum, N. (2023c). Resilient sustainable supply chain management. In *Government Impact on Sustainable and Responsible Supply Chain Management* (pp. 33–47). IGI Global Scientific Publishing. DOI: 10.4018/978-1-6684-9062-4.ch003

Taghipour, A., & Beneteau-Piet, C. (2020). Sustainable supply chain management performance. *International Journal of Innovation, Management and Technology*, *11*(6), 165–169. DOI: 10.18178/ijimt.2020.11.6.897

Taghipour, A., Fooladvand, A., Khazaei, M., & Ramezani, M. (2023a). Criteria clustering and supplier segmentation based on sustainable shared value using BWM and PROMETHEE. *Sustainability (Basel)*, *15*(11), 8670. DOI: 10.3390/su15118670

Taghipour, A., & Frayret, J. M. (2013a, May). An algorithm to improve operations planning in decentralized supply chains. In *2013 International Conference on Advanced Logistics and Transport* (pp. 100-103). IEEE. DOI: 10.1109/ICAdLT.2013.6568442

Taghipour, A., & Frayret, J. M. (2013b). Coordination of operations planning in supply chains: A review. *International Journal of Business Performance and Supply Chain Modelling*, *5*(3), 272–307. DOI: 10.1504/IJBPSCM.2013.055729

Taghipour, A., & Lu, X. (2025a). Advancing Supply Chain Innovation: Theoretical Foundations, Contemporary Developments, and Future Directions. In Ecological and Human Dimensions of AI-Based Supply Chain (pp. 1-26). IGI Global Scientific Publishing.

Taghipour, A., & Lu, X. (2025b). Navigating the artificial intelligence era: impacts of artificial intelligence on youth critical thinking, career paths, and ethical challenges. In *Ecological and Human Dimensions of AI-Based Supply Chain* (pp. 49–68). IGI Global Scientific Publishing. DOI: 10.4018/979-8-3693-7478-8.ch003

Taghipour, A., Lu, X., Derradji, M., & Sow, A. D. (2022c, July). The impact of digitalization on supply chain management: a literature review. In *Proceedings of the 12th International Conference on Information Communication and Management* (pp. 75-78). DOI: 10.1145/3551690.3551702

Taghipour, A., Lu, X., & Smahi, M. (2022b). Opportunities and challenges for society 5.0 in procurement. *Blockchain Technology in Supply Chain Management for Society*, *5*(0), 91–100. DOI: 10.1201/9781003177432-9

Taghipour, A., & Lu, X. W. (2023, August). Green Supply Chain Management: A Guide. In International Conference on Applied Economics and Business (pp. 315-328). Cham: Springer Nature Switzerland.

Taghipour, A., Rouyendegh, B. D., Ünal, A., & Piya, S. (2022a). Selection of suppliers for speech recognition products in IT projects by combining techniques with an integrated fuzzy MCDM. *Sustainability (Basel), 14*(3), 1777. DOI: 10.3390/su14031777

Taghipour, A., Sohrabi, A., Ghaedi, M., & Khazaei, M. (2023b). A robust vaccine supply chain model in pandemics: Case of Covid-19 in Iran. *Computers & Industrial Engineering, 183*, 109465. DOI: 10.1016/j.cie.2023.109465

Tliche, Y., Taghipour, A., & Canel-Depitre, B. (2019). Downstream Demand Inference in decentralized supply chains. *European Journal of Operational Research, 274*(1), 65–77. DOI: 10.1016/j.ejor.2018.09.034

Tliche, Y., Taghipour, A., Mahfod-Leroux, J., & Vosooghidizaji, M. (2023). Collaborative bullwhip effect-oriented bi-objective optimization for inference-based weighted moving average forecasting in decentralized supply chain. [IJISSCM]. *International Journal of Information Systems and Supply Chain Management, 16*(1), 1–37. DOI: 10.4018/IJISSCM.316168

Vosooghidizaji, M., Taghipour, A., & Canel-Depitre, B. (2019). A literature review on information asymmetry in supply chain coordination. *International Journal of Production Research, 58*(6), 1–6.

Vosooghidizaji, M., Taghipour, A., & Canel-Depitre, B. (2020). Information asymmetry in supply chain coordination: State of the art. *Journal of Industrial and Intelligent Information, 8*(2), 38–43. DOI: 10.18178/jiii.8.2.38-43

XiaoWen, L., & Atour, T.XiaoWen. (2025). Knowledge-driven digital innovation in supply chains: An organizational perspective. *Journal of Innovation & Knowledge, 10*(5), 100787. DOI: 10.1016/j.jik.2025.100787

Zoghlami, N., Taghipour, A., Merlo, C., & Abed, M. (2016). Management of divergent production network using decentralised multi-level capacitated lot-sizing models. *International Journal of Shipping and Transport Logistics, 8*(5), 590–604. DOI: 10.1504/IJSTL.2016.078686

Chapter 9
Conceptual Foundations and Paradigm Shifts Between Industry 4.0 and Industry 5.0

Alaa Eddine El Moussaoui
http://orcid.org/0000-0002-5749-7682
EMIO, LIREEM Laboratory, Higher School of Technology of Nador, Mohammed First University, Oujda, Morocco

Taoufiq El Moussaoui
Polydisciplinary Faculty of Sidi Bennour, Chouaib Doukkali University, El Jadida, Morocco

ABSTRACT

Industry 4.0 has transformed industrial systems through digitalization and automation, yet its focus on efficiency has raised concerns about social inclusion, sustainability, and resilience. Industry 5.0 has emerged to address these gaps, emphasizing human-centric, sustainable, and resilient value creation. This paper synthesizes the principles, technologies, and value orientations of both paradigms, showing that Industry 5.0 is a socio-technical evolution of Industry 4.0 rather than a radical break. Key differences in governance, workforce roles, and sustainability metrics are examined, along with areas of convergence that enable integrated transitions. Implementation challenges, scalability issues, and policy implications are discussed to guide managers and policymakers in developing inclusive and sustainable industrial ecosystems, while future research directions are proposed.

DOI: 10.4018/979-8-2600-3199-5.ch009

1. INTRODUCTION

The Fourth Industrial Revolution, widely known as Industry 4.0, emerged in 2011 as a central pillar of Germany's high-tech strategy. Building on prior industrial revolutions—from mechanization to electrification to automation—Industry 4.0 integrates Cyber-Physical Systems (CPS), the Industrial Internet of Things (IIoT), and advanced analytics to create highly interconnected, intelligent manufacturing environments (Wang et al., 2017 ; Yang & Gu, 2021). While this paradigm has significantly increased productivity, efficiency, and flexibility, its primary focus remains technology-driven, often underemphasizing human-centric considerations, societal impacts, and environmental sustainability.

The recent concept of Industry 5.0 complements and extends Industry 4.0 by emphasizing human-centricity, sustainability, and resilience (Alves et al., 2023; Taghipour et al., 2023). Rather than merely optimizing production, Industry 5.0 advocates for value-driven industrial practices that integrate worker well-being, environmental responsibility, and societal goals alongside technological advancement. Concepts such as the "Age of Augmentation" and "Smart Working" highlight synergistic human-machine collaboration, enabling inclusive workplaces while enhancing innovation and productivity (Villar et al., 2023).

This duality raises several critical questions: (1)To what extent does Industry 4.0 address human-centric and sustainable objectives? (2) Can the enabling technologies of Industry 4.0 fully support Industry 5.0 goals, or are additional innovations required? (3) Is Industry 5.0 a chronological continuation of Industry 4.0 or a conceptual departure emphasizing societal values?

Addressing these questions is essential for managers, policymakers, and researchers seeking to navigate the transition between technology-driven and value-driven industrial paradigms. In addition, global initiatives such as the EU Green Deal, the UN Sustainable Development Goals (SDGs), and national strategies like Made in China 2025 and Society 5.0 (Japan) illustrate how policy frameworks are shaping Industry 5.0 adoption worldwide, highlighting regional variations in implementation and priorities.

This chapter examines the conceptual foundations and paradigm shifts between Industry 4.0 and Industry 5.0, structured as follows:

(1) Foundational concepts and historical context of Industry 4.0, focusing on technological underpinnings and global impact.
(2) Emergence of Industry 5.0, emphasizing human-centric approaches, sustainability, and resilience.
(3) Comparative analysis highlighting intersections, divergences, and collective potential.

(4) Discussion and conclusion, with practical implications, policy considerations, and future research directions.

By foregrounding both technological and societal dimensions, this chapter aims to provide a balanced and integrative framework for understanding the ongoing industrial transformation and its implications for sustainable, human-centered manufacturing ecosystems.

2. INDUSTRY 4.0: A REVOLUTION IN PROGRESS REVISITED

2.1 Industry 4.0 and the RAMI 4.0 Framework: Beyond a Technical Architecture

Industry 4.0 is commonly defined as a paradigm centered on the intelligent interconnection of industrial assets through Cyber-Physical Systems (CPS), enabling decentralized decision-making, real-time responsiveness, and data-driven optimization (Dafflon et al., 2021; Javaid et al., 2023). At its core, CPS integrate computational intelligence into physical production systems, blurring the boundary between the digital and physical domains. This integration has profoundly reshaped not only manufacturing operations but also logistics, supply chain coordination, and service-oriented industrial activities (Mahfod et al., 2021; El Moussaoui et al., 2022a; El Moussaoui et al., 2025b).

Table 1. Key Dimensions of the RAMI 4.0 Framework

Dimension	Description
Hierarchy Levels	Defines organizational and functional levels in production, from products and field devices to enterprise and connected world. Supports structured information flow across all levels.
Layers	Represents the technical and functional layers of Industry 4.0 systems, including Asset, Integration, Communication, Information, Functional, and Business layers, linking physical assets to digital services.
Life Cycle & Value Stream	Covers the complete lifecycle of assets, from development and engineering to production, maintenance, and decommissioning. Aligns physical components with business processes and value creation.

A central conceptual instrument supporting the implementation of Industry 4.0 is the Reference Architecture Model Industrie 4.0 (RAMI 4.0), developed under the leadership of the German Electrical and Electronic Manufacturers' Association (ZVEI). As illustrated in Table 1, RAMI 4.0 structures Industry 4.0 systems along three complementary dimensions: Hierarchy Levels, Layers, and Life Cycle & Value Stream (Melo et al., 2021). This three-dimensional architecture enables a standardized understanding of how assets evolve across their lifecycle, how information flows across organizational levels, and how physical components are linked to digital services and business processes (Suleiman et al., 2022 ; El Moussaoui, 2025).

While RAMI 4.0 is often presented as a technical reference model, its broader significance lies in its role as a socio-technical coordination framework. By emphasizing interoperability, modularity, and scalability, RAMI 4.0 implicitly shapes organizational structures, governance mechanisms, and inter-firm collaboration. However, despite this integrative ambition, RAMI 4.0 remains primarily focused on technical coherence and operational efficiency, offering limited guidance on human agency, ethical governance, or societal outcomes—dimensions that later become central within the Industry 5.0 discourse.

2.2 Design Principles of Industry 4.0: Efficiency, Flexibility, and Interoperability

The design principles of Industry 4.0 provide the operational logic through which CPS-enabled systems deliver performance improvements (Kılıç & Atilla, 2024 ; El Moussaoui et al, 2025b). These principles include interoperability, decentralization, real-time capability, service orientation, and modularity, all of which aim to enhance flexibility and responsiveness within complex industrial environments (Mittal et al., 2018).

Interoperability ensures seamless communication between machines, humans, and external systems, while decentralized intelligence allows local units to make autonomous decisions based on real-time data. Adaptability and flexibility enable industrial systems to respond dynamically to demand fluctuations, supply disruptions, or customization requirements. Additionally, the optimization of Overall Equipment Effectiveness (OEE) remains a dominant performance objective, reflecting Industry 4.0's emphasis on productivity, availability, and quality (Taghipour & Beneteau-Piet, 2020).

Yet, these principles also reveal the normative orientation of Industry 4.0: performance is primarily measured through efficiency-driven indicators. Although data integration across product lifecycles improves transparency and traceability, social and environmental dimensions are often treated as secondary outcomes rather than core objectives. This imbalance partly explains why Industry 4.0, despite its technical sophistication, has been criticized for insufficiently addressing workforce well-being, ethical responsibility, and long-term sustainability.

2.3 From Concept to Reality: Enabling Technologies and Industrial Transformation

Industry 4.0's transformative capacity is largely driven by a constellation of enabling technologies that collectively reshape production and coordination mechanisms. According to the Boston Consulting Group, nine technological pillars underpin Industry 4.0: Big Data and analytics, autonomous robots, simulation, horizontal and vertical system integration, IIoT, cybersecurity, cloud computing, additive manufacturing, and augmented reality (AR) (Alcácer & Cruz-Machado, 2019; Taghipour, 2024).

These technologies enable predictive maintenance, digital process simulation, real-time monitoring, and enhanced human–machine interaction (Logeswaran et al., 2024). Horizontal and vertical integration, in particular, facilitate coordination across value networks and organizational hierarchies, reinforcing the systemic nature of Industry 4.0 (Taghipour and Lu, 2025). However, empirical evidence suggests that technological adoption remains uneven, with large industrial actors benefiting more rapidly than SMEs, especially in resource-constrained contexts.

While these technologies significantly enhance operational performance, they also reinforce a technology-first logic, where innovation is often justified by cost reduction, speed, and scalability. As a result, broader societal objectives—such as social inclusion, environmental regeneration, or workforce empowerment—are addressed indirectly, if at all. This limitation becomes a central motivation for the emergence of Industry 5.0.

2.4 Industry 4.0, Sustainability, and Resilience: Promises and Limitations

In response to growing environmental and societal pressures, Industry 4.0 has progressively incorporated sustainability-oriented applications, particularly in resource efficiency, energy optimization, and resilient supply chain management (Oláh et al., 2020 ; Chabane et al., 2023). Advanced monitoring systems enable real-time assessment of energy consumption and material flows, supporting waste reduction and eco-efficiency strategies (El Moussaoui et al., 2022b; El Moussaoui et al., 2025c).

Decision-support tools such as the Green Production Index assist organizations in aligning investments with environmental performance objectives (Loivet et al., 2020; Taghipour & Lu, 2023). Moreover, simulation-based approaches enhance industrial resilience by enabling rapid reconfiguration in response to disruptions, as illustrated by adaptive supplier selection during crises.

Despite these advancements, sustainability and resilience within Industry 4.0 are largely treated as optimization problems, rather than normative commitments. Environmental gains are often evaluated through efficiency metrics, while social dimensions—such as labor equity, occupational well-being, or power asymmetries—remain underexplored. This instrumental treatment of sustainability highlights a conceptual gap that Industry 5.0 explicitly seeks to address.

2.5 Human–Machine Interaction in Industry 4.0: Foundations for Augmentation

Although Industry 4.0 is frequently portrayed as technology-centric, it has introduced important shifts in human–machine relations. Operator assistance systems, collaborative robotics, and AR-based interfaces enhance situational awareness and reduce cognitive and physical strain (Alizadeh et al., 2021; El Moussaoui et al, 2022 ; Licardo et al., 2024). These developments support new forms of human–machine cooperation, moving beyond substitution toward functional collaboration.

Industry 4.0 has also contributed to the emergence of socio-technical infrastructures addressing lifelong learning, knowledge management, and flexible work organization (Marcon et al., 2022; Carayannis et al., 2023 ; El Moussaoui et al, 2025d). By automating repetitive tasks, smart systems allow workers to focus on creative, supervisory, and problem-solving activities. However, access to these benefits remains uneven, and concerns related to surveillance, skill polarization, and job displacement persist.

Consequently, while Industry 4.0 provides essential technological foundations for worker augmentation, it lacks an explicit ethical and governance framework to ensure that human empowerment becomes a primary objective rather than a by-product. This unresolved tension sets the stage for Industry 5.0, which reframes human agency, sustainability, and resilience as core industrial values rather than secondary outcomes.

3. INDUSTRY 5.0: CONCEPTS, PILLARS, AND STRATEGIC DRIVERS

3.1 Emergence of Industry 5.0: From Technology-Centric Growth to Societal Value Creation

Since 2017, scholarly discourse has increasingly questioned the adequacy of purely technology-driven industrial paradigms, paving the way for the emergence of Industry 5.0 as a value-oriented framework. This intellectual shift gained institutional momentum in 2021, when the European Commission formally introduced Industry 5.0 as a strategic vision for a sustainable, human-centric, and resilient industry (Broo et al., 2022). The initiative was shaped through consultations and expert workshops organized by the Directorate-General for Research and Innovation, reflecting growing concerns regarding environmental degradation, social inequality, and systemic vulnerability in global industrial systems (Tiron-Tudor & Deliu, 2024).

As illustrated in Table 2, Industry 5.0 does not emerge as a sudden technological rupture but rather as the latest stage in a long-term industrial evolution, following mechanization, electrification, automation, and digitalization. Unlike earlier revolutions, however, Industry 5.0 is not defined by a dominant technology but by a normative reorientation of industrial objectives. The COVID-19 pandemic, geopolitical tensions, and climate-related disruptions exposed the fragility of hyper-optimized global value chains, reinforcing the need for resilience, redundancy, and adaptive capacity (Ammar et al., 2024; Toufah et al., 2025).

Although the European Commission has played a catalytic role, the underlying principles of Industry 5.0 resonate globally. Comparable visions can be observed in Japan's Society 5.0, which emphasizes human-centered digital integration, and in Asian industrial strategies that increasingly combine automation with social stability and sustainability objectives. This broader international convergence suggests that Industry 5.0 should be understood not as a Europe-centric policy narrative, but as part of a global reassessment of industrial purpose.

Table 2. Key Features and Principles of Industry 5.0

Feature / Principle	Description
Human-Centric Approach	Focuses on placing humans at the center of industrial systems, emphasizing collaboration between humans and machines.
Societal Value Creation	Aligns industrial activities with social, environmental, and ethical objectives, promoting sustainability and social welfare.
Resilience and Adaptive Capacity	Encourages flexibility, redundancy, and robustness in industrial value chains to cope with disruptions such as pandemics, geopolitical tensions, or climate events.
Global Convergence	Reflects international alignment, including Europe's Industry 5.0 and Japan's Society 5.0, emphasizing shared goals of sustainability, human-centered digital integration, and social stability.
Normative Reorientation	Shifts focus from purely technological advancement to redefined industrial objectives that integrate ethics, social needs, and long-term sustainability.

3.2 Conceptual Foundations of Industry 5.0: Reframing the Role of Industry in Society

Industry 5.0 fundamentally challenges the assumption that industrial progress should be measured primarily through productivity, efficiency, and economic growth. Instead, it positions industry as a systemic contributor to societal well-being, environmental stewardship, and long-term resilience (Antonaci et al., 2024 ; El Moussaoui et al, 2025e). This paradigm shift reframes technology as an enabler rather than a driver, emphasizing that innovation must serve clearly articulated human and ecological values.

In contrast to Industry 4.0, where sustainability and social considerations are often addressed instrumentally, Industry 5.0 explicitly anchors industrial activity within planetary boundaries and societal expectations (Ghobakhloo et al., 2024). The European Green Deal and circular economy strategies exemplify this shift by linking industrial competitiveness to decarbonization, resource efficiency, and social inclusion (Rame et al., 2024; Gharye Mirzaei et al., 2025). Importantly, Industry 5.0 does not reject digitalization or automation; rather, it demands that these technologies be governed through ethical, inclusive, and sustainability-oriented frameworks.

This reconceptualization also responds to growing critiques of Industry 4.0, which highlight risks related to labor displacement, digital surveillance, and uneven value distribution. By foregrounding human dignity, autonomy, and participation, Industry 5.0 seeks to rebalance power relations within industrial systems and reassert the primacy of societal goals over purely technical optimization.

3.3 Core Values of Industry 5.0: Human-Centricity, Sustainability, and Resilience

The conceptual coherence of Industry 5.0 is structured around three interdependent core values—human-centricity, sustainability, and resilience—as illustrated in Table 3. These values function not merely as guiding principles but as evaluative criteria for industrial decision-making.

Table 3. Core Values of Industry 5.0

Core Value	Description
Human-Centricity	Redefines workers as co-creators of value, emphasizing safe, inclusive, and meaningful work environments. Promotes human-machine collaboration as augmentation, fostering creativity, autonomy, and cognitive support.
Sustainability	Focuses on circular resource flows, low-carbon production, and ecological regeneration. Encourages measurable sustainability indicators such as material circularity, carbon intensity, and energy autonomy.
Resilience	Enhances the capacity of industrial systems to anticipate, absorb, and recover from disruptions. Includes technological robustness, organizational adaptability, diversified supply networks, and local production capabilities.

Human-centricity redefines the role of workers from system operators to active co-creators of value. This perspective emphasizes safe, inclusive, and meaningful work environments, as well as continuous opportunities for upskilling and reskilling (Ikenga et al., 2024 ; El Moussaoui, 2025). Human-machine collaboration is reframed as augmentation rather than substitution, promoting creativity, autonomy, and cognitive support while mitigating physical and psychological strain.

Sustainability extends beyond efficiency gains to encompass circular resource flows, low-carbon production, and long-term ecological regeneration (Santiago et al., 2024). Industry 5.0 encourages the adoption of measurable sustainability indicators—such as material circularity, carbon intensity, and energy autonomy—to ensure that industrial growth remains compatible with environmental limits.

Resilience, the third pillar, addresses the capacity of industrial systems to anticipate, absorb, and recover from disruptions. This includes not only technological robustness but also organizational adaptability, diversified supply networks, and local production capabilities (El Moussaoui et al., 2022c). Together, these values form a normative framework that distinguishes Industry 5.0 from efficiency-driven industrial models and positions it as a response to systemic uncertainty.

3.4 Enabling Technologies of Industry 5.0: From Digitalization to Purpose-Driven Innovation

While Industry 5.0 is not defined by a specific technological stack, it relies on a set of enabling technologies that support its normative objectives. Advanced human–machine interaction systems, including collaborative robots and adaptive interfaces, enhance personalization and worker empowerment (Rani et al., 2024). Digital Twins and simulation technologies enable holistic system modeling, supporting sustainable design choices and resilience planning (Zafar et al., 2024).

Artificial Intelligence plays a critical role by facilitating pattern recognition, decision support, and adaptive control within complex socio-technical systems (Su et al., 2024; Taghipour & Lu, 2025). However, within Industry 5.0, AI is increasingly subject to ethical governance frameworks that emphasize transparency, accountability, and human oversight. Complementary technologies—such as bio-inspired materials, renewable energy systems, and decentralized energy storage—support circularity and carbon reduction objectives. Crucially, many of these technologies originate from Industry 4.0 infrastructures, reinforcing the view that Industry 5.0 represents not a technological break but a reorientation of technological use toward societal ends.

3.5 Implementation Challenges and Strategic Pathways

Despite its conceptual appeal, Industry 5.0 faces significant implementation challenges. Social heterogeneity in values and risk perceptions complicates technology acceptance, particularly regarding data governance, automation, and workforce transformation (Maddikunta et al., 2022). Measuring social and environmental value creation remains difficult, as standardized metrics for well-being, resilience, and circularity are still evolving (Hsu et al., 2024).

Adoption barriers are particularly acute for SMEs and industries in the Global South, where financial constraints, limited digital infrastructure, and skills shortages hinder large-scale transformation. Addressing these disparities requires targeted policy instruments, collaborative ecosystems, and scalable transition tools (Barata & Kayser, 2023). Moreover, interdisciplinary collaboration across engineering, social sciences, and policy domains is essential to align technological innovation with societal objectives. Ultimately, Industry 5.0 demands a shift from technology deployment to governance-oriented innovation, where industrial strategies are evaluated not only by efficiency gains but by their contribution to inclusive, sustainable, and resilient industrial ecosystems (Tallat et al., 2023).

4. COMPARATIVE AND CRITICAL ANALYSIS OF INDUSTRY 4.0 AND INDUSTRY 5.0

Industry 4.0 and Industry 5.0 are often portrayed as sequential phases of industrial development; however, such a linear interpretation oversimplifies the conceptual relationship between the two paradigms. Industry 4.0 emerged primarily as a response to intensifying global competition, increasing customization requirements, and rapid advances in digital technologies. Its foundational logic centers on automation, interoperability, and real-time optimization through Cyber-Physical Systems, industrial Internet of Things, artificial intelligence, and data analytics (Wang et al., 2017). Within this paradigm, performance is predominantly assessed through efficiency, productivity, cost reduction, and operational flexibility. Human labor, while not absent, is largely framed as an element to be optimized, supervised, or substituted within increasingly automated production systems.

Industry 5.0 introduces a significant normative reorientation by explicitly positioning human-centricity, sustainability, and resilience as core industrial objectives rather than peripheral considerations. Importantly, this shift does not imply a technological rupture with Industry 4.0. Instead, it represents a value-driven reinterpretation of the same digital infrastructure, redirecting advanced technologies toward human augmentation, inclusive work environments, and long-term societal value creation (Villar et al., 2023). Collaborative robotics, artificial intelligence, digital twins, and advanced analytics remain central; however, their role evolves from tools of substitution and control to instruments that enhance human creativity, decision-making, and adaptability. This conceptual distinction, illustrated by the Industry 5.0 pillars presented in Table 3, highlights a move away from purely techno-centric efficiency toward socio-technical integration.

A critical dimension differentiating the two paradigms concerns governance and ethical orientation. Frameworks associated with Industry 4.0, such as RAMI 4.0, prioritize technical interoperability, standardization, and system architecture, but they tend to underaddress questions of power asymmetry, data ownership, algorithmic transparency, and labor displacement. Industry 5.0 explicitly acknowledges these shortcomings by embedding ethical governance, responsible innovation, and participatory decision-making into industrial system design. This perspective recognizes that technological systems are not neutral artifacts but are embedded within institutional, cultural, and political contexts that shape their societal consequences. Consequently, issues related to workforce surveillance, inequality, and the distribution of value along global supply chains become central analytical concerns rather than externalities.

Sustainability and resilience further accentuate the divergence between the two paradigms. While Industry 4.0 may contribute indirectly to environmental performance through efficiency gains and waste reduction, such outcomes are often incidental rather than intentional. Industry 5.0, by contrast, integrates sustainability as an explicit design principle, emphasizing circular economy practices, carbon footprint reduction, resource efficiency, and life-cycle thinking (Gharye Mirzaei et al., 2025). This orientation aligns Industry 5.0 with broader policy frameworks such as the European Green Deal and the United Nations Sustainable Development Goals, positioning industrial systems as active contributors to environmental stewardship and societal resilience. Beyond environmental metrics, resilience within Industry 5.0 encompasses supply chain robustness, crisis adaptability, and the capacity of organizations to absorb and recover from systemic shocks—an issue that has gained prominence in light of recent global disruptions.

From a managerial perspective, the transition from Industry 4.0 to Industry 5.0 entails qualitatively different challenges. Whereas Industry 4.0 implementation is often framed as a technological and operational investment, Industry 5.0 demands organizational transformation, workforce reskilling, and cultural change. Managers must address resistance to change, manage ethical trade-offs, and balance short-term economic pressures with long-term value creation (Leng et al., 2022; Taghipour et al., 2022). These challenges are particularly pronounced for small and medium-sized enterprises and firms operating in emerging economies, where financial constraints, skill gaps, and uneven access to digital infrastructure may hinder adoption. As a result, Industry 5.0 should be understood as a context-dependent transition rather than a universally attainable industrial state.

To consolidate these conceptual and managerial distinctions, Table 4 provides a comparative synthesis of Industry 4.0 and Industry 5.0 across key analytical dimensions.

Table 4. Comparative Overview of Industry 4.0 and Industry 5.0

Dimension	Industry 4.0	Industry 5.0
Core orientation	Technology-centric efficiency	Human-centric and value-driven systems
Primary objectives	Productivity, flexibility, cost optimization	Human well-being, sustainability, resilience
Role of technology	Automation and control	Human augmentation and support
Governance focus	Technical standards and performance	Ethical governance and inclusivity
Sustainability logic	Implicit and efficiency-based	Explicit circular and environmental metrics
Managerial challenges	System integration and automation	Workforce reskilling, ethical oversight, change management

Overall, the comparative analysis suggests that Industry 5.0 should not be interpreted as a radical break from Industry 4.0, but rather as an evolutionary paradigm shift that seeks to correct the limitations of technology-dominated industrialization. By embedding normative values into digital production systems, Industry 5.0 extends the scope of industrial transformation beyond efficiency toward sustainable, resilient, and socially embedded manufacturing ecosystems. This reframing provides a critical foundation for the discussion and evaluative conclusions developed in the following section.

5. DISCUSSION AND CONCLUSION: FROM A TECHNOLOGICAL PARADIGM TO A SOCIO-TECHNICAL REORIENTATION

The comparative analysis between Industry 4.0 and Industry 5.0 highlights a fundamental transformation in the way industrial change is conceptualized, governed, and operationalized. Rather than representing a linear technological succession, Industry 5.0 emerges as a normative and socio-technical reorientation of the Industry 4.0 paradigm. While Industry 4.0 is primarily anchored in efficiency-driven digitalization and automation, Industry 5.0 reframes industrial progress through human-centric, sustainable, and resilient value creation. This distinction is not merely semantic; it reshapes managerial priorities, policy frameworks, and the ethical foundations of industrial systems.

Industry 4.0 has undeniably enabled unprecedented gains in productivity, flexibility, and system integration through cyber-physical systems, data-driven decision-making, and intelligent automation. However, as revealed through both policy critiques and recent empirical reflections, its implementation has often remained technology-centric, with social and environmental considerations treated as secondary or instrumental outcomes. Although concepts such as operator assistance, smart working environments, and socio-technical systems were present within Industry 4.0 discourse, they were largely subordinated to optimization logics. In contrast, Industry 5.0 places these dimensions at the core of industrial design, repositioning technology as a means rather than an end.

This shift becomes particularly visible when examining governance and value orientation. Industry 4.0 is largely driven by competitiveness, scalability, and cost-efficiency, whereas Industry 5.0 explicitly aligns industrial transformation with broader societal objectives, including climate neutrality, workforce well-being, and systemic resilience. In this sense, Industry 5.0 reflects a response to accumulated shortcomings exposed by global crises such as the COVID-19 pandemic, geopolitical disruptions, and accelerating environmental degradation. These events revealed the vulnerability of hyper-optimized, globally fragmented value chains and reinforced the need for more adaptive, inclusive, and locally resilient industrial ecosystems.

From a managerial perspective, the transition from Industry 4.0 to Industry 5.0 entails a profound redefinition of strategic priorities. Managers are no longer tasked solely with adopting advanced technologies but must orchestrate organizational change that integrates workforce reskilling, ethical governance, and sustainability performance. Workforce transformation represents a central challenge, as Industry 5.0 requires continuous upskilling, hybrid human–machine collaboration, and new forms of job design that preserve worker autonomy and dignity. Resistance to change, unequal access to training, and rising implementation costs particularly affect small and medium-sized enterprises, highlighting the uneven scalability of Industry 5.0 principles across industrial contexts.

Sustainability, while frequently invoked in Industry 4.0 initiatives, gains a more operational role under Industry 5.0. The latter demands measurable outcomes in terms of circular economy practices, carbon reduction, energy efficiency, and resource optimization. This necessitates the development of integrated sustainability metrics that go beyond efficiency indicators such as Overall Equipment Effectiveness. Without robust measurement frameworks, sustainability risks remaining a rhetorical ambition rather than a managerial reality. Industry 5.0 therefore challenges firms and policymakers to reconcile economic performance with environmental boundaries and long-term societal value creation.

The relationship between Industry 4.0 and Industry 5.0 should thus be understood as complementary rather than antagonistic. The technological infrastructure developed under Industry 4.0—artificial intelligence, industrial IoT, digital twins, advanced robotics—constitutes an essential foundation for realizing Industry 5.0 objectives. However, Industry 5.0 extends beyond technological deployment by introducing ethical, social, and environmental constraints that reshape how these technologies are designed, governed, and evaluated. This convergence gives rise to what can be described as a techno-social industrial transformation, where innovation is assessed not only by performance gains but also by its contribution to societal resilience and inclusiveness.

Despite its conceptual coherence, Industry 5.0 remains subject to several limitations that warrant critical reflection. First, much of the existing discourse remains policy-driven and Eurocentric, with limited empirical validation across diverse industrial regions, particularly in the Global South. Second, the practical implementation of human-centric and sustainable principles remains uneven, constrained by financial, institutional, and cultural barriers. Third, the conceptual boundaries between Industry 4.0 and Industry 5.0 are occasionally blurred in both academic and policy narratives, which risks diluting analytical clarity and managerial guidance.

Future research should therefore prioritize empirical investigations into real-world transition pathways, comparative case studies across regions and sectors, and the development of actionable assessment tools for Industry 4.0-to-Industry 5.0 transformation. Interdisciplinary approaches combining engineering, management, social sciences, and environmental studies will be essential to capture the full complexity of this paradigm shift. Particular attention should be paid to SMEs, labor dynamics, and power asymmetries embedded in digital industrial systems.

In conclusion, Industry 5.0 should not be interpreted as a radical technological rupture but as an evaluative and normative evolution of Industry 4.0. It redefines industrial progress by embedding technological innovation within a framework of human-centricity, sustainability, and resilience. This reorientation challenges industries to move beyond efficiency-driven digitalization toward a more balanced and responsible industrial future. By embracing this integrated perspective, industrial stakeholders can contribute to sustainable manufacturing ecosystems that generate economic value while enhancing societal well-being and environmental stewardship.

REFERENCES

Alcácer, V., & Cruz-Machado, V. (2019). Scanning the industry 4.0: A literature review on technologies for manufacturing systems. *Engineering Science and Technology, an International Journal, 22*(3), 899–919. DOI: 10.1016/j.jestch.2019.01.006

Alizadeh, N., Taghipour, A., & Canel-Depître, B. (2021). Which one collective strategy is appropriate for the business ecosystem? The role of political environment.

Alves, J., Lima, T. M., & Gaspar, P. D. (2023). Is industry 5.0 a human-centred approach? a systematic review. *Processes (Basel, Switzerland), 11*(1), 193. DOI: 10.3390/pr11010193

Ammar, A., Amahmoud, H., El Menzhi, K., Mkik, M., Hebaz, A., & Eddine, E. M. A. (2024, May). Critical Analysis of Logistics Transformation in Morocco Under The Auspices of Artificial Intelligence: Government Perspectives From the perspective of Innovative and Technology Driven Public Management. In 2024 IEEE 15th International Colloquium on Logistics and Supply Chain Management (LOGISTIQUA) (pp. 1-9). IEEE.

Antonaci, F. G., Olivetti, E. C., Marcolin, F., Castiblanco Jimenez, I. A., Eynard, B., Vezzetti, E., & Moos, S. (2024). Workplace Well-Being in Industry 5.0: A Worker-Centered Systematic Review. *Sensors (Basel), 24*(17), 5473. DOI: 10.3390/s24175473 PMID: 39275383

Barata, J., & Kayser, I. (2023). Industry 5.0–past, present, and near future. *Procedia Computer Science, 219*, 778–788. DOI: 10.1016/j.procs.2023.01.351

Broo, D. G., Kaynak, O., & Sait, S. M. (2022). Rethinking engineering education at the age of industry 5.0. *Journal of Industrial Information Integration, 25*, 100311. DOI: 10.1016/j.jii.2021.100311

Carayannis, E. G., Canestrino, R., & Magliocca, P. (2023). From the dark side of industry 4.0 to society 5.0: Looking "beyond the box" to developing human-centric innovation ecosystems. *IEEE Transactions on Engineering Management, 71*, 6695–6711. DOI: 10.1109/TEM.2023.3239552

Chabane, B., Komljenovic, D., & Abdul-Nour, G. (2023). Converging on human-centred industry, resilient processes, and sustainable outcomes in asset management frameworks. *Environment Systems & Decisions, 43*(4), 663–679. DOI: 10.1007/s10669-023-09943-w

Dafflon, B., Moalla, N., & Ouzrout, Y. (2021). The challenges, approaches, and used techniques of CPS for manufacturing in Industry 4.0: A literature review. *International Journal of Advanced Manufacturing Technology, 113*(7-8), 2395–2412. DOI: 10.1007/s00170-020-06572-4

El Moussaoui, A. E. (2025a). Impact of Circular Economy on Supply Chain Management: An Exploratory Study. In *Ecological and Human Dimensions of AI-Based Supply Chain* (pp. 293–314). IGI Global Scientific Publishing. DOI: 10.4018/979-8-3693-7478-8.ch013

El Moussaoui, A. E. (2025b). Predicting E-Consumer Preferences for Collection and Delivery Points Using Deep Learning. In Ecological and Human Dimensions of AI-Based Supply Chain (pp. 395-412). IGI Global Scientific Publishing.

El Moussaoui, A. E., Benbba, B., & El Amrani, L. (2022c). Distribution system design in last mile logistics: Review & research agenda. Revue Marocaine de Management, Logistique et Transport, (5).

El Moussaoui, A. E., Benbba, B., Jaegler, A., & El Andaloussi, Z. (2022a, May). City logistics: An evolutionary, successful & collaborative city. In 2022 14th international colloquium of logistics and supply chain management (LOGISTIQUA) (pp. 1-7). IEEE.

El Moussaoui, A. E., Benbba, B., Jaegler, A., El Andaloussi, Z., & El Amrani, L. (2022b, May). Last mile logistics: Challenges & improvement ways. In 2022 14th international colloquium of logistics and supply chain management (LOGISTIQUA) (pp. 1-7). IEEE.

El Moussaoui, A. E., El Moussaoui, T., Benbba, B., Jaegler, A., & El Andaloussi, Z. (2022d). Understanding the choice of collection & delivery point by the E-consumer via a machine learning model: Moroccan case study. *Procedia Computer Science, 210*, 204–211. DOI: 10.1016/j.procs.2022.10.138

El Moussaoui, A. E., Mizani, M. E., & Benlakouiri, A. (2025d, April). Transformation of Logistics in Electronic Subcontracting: A Focus on SMEs Supply Chains. In International Conference on Connected Objects and Artificial Intelligence (pp. 700-706). Cham: Springer Nature Switzerland.

El Moussaoui, A. E., Mizani, M. E., & Benlakouiri, A. (2025e, April). RFID Technology in Logistics: A Catalyst for Efficiency. In International Conference on Connected Objects and Artificial Intelligence (pp. 707-712). Cham: Springer Nature Switzerland.

El Moussaoui, T., Chakir, L., & El Moussaoui, A. E. (2025b). Exploring Information Technology (IT) Acceptance Among Supply Chain Stakeholders in Morocco's Pharmaceutical Industry. In Ecological and Human Dimensions of AI-Based Supply Chain (pp. 245-270). IGI Global Scientific Publishing.

El Moussaoui, T., Loqman, C., & El Moussaoui, A. E. (2025c). Adoption of artificial intelligence in smart cities: Literature review and bibliometric analysis. Generative AI for Cybersecurity and Privacy, 103-125.

Gharye Mirzaei, M., Goodarzian, F., Taghipour, A., & Muñuzuri, J. (2025). Sustainable closed-loop supply chain network under uncertainty considering green technologies: Toward the circular economy. *The Journal of the Operational Research Society*, •••, 1–21.

Ghobakhloo, M., Iranmanesh, M., Fathi, M., Rejeb, A., Foroughi, B., & Nikbin, D. (2024). Beyond Industry 4.0: A systematic review of Industry 5.0 technologies and implications for social, environmental and economic sustainability. *Asia-Pacific Journal of Business Administration*.

Hsu, C. H., Liu, J. C., Cai, X. Q., Zhang, T. Y., & Lv, W. Y. (2024). Enabling Sustainable Diffusion in Supply Chains Through Industry 5.0: An Impact Analysis of Key Enablers for SMEs in Emerging Economies. *Mathematics*, *12*(24), 3938. DOI: 10.3390/math12243938

Ikenga, G. U., & van der Sijde, P. (2024). Twenty-first century competencies; about competencies for industry 5.0 and the opportunities for emerging economies. *Sustainability (Basel)*, *16*(16), 7166. DOI: 10.3390/su16167166

Javaid, M., Haleem, A., Singh, R. P., & Suman, R. (2023). An integrated outlook of Cyber–Physical Systems for Industry 4.0: Topical practices, architecture, and applications. *Green Technologies and Sustainability*, *1*(1), 100001. DOI: 10.1016/j.grets.2022.100001

Kılıç, C., & Atilla, G. (2024). Industry 4.0 and sustainable business models: An intercontinental sample. *Business Strategy and the Environment*, *33*(4), 3142–3166. DOI: 10.1002/bse.3634

Licardo, J. T., Domjan, M., & Orehovački, T. (2024). Intelligent robotics—A systematic review of emerging technologies and trends. *Electronics (Basel)*, *13*(3), 542. DOI: 10.3390/electronics13030542

Logeswaran, K., Savitha, S., Suresh, P., Prasanna Kumar, K. R., Gunasekar, M., Rajadevi, R., & Jayasurya, A. S. (2024). Unifying Technologies in Industry 4.0: Harnessing the Synergy of Internet of Things, Big Data, Augmented Reality/Virtual Reality, and Blockchain Technologies. *Topics in Artificial Intelligence Applied to Industry*, *4*(0), 127–147. DOI: 10.1002/9781394216147.ch7

Loivet, W., Taghipour, A., & Kang, D. S. (2020). The rise of green supply chain management: Between complexity and necessity. *J. Econ. Bus. Manag*, *8*(1), 1–7. DOI: 10.18178/joebm.2020.8.1.604

Maddikunta, P. K. R., Pham, Q. V., Prabadevi, B., Deepa, N., Dev, K., Gadekallu, T. R., & Liyanage, M. (2022). Industry 5.0: A survey on enabling technologies and potential applications. *Journal of Industrial Information Integration*, *26*, 100257. DOI: 10.1016/j.jii.2021.100257

Mahfod, J., Khoury, B., Canel-Depitre, B., & Taghipour, A. (2021). Logistics Providers in Syria Humanitarian Operations. In Demand Forecasting and Order Planning in Supply Chains and Humanitarian Logistics (pp. 171-197). IGI Global. DOI: 10.4018/978-1-7998-3805-0.ch006

Marcon, É., Soliman, M., Gerstlberger, W., & Frank, A. G. (2022). Sociotechnical factors and Industry 4.0: An integrative perspective for the adoption of smart manufacturing technologies. *Journal of Manufacturing Technology Management*, *33*(2), 259–286. DOI: 10.1108/JMTM-01-2021-0017

Melo, P. F., Godoy, E. P., Ferrari, P., & Sisinni, E. (2021). Open source control device for industry 4.0 based on RAMI 4.0. *Electronics (Basel)*, *10*(7), 869. DOI: 10.3390/electronics10070869

Mittal, S., Khan, M. A., Romero, D., & Wuest, T. (2018). A critical review of smart manufacturing & Industry 4.0 maturity models: Implications for small and medium-sized enterprises (SMEs). *Journal of Manufacturing Systems*, *49*, 194–214. DOI: 10.1016/j.jmsy.2018.10.005

Oláh, J., Aburumman, N., Popp, J., Khan, M. A., Haddad, H., & Kitukutha, N. (2020). Impact of Industry 4.0 on environmental sustainability. *Sustainability (Basel)*, *12*(11), 4674. DOI: 10.3390/su12114674

Rame, R., Purwanto, P., & Sudarno, S. (2024). Industry 5.0 and sustainability: An overview of emerging trends and challenges for a green future. *Innovation and Green Development*, *3*(4), 100173. DOI: 10.1016/j.igd.2024.100173

Rani, S., Jining, D., Shoukat, K., Shoukat, M. U., & Nawaz, S. A. (2024). A Human–Machine Interaction Mechanism: Additive Manufacturing for Industry 5.0—Design and Management. *Sustainability (Basel), 16*(10), 4158. DOI: 10.3390/su16104158

Santiago, B. D. S., Scavarda, L. F., Gusmão Caiado, R. G., Santos, R. S., & Mattos Nascimento, D. L. D. (2024). Corporate social responsibility and circular economy integration framework within sustainable supply chain management: Building blocks for industry 5.0. *Corporate Social Responsibility and Environmental Management.*

Su, C., Tang, X., Han, Y., Wang, T., & Jiang, D. (2024). Cognitive digital twin in manufacturing process: Integrating the knowledge graph for enhanced human-centric Industry 5.0. *International Journal of Production Research*, •••, 1–22.

Suleiman, Z., Shaikholla, S., Dikhanbayeva, D., Shehab, E., & Turkyilmaz, A. (2022). Industry 4.0: Clustering of concepts and characteristics. *Cogent Engineering*, *9*(1), 2034264. DOI: 10.1080/23311916.2022.2034264

Taghipour, A. (2024). Big Data: The New Gold Mine for Supermarkets. In Applications of New Technology in Operations and Supply Chain Management (pp. 98-106). IGI Global.

Taghipour, A., Belrhazi, Y., & Damoum, N. (2023). Resilient sustainable supply chain management. In *Government Impact on Sustainable and Responsible Supply Chain Management* (pp. 33–47). IGI Global. DOI: 10.4018/978-1-6684-9062-4.ch003

Taghipour, A., & Beneteau-Piet, C. (2020). Sustainable supply chain management performance. *International Journal of Innovation, Management and Technology, 11*(6), 165–169. DOI: 10.18178/ijimt.2020.11.6.897

Taghipour, A., & Lu, X. (2025). Advancing Supply Chain Innovation: Theoretical Foundations, Contemporary Developments, and Future Directions. In Ecological and Human Dimensions of AI-Based Supply Chain (pp. 1-26). IGI Global Scientific Publishing.

Taghipour, A., & Lu, X. (2025). Navigating the Artificial Intelligence Era: Impacts of Artificial Intelligence on Youth Critical Thinking, Career Paths, and Ethical Challenges. In Ecological and Human Dimensions of AI-Based Supply Chain (pp. 49-68). IGI Global Scientific Publishing.

Taghipour, A., Lu, X., & Smahi, M. (2022). Opportunities and challenges for society 5.0 in procurement. *Blockchain Technology in Supply Chain Management for Society*, *5*(0), 91–100. DOI: 10.1201/9781003177432-9

Taghipour, A., & Lu, X. W. (2023, August). Green Supply Chain Management: A Guide. In International Conference on Applied Economics and Business (pp. 315-328). Cham: Springer Nature Switzerland.

Tallat, R., Hawbani, A., Wang, X., Al-Dubai, A., Zhao, L., Liu, Z., & Alsamhi, S. H. (2023). Navigating industry 5.0: A survey of key enabling technologies, trends, challenges, and opportunities. *IEEE Communications Surveys and Tutorials*.

Tiron-Tudor, A., & Deliu, D. (2024). The Sustainability Performance of SMEs in Industry 5.0: A Proposal for a Synergetic Digital Sustainable Development Maturity Model (SDSDMM). *Eastern European Economics*, •••, 1–45.

TOUFAH, N., EL MOUSSAOUI, A. E., & LEKHAILA, G. (2025). A Comparative Analysis of the Logistics and Economics Fields: A Literature Review. *Revue Française d'Economie et de Gestion*, *6*(8).

Villar, A., Paladini, S., & Buckley, O. (2023, July). Towards supply chain 5.0: Re-designing supply chains as resilient, sustainable, and human-centric systems in a post-pandemic world. In Operations [). Cham: Springer International Publishing.]. *Research Forum*, *4*(3), 60. DOI: 10.1007/s43069-023-00234-3

Wang, Y., Ma, H. S., Yang, J. H., & Wang, K. S. (2017). Industry 4.0: A way from mass customization to mass personalization production. *Advances in Manufacturing*, *5*(4), 311–320. DOI: 10.1007/s40436-017-0204-7

Yang, F., & Gu, S. (2021). Industry 4.0, a revolution that requires technology and national strategies. *Complex & Intelligent Systems*, *7*(3), 1311–1325. DOI: 10.1007/s40747-020-00267-9

Zafar, M. H., Langås, E. F., & Sanfilippo, F. (2024). Exploring the synergies between collaborative robotics, digital twins, augmentation, and industry 5.0 for smart manufacturing: A state-of-the-art review. *Robotics and Computer-integrated Manufacturing*, *89*, 102769. DOI: 10.1016/j.rcim.2024.102769

Zhou, K., Liu, T., & Liang, L. (2016). From cyber-physical systems to Industry 4.0: Make future manufacturing become possible. *International Journal of Manufacturing Research*, *11*(2), 167–188. DOI: 10.1504/IJMR.2016.078251

Chapter 10
From Industry 6.0 to Supply Chain 6.0: How Artificial Intelligence Is Shaping a New Era of Smart, Resilient, and Sustainable Management?

Taoufiq El Moussaoui
Polydisciplinary Faculty of Sidi Bennour, Chouaib Doukkali University, El Jadida, Morocco

Alaa Eddine El Moussaoui
http://orcid.org/0000-0002-5749-7682
EMIO, LIREEM Laboratory, Higher School of Technology of Nador, Mohammed First University, Oujda, Morocco

ABSTRACT

This chapter examines the evolution from Industry 6.0 to Supply Chain 6.0, showing how AIoT transforms industrial and supply chain systems into smart, autonomous, and sustainable networks. Industry 6.0 integrates human intelligence with AIoT for real-time monitoring, predictive analytics, and autonomous decision-making, while Supply Chain 6.0 applies these capabilities to optimize procurement, production, and distribution, improving efficiency, resilience, and sustainability. Case studies from Siemens, Amazon, Alibaba, and DHL illustrate benefits like predictive maintenance, inventory optimization, and autonomous logistics. The chapter also addresses challenges including cybersecurity, ethical AI use, and workforce adaptation, providing a framework that guides both research and practice in AIoT-driven industrial and supply chain systems.

DOI: 10.4018/979-8-2600-3199-5.ch010

1. INTRODUCTION

The accelerated diffusion of digital technologies has profoundly reshaped industrial systems and supply chain management over the past decade. Advances in information and communication technologies have progressively transformed supply chains from linear, efficiency-driven structures into complex, interconnected ecosystems characterized by real-time data exchange, advanced analytics, and cross-organizational coordination (Khang et al, 2023). These transformations have expanded firms' capabilities to integrate dispersed competencies, synchronize operational decisions, and respond more dynamically to market volatility. Within this context, supply chains are no longer perceived merely as operational backbones but as strategic platforms through which firms can achieve competitiveness, resilience, and long-term value creation (Manavalan and Jayakrishna, 2019).

Supply chains constitute the core operational infrastructure of modern organizations, encompassing procurement, supplier coordination, production planning, distribution, and customer interface management. The effectiveness of these interconnected processes directly conditions firms' performance in terms of cost efficiency, service reliability, and market responsiveness (Radhoui et al, 2021 ; Taghipour, 2023). Beyond traditional efficiency objectives, contemporary supply chain management increasingly focuses on waste reduction, inventory optimization, financial flow coordination, and risk mitigation. As highlighted by (Ganesh and Kalpana, 2022), firms capable of orchestrating these dimensions coherently are better positioned to adapt to rapid environmental changes and competitive pressures. However, the growing complexity of supply networks has exposed the limitations of conventional managerial tools, particularly in environments characterized by uncertainty, data abundance, and systemic interdependencies.

Technological innovation has emerged as a critical lever to address these limitations and to unlock new forms of supply chain intelligence. Historically, the absence of adequate analytical and digital infrastructures constrained organizations' ability to exploit the growing volumes of operational data generated across supply chain activities. Large datasets often remained underutilized due to insufficient capabilities in data acquisition, storage, and analysis (Ikegwu et al, 2022). Recent technological advances have significantly altered this situation. Organizations are now able to process structured, semi-structured, and unstructured data, transforming raw information into actionable insights that support planning, coordination, and decision-making across the entire supply chain. The proliferation of digital communication systems and interactive platforms has further intensified data generation at all supply chain stages, reinforcing the strategic role of data-driven management.

Within this digital transformation trajectory, technologies such as big data analytics, the Internet of Things (IoT), and artificial intelligence (AI) have become central enablers of advanced supply chain capabilities (Ammar et al., 2024 ; El Moussaoui et al., 2025a). Big data analytics enhances forecasting accuracy and performance monitoring, IoT enables real-time visibility and traceability of physical flows, while AI supports predictive, prescriptive, and autonomous decision-making processes. The convergence of IoT and AI into Artificial Intelligence of Things (AIoT) represents a further step toward intelligent supply networks, combining continuous data sensing with adaptive learning algorithms to optimize operations under dynamic conditions. This technological convergence has laid the foundations for digitally integrated supply chains capable of real-time coordination and proactive response.

In parallel, blockchain technology has introduced new mechanisms to enhance transparency, security, and trust within supply chain relationships (Taghipour and Merimi, 2021 ; Taghipour, 2022 ; Lu et al, 2023). By enabling immutable and verifiable transaction records, blockchain addresses long-standing challenges related to information asymmetry, traceability, and accountability among supply chain partners. Moreover, the expansion of online platforms and digital ecosystems has facilitated new forms of collaboration and interaction, generating rich datasets on customer behavior, market trends, and operational performance. Collectively, these developments have been conceptualized under the paradigm of Supply Chain 4.0, which emphasizes digital integration, connectivity, and automation as drivers of efficiency and responsiveness (Lu and Taghipour, 2023 ; Sahraoui et al, 2023 ; Shafik, 2024).

Building on this digital foundation, the emergence of Industry 5.0 has shifted attention toward human-centric, sustainable, and resilient industrial systems. Within this context, Supply Chain 5.0 extends digital supply chain models by explicitly integrating human intelligence, ethical considerations, and sustainability objectives aligned with the United Nations Sustainable Development Goals defined in 2015 (Duggal et al., 2022). While this paradigm addresses important societal and environmental concerns, recent technological acceleration suggests that existing frameworks may no longer fully capture the depth of transformation enabled by advanced artificial intelligence, real-time autonomy, and cognitive systems. This evolution has given rise to the emerging concept of Supply Chain 6.0, which represents a qualitative shift rather than a simple extension of previous models.

Supply Chain 6.0 is characterized by hyper-intelligent, self-adaptive, and resilient systems that integrate artificial intelligence, big data analytics, IoT, blockchain, and advanced computational models into a unified decision-making architecture. Unlike earlier paradigms, Supply Chain 6.0 emphasizes the fusion of artificial and natural intelligence, enabling supply networks to anticipate disruptions, learn from complex environments, and autonomously coordinate responses across organizational boundaries. By combining speed, accuracy, transparency, and security, this paradigm aims to minimize operational errors while enhancing resilience and sustainability under conditions of uncertainty (Mathiyazhagan et al, 2022). Despite its growing relevance, Supply Chain 6.0 remains underexplored in academic literature, with limited conceptual clarity regarding its distinguishing features, theoretical foundations, and managerial implications.

In response to these gaps, this chapter seeks to clarify the conceptual transition from Industry 6.0 to Supply Chain 6.0 by synthesizing recent developments in artificial intelligence and digital technologies within a coherent analytical framework. Specifically, the chapter aims to (i) position Supply Chain 6.0 relative to prior paradigms, (ii) examine the role of Artificial Intelligence of Things (AIoT) as a systemic backbone of next-generation supply chains, and (iii) discuss the implications of this transformation for resilience, sustainability, and strategic management. By adopting a conceptual synthesis approach grounded in recent literature, the chapter contributes to advancing scholarly understanding of how AI-driven systems are reshaping supply chain design and governance.

The remainder of the chapter is structured as follows. Section 2, From Industry 4.0 to Industry 6.0: The Evolution Toward Intelligent and Human-Centered Systems, examines the industrial paradigms underlying the emergence of Industry 6.0. Section 3, Artificial Intelligence of Things (AIoT): The Engine of Future Industrial Transformation, analyzes AIoT as an integrative technological foundation. Section 4, Supply Chain 6.0: Toward Smart, Autonomous, and Sustainable Supply Networks, explores the defining characteristics and applications of Supply Chain 6.0. Finally, Section 5 concludes by synthesizing key insights, discussing implications, limitations, and outlining directions for future research.

2. FROM INDUSTRY 4.0 TO INDUSTRY 6.0: THE EVOLUTION TOWARD INTELLIGENT AND HUMAN-CENTERED SYSTEMS

The industrial landscape has evolved through successive technological revolutions, each reshaping the way operations, decision-making, and human roles are integrated. Industry 4.0 marked a pivotal shift toward digitization and automation, leveraging cyber-physical systems, IoT, cloud computing, and big data to enhance operational efficiency and connectivity (Taghipour, 2024; Lu and Taghipour, 2025). Decision-making during this phase remained largely algorithmic, and ethical or sustainability considerations were limited (XiaoWen and Atour, 2025).

Building upon this foundation, Industry 5.0 introduced human-centric approaches, combining advanced technologies with human creativity and judgment. This era emphasized collaborative robotics, AI-assisted decision-making, and sustainable production, addressing social and environmental concerns while enhancing resilience (Vijay et al, 2024). Despite these improvements, operational systems still faced limitations in predictive capability and adaptability under high uncertainty.

Industry 6.0 represents a transformative leap, integrating hybrid intelligence, anti-fragility, and ethical governance into industrial systems. Human cognition interacts dynamically with AI, quantum computing, robotics, and IoT, producing self-optimizing and predictive operations capable of adapting to unforeseen disruptions (Alhakimi, 2024; Raj and Raman, 2017). Anti-fragile designs allow systems to not only withstand stress but improve under challenging conditions, converting volatility into operational strength. Ethical governance ensures that AI deployment aligns with societal values, privacy, and ESG principles, embedding responsibility directly into industrial processes (Taghipour and Frayret, 2013 ; XiaoWen and Atour, 2025; Taghipour and Merimi, 2021). Quantum computing accelerates complex calculations and enhances AI models, enabling real-time optimization across manufacturing, logistics, and supply chain networks. Advanced robotics, augmented by AI, execute complex adaptive tasks in collaboration with human operators, while IoT and satellite systems provide real-time global visibility and control (Raj and Raman, 2017). Collectively, these technologies enable Industry 6.0 systems to achieve operational excellence while integrating sustainability, ethics, and human insight.

To clarify the progression, Table 1 summarizes the key distinctions across these industrial paradigms, emphasizing technological capabilities, decision-making, human involvement, and sustainability considerations.

Table 1. Comparative Overview of Industry 4.0, 5.0, and 6.0

Dimension	**Industry 4.0**	**Industry 5.0**	**Industry 6.0**
Core Focus	Automation, digitization	Human-centric, sustainability	Hybrid intelligence, anti-fragility, ethical governance
Key Technologies	IoT, CPS, cloud, big data	Collaborative robots, AI-assisted decision-making	Quantum computing, AI, advanced robotics, ethical AI frameworks
Decision-Making	Algorithm-driven	Human-machine collaboration	Co-created hybrid intelligence
Adaptability	System optimization	Responsive to human input	Predictive, adaptive, anti-fragile systems
Sustainability	Operational efficiency	Social and environmental focus	Integrated ESG compliance, ethical oversight
Human Role	Minimal	Central to operations	Cognitive partner and ethical supervisor
Outcome	Efficient, connected operations	Personalized, resilient, sustainable production	Resilient, adaptive, ethical, globally interconnected ecosystems

The table demonstrates a clear trajectory from efficiency-driven automation to a holistic integration of technology, human intelligence, and ethical oversight. Industry 6.0 systems not only optimize operational processes but also enhance resilience, sustainability, and decision-making transparency. This integrated approach allows industries to anticipate disruptions, adapt dynamically, and maintain ethical, socially responsible operations on a global scale (Taghipour, 2024; Vijay et al, 2024). In brief, the evolution toward Industry 6.0 represents a comprehensive paradigm shift, where human cognition, advanced technologies, and ethical governance converge. This framework provides industries with a resilient, adaptive, and sustainable blueprint capable of navigating future complexities while maximizing operational efficiency and societal impact.

3. ARTIFICIAL INTELLIGENCE OF THINGS (AIOT): THE ENGINE OF FUTURE INDUSTRIAL TRANSFORMATION

The evolution of industrial and supply chain ecosystems is increasingly driven by the seamless integration of intelligent connectivity, predictive analytics, and autonomous decision-making. At the core of this transformation lies the Internet of Things (IoT), which connects billions of devices—from industrial machinery, sensors, and robotics to wearable and smart devices—allowing real-time data collection, transmission, and analysis (Younis, 2018). By converting traditional supply chains into dynamic, adaptive networks, IoT enables organizations to continuously monitor operations, optimize resource allocation, and enhance operational efficiency across manufacturing, logistics, healthcare, and urban infrastructure. Siemens' Amberg Electronics Factory in Germany exemplifies this transformation: IoT-enabled sensors monitor production lines and predict equipment failures, achieving near-zero defect rates and increasing uptime while reducing waste (Melnyk et al, 2022). Similarly, Amazon's fulfillment centers in the United States integrate IoT devices with robotics and AI algorithms to improve throughput by 25% and reduce operational costs by 20%, while DHL employs IoT-driven platforms for route optimization, improving on-time delivery by 15% and reducing carbon emissions by 12% (Chi et al, 2023; Oskounejad and Nozari, 2024). These examples highlight how IoT provides the foundational layer for operational visibility, efficiency, and data-driven decision-making.

Building upon IoT, the Internet of Everything (IoE) expands connectivity to human actors, organizational processes, and social interactions, forming a holistic ecosystem in which people, devices, and systems collaborate intelligently (Baker and Xiang, 2023). Unlike the device-centric focus of IoT, IoE integrates human cognition, behavioral patterns, and social dynamics, enabling richer insights and more robust operational strategies. Smart city initiatives in Singapore and Barcelona illustrate these capabilities: IoE frameworks dynamically optimize traffic flow, monitor energy usage, and improve public service delivery, producing measurable improvements in resource efficiency and citizen quality of life. Within industrial ecosystems, IoE facilitates real-time synchronization of production, distribution, and maintenance processes, fostering operational agility, resilience, and sustainability while reducing latency in decision-making.

The convergence of Artificial Intelligence (AI) and the Internet of Things (IoT), known as Artificial Intelligence of Things (AIoT), represents the central engine of Industry 6.0, combining vast data streams with machine learning, predictive analytics, and autonomous decision-making capabilities (Melnyk et al., 2022; El Moussaoui et al., 2025b). AIoT enables systems to self-optimize, anticipate disruptions, and dynamically adapt to changing operational conditions. In manufacturing, Siemens' Smart Factory leverages AIoT for predictive maintenance and intelligent production scheduling, reducing unplanned downtime by 30% and achieving near-zero defects. In logistics, Amazon integrates AIoT with robotic order fulfillment systems to optimize inventory and delivery processes, increasing throughput by 25% and lowering operational costs by 20%. Similarly, Alibaba's Cainiao network employs AIoT for real-time monitoring, predictive routing, and data-driven operational transparency, reducing last-mile delivery times by 22%. DHL's global smart warehouses use AIoT-enabled analytics for route planning, inventory forecasting, and energy optimization, achieving a 15% improvement in on-time deliveries while reducing environmental impact (Chi et al., 2023; Oskounejad & Nozari, 2024; Toufah et al., 2025). These real-world mini-cases illustrate how AIoT transforms industrial operations into self-learning, autonomous, and predictive systems that generate measurable gains in efficiency, resilience, and sustainability, as illustrated in Table 2.

Table 2. Real-World Applications of AIoT in Industrial and Logistics Ecosystems

Company	Sector	AIoT Application	Key Outcomes
Siemens Smart Factory	Manufacturing	IoT sensors + AI for predictive maintenance & intelligent production scheduling	30% reduction in unplanned downtime Near-zero defect rate
Amazon Fulfillment Centers	Logistics	Automated AIoT-enabled robotics & order fulfillment	25% increase in throughput 20% reduction in operational costs
DHL Smart Warehouses	Supply Chain	AIoT analytics for route planning, inventory forecasting, energy optimization	15% improvement in on-time delivery 12% reduction in operational costs
Alibaba Cainiao Network	E-commerce Logistics	AIoT for real-time monitoring, predictive routing, operational transparency	22% reduction in last-mile delivery time Increased operational transparency

Table 3. Technological Progression from IoT to AIoT in Industrial Ecosystems

Dimension	IoT (Internet of Things)	IoE (Internet of Everything)	AIoT (Artificial Intelligence of Things)
Connectivity Scope	Connected devices and sensors	Devices, people, processes, and data	Fully integrated intelligent ecosystem
Primary Function	Data collection and monitoring	System-wide data integration and interaction	Predictive analytics and autonomous optimization
Role of Human Cognition	External system operator	Integrated participant in digital processes	Collaborative intelligence between humans and AI
Level of Automation	Basic automation and control	Coordinated and interconnected systems	Self-learning, adaptive, and autonomous systems
Decision-Making Logic	Reactive and rule-based	Coordinated and data-informed	Real-time, predictive, and adaptive decision-making
Operational Impact	Improved visibility and efficiency	Enhanced synchronization and resilience	Operational intelligence, sustainability, and dynamic performance optimization
Strategic Contribution	Digital transformation foundation	Ecosystem integration layer	Central engine of Industry 6.0 enabling resilience and sustainability

In Table 3, we can see the progression from basic device connectivity (IoT) to a fully integrated ecosystem (AIoT), highlighting the interplay between human cognition, automated systems, and predictive intelligence. The table emphasizes

AIoT as the central engine of operational intelligence, resilience, and sustainability, enabling real-time, adaptive decision-making across industrial sectors.

The operational capabilities of AIoT can be understood through a layered architecture, which links technological functions to measurable industrial impacts. Table 4 demonstrates how AIoT transforms raw data into actionable insights that drive predictive operations, adaptive decision-making, and sustainable practices. The governance layer ensures compliance with ethical standards and ESG objectives, reinforcing accountability while minimizing risks associated with autonomous systems (Alhakimi, 2024).

Table 4. AIoT Operational Architecture and Industrial Impact

Layer	Function	Key Technologies	Operational Impact
Perception	Data acquisition from sensors and devices	IoT sensors, RFID, wearables, industrial devices	Real-time monitoring, continuous operational visibility
Network	Integration and data transmission	5G/6G, cloud computing, IoE platforms	Seamless communication, centralized data processing
Intelligence	Data analysis, prediction, and learning	AI, machine learning, deep learning	Predictive maintenance, demand forecasting, adaptive optimization
Application	Autonomous decision-making and optimization	AIoT platforms, robotics, smart contracts	Self-optimizing processes, error reduction, increased efficiency
Governance	Security, ethics, and sustainability oversight	Cybersecurity, blockchain, ESG frameworks	Ethical AI deployment, regulatory compliance, ESG alignment

AIoT adoption is accompanied by critical challenges, including cybersecurity threats, data privacy concerns, algorithmic bias, workforce reskilling, and platform interoperability (Vijay et al, 2024 ; XiaoWen and Atour, 2025). Firms must establish robust governance, ethical oversight, and continuous training programs to ensure effective collaboration between humans and autonomous systems. Standardization and regulatory compliance are essential to support cross-border operations and international supply chain coordination, particularly when AIoT systems operate across multiple jurisdictions and industries.

In addition to the operational and governance dimensions, AIoT can be applied to multiple sectors beyond manufacturing and logistics. In healthcare, AIoT enables real-time patient monitoring, predictive diagnosis, and personalized treatment plans, improving patient outcomes and optimizing hospital resources (Melnyk et al, 2022). In agriculture, AIoT-driven precision farming systems use sensor data and machine learning algorithms to optimize irrigation, nutrient application, and crop monitoring, increasing yields while reducing water and chemical usage. In energy, smart grids integrate AIoT to monitor electricity flows, balance demand and supply, and reduce waste, supporting environmental sustainability (Oskounejad and Nozari, 2024). These applications highlight AIoT's versatility in enabling smart, resilient, and sustainable systems across sectors.

In conclusion, AIoT forms the central engines of Industry 6.0, integrating people, devices, and processes with advanced analytics to create autonomous, predictive, and resilient industrial ecosystems. Empirical evidence from Siemens, Amazon, DHL, and Alibaba illustrates measurable improvements in operational efficiency, risk mitigation, and sustainability outcomes (Melnyk et al, 2022 ; Baker and Xiang, 2023; Chi et al, 2023). By embedding AIoT capabilities within industrial and supply chain operations, organizations can anticipate disruptions, optimize processes, and achieve strategic, human-centered, and environmentally responsible performance.

4. SUPPLY CHAIN 6.0: TOWARD SMART, AUTONOMOUS, AND SUSTAINABLE SUPPLY NETWORKS

Building on the AIoT frameworks introduced in Section 3, Supply Chain 6.0 represents the direct application of Artificial Intelligence of Things to global supply networks. While Section 3 described how AIoT enables real-time data collection, predictive analytics, and autonomous decision-making in industrial operations, Supply Chain 6.0 demonstrates how these capabilities transform the supply chain into a fully interconnected, intelligent, and adaptive ecosystem.

In procurement, Supply Chain 6.0 leverages AIoT to enable intelligent, data-driven supplier selection, automated ordering, and real-time decision-making. Unilever's procurement platform, for example, integrates IoT-enabled sensors, AI-driven analytics, and predictive algorithms to determine optimal order quantities, dynamically select suppliers based on historical performance and pricing, and automatically adjust delivery schedules. This approach minimizes waste, prevents shortages, and accelerates procurement cycles (Allal-Chérif et al, 2021). Similarly, Amazon's fulfillment centers use AIoT within their Supply Chain 6.0 framework to optimize inventory management and warehouse operations, achieving a 25% increase in throughput and a 20% reduction in operational costs (Chi et al, 2023; Oskounejad and Nozari, 2024). By embedding AIoT at the procurement layer, Supply Chain 6.0 enables organizations to operate with unprecedented efficiency, agility, and resilience.

In the production domain, Supply Chain 6.0 integrates AIoT-enabled Smart Factories, connecting machines, sensors, and analytics systems to facilitate real-time monitoring, predictive maintenance, and adaptive scheduling. Siemens' Smart Factory in Germany demonstrates this concept: IoT sensors continuously monitor equipment health, AI predicts maintenance needs, and adaptive scheduling automatically aligns production with real-time demand, reducing downtime by 30% and achieving near-zero defect rates (Hassebo and Tealab, 2023). Within the Supply Chain 6.0 framework, production systems communicate seamlessly with procurement, warehousing, and distribution units, ensuring synchronization across all stages of the value chain and enabling proactive responses to disruptions or fluctuations in demand.

Supply Chain 6.0 also transforms warehousing and distribution through AIoT-enabled automation and predictive analytics. DHL's smart warehouses employ robotics, IoT sensors, and AI analytics to optimize inventory management, automate replenishment, and improve retrieval efficiency (Oskounejad and Nozari, 2024). Amazon and Alibaba further illustrate how Supply Chain 6.0 integrates AIoT to dynamically plan delivery routes, monitor environmental conditions during transit, and ensure timely, sustainable deliveries (Chi et al, 2023; Reis, 2023). These capabilities allow companies to reduce costs, lower emissions, and enhance customer satisfaction, all while maintaining a highly responsive and adaptive supply network. The operational architecture of Supply Chain 6.0 can be summarized in the following table:

Table 5. AIoT-Enabled Supply Chain 6.0 Operational Architecture

Layer	Function	Key Technologies	AIoT Impact in Supply Chain 6.0
Procurement	Smart supplier selection & automated ordering	AIoT platforms, IoT sensors, big data	Optimal procurement, reduced lead times, cost minimization
Production	Real-time monitoring & adaptive scheduling	AIoT, predictive maintenance, MRP systems	Reduced downtime, high quality, energy efficiency
Warehouse	Intelligent inventory management & automation	Robotics, AI, IoT, autonomous vehicles	Accurate stock levels, efficient retrieval, lower costs
Distribution	Dynamic routing & predictive delivery	AI algorithms, IoT sensors, autonomous transport	Timely deliveries, lower emissions, customer satisfaction
Governance	Security, compliance, and sustainability oversight	Cybersecurity, blockchain, ESG frameworks	Ethical AI, regulatory compliance, ESG alignment

Table 5 highlights how Supply Chain 6.0 applies AIoT to transform raw data into actionable insights across procurement, production, warehousing, and distribution. The governance layer ensures ethical AI deployment, regulatory compliance, and ESG alignment (Alhakimi, 2024).

Taken together, Supply Chain 6.0 operationalizes the AIoT frameworks discussed in Section 3, creating smart, autonomous, and resilient supply networks. Mini-case examples—Unilever for procurement, Siemens for production, DHL for warehousing, and Amazon/Alibaba for distribution—demonstrate measurable improvements in efficiency, adaptability, and sustainability. By embedding AIoT across every layer of the supply chain, Supply Chain 6.0 ensures predictive capabilities, operational intelligence, and human-centered innovation across the value chain (Chi et al, 2023 ; Reis, 2023 ; Afrin et al, 2024; XiaoWen & Atour, 2025).

5. CONCLUSION

The evolution from Industry 6.0 to Supply Chain 6.0 marks a transformative period in industrial and supply chain management, driven by the integration of Artificial Intelligence of Things (AIoT), advanced robotics, IoT, and big data analytics. Industry 6.0 establishes adaptive industrial ecosystems in which human cognition and AIoT-enabled systems interact seamlessly, enabling real-time monitoring, predictive analytics, and autonomous decision-making across global operations. These systems leverage AIoT to transform operational decisions into a dynamic synergy between human insight and machine intelligence, enhancing resilience, responsiveness, and sustainability across industrial and supply chain networks.

AIoT functions as the operational backbone of these transformations, connecting devices, processes, and human actors within integrated ecosystems. Empirical examples, such as Siemens' Smart Factory, Amazon's fulfillment centers, Alibaba's Cainiao network, and DHL's global warehouses, demonstrate how AIoT facilitates predictive maintenance, autonomous inventory management, optimized routing, and real-time operational analytics, delivering measurable improvements in efficiency, throughput, and sustainability. By applying a layered operational architecture encompassing perception, network, intelligence, application, and governance, organizations gain continuous operational visibility, ethical oversight, regulatory alignment, and ESG integration.

Within Supply Chain 6.0, these AIoT capabilities create intelligent, autonomous, and predictive networks that continuously optimize procurement, production, and distribution. Procurement systems utilize real-time data to determine optimal order quantities, select suppliers, and manage transactions automatically, while production systems achieve near-zero defects through predictive scheduling, quality integration, and real-time cross-departmental communication. Distribution and sales processes leverage AIoT to optimize delivery routes, monitor product conditions, and align stock levels with market demand, resulting in improved customer experiences, operational efficiency, and environmental performance. Collectively, these practices position Supply Chain 6.0 as a fully intelligent, resilient, and sustainable framework capable of responding proactively to market fluctuations and environmental constraints.

This chapter contributes a comprehensive framework linking Industry 6.0 principles, AIoT capabilities, and Supply Chain 6.0 practices, illustrating how emerging technologies enable smart, resilient, and sustainable operations. The integration of empirical examples provides actionable insights for both academics and practitioners, emphasizing operational, ethical, and sustainability dimensions. Nonetheless, the framework is constrained by the focus on advanced firms with high technological readiness, limiting its immediate applicability to smaller organizations or less developed regions. Rapid technological evolution further necessitates continuous adaptation of strategies and systems.

Future research could explore AIoT adoption in diverse industrial and geographic contexts, including small and medium-sized enterprises and emerging markets, while examining human-AI collaboration, ethical implementation, and cybersecurity strategies in autonomous supply networks. Further investigation into integrating circular economy principles, resilience measures, and sustainability metrics would enhance understanding of AIoT-enabled supply chains. Longitudinal studies tracking predictive, self-optimizing, and fully autonomous networks would also refine both theoretical and practical frameworks.

Overall, the convergence of Industry 6.0 principles with AIoT technologies within Supply Chain 6.0 establishes a new paradigm for industrial and supply chain management. Intelligent automation, predictive analytics, and real-time decision-making enable organizations to enhance operational excellence, anticipate disruptions, and achieve sustainable, socially responsible outcomes. This integrated framework offers a foundation for practical implementation and academic research, shaping a new era of smart, resilient, and human-centered supply chains.

REFERENCES

Afrin, S., Roksana, S., & Akram, R. (2024). AI-Enhanced Robotic Process Automation: A Review of Intelligent Automation Innovations. *IEEE Access : Practical Innovations, Open Solutions.*

Alhakimi, A. M. (2024). The Power of Technology in Industrial Revolution 5.0. In Utilizing Renewable Energy, Technology, and Education for Industry 5.0 (pp. 400-443). IGI Global.

Allal-Chérif, O., Simón-Moya, V., & Ballester, A. C. C. (2021). Intelligent purchasing: How artificial intelligence can redefine the purchasing function. *Journal of Business Research*, *124*, 69–76. DOI: 10.1016/j.jbusres.2020.11.050

Ammar, A., Amahmoud, H., El Menzhi, K., Mkik, M., Hebaz, A., & Eddine, E. M. A. (2024, May). Critical Analysis of Logistics Transformation in Morocco Under The Auspices of Artificial Intelligence: Government Perspectives From the perspective of Innovative and Technology Driven Public Management. In 2024 IEEE 15th International Colloquium on Logistics and Supply Chain Management (LOGISTIQUA) (pp. 1-9). IEEE.

Baker, S., & Xiang, W. (2023). Artificial intelligence of things for smarter healthcare: A survey of advancements, challenges, and opportunities. *IEEE Communications Surveys and Tutorials*, *25*(2), 1261–1293. DOI: 10.1109/COMST.2023.3256323

Chi, C., Yin, Z., Liu, Y., & Chai, S. (2023). A trusted cloud-edge decision architecture based on blockchain and mlp for aiot. *IEEE Internet of Things Journal.*

Duggal, A. S., Malik, P. K., Gehlot, A., Singh, R., Gaba, G. S., Masud, M., & Al-Amri, J. F. (2022). A sequential roadmap to Industry 6.0: Exploring future manufacturing trends. *IET Communications*, *16*(5), 521–531. DOI: 10.1049/cmu2.12284

El Moussaoui, T., Chakir, L., & El Moussaoui, A. E. (2025b). Exploring Information Technology (IT) Acceptance Among Supply Chain Stakeholders in Morocco's Pharmaceutical Industry. In Ecological and Human Dimensions of AI-Based Supply Chain (pp. 245-270). IGI Global Scientific Publishing.

El Moussaoui, T., Loqman, C., & El Moussaoui, A. E. (2025a). Adoption of artificial intelligence in smart cities: Literature review and bibliometric analysis. Generative AI for Cybersecurity and Privacy, 103-125.

Ganesh, A. D., & Kalpana, P. (2022). Future of artificial intelligence and its influence on supply chain risk management–A systematic review. *Computers & Industrial Engineering*, *169*, 108206. DOI: 10.1016/j.cie.2022.108206

Hassebo, A., & Tealab, M. (2023). Global models of smart cities and potential IoT applications: A review. *IoT*, *4*(3), 366–411. DOI: 10.3390/iot4030017

Ikegwu, A. C., Nweke, H. F., Anikwe, C. V., Alo, U. R., & Okonkwo, O. R. (2022). Big data analytics for data-driven industry: A review of data sources, tools, challenges, solutions, and research directions. *Cluster Computing*, *25*(5), 3343–3387. DOI: 10.1007/s10586-022-03568-5

Khang, A., Jadhav, B., & Birajdar, S. (2023). Industry revolution 4.0: workforce competency models and designs. In *Designing workforce management systems for industry 4.0* (pp. 11–34). CRC Press. DOI: 10.1201/9781003357070-2

Lu, X., & Taghipour, A. (2023). A French Guide for Businesses and Governments to Integrate the Concept of Sustainable Development Into Their Supply Chains. In *Government Impact on Sustainable and Responsible Supply Chain Management* (pp. 1–12). IGI Global. DOI: 10.4018/978-1-6684-9062-4.ch001

Lu, X., & Taghipour, A. (2025). The Future of Marketing: Integrating Big Data and AI for Personalized Customer Engagement. In Ecological and Human Dimensions of AI-Based Supply Chain (pp. 97-110). IGI Global Scientific Publishing.

Lu, X. W., Tliche, Y., Vosooghidizaji, M., & Taghipour, A. (2023). Cryptocurrencies and Blockchain Applications. In Blockchain Applications in Cryptocurrency for Technological Evolution (pp. 1-13). IGI Global.

Manavalan, E., & Jayakrishna, K. (2019). A review of Internet of Things (IoT) embedded sustainable supply chain for industry 4.0 requirements. *Computers & Industrial Engineering*, *127*, 925–953. DOI: 10.1016/j.cie.2018.11.030

Mathiyazhagan, K., Taghipour, A., & Agarwal, V. (Eds.). (2022). *Blockchain Technology in Supply Chain Management for Society 5.0*. CRC Press. DOI: 10.1201/9781003177432

Melnyk, S. A., Schoenherr, T., Speier-Pero, C., Peters, C., Chang, J. F., & Friday, D. (2022). New challenges in supply chain management: Cybersecurity across the supply chain. *International Journal of Production Research*, *60*(1), 162–183. DOI: 10.1080/00207543.2021.1984606

Oskounejad, M. M., & Nozari, H. (Eds.). (2024). *Advanced Businesses in Industry 6.0*. IGI Global. DOI: 10.4018/979-8-3693-3108-8

Radhoui, H., Taghipour, A., & Canel-Depitre, B. (2021). Mixed delivery and pickup vehicle routing problem with limited flow and assignment of drones in an urban network. In *Demand Forecasting and Order Planning in Supply Chains and Humanitarian Logistics* (pp. 225–249). IGI Global. DOI: 10.4018/978-1-7998-3805-0.ch008

Raj, P., & Raman, A. C. (2017). *The Internet of Things: Enabling technologies, platforms, and use cases*. Auerbach Publications.

Reis, J. (2023). Exploring Applications and Practical Examples by Streamlining Material Requirements Planning (MRP) with Python. *Logistics (Basel)*, *7*(4), 91. DOI: 10.3390/logistics7040091

Sahraoui, A., Tran, N. K., Tliche, Y., Kacem, A., & Taghipour, A. (2023). Examining ICT Innovation for Sustainable Terminal Operations in Developing Countries: A Case Study of the Port of Radès in Tunisia. *Sustainability (Basel)*, *15*(11), 9123. DOI: 10.3390/su15119123

Shafik, W. (2024). Artificial intelligence and internet of things roles in sustainable next-generation manufacturing: An overview of emerging trends in Industry 6.0. *Advances in Business Information Systems and Analytics*, *6*(0), 207–239. DOI: 10.4018/979-8-3693-3140-8.ch012

Taghipour, A. (Ed.). (2022). *Blockchain Applications in Cryptocurrency for Technological Evolution*. IGI Global. DOI: 10.4018/978-1-6684-6247-8

Taghipour, A. (Ed.). (2023). *Government Impact on Sustainable and Responsible Supply Chain Management*. IGI Global. DOI: 10.4018/978-1-6684-9062-4

Taghipour, A. (2024). Big Data: The New Gold Mine for Supermarkets. In Applications of New Technology in Operations and Supply Chain Management (pp. 98-106). IGI Global.

Taghipour, A., & Frayret, J. M. (2013). Coordination of operations planning in supply chains: A review. *International Journal of Business Performance and Supply Chain Modelling*, *5*(3), 272–307. DOI: 10.1504/IJBPSCM.2013.055729

Taghipour, A., & Merimi, M. (2021, March). Digital transformation of supply chains during crisis: covid-19. In 11th Annual International Conference on Industrial Engineering and Operations Management, IEOM (pp. 7493-7501). DOI: 10.46254/AN11.20211298

TOUFAH, N., EL MOUSSAOUI, A. E., & LEKHAILA, G. (2025). A Comparative Analysis of the Logistics and Economics Fields: A Literature Review. *Revue Française d'Economie et de Gestion*, *6*(8).

Vijay, A. J., William, B. N. J., Haruna, A. A., & Prasad, D. D. (2024). Exploring the synergy of IIoT, AI, and data analytics in Industry 6.0. In *Industry 6.0* (pp. 1–36). CRC Press. DOI: 10.1201/9781003517993-1

XiaoWen, L., & Atour, T.XiaoWen. (2025). Knowledge-driven digital innovation in supply chains: An organizational perspective. *Journal of Innovation & Knowledge*, *10*(5), 100787. DOI: 10.1016/j.jik.2025.100787

Younis, M. (2018). Internet of everything and everybody: Architecture and service virtualization. *Computer Communications*, *131*, 66–72. DOI: 10.1016/j.comcom.2018.07.008

Chapter 11
Sustainable Sport Supply Chains:
Managing Equipment, Events, and Athlete Performance

Mojgan Bazhrang
http://orcid.org/0009-0002-9720-0481
University of Quebec, Canada

ABSTRACT

The sports industry is a massive global sector that excites fans, generates billions, and relies on complex supply chains, from making equipment to transporting athletes and hosting major events. Growing pressure for sustainability demands these chains address climate impact, social responsibility, and economic value. This chapter reviews how brands, federations, global events, and athlete logistics contribute to emissions, labor use, and financial outcomes. It offers a framework for assessing sustainability in sport supply chains and highlights examples like the Olympics, FIFA World Cup, and apparel makers. The chapter argues that real change requires shared governance, digital tools such as AI and IoT, and circular models that cut waste and extend product lifecycles. Sport can lead global sustainability if climate goals, social equity, and economic performance guide supply-chain decisions.

1. INTRODUCTION

Sport is among the most influential global industries, with an estimated economic value exceeding $500 billion annually when counting professional leagues, apparel, events, tourism, and media broadcasting (PwC, 2023). Because sports engage consumers emotionally and culturally, their environmental and social footprint is

DOI: 10.4018/979-8-2600-3199-5.ch011

both extensive and highly visible. Sporting events require stadium infrastructure, transportation systems, security personnel, medical supplies, and hospitality services. Supply chains support every aspect of these operations, from the sourcing of raw materials such as polyester and rubber for equipment, to logistics networks that enable athletes and fans to travel across borders.

However, this dynamic consumption and movement comes at ecological and social cost. Studies show that a single mega-event, such as the FIFA World Cup or the Olympic Games, generates between 1.4 and 3.6 million tons of CO_2 emissions (Collins et al., 2021). Fan transportation alone may account for 60% to 80% of total event emissions (Preuss, 2019). Apparel manufacturing for global brands such as Nike and Adidas is still concentrated in regions where labor conditions and environmental regulations are fragile (Kumar & Bansal, 2022). Meanwhile, elite athletes frequently travel long distances for competitions, creating logistics patterns that add to emissions and physical strain.

The concept of sustainable sport supply chains, therefore, has emerged as a response to a rapidly changing environmental and social landscape. Sustainability expectations are rising among governments, investors, and civil society. The Paris Agreement and subsequent carbon neutrality targets have forced events like Paris 2024 to announce zero-waste goals and low-carbon procurement models. At the same time, social accountability,fair labor, diversity, accessibility, and safety, has become part of the reputational fabric of sporting organizations. Finally, economic resilience of leagues and events has been challenged by COVID-19, geopolitical instability, and supply chain disruptions.

The central research question of this chapter is therefore:

How can sport supply chains be managed to simultaneously achieve climate action, social accountability, and economic value?

Existing literature on sustainable supply chain management (SSCM) has explored manufacturing, retail, and urban logistics, but sport, despite its societal visibility, remains understudied. This chapter addresses this gap by integrating operational research, sustainability science, sport management, and logistics strategy.

The contribution of this chapter is threefold:

- It introduces a new multi-layer supply chain model specific to sport (equipment → athlete → venue → event → spectator).
- It synthesizes fragmented research across sustainability domains and applies them to sport contexts.

- It provides real-world case studies demonstrating how sustainability strategies succeed or fail.

This introduction establishes that sport is an important sustainability frontier: because millions of people witness sport every day, sustainable practices in sport can influence culture and behavior on a global scale. If sports organizations implement circular economy models, reduce carbon emissions, and uphold fair labor, they can become role models for corporate responsibility across industries.

The sections that follow deepen this examination through literature review, framework development, and applied analysis.

2. LITERATURE REVIEW

2.2 Sustainable Supply Chain Management (SSCM): Concepts and Theoretical Foundations

Sustainable supply chain management is defined as "the strategic, transparent integration and pursuit of an organization's social, environmental, and economic goals in the systemic coordination of key interorganizational business processes" (Carter & Rogers, 2008). The core theoretical models used to assess sustainable supply chains include:

- **Triple Bottom Line (TBL):** people, planet, profit (Elkington, 1997)
- **Circular Economy (CE):** reduce, reuse, recycle loops to eliminate waste (Geissdoerfer et al., 2017)
- **Environmental, Social & Governance (ESG):** criteria - corporate reporting standards (Alizadeh et al., 2021)
- **Life-Cycle Assessment (LCA):** measurement of total ecological impact of a product or service (Vosooghidizaji et al., 2019)
- **Stakeholder Theory:** aligning the interests of diverse actor groups (Zoghlami et al., 2016)
- **Resilience Theory:** ability to adapt to shocks (pandemics, supply delays) (Taghipour et al., 2023).

Sport intersects with each of these frameworks. For example, carbon neutrality goals in mega-events apply TBL and LCA; social inclusion in grassroots sport relies on social accountability; and stadium procurement uses circular economy thinking to reuse materials (e.g., Paris 2024 sourcing 90% recycled materials).

2.3 Climate Change and the Environmental Burden of Sports

The climate impact of sport is increasingly documented. Collins et al. (2021) estimate that Olympic Games emissions historically range between 1.4 and 3.6 million tons of CO_2, depending on host location, construction, and number of spectators. Several research insights shape this field:

- **Travel-related emissions dominate:** Preuss (2019) finds that 60–80% of total greenhouse gases in sports events come from fan mobility.
- **Construction is the second-largest contributor:** stadiums, Olympic villages, and temporary infrastructure generate emissions via steel, cement, and energy use (Gössling & Scott, 2021).
- **Equipment materials are carbon-intensive:** Polyester, rubber, and plastics have high embodied energy and require fossil-fuel extraction (Niinimäki et al., 2020).
- **Operational energy matters:** lighting, heating, cooling, and turf maintenance remain significant contributors (Aouadni et al., 2024).

Sports organizations are beginning to measure climate impacts using GHG Protocol scopes (Table 1):

Table 1. Protocol scopes

Scope	Example in sport
Scope 1	emissions from stadium generators, facility vehicles
Scope 2	electricity purchased for lighting fields, VR broadcasts
Scope 3	athlete and fan travel, apparel manufacturing, supply chain

Recent policy movements such as carbon labeling and mandatory ESG reporting (EU CSRD, California GHG disclosure) are pushing sports federations to adopt more rigorous measurement.

2.4 Social Accountability in the Sport Supply Chain

Social sustainability involves labor rights, health and safety, equity, and community impacts. In sport, this manifests across multiple dimensions:

- **Apparel factory labor:** Sweatshop scandals have historically implicated Nike and Adidas (Locke, 2013). Though progress has been made, research shows subcontractor auditing remains inconsistent (Kumar & Bansal, 2022).

- **Infrastructure labor exploitation:** Construction of stadiums for Qatar 2022 involved migrant worker exploitation, poor living conditions, and fatalities (Human Rights Watch, 2021).
- **Accessibility and inclusivity:** Sustainable design includes disability access, gender equity, and affordability for low-income communities (Misener & Darcy, 2014).
- **Athlete welfare as a supply chain output:** Increasingly, athlete mental health, travel fatigue, and injury prevention are viewed as ethical obligations.

Unlike traditional supply chains, sport also has a community role, e.g., clubs functioning as social cohesion institutions. Thus, social accountability also includes legacy impacts, what remains after the event ends.

2.5 Economic Value and Financial Sustainability

Economics of sport is driven by:

- broadcasting and media rights
- sponsorship and brand value
- ticketing and tourism revenue
- merchandise sales
- ancillary economic spillovers (jobs, transport, food services)

However, research shows that mega-events frequently fail to deliver promised economic benefits. Zimbalist (2015) demonstrates that most host cities incur long-term debt. Tokyo 2020 exceeded budgets; Brazil 2014 stadiums are under-utilized today.

Yet, sustainable supply chain design can enhance economic ROI (Table 2):

Table 2. Sustainable supply chain and economic effects

Strategy	**Economic effect**
Circular procurement (reuse materials)	reduces capex / waste costs
Local sourcing	keeps money in region, supporting SMEs
Smart logistics	lowers transport cost, reduces delay costs
Renewable-energy facilities	decreases long-term operating expenses

The literature lacks integration across climate, social, and economic domains, which positions this chapter to fill that gap.

3. METHODOLOGY AND CONCEPTUAL FRAMEWORK

Because this is not an empirical study but a conceptual chapter, its methodology is integrative synthesis, drawing on interdisciplinary sources to produce a framework.

3.1 Analytical Approach

The chapter adopts:

- **system mapping** identifying actors (brands, federations, athletes, fans, suppliers)
- **multi-layer chain analysis** moving from equipment → athlete → event → spectator
- **TBL + LCA metrics** carbon (CO_2e), social score, cost/performance KPIs
- **case synthesis** cross-case comparison (Olympics, World Cup, NBA, etc.)

3.2 Multi-Layer Sport Supply Chain Framework

This chapter models the sport supply chain in five interconnected layers:

1 **Equipment & Apparel Layer:** materials, production, distribution
2 **Athlete Performance Layer:** nutrition, travel, medical logistics
3 **Venue Layer:** stadium construction, turf, energy infrastructure
4 **Event Management Layer:** scheduling, security, waste, catering, ticketing
5 **Spectator & Media Layer:** travel, accommodation, digital streaming demand

Each layer influences sustainability objectives differently (Table 3):

Table 3. Sportive layers and their influences

Layer	Climate	Social	Economic
Equipment	plastics extraction, production energy	factory labor	brand sales
Athlete	air travel emissions	wellbeing, fair conditions	sponsorship value
Venue	cement & steel, energy	migrant labor risks	capex investment
Event Mgmt	operational emissions & waste	volunteer labor	ticketing & merch
Spectator	mobility footprint	accessibility & pricing	tourism economy

3.3 Conceptual Model

Sustainable sport supply chain performance (climate action, social accountability, and economic resilience), moderated by digital innovation and stakeholder governance.

Inputs: materials, energy, capital, labor
Transformation: production, travel, events
Outputs: performance, experience, carbon, social legacy, profit
Moderators: digitalization, policy, ESG pressure, fan expectations

4. SUSTAINABLE SPORT SUPPLY CHAINS

4.1 Equipment & Apparel Supply Chains

4.1.1 Overview

The production of sport apparel and equipment represents one of the most visible aspects of the sport supply chain. Major brands like Nike, Adidas, Puma, Under Armour, and Decathlon collectively control a global market exceeding $350 billion in sportswear and equipment (Statista, 2023). However, their supply chains are complex, geographically fragmented, and carbon-intensive.

Most sport equipment and apparel follows a globalized sourcing pattern:

- Polyester, elastane, rubber, EVA foam → sourced from petrochemical sectors in China, India, Gulf states
- Manufacturing → largely outsourced to Southeast Asia (Vietnam, Cambodia, Bangladesh)
- Distribution → global logistics hubs (Rotterdam, Singapore, Los Angeles)
- Retail → physical and online channels in Europe, USA, and Asia

This structure embeds scope 3 emissions, labor compliance risks, and long transportation routes, all of which raise sustainability concerns.

4.1.2 Climate Action Opportunities

To address climate impacts, sport apparel companies are adopting:

- **Recycled materials:** Adidas's "Ocean Plastic" shoes made from marine waste (Parley partnership)

- **Bio-based fibers:** Nike experimenting with plant-based leather substitutes
- **Closed-loop design:** Decathlon renting, repairing, and reselling bicycles and outdoor gear
- **Regionalized production:** reducing emissions from long-distance shipping

Lifecycle assessments show that raw material extraction and processing account for 45–60% of footwear's total CO_2 (Niinimäki et al., 2020). Switching to recycled polyester reduces emissions by 30–40% per unit (H&M Foundation, 2022). This demonstrates how carbon action is measurable at the product level.

4.1.3 Social Accountability

Sport apparel has been criticized for labor exploitation. Nike's early 2000s factory violations became a global scandal; academic studies show improvements since transparency reporting began (Locke, 2013). However, multi-tier subcontracting continues, meaning that tier 2–3 suppliers (dye houses, fiber processing) may still violate safety standards (Kumar & Bansal, 2022).

Best practices include:

- **Worker councils and collective audits**
- **Living wage agreements:** Adidas partnerships with Fair Labor Association
- **Gender equity programs in factories**
- **Training and upskilling**

A sustainable supply chain must guarantee that performance apparel used in sport is not made under conditions that harm workers, or else the legitimacy of the sport itself is compromised.

4.1.4 Economic Value

Sport apparel fuels sponsorships that sustain entire leagues. Jerseys, merchandise, and branded equipment generate economic multipliers, every $1 in merchandise can generate $3–$4 in tourism or media-driven spending (PwC, 2023). Sustainable apparel also has a brand premium: products marketed as eco-responsible sell up to 20% faster (McKinsey, 2021).

Thus, sustainability is not only ethical, it is profitable.

4.2 Stadiums & Infrastructure: Climate, Labor, and Legacy

4.2.1 Stadium Construction and Climate Burden

Stadiums require steel, aluminum, concrete — materials responsible for ~8% of global CO_2 emissions (IEA, 2022). For Qatar 2022, the construction of seven new stadiums accounted for over 65% of total event emissions (Human Rights Watch, 2021).

Climate innovations include:

- Modular stadiums: Qatar's Stadium 974 dismantled & reusable
- Net-zero stadiums powered by solar and geothermal (e.g., LA SoFi Stadium pilot)
- BIM modeling to reduce waste in construction
- Passive cooling and turf irrigation optimization (AI-controlled grass hydration)

4.2.2 Social Accountability: Labor Rights

The most controversial aspect of sport infrastructure is migrant labor. Academic research and journalism uncovered:

- Worker deaths in Qatar under dangerous heat
- Passport confiscation
- Unpaid wages
- Poor living conditions

Sustainable supply chains require binding labor governance, including:

- Contract transparency
- Worker grievance channels
- Wage escrow policies
- Independent auditing

Without these, stadiums symbolize *inequality and injustice*, contradicting sport's social purpose.

4.2.3 Economic Value & Event Legacy

Stadiums often become "white elephants", unused after events. Brazil 2014 stadiums today sit empty, costing governments millions annually (Zimbalist, 2015).

Sustainable stadium economics must include:

- Multi-use facilities (concerts, conferences)
- Community-access hours
- Modular seating
- Conversion to schools/housing post-event

Legacy planning, begins before construction, not after abandonment.

4.3 Event Mobility & Logistics: The Core Carbon Driver

When examining sustainability in sport supply chains, mobility is the elephant in the room.

Research repeatedly shows:

Fan travel accounts for 60–80% of event emissions (Preuss, 2019).

4.3.1 Key Drivers of Carbon in Sport Mobility

- Long-haul flights for overseas fans
- Private buses and cars for regional events
- Transport of equipment and broadcast teams
- Athlete travel, seasonal tournament circuits

4.3.2 Mitigation Strategies (Table 4)

Table 4. Mitigation strategies

Strategy	Example
Rail-friendly scheduling	Paris 2024 — events clustered near rail hubs
Virtual spectator experience	NBA VR live-stream
Carbon ticketing	Fans pay offset fee
Local fan priority	Selling 70% tickets within 200 km

4.3.3 The Problem of Athlete Travel

Elite athletes follow travel schedules that damage climate, and physical health:

- Rugby players: 50,000 km annual flying
- Tennis ATP tour: 100,000 km a year
- Jet lag → sleep disruption → injury risk

A "sustainable performance logistics protocol" could:

- Cluster tournaments geographically
- Replace flights with trains within Europe
- Build sleep-aware competition calendars

This is supply chain planning meeting sports medicine.

4.4 The Athlete-Centered Supply Chain

Sport supply chains are often conceptualized from the perspective of equipment and event logistics, but athletes themselves are nodes in the supply chain, relying on coordinated flows of:

- Nutrition
- Medical supplies
- Training technologies
- Travel itineraries
- Data & analytics
- Sponsorship materials

4.4.1 Nutrition Logistics

Elite athletes consume specialized diets requiring controlled sourcing, organic foods, supplements, hydration solutions.
Sustainability enters when:

- food is sourced local vs. imported
- packaging waste is reduced
- nutrition aligns with climate-friendly diets (plant-forward menus)

Recent IOC recommendations suggest low-carbon dietary models for athletes during competition (IOC, 2022). Paris 2024 committed to 50% plant-based menus for delegations, a first in Olympic history (Paris 2024 Committee, 2023).

4.4.2 Medical & Performance Technology Supply Chains

Sports medicine is increasingly tech-driven: MRI, GPS trackers, wearable sensors, cryotherapy devices.

These items require:

- stable cold chain logistics (for biological samples)
- sterilization protocols
- rapid distribution during emergencies

Sustainability concerns emerge around single-use plastics (bandages, syringes), energy consumption for equipment, and ethical sourcing of pharmaceuticals.

4.4.3 Athlete Travel and Sleep Logistics

Travel schedules affect performance and recovery. A logistics model integrating sleep science can reduce injury rates by up to 25% (Fullagar et al., 2021). Sustainable supply chain design can (Goodarzian et al., 2024; Lu and Taghipour, 2023; Sahraoui et al., 2023):

- reduce unnecessary flights
- plan itineraries with rest-buffer windows
- prioritize rail transport where feasible

Athlete welfare becomes part of social sustainability, expanding the concept beyond factory workers to include performance participants.

4.5 Reverse Logistics, Circularity & Waste Reduction in Sport

4.5.1 Circular Equipment Systems

Sport generates massive waste: jerseys, shoes, balls, nets, promotional banners. Circular economy principles enable:

- rental models (ski equipment)
- repair/refurbish facilities

- upcycling, 2020 Tokyo medals made of recycled electronics
- donation programs, jerseys reused by youth clubs

4.5.2 Waste in Mega-Events

Mega-events produce tons of waste daily:

- single-use plastic cups
- packaging from food vendors
- signage & temporary structures

Tokyo 2020 and Paris 2024 implemented:

- zero single-use plastic
- QR menus instead of paper
- reusable cup return systems

Studies show that 30–50% waste reduction is possible through supply chain redesign (Collins et al., 2021).

4.5.3 Reverse Fan Logistics

Fans are customers, but also assets for waste recovery. Systems such as:

- bottle deposit-return
- ticket-for-recycling programs
- gamification apps

have shown up to 60% increased recycling engagement (Circular Fan Initiative, UEFA, 2022).

4.6 Digital Transformation of Sustainable Sport Supply Chains

Digital tools allow sustainability metrics to be measured, optimized, and verified (Taghipour and Lu, 2025; Taghipour and Merimi, 2021).

4.6.1 Artificial Intelligence

AI applications include:

- demand forecasting for concessions → reducing food waste
- seating distribution optimization → reducing fan mobility
- predictive maintenance for stadium energy systems
- athlete fatigue prediction algorithms

4.6.2 IoT (Internet of Things)

Sensors installed in stadiums can measure:

- energy consumption
- water usage on fields
- temperature & occupancy
- waste bin fill levels

This supports real-time emission dashboards.

4.6.3 Blockchain for Traceability

Blockchain allows:

- transparency in apparel manufacturing
- anti-counterfeit protection for jerseys
- carbon footprint tagging per product

UEFA pilot-tested blockchain ticketing to reduce fraud and unnecessary print waste (UEFA, 2021).

4.6.4 Data Governance

Digitalization introduces ethical considerations:

- athlete biometric data privacy
- surveillance in stadiums
- fan data monetization

Sustainable supply chains must integrate data ethics within environmental and social criteria.

4.7 Governance: Who Controls Sustainability in Sport?

Sustainability depends on aligned incentives. Currently, incentives are fragmented (Table 5):

Table 5. Sustainability incentives

Actor	Role	Barrier
Governments	regulate carbon, labor	short-term political cycles
Sport Federations	set competition rules	rarely enforce ESG
Brands	innovate product	profit pressures
Athletes	influence culture	limited decision power
Fans	demand sustainability	lack information

Effective governance requires shared accountability, including:

- ESG reporting standards for events
- procurement rules mandating circular materials
- labor certification requirements
- revenue models rewarding low-carbon operations

5. CASE STUDIES: LESSONS FROM GLOBAL SPORT SUPPLY CHAINS

This chapter now contextualizes theory through four comparative case studies, illustrating how climate action, social accountability, and economic value evolve across different sport systems.

5.1 Tokyo 2020: A Benchmark for Circularity and Carbon-Conscious Design

Tokyo 2020, postponed due to the COVID-19 pandemic, became a unique experiment in constrained, sustainability-oriented planning. With limited spectators allowed, direct transportation emissions were significantly reduced — but construction and operational logistics remained major contributors.

Sustainability Actions Taken (Table 6).

Table 6. Sustainability Actions

Category	Interventions
Circular economy	6,000+ podiums made from recycled plastic; medals made from recycled e-waste
Event operations	Recyclable cardboard beds for athletes; renewable-energy-based venues
Digitalization	Cloud-based broadcasting reduced equipment transport
Fan strategy	Virtual fan experience → lowered spectator CO_2

Tokyo's most innovative achievement was its national e-waste collection program, 78,985 tons of phones and electronics collected across Japan, melted down to produce 100% recycled medals (Tokyo Committee, 2021). This presented a social-economic-environmental triple win:

- engaged citizens → social cohesion
- saved mining inputs → climate action
- lowered sourcing cost → economic value

Weaknesses

Construction still generated more than 2.7 million tons of emissions (Collins et al., 2021), demonstrating that late-stage sustainability (operational tweaks) is insufficient without early supply-chain design transformation.

5.2 FIFA World Cup Qatar 2022: Social Sustainability Failure Despite Climate Innovation

Qatar 2022 was marketed as the first "carbon-neutral World Cup", implementing solar-powered stadiums and modular infrastructure (Stadium 974). However, human-rights organizations documented serious labor violations among migrant workers:

- unpaid wages
- confiscated passports
- excessive heat exposure
- deaths linked to construction labor (Human Rights Watch, 2021)

This case illustrates a sustainability paradox:

A sport supply chain cannot be sustainable if climate goals are achieved at the expense of people.

Even where climate-forward design occurred, governance lacked social-equity mechanisms, demonstrating the need for binding ESG compliance, not voluntary pledges.

Climate Strategy Highlights

- Modular stadium → assembled from shipping containers
- Solar-cooled venues
- Water-reuse systems for turf

Economic Outcomes

Tourism and reputation gained; however, long-term stadium utility remains unclear. Several facilities risk becoming white-elephants, echoing Brazil 2014 mistakes.

5.3 Paris 2024: Blueprint for Local Procurement and Zero-Waste Event Management

Paris 2024 presents the most ambitious sustainability agenda in modern sports:

- **–50% carbon footprint target** vs. London 2012
- **95% of venues repurposed or temporary**
- **Local sourcing for 70% of food supply**
- **Second-life plan** for temporary stadium seating

Social Accountability Features

- Accessibility design → 100% venues wheelchair-friendly
- Volunteer well-being protocols
- Gender-balanced organizational leadership

Economic-Social-Climate Alignment

Paris integrates the triple-bottom-line model better than any prior event (Table 7):

Table 7. Paris integrates the triple-bottom-line model

Strategy	Climate	Social	Economic
Local sourcing	↓ food transport CO_2	supports local farms	generates local jobs
Temporary venues	↓ concrete emissions	reduces displacement	limits long-term debt
Fan mobility plan	encourages train travel	increases social inclusion	boosts public transit ROI

Paris 2024 is often described not as a sports event, but as a supply-chain-managed sustainability demonstration, where logistics is the invisible backbone.

5.4 NBA & NFL: Micro-Scale Sustainability Through Organizational Policy

Unlike mega-events, U.S. leagues such as the NBA and NFL focus on continuous annual operations, providing a different sustainability lens.

NBA Initiatives

- "NBA Green" program, recycling waste at arenas
- Partnerships with Nike to reduce apparel footprint
- Community solar projects
- Youth sport recycling drives

NBA demonstrates how leagues can leverage brand power to influence young populations' ecological behavior.

NFL Initiatives

- Stadium solar fields (Philadelphia Eagles)
- Food redistribution to local shelters
- Electronic ticketing reducing paper waste

However, player travel remains carbon-intensive, and leagues have yet to meaningfully change scheduling to reduce emissions. This suggests economic priorities still outweigh climate action, highlighting opportunity for future policy.

Case Study Synthesis

Across cases, successful sustainable sport supply chains exhibit:

1. Early integration into procurement & infrastructure

Late-stage recycling is insufficient, sustainability must enter before construction, at the design phase.

2. Social responsibility must be non-negotiable

Climate-positive outcomes cannot justify labor harm, ESG must be all-dimensional.

3. Localized value creation increases resilience

The more goods and services sourced locally, the more climate-friendly, equitable, and economically valuable the system becomes.

4. Digital tools improve measurement → accountability

What gets measured gets managed.

5. Cultural leverage of sport matters

Sport is a behavior-shaping mechanism, fans can be mobilized to participate in sustainability initiatives.

6. FUTURE DIRECTIONS

As global attention intensifies around sustainability, sport supply chains must evolve in several directions:

6.1 Green Sponsorship as Financial Engine

Future events could prioritize sponsors with ESG credibility, replacing fossil-fuel-linked companies with circular economy brands. This may require regulatory intervention, since sponsorship is a major revenue stream.

6.2 Smart Stadia and the Internet of Things

Future arenas will:

- Self-regulate temperature
- Auto-track food waste
- Display live carbon dashboards
- Use AI to optimize fan seating to reduce transport emissions

Such innovation will turn stadiums into digital sustainability laboratories.

6.3 Athlete-Centric Sustainable Mobility

Federations may:

- Regionally cluster tournaments
- Incentivize train travel
- Introduce "rest carbon credit days" into scheduling

This approach aligns performance science with green logistics, creating shared value.

6.4 Universal ESG Standards for Sport

Today, sustainability depends on voluntary commitment. A future direction is:

- mandatory sustainability certification for events
- GHG-based event licensing
- labor compliance scorecards
- carbon-tagged ticketing systems

Institutions like IOC, FIFA, UEFA could lead, or governments may impose standards.

7. CONCLUSION

Sport, traditionally celebrated for physical performance and emotional unity, is now confronted with a new arena of competition, sustainability. At the heart of this challenge lies the sport supply chain: a powerful but often invisible system that shapes climate emissions, labor conditions, and economic outcomes.

This chapter demonstrates that sustainable sport supply chains are possible, but require integrated action across five layers: equipment, athletes, venues, event management, and fans. When environmental goals are aligned with social accountability and economic value, sport becomes a tool for global transformation.

Mega-events like Tokyo 2020 and Paris 2024 show progress, while the Qatar World Cup highlights the cost of neglecting social sustainability. Apparel companies demonstrate that carbon reduction and commercial success can coexist. Digital tools expand the frontier of measurement and accountability.

Ultimately, sport is more than entertainment, it is a cultural platform capable of influencing global social norms. If sport chooses sustainability, billions of spectators may follow.

8. REFERENCES

Alizadeh, N., Taghipour, A., & Canel-Depître, B. (2021). Which one collective strategy is appropriate for the business ecosystem? The role of political environment.

Aouadni, S., Aouadni, I., & Taghipour, A. (2024). Using ordinal priority approach with confidence-level measurement for third-party logistics provider selection in the tunisian healthcare sector. In *Applications of New Technology in Operations and Supply Chain Management* (pp. 404–429). IGI Global. DOI: 10.4018/979-8-3693-1578-1.ch020

Carter, C. R., & Rogers, D. S. (2008). A framework of sustainable supply chain management. *International Journal of Physical Distribution & Logistics Management, 38*(5), 360–387. DOI: 10.1108/09600030810882816

Collins, A., Jones, C., & Munday, M. (2021). Assessing the environmental impacts of mega sporting events. *Journal of Sustainable Tourism*, *29*(3), 455–472.

Elkington, J. (1997). *Cannibals with Forks: The Triple Bottom Line of 21st Century Business*. Capstone Publishing.

Fullagar, H. H., Duffield, R., & Skorski, S. (2021). The impact of travel fatigue and sleep on sport performance. *Sports Medicine (Auckland, N.Z.)*, *51*(2), 251–268.

Geissdoerfer, M., Savaget, P., Bocken, N., & Hultink, E. (2017). The Circular Economy – a new sustainability paradigm. *Journal of Cleaner Production, 143*, 757–768. DOI: 10.1016/j.jclepro.2016.12.048

Goodarzian, F., Abraham, A., Muñuzuri, J., Taghipour, A., & Ghasemi, P. (2024). A Benders decomposition approach for a new sustainable pharmaceutical supply chain network: A case study in France. *Annals of Operations Research*, •••, 1–39.

Gössling, S., & Scott, D. (2021). Sports tourism and climate change. *Current Issues in Tourism*, *24*(1), 1–17.

Human Rights Watch. (2021). Migrant Worker Deaths Unexplained.

IOC. (2022). *Sustainability Strategy for 2030*. International Olympic Committee.

Kumar, S., & Bansal, P. (2022). Supply chain labour risks in the textile industry. *Business and Society Review*, *127*(4), 721–740.

Locke, R. (2013). *The Promise and Limits of Private Power: Promoting Labor Standards in a Global Economy*. Cambridge University Press. DOI: 10.1017/CBO9781139381840

Lu, X., & Taghipour, A. (2023). A French Guide for Businesses and Governments to Integrate the Concept of Sustainable Development Into Their Supply Chains. In *Government Impact on Sustainable and Responsible Supply Chain Management* (pp. 1–12). IGI Global. DOI: 10.4018/978-1-6684-9062-4.ch001

Misener, L., & Darcy, S. (2014). *Managing Disability Sport: From Theory to Practice*. Routledge.

Niinimäki, K.. (2020). Environmental impact of polyester manufacturing. *Textile Research Journal, 90*(3), 281–296.

Paris 2024 Committee. (2023). *Official Sustainability Report*.

Preuss, H. (2019). Event visitor carbon footprinting. *European Sport Management Quarterly, 19*(5), 628–651.

PwC. (2023). *Global Sports Industry Outlook*.

Sahraoui, A., Tran, N. K., Tliche, Y., Kacem, A., & Taghipour, A. (2023). Examining ICT Innovation for Sustainable Terminal Operations in Developing Countries: A Case Study of the Port of Radès in Tunisia. *Sustainability (Basel), 15*(11), 9123. DOI: 10.3390/su15119123

Statista. (2023). *Global Sports Apparel Revenue*.

Taghipour, A., Belrhazi, Y., & Damoum, N. (2023). Resilient sustainable supply chain management. In *Government Impact on Sustainable and Responsible Supply Chain Management* (pp. 33–47). IGI Global. DOI: 10.4018/978-1-6684-9062-4.ch003

Taghipour, A., & Lu, X. (2025). Navigating the Artificial Intelligence Era: Impacts of Artificial Intelligence on Youth Critical Thinking, Career Paths, and Ethical Challenges. In Ecological and Human Dimensions of AI-Based Supply Chain (pp. 49-68). IGI Global Scientific Publishing.

Taghipour, A., & Merimi, M. (2021, March). Digital transformation of supply chains during crisis: covid-19. In 11th Annual International Conference on Industrial Engineering and Operations Management, IEOM (pp. 7493-7501). DOI: 10.46254/AN11.20211298

UEFA. (2021). *Blockchain Ticketing Pilot Report*.

Vosooghidizaji, M., Taghipour, A., & Canel-Depitre, B. (2019). A literature review on information asymmetry in supply chain coordination. *International Journal of Production Research, 58*(6), 1–6.

Zimbalist, A. (2015). *Circus Maximus: The Economic Gamble Behind Hosting the Olympics and the World Cup*. Brookings Press. DOI: 10.5040/9780815751694

Zoghlami, N., Taghipour, A., Merlo, C., & Abed, M. (2016). Management of divergent production network using decentralised multi-level capacitated lot-sizing models. *International Journal of Shipping and Transport Logistics*, *8*(5), 590–604. DOI: 10.1504/IJSTL.2016.078686

Compilation of References

Afrin, S., Roksana, S., & Akram, R. (2024). AI-Enhanced Robotic Process Automation: A Review of Intelligent Automation Innovations. *IEEE Access : Practical Innovations, Open Solutions.*

Ahmadi, T., Hesaraki, A. F., & Morsch, J. P. M. (2024). Exploring it-driven supply chain capabilities and resilience: The roles of supply chain risk management and complexity. *Supply Chain Management, 30*(1), 50–66. Advance online publication. DOI: 10.1108/SCM-11-2023-0561

Ahmed Batki, A., & Phudinawala, H. (2024). A Comparative Study on How AI is Partnering with Nature for a Sustainable Future. *International Journal for Multidisciplinary Research, 6*(3), 1–9. DOI: 10.1093/polsoc/puae040

Ahmed Eljetchtimi. (2026). Morocco targets $10 billion AI contribution to GDP by 2030 | Reuters. Retrieved January 27, 2026, from https://www.reuters.com/sustainability/climate-energy/morocco-targets-10-billion-ai-contribution-gdp-by-2030-2026-01-12/

Ahmed, W. A. H., & MacCarthy, B. L. (2023). Blockchain-enabled supply chain traceability – How wide? How deep? *International Journal of Production Economics, 263*, 108963. DOI: 10.1016/j.ijpe.2023.108963

Alabdali, M. A., Yaqub, M. Z., & Windsperger, J. (2025). Algorithmic management and green technologies: Enhancing supply chain resilience through transformation. *Cleaner Logistics and Supply Chain, 17*, 100281. DOI: 10.1016/j.clscn.2025.100281

Alcácer, V., & Cruz-Machado, V. (2019). Scanning the industry 4.0: A literature review on technologies for manufacturing systems. *Engineering Science and Technology, an International Journal, 22*(3), 899–919. DOI: 10.1016/j.jestch.2019.01.006

Alhakimi, A. M. (2024). The Power of Technology in Industrial Revolution 5.0. In Utilizing Renewable Energy, Technology, and Education for Industry 5.0 (pp. 400-443). IGI Global.

Ali, A., Mahfouz, A., & Arisha, A. (2017). Analysing supply chain resilience: Integrating the constructs in a concept mapping framework via a systematic literature review. *Supply Chain Management, 22*(1), 16–39. DOI: 10.1108/SCM-06-2016-0197

Alizadeh, N., Taghipour, A., & Canel-Depître, B. (2021). Which one collective strategy is appropriate for the business ecosystem? The role of political environment.

Aljoghaiman, A., & Ghouri, A. M. (2024). Management information system and digital supply chain influence on supply chain resilience through supply chain risk management. *International Journal of Construction Supply Chain Management, 14*(1), 96–118. DOI: 10.14424/ijcscm202414106

Allal-Chérif, O., Simón-Moya, V., & Ballester, A. C. C. (2021). Intelligent purchasing: How artificial intelligence can redefine the purchasing function. *Journal of Business Research, 124*, 69–76. DOI: 10.1016/j.jbusres.2020.11.050

Alquraish, M. (2025). Digital Transformation, Supply Chain Resilience, and Sustainability: A Comprehensive Review with Implications for Saudi Arabian Manufacturing. *Sustainability (Basel), 17*(10), 4495. DOI: 10.3390/su17104495

Alvarenga, M. Z., de Oliveira, M. P. V., & de Oliveira, T. A. G. F. (2023). The impact of using digital technologies on supply chain resilience and robustness: The role of memory under the covid-19 outbreak. *Supply Chain Management, 28*(5), 825–842. Advance online publication. DOI: 10.1108/SCM-06-2022-0217

Alves, J., Lima, T. M., & Gaspar, P. D. (2023). Is industry 5.0 a human-centred approach? a systematic review. *Processes (Basel, Switzerland), 11*(1), 193. DOI: 10.3390/pr11010193

Alzoubi, H. M., Tan, C. L., El Khatib, M., Alshurideh, M. T., Shwedeh, F., Yanamandra, R., & Lee, K. L. (2025). Smart Government Initiatives: Transforming Global Supply Chains through Digital Change. *International Review of Management and Marketing, 15*(3), 209–217. DOI: 10.32479/irmm.18962

Ammar, A., Amahmoud, H., El Menzhi, K., Mkik, M., Hebaz, A., & Eddine, E. M. A. (2024). Critical Analysis of Logistics Transformation in Morocco under the Auspices of Artificial Intelligence: Government Perspectives from the perspective of Innovative and Technology Driven Public Management. *2024 IEEE 15th International Colloquium of Logistics and Supply Chain Management, LOGISTIQUA 2024*. DOI: 10.1109/LOGISTIQUA61063.2024.10571402

Ammar, A., Amahmoud, H., El Menzhi, K., Mkik, M., Hebaz, A., & Eddine, E. M. A. (2024, May). Critical Analysis of Logistics Transformation in Morocco Under The Auspices of Artificial Intelligence: Government Perspectives From the perspective of Innovative and Technology Driven Public Management. In 2024 IEEE 15th International Colloquium on Logistics and Supply Chain Management (LOGISTIQUA) (pp. 1-9). IEEE.

Antonaci, F. G., Olivetti, E. C., Marcolin, F., Castiblanco Jimenez, I. A., Eynard, B., Vezzetti, E., & Moos, S. (2024). Workplace Well-Being in Industry 5.0: A Worker-Centered Systematic Review. *Sensors (Basel)*, *24*(17), 5473. DOI: 10.3390/s24175473 PMID: 39275383

Aouadni, S., Aouadni, I., & Taghipour, A. (2024). Using ordinal priority approach with confidence-level measurement for third-party logistics provider selection in the tunisian healthcare sector. In *Applications of New Technology in Operations and Supply Chain Management* (pp. 404–429). IGI Global. DOI: 10.4018/979-8-3693-1578-1.ch020

Aslam, H., Blome, C., Roscoe, S., & Azhar, T. M. (2018). Dynamic supply chain capabilities. *International Journal of Operations & Production Management*, *38*(12), 2266–2285. DOI: 10.1108/IJOPM-09-2017-0555

Bag, S., Rahman, M. S., Routray, S., Roubaud, D., & Mangla, S. K. (2025). Integrating Big Data and Artificial Intelligence Technology to Build Renewable Energy Supply Chain Resilience: An Empirical Study. *Business Strategy and the Environment*, *34*(7), 8847–8869. DOI: 10.1002/bse.70052

Baker, S., & Xiang, W. (2023). Artificial intelligence of things for smarter healthcare: A survey of advancements, challenges, and opportunities. *IEEE Communications Surveys and Tutorials*, *25*(2), 1261–1293. DOI: 10.1109/COMST.2023.3256323

Balaji, K. (2025). Harnessing AI and Blockchain in Sustainability Assurance: Trends Shaping the Future of Verification. In Navigating Trust in Sustainability Reporting and Assurance (pp. 215-242). IGI Global Scientific Publishing.

Barata, J., & Kayser, I. (2023). Industry 5.0–past, present, and near future. *Procedia Computer Science*, *219*, 778–788. DOI: 10.1016/j.procs.2023.01.351

Barney, J. (1991). Firm resources and sustained competitive advantage. *Journal of Management*, *17*(1), 99–120. DOI: 10.1177/014920639101700108

Belhadi, A., Kamble, S. S., Venkatesh, M., Chiappetta Jabbour, C. J., & Benkhati, I. (2022). Building supply chain resilience and efficiency through additive manufacturing: An ambidextrous perspective on the dynamic capability view. *International Journal of Production Economics, 249*, 108516. DOI: 10.1016/j.ijpe.2022.108516

Benabdeljlil, N., & Kerzazi, L. (2025). Corporate social responsibility imperatives in the Moroccan textile-clothing sector: Ways of implementation and impact on local value chains. *IDOS Discussion Papers*. DOI: 10.23661/IDP18.2025

Benda, N. C., Veinot, T. C., Sieck, C. J., & Ancker, J. S. (2020). Broadband internet access is a social determinant of health! *American Journal of Public Health, 110*(8), 1123–1125. DOI: 10.2105/AJPH.2020.305784 PMID: 32639914

Beske, P. (2012). Dynamic capabilities and sustainable supply chain management. *International Journal of Physical Distribution & Logistics Management, 42*(4), 372–387. DOI: 10.1108/09600031211231344

BharatNet. (2024, August 5). 95% Indian villages have internet connectivity [Press release].

Biggs, R. (Oonsie), Rhode, C., Archibald, S., Kunene, L. M., Mutanga, S. S., Nkuna, N., Ocholla, P. O., & Phadima, L. J. (2015). Strategies for managing complex social-ecological systems in the face of uncertainty: examples from South Africa and beyond. *Ecology and Society, 20*(1). https://www.jstor.org/stable/26269769

Bouanba, N., Barakat, O., & Bendou, A. (2022). Artificial Intelligence & Agile Innovation: Case of Moroccan Logistics Companies. *Procedia Computer Science, 203*, 444–449. DOI: 10.1016/j.procs.2022.07.059

Boulitama, O., Rahli, D., & Haoucha, M. (2022). Digital solutions and Moroccan companies during the Covid-19 pandemic. *2022 IEEE 14th International Conference of Logistics and Supply Chain Management, LOGISTIQUA 2022*. Institute of Electrical and Electronics Engineers Inc. DOI: 10.1109/LOGISTIQUA55056.2022.9938069

Boulitama, O., Rahli, D., & Sabri, K. (2021). *L'impact de la covid-19 sur la chaine logistique marocaine The impact of covid-19 on the Moroccan supply chain. 2*(3), 165–181. DOI: 10.5281/zenodo.4817869

Boulitama, O., Lhamidi, S., Taifi, R., & Brahim, S. (2025). Digital transformation and supply chain capabilities: A sectoral maturity perspective in morocco. *Polish Journal of Management Studies, 32*(1), 61–80. DOI: 10.17512/pjms.2025.32.1.04

Brandon-Jones, E., Squire, B., Autry, C., & Petersen, K. J. (2014). A contingent resource-based perspective of supply chain resilience and robustness. *The Journal of Supply Chain Management, 50*(3), 55–73. DOI: 10.1111/jscm.12050

Broo, D. G., Kaynak, O., & Sait, S. M. (2022). Rethinking engineering education at the age of industry 5.0. *Journal of Industrial Information Integration, 25*, 100311. DOI: 10.1016/j.jii.2021.100311

Brusset, X., & Teller, C. (2017). Supply chain capabilities, risks, and resilience. *International Journal of Production Economics, 184*, 59–68. DOI: 10.1016/j.ijpe.2016.09.008

Büchi, G., Cugno, M., & Castagnoli, R. (2020). Smart factory performance and Industry 4.0. *Technological Forecasting and Social Change, 150*, 119790. Advance online publication. DOI: 10.1016/j.techfore.2019.119790

Busse, C., Meinlschmidt, J., & Foerstl, K. (2017). Supplier development and supplier sustainability: A systematic review. *The Journal of Supply Chain Management.*

Carayannis, E. G., Canestrino, R., & Magliocca, P. (2023). From the dark side of industry 4.0 to society 5.0: Looking "beyond the box" to developing human-centric innovation ecosystems. *IEEE Transactions on Engineering Management, 71*, 6695–6711. DOI: 10.1109/TEM.2023.3239552

Carter, C. R., & Rogers, D. S. (2008). A framework of sustainable supply chain management. *International Journal of Physical Distribution & Logistics Management, 38*(5), 360–387. DOI: 10.1108/09600030810882816

Cath, C. (2018). Governing artificial intelligence: Ethical, legal and technical opportunities and challenges. *Philosophical Transactions. Series A, Mathematical, Physical, and Engineering Sciences, 376*(2133), 20180080. DOI: 10.1098/rsta.2018.0080 PMID: 30322996

Cauchois, R., Taghipour, A., Kang, D., Zoghlami, N., & Abed, M. (2017). Advanced solutions for a supply chain with stochastic information. *Journal of Advanced Management Science, 5*(1), 9–13. DOI: 10.18178/joams.5.1.9-13

Chabane, B., Komljenovic, D., & Abdul-Nour, G. (2023). Converging on human-centred industry, resilient processes, and sustainable outcomes in asset management frameworks. *Environment Systems & Decisions, 43*(4), 663–679. DOI: 10.1007/s10669-023-09943-w

Charmaz, K. (2006). *Constructing grounded theory: A practical guide through qualitative analysis*. sage.

Chatterjee, S. (2020). AI strategy of India: policy framework, adoption challenges and actions for government. *Transforming Government: People. Transforming Government, 14*(5), 757–775. DOI: 10.1108/TG-05-2019-0031

Chaudhary, A. (2021). Rural-urban disparities in digital access: Barriers to ICT adoption. *Indian Journal of Development Research, 15*(2), 23–34.

Chauhan, M., & Sahoo, D. R. (2024). Towards a greener tomorrow: Exploring the potential of AI, blockchain, and IoT in sustainable development. *Nature Environment and Pollution Technology, 23*(2), 1105–1113. DOI: 10.46488/NEPT.2024.v23i02.044

Chau, L., Anh, L., & Duc, V. (2025). Valuing ESG: How financial markets respond to corporate sustainability. *International Business Review, 34*(3), 102418. DOI: 10.1016/j.ibusrev.2025.102418

Chbaik, N., Khiat, A., Bahnasse, A., & Ouajji, H. (2022). The Application of Smart Supply Chain Technologies in The Moroccan Logistics. *Procedia Computer Science, 198*, 578–583. DOI: 10.1016/j.procs.2021.12.289

Chen, G., & Yu, Z. (2024). Digital finance, value cocreation, and supply chain resilience: Evidence from listed manufacturing firms in China. *Finance Research Letters, 70*, 106322. Advance online publication. DOI: 10.1016/j.frl.2024.106322

Chi, C., Yin, Z., Liu, Y., & Chai, S. (2023). A trusted cloud-edge decision architecture based on blockchain and mlp for aiot. *IEEE Internet of Things Journal.*

Chinta, P. C. R., Jha, K. M., Velaga, V., Moore, C., Routhu, K., & SADARAM, G. (2024). Harnessing Big Data and AI-Driven ERP Systems to Enhance Cybersecurity Resilience in Real-Time Threat Environments. Available at SSRN 5151788.

Chittipaka, V., Kumar, S., Sivarajah, U., Bowden, J. L. H., & Baral, M. M. (2023). Blockchain Technology for Supply Chains operating in emerging markets: An empirical examination of technology-organization-environment (TOE) framework. *Annals of Operations Research, 327*(1), 465–492. DOI: 10.1007/s10479-022-04801-5

Choi, T. Y., Dooley, K. J., & Rungtusanatham, M. (2001). Supply networks and complex adaptive systems: Control versus emergence. *Journal of Operations Management, 19*(3), 351–366. DOI: 10.1016/S0272-6963(00)00068-1

Chopra, S., & Sodhi, M. S. (2014). Reducing the risk of supply chain disruptions. *MIT Sloan Management Review, 55*(3), 73–80.

Chowdhury, M. M. H., & Quaddus, M. (2016). Supply chain readiness, response and recovery for resilience. *Supply Chain Management, 21*(6), 709–731. DOI: 10.1108/SCM-12-2015-0463

Chowdhury, M. M. H., & Quaddus, M. (2017). Supply chain resilience: Conceptualization and scale development using dynamic capability theory. *International Journal of Production Economics, 188*(188), 185–204. DOI: 10.1016/j.ijpe.2017.03.020

Christopher, M., & Peck, H. (2004). Building the Resilient Supply Chain. *International Journal of Logistics Management, 15*(2), 1–14. DOI: 10.1108/09574090410700275

Christou, E. Kostas Alexandris, & A. F. (2018). TOURMAN 2018 Conference Proceedings.

Collins, A., Jones, C., & Munday, M. (2021). Assessing the environmental impacts of mega sporting events. *Journal of Sustainable Tourism, 29*(3), 455–472.

Common Service Centres. (2025). In *Wikipedia*. Retrieved September 1, 2025, from https://en.wikipedia.org/wiki/Common_Service_Centres

Crandall, A., Rahim, H. A., Yount, K. M., Borghei, N. S., Taghipour, A., Roudsari, R. L., ... & Nelson, B. D. (1995). WHO journals. Information for authors, 1.

Culot, G., Podrecca, M., & Nassimbeni, G. (2024, November 1). Artificial intelligence in supply chain management: A systematic literature review of empirical studies and research directions. *Computers in Industry*, Vol. 162. Elsevier B.V. DOI: 10.1016/j.compind.2024.104132

Dafflon, B., Moalla, N., & Ouzrout, Y. (2021). The challenges, approaches, and used techniques of CPS for manufacturing in Industry 4.0: A literature review. *International Journal of Advanced Manufacturing Technology, 113*(7-8), 2395–2412. DOI: 10.1007/s00170-020-06572-4

Day, J. M. (2013). Fostering emergent resilience: The complex adaptive supply network of disaster relief. *International Journal of Production Research, 52*(7), 1970–1988. DOI: 10.1080/00207543.2013.787496

Demir, S. B. (2018). Predatory journals: Who publishes in them and why? *Journal of Informetrics, 12*(4), 1296–1311. DOI: 10.1016/j.joi.2018.10.008

Drazin, R. (1991). The processes of technological innovation. *The Journal of Technology Transfer 1991 16:1, 16*(1), 45–46. DOI: 10.1007/BF02371446

Dua, G. K. (2025). Enhancing Sustainable Development through Blockchain and Artificial Intelligence: Optimizing the Supply Chain and Mitigating Environmental Footprints. In Global Partnerships and Governance of Supply Chain Systems (pp. 157-188). IGI Global Scientific Publishing.

Dubey, R., Bryde, D. J., Dwivedi, Y. K., Graham, G., Foropon, C., & Papadopoulos, T. (2023). Dynamic digital capabilities and supply chain resilience: The role of government effectiveness. *International Journal of Production Economics, 258*(4), 108790. DOI: 10.1016/j.ijpe.2023.108790

Duggal, A. S., Malik, P. K., Gehlot, A., Singh, R., Gaba, G. S., Masud, M., & Al-Amri, J. F. (2022). A sequential roadmap to Industry 6.0: Exploring future manufacturing trends. *IET Communications, 16*(5), 521–531. DOI: 10.1049/cmu2.12284

Eckstein, D., Goellner, M., Blome, C., & Henke, M. (2015). The performance impact of supply chain agility and supply chain adaptability: The moderating effect of product complexity. *International Journal of Production Research, 53*(10), 3028–3046. DOI: 10.1080/00207543.2014.970707

Eisenhardt, K. M., & Martin, J. A. (2000). Dynamic capabilities: What are they? *Strategic Management Journal, 21*(10/11), 1105–1121. https://www.jstor.org/stable/3094429. DOI: 10.1002/1097-0266(200010/11)21:10/11<1105::AID-SMJ133>3.0.CO;2-E

El Hafdaoui, H., Khallaayoun, A., & Ouazzani, K. (2024). Long-term low carbon strategy of Morocco: A review of future scenarios and energy measures. *Results in Engineering, 21*, 101724. DOI: 10.1016/j.rineng.2023.101724

El Moussaoui, A. E. (2025b). Predicting E-Consumer Preferences for Collection and Delivery Points Using Deep Learning. In Ecological and Human Dimensions of AI-Based Supply Chain (pp. 395-412). IGI Global Scientific Publishing.

El Moussaoui, A. E., Benbba, B., & El Amrani, L. (2022c). Distribution system design in last mile logistics: Review & research agenda. Revue Marocaine de Management, Logistique et Transport, (5).

El Moussaoui, A. E., Benbba, B., Jaegler, A., & El Andaloussi, Z. (2022a, May). City logistics: An evolutionary, successful & collaborative city. In 2022 14th international colloquium of logistics and supply chain management (LOGISTIQUA) (pp. 1-7). IEEE.

El Moussaoui, A. E., Benbba, B., Jaegler, A., El Andaloussi, Z., & El Amrani, L. (2022b, May). Last mile logistics: Challenges & improvement ways. In 2022 14th international colloquium of logistics and supply chain management (LOGISTIQUA) (pp. 1-7). IEEE.

El Moussaoui, A. E., Mizani, M. E., & Benlakouiri, A. (2025d, April). Transformation of Logistics in Electronic Subcontracting: A Focus on SMEs Supply Chains. In International Conference on Connected Objects and Artificial Intelligence (pp. 700-706). Cham: Springer Nature Switzerland.

El Moussaoui, A. E., Mizani, M. E., & Benlakouiri, A. (2025e, April). RFID Technology in Logistics: A Catalyst for Efficiency. In International Conference on Connected Objects and Artificial Intelligence (pp. 707-712). Cham: Springer Nature Switzerland.

El Moussaoui, T., Chakir, L., & El Moussaoui, A. E. (2025b). Exploring Information Technology (IT) Acceptance Among Supply Chain Stakeholders in Morocco's Pharmaceutical Industry. In Ecological and Human Dimensions of AI-Based Supply Chain (pp. 245-270). IGI Global Scientific Publishing.

El Moussaoui, T., Loqman, C., & El Moussaoui, A. E. (2025a). Adoption of artificial intelligence in smart cities: Literature review and bibliometric analysis. Generative AI for Cybersecurity and Privacy, 103-125.

El Moussaoui, T., Loqman, C., & El Moussaoui, A. E. (2025c). Adoption of artificial intelligence in smart cities: Literature review and bibliometric analysis. Generative AI for Cybersecurity and Privacy, 103-125.

El Moussaoui, A. E., El Moussaoui, T., Benbba, B., Jaegler, A., & El Andaloussi, Z. (2022d). Understanding the choice of collection & delivery point by the E-consumer via a machine learning model: Moroccan case study. *Procedia Computer Science*, *210*, 204–211. DOI: 10.1016/j.procs.2022.10.138

Elkington, J. (1997). *Cannibals with Forks: The Triple Bottom Line of 21st Century Business*. Capstone.

El-Nemr, N., Canel-Depitre, B., & Taghipour, A. (2017, September). Determinants of hotel room rates. In Marketing Trends Congress. Luxury Industries Conference London 2017.

Engin, Z., Crowcroft, J., Hand, D., & Treleaven, P. (2025). The Algorithmic State Architecture (ASA): an integrated framework for AI-enabled government. *arXiv preprint arXiv:2503.08725*.

European Commission. (2021). *Industry 5.0: Towards A Sustainable*. Human-Centric Industrial Future.

European Commission. (2023). *Corporate Sustainability Reporting Directive (CSRD)*. https://eur-lex.europa.eu

Fakhraddine, M., Zerrad, N., Berhili, H., & Morchid, M. (2025). Digital transformation in Moroccan agriculture: Applications, used technologies, impacts on marketing, limitations, and orientations for future research. *Smart Agricultural Technology*, *11*, 100978. DOI: 10.1016/j.atech.2025.100978

Farouk, I. I. El, Moufad, I., Frichi, Y., Arif, J., & Jawab, F. (2020). Proposing a Supply Chain Collaboration Framework for Synchronous Flow Implementation in the Automotive Industry: A Moroccan Case Study. *Information 2020, Vol. 11, 11*(9). DOI: 10.3390/info11090431

Faruquee, M., Paulraj, A., & Irawan, C. A. (2021). Strategic supplier relationships and supply chain resilience: Is digital transformation that precludes trust beneficial? *International Journal of Operations & Production Management, 41*(7), 1192–1219. DOI: 10.1108/IJOPM-10-2020-0702

Fiskel, J., Polyviou, M., Croxton, K. L., & Pettit, T. J. (2015). From risk to resilience: Learning to deal with disruption. *MIT Sloan Management Review, 56*(2), 79–86.

Fiss, P. C. (2011). Building better causal theories: A fuzzy set approach to typologies in organization research. *Academy of Management Journal, 54*(2), 393–420. DOI: 10.5465/amj.2011.60263120

Flick, U. (2022). *An introduction to qualitative research* (6th ed.). SAGE Publications.

Floridi, L., & Cowls, J. (2019). A unified framework for AI ethics. *Harvard Data Science Review*. Advance online publication. DOI: 10.1162/99608f92.8cd550d1

Fullagar, H. H., Duffield, R., & Skorski, S. (2021). The impact of travel fatigue and sleep on sport performance. *Sports Medicine (Auckland, N.Z.), 51*(2), 251–268.

Ganesh, A. D., & Kalpana, P. (2022). Future of artificial intelligence and its influence on supply chain risk management–A systematic review. *Computers & Industrial Engineering, 169*, 108206. DOI: 10.1016/j.cie.2022.108206

Gao, Y., Li, Z., & Kang, D. S. (2018). Supply chain coordination: A review. *Journal of Advanced Management Science, 6*(4), 213–217. DOI: 10.18178/joams.6.4.213-217

Geissdoerfer, M., Savaget, P., Bocken, N. M., & Hultink, E. J. (2017). The Circular Economy–A new sustainability paradigm? *Journal of Cleaner Production, 143*, 757–768. DOI: 10.1016/j.jclepro.2016.12.048

Gharye Mirzaei, M., Goodarzian, F., Mokhtari, K., & Ansaripoor, A. H. (2025). IoT-based platform application for Optimizing Sustainable Blood Supply Chain Network under Uncertainty. *Fariba and Mokhtari, Kourosh and Ansaripoor, Amir H., IoT-based platform application for Optimizing Sustainable Blood Supply Chain Network under Uncertainty.*

Gharye Mirzaei, M., Goodarzian, F., Taghipour, A., & Muñuzuri, J. (2025). Sustainable closed-loop supply chain network under uncertainty considering green technologies: Toward the circular economy. *The Journal of the Operational Research Society*, •••, 1–21.

Ghobakhloo, M., Iranmanesh, M., Fathi, M., Rejeb, A., Foroughi, B., & Nikbin, D. (2024). Beyond Industry 4.0: A systematic review of Industry 5.0 technologies and implications for social, environmental and economic sustainability. *Asia-Pacific Journal of Business Administration.*

Ghosh, O., & Pandey, A. (2026). Accountability, Responsibility, and Liability in AI and Data Ecosystems: Centering Transparency Through End-to-End Governance. In *Centering Transparency and Trust in Data and AI Ecosystems* (pp. 1-26). IGI Global Scientific Publishing.

Glaa, B., Zoghlami, N., & Taghipour, A. (2014, May). Outsourcing and off-shoring healthcare services: A way to cut the costs and improve quality. In 2014 international conference on advanced logistics and transport (ICALT) (pp. 189-194). IEEE.

Goodarzian, F., Abraham, A., Muñuzuri, J., Taghipour, A., & Ghasemi, P. (2024). A Benders decomposition approach for a new sustainable pharmaceutical supply chain network: A case study in France. *Annals of Operations Research*, •••, 1–39.

Gössling, S., & Scott, D. (2021). Sports tourism and climate change. *Current Issues in Tourism*, *24*(1), 1–17.

Gouiferda, F., & Iddik, S. (2025). Digitalization and environmental sustainability ramifications on the Moroccan companies' resilience. *Management and Sustainability*, 1–27. https://doi.org/DOI: 10.1108/MSAR-02-2025-0074/1312706

Greif, L., Röckel, F., Kimmig, A., & Ovtcharova, J. (2025). A systematic review of current AI techniques used in the context of the SDGs. *International Journal of Environmental Research*, *19*(1), 1. DOI: 10.1007/s41742-024-00668-5

GSMA. (2022). *The mobile gender gap report 2022*. GSMA. https://www.gsma.com/r/gender-gap

Han, Y., & Fang, X. (2024). Systematic review of adopting blockchain in supply chain management: Bibliometric analysis and theme discussion. *International Journal of Production Research*, *62*(3), 991–1016. DOI: 10.1080/00207543.2023.2236241

Haricha, K., Khiat, A., Issaoui, Y., Bahnasse, A., & Ouajji, H. (2020). Towards smart manufucturing: Implementation and benefits. *Procedia Computer Science*, *177*, 639–644. DOI: 10.1016/j.procs.2020.10.091

Hassebo, A., & Tealab, M. (2023). Global models of smart cities and potential IoT applications: A review. *IoT*, *4*(3), 366–411. DOI: 10.3390/iot4030017

Hirsch, K., Niemann, W., & Swart, B. (2024). Artificial intelligence and information systems capabilities for supply chain resilience: A study in the South African fast-moving consumer goods industry. *Journal of Transport and Supply Chain Management, 18*(0), 1–16. DOI: 10.4102/JTSCM.v18i0.1025

Hitt, M. A. (2019). Relevance of strategic management theory and research for supply chain management. *The Journal of Supply Chain Management, 47*(1), 9–13. DOI: 10.1111/j.1745-493X.2010.03210.x

Hong, J., Zhang, Y., & Ding, M. (2018). Sustainable supply chain management practices, supply chain dynamic capabilities, and enterprise performance. *Journal of Cleaner Production, 172*(1), 3508–3519. DOI: 10.1016/j.jclepro.2017.06.093

Hossain, M. I., Talapatra, S., Saha, P., & Belal, H. M. (2024). From Theory to Practice: Leveraging Digital Twin Technologies and Supply Chain Disruption Mitigation Strategies for Enhanced Supply Chain Resilience with Strategic Fit in Focus. *Global Journal of Flexible Systems Managment, 26*(1), 87–109. DOI: 10.1007/s40171-024-00424-w

Hsu, C. H., Liu, J. C., Cai, X. Q., Zhang, T. Y., & Lv, W. Y. (2024). Enabling Sustainable Diffusion in Supply Chains Through Industry 5.0: An Impact Analysis of Key Enablers for SMEs in Emerging Economies. *Mathematics, 12*(24), 3938. DOI: 10.3390/math12243938

Human Rights Watch. (2021). Migrant Worker Deaths Unexplained.

Huong, D. G., Azmat, M., & Hadeed, R. (2025). Exploring big data analytics adoption for sustainable manufacturing supply Chains: Insights from a TOE-guided systematic review. *Cleaner Logistics and Supply Chain, 16*, 100256. DOI: 10.1016/j.clscn.2025.100256

Idrissi, Z. K., Lachgar, M., & Hrimech, H. (2024). Blockchain, IoT and AI in logistics and transportation: A systematic review. *Transport Economics and Management, 2*, 275–285. DOI: 10.1016/j.team.2024.09.002

Ikegwu, A. C., Nweke, H. F., Anikwe, C. V., Alo, U. R., & Okonkwo, O. R. (2022). Big data analytics for data-driven industry: A review of data sources, tools, challenges, solutions, and research directions. *Cluster Computing, 25*(5), 3343–3387. DOI: 10.1007/s10586-022-03568-5

Ikenga, G. U., & van der Sijde, P. (2024). Twenty-first century competencies; about competencies for industry 5.0 and the opportunities for emerging economies. *Sustainability (Basel), 16*(16), 7166. DOI: 10.3390/su16167166

Ikram, M., & Sadki, J. E. (2024). Resilient and sustainable green technology strategies: A study of Morocco's path toward sustainable development. *Sustainable Futures : An Applied Journal of Technology, Environment and Society, 8*, 100327. DOI: 10.1016/j.sftr.2024.100327

India, D. (2025). In *Wikipedia*. Retrieved September 1, 2025, from https://en.wikipedia.org/wiki/Digital_India

India, T. O. (2025, August 7). Over 1,900 villages in Odisha lack mobile connectivity: MoS. *The Times of India*. https://timesofindia.indiatimes.com/city/bhubaneswar/over-1900-villages-in-odisha-lack-mobile-connectivity-mos/articleshow/123173827.cms

India, T. O. (2025a, July 19). State far behind in school digital access, reveals govt data. *The Times of India*. https://timesofindia.indiatimes.com/city/bhopal/state-far-behind-in-school-digital-access-reveals-govt-data/articleshow/122789651.cms

Internet and Mobile Association of India. (2022). *Internet in India 2022*. IAMAI & KANTAR. https://www.iamai.in

IOC. (2022). *Sustainability Strategy for 2030*. International Olympic Committee.

Iqbal, R. (2021). Gendering of smartphone ownership and autonomy among youth: Narratives from rural India [Preprint]. *arXiv*. https://arxiv.org/abs/2108.09788

Issaoui, Y., Khiat, A., Bahnasse, A., & Ouajji, H. (2019). Smart logistics : Study of the application of blockchain technology. *Procedia Computer Science, 160*, 266–271. Elsevier B.V. DOI: 10.1016/j.procs.2019.09.467

Ivanov, D. (2017). Revealing interfaces of supply chain resilience and sustainability: A simulation study. *International Journal of Production Research, 56*(10), 3507–3523. DOI: 10.1080/00207543.2017.1343507

Ivanov, D., & Dolgui, A. (2019). New Disruption Risk Management Perspectives in Supply chains: Digital twins, the Ripple effect, and Resileanness. *IFAC-PapersOnLine, 52*(13), 337–342. DOI: 10.1016/j.ifacol.2019.11.138

Ivanov, D., & Dolgui, A. (2020). A digital supply chain twin for managing disruptions. *International Journal of Production Research.*

Ivanov, D., Dolgui, A., Das, A., & Sokolov, B. (2019). Digital supply chain twins: Managing the ripple effect, resilience, and disruption risks by data-driven optimization, simulation, and visibility. In *Handbook of ripple effects in the supply chain* (pp. 309–332). Springer International Publishing.

Ivanov, D., Dolgui, A., & Sokolov, B. (2019). The impact of digital technology and Industry 4.0 on the ripple effect and supply chain risk analytics. *International Journal of Production Research, 57*(3), 829–846. https://www.tandfonline.com/doi/abs/10.1080/00207543.2018.1488086. DOI: 10.1080/00207543.2018.1488086

Ivanov, D., Tsipoulanidis, A., & Schönberger, J. (2019). Supply chain risk management and resilience. In *Global Supply Chain and Operations Management* (pp. 455–479). Springer., DOI: 10.1007/978-3-319-94313-8_15

Jabbar, A., Akhtar, P., & Ali, S. I. (2025). The interplay between blockchain and big data analytics for enhancing supply chain value creation in micro, small, and medium enterprises. *Annals of Operations Research, 350*(2), 649–671. DOI: 10.1007/s10479-024-06415-5

Jam, F. A., Ali, I., Albishri, N., Mammadov, A., & Mohapatra, A. K. (2025). How does the adoption of digital technologies in supply chain management enhance supply chain performance? A mediated and moderated model. *Technological Forecasting and Social Change, 219*, 124225. Advance online publication. DOI: 10.1016/j.techfore.2025.124225

Janjua, N. A., Sahibzada, U. F., & Rafi-ul-Shan, P. M. (2025). Advancing sustainable development goals through green inclusive leadership in hospitality industry: A dual study perspective. *Current Issues in Tourism*, •••, 1–22. DOI: 10.1080/13683500.2025.2469749

Javaid, M., Haleem, A., Singh, R. P., & Suman, R. (2023). An integrated outlook of Cyber–Physical Systems for Industry 4.0: Topical practices, architecture, and applications. *Green Technologies and Sustainability, 1*(1), 100001. DOI: 10.1016/j.grets.2022.100001

Jebbad, R., Sierra, J. P., Mösso, C., Mestres, M., & Sánchez-Arcilla, A. (2022). Assessment of harbour inoperability and adaptation cost due to sea level rise. Application to the port of Tangier-Med (Morocco). *Applied Geography (Sevenoaks, England), 138*, 102623. Advance online publication. DOI: 10.1016/j.apgeog.2021.102623

Jeffrie, N. (2025, April 14). The mobile gender gap in South Asia is now widening. *GSMA – Mobile for Development*. https://www.gsma.com/mobilefordevelopment

Jelti, F., & Saadani, R. (2024). Energy efficiency analysis of heavy goods vehicles in road transportation: The case of Morocco. *Case Studies on Transport Policy, 17*, 101260. DOI: 10.1016/j.cstp.2024.101260

Jia, L., & Li, J. (2024). How does digital collaboration impact supply chain resilience. *Finance Research Letters, 66*, 105684–105684. DOI: 10.1016/j.frl.2024.105684

Jiang, Y., Feng, T., & Huang, Y. (2023). Antecedent configurations toward supply chain resilience: The joint impact of supply chain integration and big data analytics capability. *Journal of Operations Management, 70*(2), 257–284. Advance online publication. DOI: 10.1002/joom.1282

Jobin, A., Ienca, M., & Vayena, E. (2019). The global landscape of AI ethics guidelines. *Nature Machine Intelligence, 1*(9), 389–399. DOI: 10.1038/s42256-019-0088-2

Joshi, D. (2024). AI governance in India–law, policy and political economy. *Communication Research and Practice, 10*(3), 328–339. DOI: 10.1080/22041451.2024.2346428

Jüttner, U., & Maklan, S. (2011). Supply chain resilience in the global financial crisis: An empirical study. *Supply Chain Management, 16*(4), 246–259. DOI: 10.1108/13598541111139062

Kalkha, H., Khiat, A., Bahnasse, A., Ouajji, H., Kalkha, H., Khiat, A., & Ouajji, H. (2023). The Rising Trends of Smart E-Commerce Logistics. *IEEE Access : Practical Innovations, Open Solutions, 11*, 33839–33857. DOI: 10.1109/ACCESS.2023.3252566

Kar, T.. (2024). The digital revolution in India: Bridging the gap in rural technology adoption. *Journal of Innovation and Entrepreneurship, 13*(1), 29. Advance online publication. DOI: 10.1186/s13731-024-00380-w

Kayikci, Y., Gozacan-Chase, N., Rejeb, A., & Mathiyazhagan, K. (2022). Critical success factors for implementing blockchain-based circular supply chain. *Business Strategy and the Environment, 31*(7), 3595–3615. DOI: 10.1002/bse.3110

Khang, A., Jadhav, B., & Birajdar, S. (2023). Industry revolution 4.0: workforce competency models and designs. In *Designing workforce management systems for industry 4.0* (pp. 11–34). CRC Press. DOI: 10.1201/9781003357070-2

Kılıç, C., & Atilla, G. (2024). Industry 4.0 and sustainable business models: An intercontinental sample. *Business Strategy and the Environment, 33*(4), 3142–3166. DOI: 10.1002/bse.3634

Klimek, P., Varga, J., Jovanovic, A. S., & Székely, Z. (2019). Quantitative resilience assessment in emergency response reveals how organizations trade efficiency for redundancy. *Safety Science, 113*, 404–414. DOI: 10.1016/j.ssci.2018.12.017

Köhler, S., & Pizzol, M. (2020). Life cycle sustainability and AI. *Journal of Cleaner Production.*

Konopik, J., Jahn, C., Schuster, T., Hoßbach, N., & Pflaum, A. (2022). Mastering the digital transformation through organizational capabilities: A conceptual framework. *Digital Business, 2*(2), 100019. https://doi.org/https://doi.org/10.1016/j.digbus.2021.100019

Kovács, G., & Spens, K. M. (2011). Humanitarian logistics and supply chain management: The start of a new journal. *Journal of Humanitarian Logistics and Supply Chain Management*, *1*(1), 5–14. DOI: 10.1108/20426741111123041

Kumar, S., & Bansal, P. (2022). Supply chain labour risks in the textile industry. *Business and Society Review*, *127*(4), 721–740.

Lauterbach, A. (2019). Artificial intelligence and policy: Quo vadis? *Digital Policy. Regulation & Governance*, *21*(3), 238–263.

Lebosse, S., Taghipour, A., & Canel-Depitre, B. (2017). Quick response to fluctuations in supply chains: A review. *Journal of Advanced Management Science*, *5*(5), 394–400. DOI: 10.18178/joams.5.5.394-400

Lhamidi, S., & Boulitama, O. (2025). Adoption of Industry 4.0 Technologies in Moroccan Supply Chains: A Bayesian Network and Sectoral Analysis. *16th International Conference on Logistics and Supply Chain Management - LOGISTIQUA 2025*, 28–30. DOI: 10.1109/LOGISTIQUA66323.2025.11122847

Licardo, J. T., Domjan, M., & Orehovački, T. (2024). Intelligent robotics—A systematic review of emerging technologies and trends. *Electronics (Basel)*, *13*(3), 542. DOI: 10.3390/electronics13030542

Ling-yee, L. (2007). Marketing resources and performance of exhibitor firms in trade shows: A contingent resource perspective. *Industrial Marketing Management*, *36*(3), 360–370. DOI: 10.1016/j.indmarman.2005.11.001

Li, P., Chen, Y., & Guo, X. (2025). Digital Transformation and Supply Chain Resilience. *International Review of Economics & Finance*, *99*, 104033. DOI: 10.1016/j.iref.2025.104033

Liu, Q., & Wang, H. (2025). Digital transformation, innovation capability, and ESG performance. *Finance Research Letters*, *78*, 107166. DOI: 10.1016/j.frl.2025.107166

Liu, Y., Song, J., Zhou, B., & Liu, J. (2025). Artificial intelligence applications and corporate ESG performance. *International Review of Economics & Finance*, *104*, 104559. https://doi.org/https://doi.org/10.1016/j.iref.2025.104559. DOI: 10.1016/j.iref.2025.104559

Live Mint. (2025, June 4). UPI fuels rural women's digital leap—but few own their phones (P. Srivastava & P. Bhattacharya).

Locke, R. (2013). *The Promise and Limits of Private Power: Promoting Labor Standards in a Global Economy*. Cambridge University Press. DOI: 10.1017/CBO9781139381840

Logeswaran, K., Savitha, S., Suresh, P., Prasanna Kumar, K. R., Gunasekar, M., Rajadevi, R., & Jayasurya, A. S. (2024). Unifying Technologies in Industry 4.0: Harnessing the Synergy of Internet of Things, Big Data, Augmented Reality/Virtual Reality, and Blockchain Technologies. *Topics in Artificial Intelligence Applied to Industry*, *4*(0), 127–147. DOI: 10.1002/9781394216147.ch7

Loivet, W., Taghipour, A., & Kang, D. S. (2020). The rise of green supply chain management: Between complexity and necessity. *J. Econ. Bus. Manag*, *8*(1), 1–7. DOI: 10.18178/joebm.2020.8.1.604

Loivet, W., Taghipour, A., & Kang, D. S. (2020). The rise of green supply chain management: Between complexity and necessity. Journal of Economics. *Business and Management*, *8*(1), 1–7.

Lu, X. W., Tliche, Y., Vosooghidizaji, M., & Taghipour, A. (2023). Cryptocurrencies and Blockchain Applications. In Blockchain Applications in Cryptocurrency for Technological Evolution (pp. 1-13). IGI Global.

Lu, X., & Taghipour, A. (2025). The Future of Marketing: Integrating Big Data and AI for Personalized Customer Engagement. In Ecological and Human Dimensions of AI-Based Supply Chain (pp. 97-110). IGI Global Scientific Publishing.

Lu, X., & Taghipour, A. (2023). A French Guide for Businesses and Governments to Integrate the Concept of Sustainable Development Into Their Supply Chains. In *Government Impact on Sustainable and Responsible Supply Chain Management* (pp. 1–12). IGI Global. DOI: 10.4018/978-1-6684-9062-4.ch001

Lu, X., & Taghipour, A. (2025a). A review of supply chain digitalization and emerging research paradigms. *Logistics (Basel)*, *9*(2), 47. DOI: 10.3390/logistics9020047

Madanchian, M., & Taherdoost, H. (2025). Barriers and enablers of AI adoption in human resource management: A critical analysis of organizational and technological factors. *Information (Basel)*, *16*(1), 51. DOI: 10.3390/info16010051

Maddikunta, P. K. R., Pham, Q. V., Prabadevi, B., Deepa, N., Dev, K., Gadekallu, T. R., & Liyanage, M. (2022). Industry 5.0: A survey on enabling technologies and potential applications. *Journal of Industrial Information Integration*, *26*, 100257. DOI: 10.1016/j.jii.2021.100257

Maersk. (2022). *Annual Sustainability and Climate Report.*

Mahfod, J., Canel-Depitre, B., & Taghipour, A. (2019). Quality function deployment-ELECTRE in supplier evaluation. Journal of advanced management science, 7(4).

Mahfod, J., Khoury, B., Canel-Depitre, B., & Taghipour, A. (2021). Logistics Providers in Syria Humanitarian Operations. In Demand Forecasting and Order Planning in Supply Chains and Humanitarian Logistics (pp. 171-197). IGI Global. DOI: 10.4018/978-1-7998-3805-0.ch006

Ma, J., Ni, J., Zhao, Y., & Wu, J. (2025). Environmental regulation, digital technology application and low-carbon supply chain resilience: Evidence from China. *Journal of Environmental Management, 389*, 126087. DOI: 10.1016/j.jenvman.2025.126087 PMID: 40494230

Manavalan, E., & Jayakrishna, K. (2019). A review of Internet of Things (IoT) embedded sustainable supply chain for industry 4.0 requirements. *Computers & Industrial Engineering, 127*, 925–953. DOI: 10.1016/j.cie.2018.11.030

Marcon, É., Soliman, M., Gerstlberger, W., & Frank, A. G. (2022). Sociotechnical factors and Industry 4.0: An integrative perspective for the adoption of smart manufacturing technologies. *Journal of Manufacturing Technology Management, 33*(2), 259–286. DOI: 10.1108/JMTM-01-2021-0017

Markolf, S. A., Helmrich, A., Kim, Y., Hoff, R., & Chester, M. (2022). Balancing efficiency and resilience objectives in pursuit of sustainable infrastructure transformations. *Current Opinion in Environmental Sustainability, 56*, 101181. DOI: 10.1016/j.cosust.2022.101181

Massari, G. F., Nacchiero, R., & Giannoccaro, I. (2025). Transformative supply chains: The enabling role of digital technologies. *International Journal of Production Economics, 283*, 109562. DOI: 10.1016/j.ijpe.2025.109562

Mathiyazhagan, K., Taghipour, A., & Agarwal, V. (Eds.). (2022). Blockchain technology in supply chain management for society 5.0. CRC Press. Lu, X., & Taghipour, A. (2023). A French Guide for Businesses and Governments to Integrate the Concept of Sustainable Development Into Their Supply Chains. In Government Impact on Sustainable and Responsible Supply Chain Management (pp. 1-12). IGI Global Scientific Publishing. Lu, X. W., Tliche, Y., Vosooghidizaji, M., & Taghipour, A. (2023). Cryptocurrencies and Blockchain Applications. In Blockchain Applications in Cryptocurrency for Technological Evolution (pp. 1-13). IGI Global Scientific Publishing.

Mathiyazhagan, K., Taghipour, A., & Agarwal, V. (Eds.). (2022). *Blockchain Technology in Supply Chain Management for Society 5.0*. CRC Press. DOI: 10.1201/9781003177432

Mbiatem, J., Taghipour, A., & Canel-Depitre, B. (2018, August). Supplier selection approaches for decision makers. In *Proceedings of the 8th International Conference on Information Communication and Management* (pp. 108-112).

McKinsey & Company. (2021). *The Future of Digital Supply Chain Transformation.*

Meher, S., & Sahoo, P. (2021). Digital divide in India: Dimensions and determinants. *Economic and Political Weekly*, *56*(24), 45–53.

Melnyk, S. A., Schoenherr, T., Speier-Pero, C., Peters, C., Chang, J. F., & Friday, D. (2022). New challenges in supply chain management: Cybersecurity across the supply chain. *International Journal of Production Research*, *60*(1), 162–183. DOI: 10.1080/00207543.2021.1984606

Melo, P. F., Godoy, E. P., Ferrari, P., & Sisinni, E. (2021). Open source control device for industry 4.0 based on RAMI 4.0. *Electronics (Basel)*, *10*(7), 869. DOI: 10.3390/electronics10070869

Merimi, M., & Taghipour, A. (2021). Accelerating the digitalization of the supply chain: An empirical research about COVID-19 crisis. In *Digitalization of decentralized supply chains during global crises* (pp. 1–24). IGI Global Scientific Publishing. DOI: 10.4018/978-1-7998-6874-3.ch001

Metwally, M., & Ahmed, A. (2024). The Interplay between Digital Technologies, Supply Chain Resilience, Robustness and Sustainable Environmental Performance: Does Supply Chain Complexity Matter? *Sustainability (Basel)*, *16*(14), 6175–6175. DOI: 10.3390/su16146175

Ministry of Electronics and Information Technology (MeitY). (2015). *Digital India Programme*. Government of India.

Ministry of Electronics and Information Technology (MeitY). (2019). *Pradhan Mantri Gramin Digital Saksharta Abhiyan (PMGDISHA)*. Government of India.

Misener, L., & Darcy, S. (2014). *Managing Disability Sport: From Theory to Practice*. Routledge.

Mittal, S., Khan, M. A., Romero, D., & Wuest, T. (2018). A critical review of smart manufacturing & Industry 4.0 maturity models: Implications for small and medium-sized enterprises (SMEs). *Journal of Manufacturing Systems*, *49*, 194–214. DOI: 10.1016/j.jmsy.2018.10.005

Mohammaddust, F., Rezapour, S., Farahani, R. Z., Mofidfar, M., & Hill, A. (2017). Developing lean and responsive supply chains: A robust model for alternative risk mitigation strategies in supply chain designs. *International Journal of Production Economics, 183*, 632–653. DOI: 10.1016/j.ijpe.2015.09.012

Moitra, A., Kumar, A., & Seth, A. (2021). An analysis of impact pathways arising from a mobile-based community media platform in rural India (Mobile Vaani). *arXiv*. https://arxiv.org/abs/2106.15917

Mood, M., Ghamary, M., & Youshanlouei, H. R. (2025). The Role of Governments, Employers, and Platforms to Cope with the Skill Gaps in Industry 4.0. In *Ecological and Human Dimensions of AI-Based Supply Chain* (pp. 111–162). IGI Global Scientific Publishing. DOI: 10.4018/979-8-3693-7478-8.ch006

Moore, M.-L., Tjornbo, O., Enfors, E., Knapp, C., Hodbod, J., Baggio, J. A., Norström, A., Olsson, P., & Biggs, D. (2014). Studying the complexity of change: Toward an analytical framework for understanding deliberate social-ecological transformations. *Ecology and Society, 19*(4), 10. https://www.jstor.org/stable/26269689. DOI: 10.5751/ES-06966-190454

Mukherjee, S., Mukherjee, S., Ferraris, A., & Stehlikova, B. (2025). Enhancing health-care service delivery through AI-integrated knowledge management systems. *Journal of Knowledge Management, 29*(10), 3379–3409. DOI: 10.1108/JKM-01-2025-0119

Mulligan, C., Morsfield, S., & Cheikosman, E. (2024). Blockchain for sustainability: A systematic literature review for policy impact. *Telecommunications Policy, 48*(2), 102676. DOI: 10.1016/j.telpol.2023.102676

Mustapha, I., Khan, N., Qureshi, M. I., Sikandar, H., Hassan, M., & Simarmata, J. (2024). Revolutionizing supply chain processes: harnessing the power of IoT and blockchain technology to enhance opportunities. In *Innovative Technologies for Enhancing Experiences and Engagement* (pp. 87–94). Springer Nature Switzerland. DOI: 10.1007/978-3-031-55558-9_10

Nadia, E. N., Beatrice, C. D., & Atour, T. (2020). Luxury hotels' eco-friendly activities & customers' preferences and willingness to pay for green hotels. *Journal of Advanced Management Science, 8*(1), 1–24.

Nadia, E. N., Beatrice, C. D., & Atour, T. (2021). The determinants of hotel room rates in Beirut: A hedonic pricing model. International Journal of Trade. *Economics and Finance, 12*(2), 33–42.

Nazrul, I. M., & Rahman, H. A. (2021). Sustaining the Environment: A case study of the Garment Industry in Bangladesh. *International Journal of Academic Research in Business & Social Sciences, 11*(8), 947–963. DOI: 10.6007/IJARBSS/v11-i8/10789

Nelson, R. R., & Winter, S. G. (1982). *An evolutionary theory of economic change.* Belknap Press of Harvard University Press.

Neri, A., Negri, M., Cagno, E., Kumar, V., & Garza-Reyes, J. A. (2023). What digital-enabled dynamic capabilities support the circular economy? A multiple case study approach. *Business Strategy and the Environment, 32*(7), 5083–5101. DOI: 10.1002/bse.3409

Neto, O., Amorim, M., Carlos De Oliveira Matias, J., Fernando, L., Pinto, R., Bouazza, S., … Hachimi, H. (2023). Maritime Bilateral Connectivity Analysis for Sustainable Maritime Growth: Case of Morocco. *Sustainability 2023, Vol. 15, Page 4993, 15*(6), 4993. DOI: 10.3390/su15064993

Niinimäki, K.. (2020). Environmental impact of polyester manufacturing. *Textile Research Journal, 90*(3), 281–296.

Nikookar, E., Stevenson, M., & Varsei, M. (2024). Building an antifragile supply chain: A capability blueprint for resilience and post-disruption growth. *The Journal of Supply Chain Management, 60*(1), 13–31. Advance online publication. DOI: 10.1111/jscm.12313

Ning, Y., Li, L., Xu, S. X., & Yang, S. (2022). How do digital technologies improve supply chain resilience in the COVID-19 pandemic? Evidence from Chinese manufacturing firms. *Frontiers of Engineering Management, 10*(1), 39–50. DOI: 10.1007/s42524-022-0230-4

OECD. (2018). *Due Diligence Guidance for Responsible Business Conduct.*

OECD. (2019). *Recommendation of the Council on Artificial Intelligence.* OECD. OECD AI Principles

OECD. (2024). *Governing with artificial intelligence: Are governments ready? OECD Artificial Intelligence Papers, 20.* OECD Publishing., DOI: 10.1787/26324bc2-

OECD. (2025). *Governing with artificial intelligence: The state of play and way forward in core government functions.* OECD Publishing., DOI: 10.1787/795de142-

OECD. (2025). *Steering AI's future: Strategies for anticipatory governance. OECD Artificial Intelligence Papers, 32.* OECD Publishing., DOI: 10.1787/5480ff0a-

Ojadi, J. O., Odionu, C., Onukwulu, E., & Owulade, O. (2024). Big data analytics and AI for optimizing supply chain sustainability and reducing greenhouse gas emissions in logistics and transportation. *International Journal of Multidisciplinary Research and Growth Evaluation*, *5*(1), 1536–1548. DOI: 10.54660/.IJMRGE.2024.5.1.1536-1548

Oláh, J., Aburumman, N., Popp, J., Khan, M. A., Haddad, H., & Kitukutha, N. (2020). Impact of Industry 4.0 on environmental sustainability. *Sustainability (Basel)*, *12*(11), 4674. DOI: 10.3390/su12114674

Olawade, D. B., Wada, O. Z., Ige, A. O., Egbewole, B. I., Olojo, A., & Oladapo, B. I. (2024). Artificial intelligence in environmental monitoring: Advancements, challenges, and future directions. *Hygiene and Environmental Health Advances*, *12*, 100114. DOI: 10.1016/j.heha.2024.100114

Omisola, J. O., Bihani, D., Daraojimba, A. I., Osho, G. O., Ubamadu, B. C., & Etukudoh, E. A. (2023). Blockchain in supply chain transparency: A conceptual framework for real-time data tracking and reporting using blockchain and AI. International Journal of Multidisciplinary Research and Growth Evaluation, 4.

Organisation for Economic Co-operation and Development. (2024). *Keys to resilient supply chains: OECD policy toolkit – Increasing supply chain resilience*. OECD Publishing.

Organisation for Economic Co-operation and Development. (2025). *OECD Supply Chain Resilience Review: Navigating Risks*. OECD Publishing.

Oskounejad, M. M., & Nozari, H. (Eds.). (2024). *Advanced Businesses in Industry 6.0*. IGI Global. DOI: 10.4018/979-8-3693-3108-8

Oyedijo, A., Yang, Y., Koukpaki, A. S. F., & Mishra, N. (2023). The role of fairness in multi-tier sustainable supply chains. *International Journal of Production Research*, *61*(14), 4893–4917. DOI: 10.1080/00207543.2021.1928319

Panigrahi, S. S., Bahinipati, B., & Jain, V. (2019). Sustainable supply chain management: A review of literature and implications for future research. *Management of Environmental Quality*, *30*(5), 1001–1049. DOI: 10.1108/MEQ-01-2018-0003

Paramesha, M., Rane, N., & Rane, J. (2024). Big data analytics, artificial intelligence, machine learning, internet of things, and blockchain for enhanced business intelligence. Artificial Intelligence, Machine Learning, Internet of Things, and Blockchain for Enhanced Business Intelligence (June 6, 2024).

Paris 2024 Committee. (2023). *Official Sustainability Report*.

Pathak, S. D., Day, J. M., Nair, A., Sawaya, W. J., & Kristal, M. M. (2007). Complexity and Adaptivity in Supply Networks: Building Supply Network Theory Using a Complex Adaptive Systems Perspective*. *Decision Sciences, 38*(4), 547–580. DOI: 10.1111/j.1540-5915.2007.00170.x

Pathrose, A. P., & Seethalakshmi, M. (2025). Impact of the Digital India program in rural villages: A survey-based study. *Vidhyayana – An International Multidisciplinary Peer-Reviewed E-Journal, 10*(si3). DOI: 10.58213/vidhyayana.v10isi3.2213

Pavlou, P. A., & El Sawy, O. A. (2011). Understanding the Elusive Black Box of Dynamic Capabilities. *Decision Sciences, 42*(1), 239–273. DOI: 10.1111/j.1540-5915.2010.00287.x

Pettit, T. J., Fiksel, J., & Croxton, K. L. (2010). ENSURING SUPPLY CHAIN RESILIENCE: DEVELOPMENT OF a CONCEPTUAL FRAMEWORK. *Journal of Business Logistics, 31*(1), 1–21. DOI: 10.1002/j.2158-1592.2010.tb00125.x

Piprani, A. Z., Nazir, S., Najmi, A., Watabe, M., & Jaafar, N. I. (2025). Digital Capabilities and Supply Chain Resilience: Is Supply Chain Mapping the Missing Link? *Business Strategy & Development, 8*(3), 1–12. DOI: 10.1002/bsd2.70148

PMGDISHA. (n.d.). How PMGDISHA is empowering rural India digitally. Retrieved September 1, 2025, from https://www.pmgdisha.in

Ponomarov, S. Y., & Holcomb, M. C. (2009). Understanding the concept of supply chain resilience. *International Journal of Logistics Management, 20*(1), 124–143. DOI: 10.1108/09574090910954873

Ponputtha, W., Wannapiroon, P., & Nilsook, P. (2021). Creative history learning model using digital storytelling through cloud learning. International Journal of E-Education, e-Business, e-. *Management Learning, 11*(2), 42–50. DOI: 10.17706/ijeeee.2021.11.2.42-50

Ponputtha, W., Wannapiroon, P., Nilsook, P., Taghipour, A., Murat, S., Huang, P., & Chou, T. C. (2021). Creative history learning model using digital storytelling through cloud learning to enhance analytical thinking. International Journal of e-Education, e-Business, e-. *Management Learning, 11*(2), 42–50.

Pour Mohammadi, M., Ghorbani, R., & Taghipour, A. (2014). Factors affecting the price of housing in the city of Tabriz using hedonic model. *Geographical Planning of Space Quarterly Journal, 3*(9), 83–104.

Prasittisopin, L. (2025). Artificial intelligence-driven materiality: A systematic review and perspective. *Engineering and Science, 35*, 1587. DOI: 10.30919/es1587

Pratap, S., Jauhar, S. K., Gunasekaran, A., & Kamble, S. S. (2024). Optimizing the IoT and big data embedded smart supply chains for sustainable performance. *Computers & Industrial Engineering*, *187*, 109828. DOI: 10.1016/j.cie.2023.109828

Preiser, R., Schlüter, M., Biggs, R., García, M. M., Haider, J., Hertz, T., & Klein, L. (2021). Complexity-based social-ecological systems research: Philosophical foundations and practical implications. In *The Routledge Handbook of Research Methods for Social-Ecological Systems* (pp. 27–46). Routledge. DOI: 10.4324/9781003021339-3

Press Information Bureau. (2022, December 7). National telemedicine service of India – eSanjeevani achieves 80 million teleconsultations. *IBEF*. https://www.ibef.org

Preuss, H. (2019). Event visitor carbon footprinting. *European Sport Management Quarterly*, *19*(5), 628–651.

PwC. (2023). *Global Sports Industry Outlook.*

PwC. (2023). *Global Supply Chain Outlook Report.*

Qader, G., Junaid, M., Abbas, Q., & Mubarik, M. S. (2022). Industry 4.0 enables supply chain resilience and supply chain performance. *Technological Forecasting and Social Change*, *185*, 122026. Advance online publication. DOI: 10.1016/j.techfore.2022.122026

Qu, C., & Kim, E. (2024). Reviewing the roles of AI-integrated technologies in sustainable supply chain management: Research propositions and a framework for future directions. *Sustainability (Basel)*, *16*(14), 6186. DOI: 10.3390/su16146186

Queiroz, M. M., Fosso Wamba, S., De Bourmont, M., & Telles, R. (2021). Blockchain adoption in operations and supply chain management: Empirical evidence from an emerging economy. *International Journal of Production Research*, *59*(20), 6087–6103. DOI: 10.1080/00207543.2020.1803511

Radhoui, H., Taghipour, A., & Canel-Depitre, B. (2019). The distribution and pickup of goods: A literature review and survey. Hierarchical Planning and Information Sharing Techniques in Supply Chain Management, 46-85.

Radhoui, H., Taghipour, A., & Canel-Depitre, B. (2021). Mixed delivery and pickup vehicle routing problem with limited flow and assignment of drones in an urban network. Demand Forecasting and Order Planning in Supply Chains and Humanitarian Logistics, 225-249.

Radhoui, H., Taghipour, A., & Canel-Depitre, B. (2021). Mixed delivery and pickup vehicle routing problem with limited flow and assignment of drones in an urban network. In *Demand Forecasting and Order Planning in Supply Chains and Humanitarian Logistics* (pp. 225–249). IGI Global. DOI: 10.4018/978-1-7998-3805-0.ch008

Raj, P., & Raman, A. C. (2017). *The Internet of Things: Enabling technologies, platforms, and use cases.* Auerbach Publications.

Rame, R., Purwanto, P., & Sudarno, S. (2024). Industry 5.0 and sustainability: An overview of emerging trends and challenges for a green future. *Innovation and Green Development, 3*(4), 100173. DOI: 10.1016/j.igd.2024.100173

Rani, S., Jining, D., Shoukat, K., Shoukat, M. U., & Nawaz, S. A. (2024). A Human–Machine Interaction Mechanism: Additive Manufacturing for Industry 5.0—Design and Management. *Sustainability (Basel), 16*(10), 4158. DOI: 10.3390/su16104158

Rao, S., & Jena, R. K. (2020). E-governance and digital literacy in rural India: A transformative study. *Government Information Quarterly, 37*(3), 101449. DOI: 10.1016/j.giq.2020.101449

Reis, J. (2023). Exploring Applications and Practical Examples by Streamlining Material Requirements Planning (MRP) with Python. *Logistics (Basel), 7*(4), 91. DOI: 10.3390/logistics7040091

Ren, Z., Taghipour, A., & Canel-Depitre, B. (2016, October). Information sharing in supply chain under uncertainty. In 2016 6th International Conference on Information Communication and Management (ICICM) (pp. 67-71). IEEE. DOI: 10.1109/INFOCOMAN.2016.7784217

Riad, M., Naimi, M., & Okar, C. (2024). Enhancing supply chain resilience through artificial intelligence: Developing a comprehensive conceptual framework for AI implementation and supply chain optimization. *Logistics (Basel), 8*(4), 111. DOI: 10.3390/logistics8040111

Richey, R. G. (2009). The supply chain crisis and disaster pyramid. *International Journal of Physical Distribution & Logistics Management, 39*(7), 619–628. DOI: 10.1108/09600030910996288

Romero, I. (2025). Information technology as a driver of organizational change in SMEs: A study of key determinants. *Journal of Organizational Change Management, 38*(3), 625–643. https://doi.org/https://doi.org/10.1108/JOCM-11-2024-0702. DOI: 10.1108/JOCM-11-2024-0702

Roumeliotis, C., Dasygenis, M., Lazaridis, V., & Dossis, M. (2024). Blockchain and digital twins in smart industry 4.0: The use case of supply chain-a review of integration techniques and applications. *Designs*, *8*(6), 105. DOI: 10.3390/designs8060105

Ruiz-Benítez, R., López, C., & Real, J. C. (2018). The lean and resilient management of the supply chain and its impact on performance. *International Journal of Production Economics*, *203*, 190–202. DOI: 10.1016/j.ijpe.2018.06.009

Saari, A., Sinclair, S., Leshinsky, R., & Junnila, S. (2025). Best practices for blockchain-driven digital transformation in cross-industry settings. *Digital Business*, *5*(2), 100127. https://doi.org/https://doi.org/10.1016/j.digbus.2025.100127

Sahoo, S., Kumar, S., Sivarajah, U., Lim, W. M., Westland, J. C., & Kumar, A. (2024). Blockchain for sustainable supply chain management: Trends and ways forward. *Electronic Commerce Research*, *24*(3), 1563–1618. DOI: 10.1007/s10660-022-09569-1

Sahraoui, A., Tran, N. K., Tliche, Y., Kacem, A., & Taghipour, A. (2023). Examining ICT Innovation for Sustainable Terminal Operations in Developing Countries: A Case Study of the Port of Radès in Tunisia. *Sustainability (Basel)*, *15*(11), 9123. DOI: 10.3390/su15119123

Salemink, K., Strijker, D., & Bosworth, G. (2017). Rural development in the digital age: A systematic literature review on unequal ICT availability, adoption, and use in rural areas. *Journal of Rural Studies*, *54*, 360–371. DOI: 10.1016/j.jrurstud.2015.09.001

Sánchez-Flores, R. B., Cruz-Sotelo, S. E., Ojeda-Benitez, S., & Ramírez-Barreto, M. E. (2020). Sustainable supply chain management—A literature review on emerging economies. *Sustainability (Basel)*, *12*(17), 6972. DOI: 10.3390/su12176972

Santiago, B. D. S., Scavarda, L. F., Gusmão Caiado, R. G., Santos, R. S., & Mattos Nascimento, D. L. D. (2024). Corporate social responsibility and circular economy integration framework within sustainable supply chain management: Building blocks for industry 5.0. *Corporate Social Responsibility and Environmental Management*.

Sarma, M., & Pais, J. (2019). Financial inclusion and development in India: An assessment. *Journal of Economic Development Studies*, *7*(1), 43–57. DOI: 10.2139/ssrn.3400822

Saxena, R., Shoeb, M., Srivastava, A. K., Hayat, M., & Yadav, A. (2024). Harnessing Artificial Intelligence for Business Sustainability: Strategies for a Resilient and Adaptive Future. Library of Progress-Library Science, Information Technology & Computer, 44(3).

Sentinel Digital Desk. (2025, August 26). 3,841 villages in Northeast remain out of mobile network coverage. *The Sentinel - of This Land, for Its People*. https://www.sentinelassam.com/topheadlines/3841-villages-in-northeast-remain-out-of-mobile-network-coverage

Seuring, S., & Müller, M. (2008). From a literature review to a conceptual framework for sustainable supply chain management. *Journal of Cleaner Production, 16*(15), 1699–1710. DOI: 10.1016/j.jclepro.2008.04.020

Shafik, W. (2024). Artificial intelligence and internet of things roles in sustainable next-generation manufacturing: An overview of emerging trends in Industry 6.0. *Advances in Business Information Systems and Analytics*, *6*(0), 207–239. DOI: 10.4018/979-8-3693-3140-8.ch012

Shah, R., & Ward, P. T. (2007). Defining and Developing Measures of Lean Production. *Journal of Operations Management, 25*(4), 785–805. DOI: 10.1016/j.jom.2007.01.019

Sharma, S. K., Dwivedi, Y. K., Metri, B., Lal, B., & Elbanna, A. (2023). Transfer, Diffusion and Adoption of Next-Generation Digital Technologies. In *Proceedings of the IFIP WG* (Vol. 8).

Sharma, V., Vashishth, T. K., Kumar, B., Sharma, K. K., Vidyant, S., & Chaudhary, S. (2023, December). Health Interpretation of Covid-19 Patients using Artificial Intelligence. In *2023 International Conference on Artificial Intelligence for Innovations in Healthcare Industries (ICAIIHI)* (Vol. 1, pp. 1-5). IEEE Computer Society. DOI: 10.1109/ICAIIHI57871.2023.10488924

Sheffi, Y. (2015). *The power of resilience: How the best companies manage the unexpected*. The MIT Press. DOI: 10.7551/mitpress/9780262029797.001.0001

Shen, B. (2014). Sustainable fashion supply chain: Lessons from H&M. *Sustainability (Basel)*, *6*(9), 6236–6249. DOI: 10.3390/su6096236

Singh, A. (2021). ICT-driven rural empowerment: Lessons from India. *Journal of Rural Studies*, *82*, 145–154. DOI: 10.1016/j.jrurstud.2021.01.020

Singh, D., Sharma, A., Singh, R. K., & Rana, P. S. (2025). Augmenting supply chain resilience through AI and big data. *Business Process Management Journal*, *31*(2), 631–657. DOI: 10.1108/BPMJ-04-2024-0260

Singh, R. K. (2025). Transforming humanitarian supply chains with digital twin technology: A study on resilience and agility. *International Journal of Logistics Management*, *36*(4), 1119–1135. DOI: 10.1108/IJLM-08-2024-0504

Sirmon, D. G., Hitt, M. A., Ireland, R. D., & Gilbert, B. A. (2010). Resource Orchestration to Create Competitive Advantage. *Journal of Management, 37*(5), 1390–1412. DOI: 10.1177/0149206310385695

Statista. (2023). *Global Sports Apparel Revenue.*

Stix, C. (2021). Actionable principles for artificial intelligence policy: Three pathways. *Science and Engineering Ethics, 27*(1), 15. DOI: 10.1007/s11948-020-00277-3 PMID: 33608756

Stroumpoulis, A., Kopanaki, E., & Chountalas, P. T. (2024). Enhancing sustainable supply chain management through digital transformation: A comparative case study analysis. *Sustainability (Basel), 16*(16), 6778. DOI: 10.3390/su16166778

Su, C., Tang, X., Han, Y., Wang, T., & Jiang, D. (2024). Cognitive digital twin in manufacturing process: Integrating the knowledge graph for enhanced human-centric Industry 5.0. *International Journal of Production Research*, •••, 1–22.

Suleiman, Z., Shaikholla, S., Dikhanbayeva, D., Shehab, E., & Turkyilmaz, A. (2022). Industry 4.0: Clustering of concepts and characteristics. *Cogent Engineering, 9*(1), 2034264. DOI: 10.1080/23311916.2022.2034264

Taghipour, A. (2009). Evaluation de la collaboration dans une chaîne d'approvisionnement. Revue française de gestion industrielle, 28(1), 26-42.

Taghipour, A. (2024). Big Data: The New Gold Mine for Supermarkets. In Applications of New Technology in Operations and Supply Chain Management (pp. 98-106). IGI Global Scientific Publishing.

Taghipour, A. (2024). Big Data: The New Gold Mine for Supermarkets. In Applications of New Technology in Operations and Supply Chain Management (pp. 98-106). IGI Global.

Taghipour, A., & Frayret, J. M. (2011). Supply chain coordination planning: A review. Work paper, École polytechnique de Montréal.

Taghipour, A., & Lu, X. (2025). Advancing Supply Chain Innovation: Theoretical Foundations, Contemporary Developments, and Future Directions. In Ecological and Human Dimensions of AI-Based Supply Chain (pp. 1-26). IGI Global Scientific Publishing.

Taghipour, A., & Lu, X. (2025). Advancing Supply Chain Innovation: Theoretical Foundations, Contemporary Developments, and Future Directions. In *Ecological and Human Dimensions of AI-Based Supply Chain* (pp. 1–26). IGI Global Scientific Publishing. DOI: 10.4018/979-8-3693-7478-8.ch001

Taghipour, A., & Lu, X. (2025). Navigating the Artificial Intelligence Era: Impacts of Artificial Intelligence on Youth Critical Thinking, Career Paths, and Ethical Challenges. In Ecological and Human Dimensions of AI-Based Supply Chain (pp. 49-68). IGI Global Scientific Publishing.

Taghipour, A., & Lu, X. (2025a). Advancing Supply Chain Innovation: Theoretical Foundations, Contemporary Developments, and Future Directions. In Ecological and Human Dimensions of AI-Based Supply Chain (pp. 1-26). IGI Global Scientific Publishing.

Taghipour, A., & Lu, X. W. (2023, August). Green Supply Chain Management: A Guide. In International Conference on Applied Economics and Business (pp. 315-328). Cham: Springer Nature Switzerland.

Taghipour, A., & Merimi, M. (2021, March). Digital transformation of supply chains during crisis: covid-19. In 11th Annual International Conference on Industrial Engineering and Operations Management, IEOM (pp. 7493-7501). DOI: 10.46254/AN11.20211298

Taghipour, A., Abed, M., & Zoghlami, N. (2015, May). Design for remanufacturing respecting reverse logistics processes: A review. In 2015 4th international conference on advanced logistics and transport (ICALT) (pp. 299-304). IEEE. DOI: 10.1109/ICAdLT.2015.7136602

Taghipour, A. (Ed.). (2020). *Demand forecasting and order planning in supply chains and humanitarian logistics*. IGI Global.

Taghipour, A. (Ed.). (2022). *Blockchain Applications in Cryptocurrency for Technological Evolution*. IGI Global. DOI: 10.4018/978-1-6684-6247-8

Taghipour, A., & Beneteau-Piet, C. (2020). Sustainable supply chain management performance. *International Journal of Innovation, Management and Technology*, *11*(6), 165–169. DOI: 10.18178/ijimt.2020.11.6.897

Taghipour, A., Fooladvand, A., Khazaei, M., & Ramezani, M. (2023a). Criteria clustering and supplier segmentation based on sustainable shared value using BWM and PROMETHEE. *Sustainability (Basel)*, *15*(11), 8670. DOI: 10.3390/su15118670

Taghipour, A., & Frayret, J. M. (2013). Coordination of operations planning in supply chains: A review. *International Journal of Business Performance and Supply Chain Modelling*, *5*(3), 272–307. DOI: 10.1504/IJBPSCM.2013.055729

Taghipour, A., & Frayret, J. M. (2013a, May). An algorithm to improve operations planning in decentralized supply chains. In *2013 International Conference on Advanced Logistics and Transport* (pp. 100-103). IEEE. DOI: 10.1109/ICAdLT.2013.6568442

Taghipour, A., & Lu, X. (2025b). Navigating the artificial intelligence era: impacts of artificial intelligence on youth critical thinking, career paths, and ethical challenges. In *Ecological and Human Dimensions of AI-Based Supply Chain* (pp. 49–68). IGI Global Scientific Publishing. DOI: 10.4018/979-8-3693-7478-8.ch003

Taghipour, A., Lu, X., Derradji, M., & Sow, A. D. (2022b, July). The impact of digitalization on supply chain management: a literature review. In *Proceedings of the 12th International Conference on Information Communication and Management* (pp. 75-78). DOI: 10.1145/3551690.3551702

Taghipour, A., Lu, X., & Smahi, M. (2022a). Opportunities and challenges for society 5.0 in procurement. *Blockchain Technology in Supply Chain Management for Society*, *5*(0), 91–100. DOI: 10.1201/9781003177432-9

Taghipour, A., Rouyendegh, B. D., Ünal, A., & Piya, S. (2022c). Selection of suppliers for speech recognition products in IT projects by combining techniques with an integrated fuzzy MCDM. *Sustainability (Basel)*, *14*(3), 1777. DOI: 10.3390/su14031777

Taghipour, A., Sohrabi, A., Ghaedi, M., & Khazaei, M. (2023b). A robust vaccine supply chain model in pandemics: Case of Covid-19 in Iran. *Computers & Industrial Engineering*, *183*, 109465. DOI: 10.1016/j.cie.2023.109465

Tallat, R., Hawbani, A., Wang, X., Al-Dubai, A., Zhao, L., Liu, Z., & Alsamhi, S. H. (2023). Navigating industry 5.0: A survey of key enabling technologies, trends, challenges, and opportunities. *IEEE Communications Surveys and Tutorials*.

Teece, D. J. (2025). Explicating Dynamic Capabilities: The Nature and Microfoundations of (Sustainable) Enterprise Performance. SSRN *Electronic Journal*, *28*(13), 1319–1350. DOI: 10.2139/ssrn.5131710

Teixeira, A. R., Ferreira, J. V., & Ramos, A. L. (2025). Intelligent Supply Chain Management: A Systematic Literature Review on Artificial Intelligence Contributions. *Information 2025, Vol. 16*, *16*(5). DOI: 10.3390/info16050399

Testa, F., Boiral, O., & Iraldo, F. (2018). Internalization of environmental practices and institutional complexity: Can stakeholders pressures encourage greenwashing? *Journal of Business Ethics*, *147*(2), 287–307. DOI: 10.1007/s10551-015-2960-2

Thakur, A. (2025). Innovation through collaboration leveraging knowledge sharing for global R&D success. In *Research and development practices in innovation* (pp. 127–164). IGI Global Scientific Publishing. DOI: 10.4018/979-8-3373-0812-8.ch006

Tiron-Tudor, A., & Deliu, D. (2024). The Sustainability Performance of SMEs in Industry 5.0: A Proposal for a Synergetic Digital Sustainable Development Maturity Model (SDSDMM). *Eastern European Economics*, •••, 1–45.

Tiwari, S., Wee, H. M., & Daryanto, Y. (2018). Big data analytics in supply chain management between 2010 and 2016: Insights to industries. *Computers & Industrial Engineering*, *115*, 319–330. DOI: 10.1016/j.cie.2017.11.017

Tliche, Y., Taghipour, A., & Canel-Depitre, B. (2019). Downstream Demand Inference in decentralized supply chains. *European Journal of Operational Research*, *274*(1), 65–77. DOI: 10.1016/j.ejor.2018.09.034

Tliche, Y., Taghipour, A., Mahfod-Leroux, J., & Vosooghidizaji, M. (2023). Collaborative bullwhip effect-oriented bi-objective optimization for inference-based weighted moving average forecasting in decentralized supply chain. [IJISSCM]. *International Journal of Information Systems and Supply Chain Management*, *16*(1), 1–37. DOI: 10.4018/IJISSCM.316168

Tortorella, G., Gloet, M., Samson, D., Kurnia, S., Fogliatto, F. S., & Anzanello, M. J. (2024). Food supply chain resilience through digital transformation: A mixed-method approach. *International Journal of Logistics Management*, *36*(2), 381–412. DOI: 10.1108/IJLM-01-2024-0030

TOUFAH, N., EL MOUSSAOUI, A. E., & LEKHAILA, G. (2025). A Comparative Analysis of the Logistics and Economics Fields: A Literature Review. *Revue Française d'Economie et de Gestion*, *6*(8).

Tripathi, R. (2020). Affordability and awareness issues in rural connectivity. *Asian Journal of Technology and Society*, *4*(1), 67–75.

Truant, E., Borlatto, E., Crocco, E., & Sahore, N. (2024). Environmental, social and governance issues in supply chains. A systematic review for strategic performance. *Journal of Cleaner Production*, *434*, 140024. DOI: 10.1016/j.jclepro.2023.140024

Tukamuhabwa, B. R., Stevenson, M., Busby, J., & Zorzini, M. (2015). Supply chain resilience: Definition, review and theoretical foundations for further study. *International Journal of Production Research*, *53*(18), 5592–5623. DOI: 10.1080/00207543.2015.1037934

Ubaldi, B., Le Fevre, E. M., Petrucci, E., Marchionni, P., Biancalana, C., Hiltunen, N., ... & Yang, C. (2019). State of the art in the use of emerging technologies in the public sector. *OECD working papers on public governance*, (31), 1-74.

UEFA. (2021). *Blockchain Ticketing Pilot Report*.

UN Human Rights Council. (2011). *UN Guiding Principles on Business and Human Rights.*

UNESCO. (2022). *Digital literacy for inclusive societies: Policy insights*. UNESCO. https://unesdoc.unesco.org

Unilever. (2022). *Sustainable Procurement and Logistics Innovations.*

van Dijk, J. (2020). *The digital divide*. Polity Press.

Van Nguyen, T., Cong Pham, H., Nhat Nguyen, M., Zhou, L., & Akbari, M. (2023). Data-driven review of blockchain applications in supply chain management: Key research themes and future directions. *International Journal of Production Research, 61*(23), 8213–8235. DOI: 10.1080/00207543.2023.2165190

Vashishth, T. K., Sharma, V., Kaushik, V., & Sharma, K. K. (2025). Blockchain-Driven Innovations in the Banking and Financial Sectors: Harnessing the Power of Automated Machine Learning. In Utilizing AI and Machine Learning in Financial Analysis (pp. 555-578). IGI Global Scientific Publishing.

Vashishth, T. K., Sharma, V., Sharma, K. K., Kumar, B., Chaudhary, S., & Panwar, R. (2024a). Security and Privacy Challenges in Blockchain-Based Supply Chain Management: A Comprehensive Analysis. In Achieving Secure and Transparent Supply Chains with Blockchain Technology (pp. 70-91). IGI Global. DOI: 10.4018/979-8-3693-0482-2.ch005

Vashishth, T. K., Sharma, V., Sharma, K. K., Kumar, B., Chaudhary, S., & Panwar, R. (2024b). Waste-to-Energy Solutions Harnessing IoT and ML for Sustainable Power Generation in Smart Cities. In Methodologies, Frameworks, and Applications of Machine Learning (pp. 125-146). IGI Global. DOI: 10.4018/979-8-3693-1062-5.ch007

Velluti, S. (2024). Labour standards in global garment supply chains and the proposed EU corporate sustainability due diligence directive. *European Labour Law Journal, 15*(4), 822–850. DOI: 10.1177/20319525241239283

Vijay, A. J., William, B. N. J., Haruna, A. A., & Prasad, D. D. (2024). Exploring the synergy of IIoT, AI, and data analytics in Industry 6.0. In *Industry 6.0* (pp. 1–36). CRC Press. DOI: 10.1201/9781003517993-1

Villar, A., Paladini, S., & Buckley, O. (2023, July). Towards supply chain 5.0: Redesigning supply chains as resilient, sustainable, and human-centric systems in a post-pandemic world. In Operations [). Cham: Springer International Publishing.]. *Research Forum, 4*(3), 60. DOI: 10.1007/s43069-023-00234-3

Vosooghidizaji, M., Taghipour, A., & Canel-Depitre, B. (2019). A literature review on information asymmetry in supply chain coordination. *International Journal of Production Research, 58*(6), 1–6.

Vosooghidizaji, M., Taghipour, A., & Canel-Depitre, B. (2020). Information asymmetry in supply chain coordination: State of the art. *Journal of Industrial and Intelligent Information, 8*(2), 38–43. DOI: 10.18178/jiii.8.2.38-43

Vosooghidizaji, M., Taghipour, A., & Canel-Depitre, B. (2020). Supply chain coordination under information asymmetry: A review. *International Journal of Production Research, 58*(6), 1805–1834. DOI: 10.1080/00207543.2019.1685702

Wang, C. L., & Ahmed, P. K. (2007). Dynamic capabilities: A review and research agenda. *International Journal of Management Reviews, 9*(1), 31–51. DOI: 10.1111/j.1468-2370.2007.00201.x

Wang, H., Chen, Y., Xie, J., & Liu, C. (2025). Research on digital empowerment, innovation vitality and manufacturing supply chain resilience mechanism. *PLoS One, 20*(2), e0316183–e0316183. DOI: 10.1371/journal.pone.0316183 PMID: 39937796

Wang, Y., Ma, H. S., Yang, J. H., & Wang, K. S. (2017). Industry 4.0: A way from mass customization to mass personalization production. *Advances in Manufacturing, 5*(4), 311–320. DOI: 10.1007/s40436-017-0204-7

Whig, P., Remala, R., Mudunuru, K. R., & Quraishi, S. J. (2024). Integrating AI and quantum technologies for sustainable supply chain management. In *Quantum computing and supply chain management: A new era of optimization* (pp. 267–283). IGI Global. DOI: 10.4018/979-8-3693-4107-0.ch018

Wieland, A. (2021). Dancing the Supply Chain: Toward Transformative Supply Chain Management. *The Journal of Supply Chain Management, 57*(1), 58–73. Advance online publication. DOI: 10.1111/jscm.12248

Wieland, A. (2021). The responsible supply chain. *Journal of Business Ethics.*

Wieland, A., Stevenson, M., Melnyk, S. A., Davoudi, S., & Schultz, L. (2023). Thinking differently about supply chain resilience: What we can learn from social-ecological systems thinking. *International Journal of Operations & Production Management, 43*(1), 1–21. DOI: 10.1108/IJOPM-10-2022-0645

World Bank. (2021). *Digital development in South Asia: Bridging the connectivity divide.* World Bank. https://www.worldbank.org

World Economic Forum. (2020). *Shaping the Future of Technology Governance: AI in Supply Chains.*

Wu, H., Li, G., & Zheng, H. (2024). How does digital intelligence technology enhance supply chain resilience? Sustainable framework and agenda. *Annals of Operations Research*, •••, 1–23.

Wu, L., Huang, J., Wang, M., & Kumar, A. (2024). Unleashing supply chain agility: Leveraging data network effects for digital transformation. *International Journal of Production Economics*, *277*, 109402. DOI: 10.1016/j.ijpe.2024.109402

XiaoWen, L., & Atour, T. (2025). Knowledge-driven digital innovation in supply chains: An organizational perspective. *Journal of Innovation & Knowledge*, *10*(5), 100787. DOI: 10.1016/j.jik.2025.100787

Xue, J., & Li, G. (2023). Balancing resilience and efficiency in supply chains: Roles of disruptive technologies under Industry 4.0. *Frontiers of Engineering Management*, *10*(1), 171–176. DOI: 10.1007/s42524-022-0247-8

Yang, F., & Gu, S. (2021). Industry 4.0, a revolution that requires technology and national strategies. *Complex & Intelligent Systems*, *7*(3), 1311–1325. DOI: 10.1007/s40747-020-00267-9

Yebenes, J., & Zorrilla, M. (2019). Towards a Data Governance Framework for Third Generation Platforms. *Procedia Computer Science*, *151*, 614–621. https://doi.org/https://doi.org/10.1016/j.procs.2019.04.082. DOI: 10.1016/j.procs.2019.04.082

Yi, Z., & Ayangbah, S. (2024). The impact of AI innovation management on organizational productivity and economic growth: An analytical study. *International Journal of Business Management and Economic Research*, *7*(3), 61–84.

Younis, M. (2018). Internet of everything and everybody: Architecture and service virtualization. *Computer Communications*, *131*, 66–72. DOI: 10.1016/j.comcom.2018.07.008

Yu, X., Fan, L., & Yu, Y. (2025). Artificial Intelligence and Corporate ESG Performance: A Mechanism Analysis Based on Corporate Efficiency and External Environment. *Sustainability 2025, Vol. 17, 17*(9). DOI: 10.3390/su17093819

Yuan, Y., Tan, H., & Liu, L. (2023). The effects of digital transformation on supply chain resilience: A moderated and mediated model. *Journal of Enterprise Information Management*, *37*(2), 488–510. DOI: 10.1108/JEIM-09-2022-0333

Yu, Y., Xu, L., & Wen, X. (2025). The Impact of Digital Transformation on Supply Chain Resilience in Manufacturing: The Mediating Role of Supply Chain Integration. *Sustainability (Basel)*, *17*(9), 1–21. DOI: 10.3390/su17093873

Zafar, M. H., Langås, E. F., & Sanfilippo, F. (2024). Exploring the synergies between collaborative robotics, digital twins, augmentation, and industry 5.0 for smart manufacturing: A state-of-the-art review. *Robotics and Computer-integrated Manufacturing*, *89*, 102769. DOI: 10.1016/j.rcim.2024.102769

Zamani, E. D., Smyth, C., Gupta, S., & Dennehy, D. (2023). Artificial intelligence and big data analytics for supply chain resilience: A systematic literature review. *Annals of Operations Research*, *327*(2), 605–632. DOI: 10.1007/s10479-022-04983-y PMID: 36212520

Zejjari, I., & Benhayoun, I. (2024). Bibliometric analysis of Artificial Intelligence in marketing: Revealing publication trends using bibliometrix R-Tool. In *Artificial Intelligence, Digitalization and Regulation: A Legal Framework for Business* (pp. 737–750). Springer Nature Switzerland. DOI: 10.1007/978-3-031-67531-7_59

Zhang, J., Miao, X., & Shang, T. (2025). Impact Mechanism of Digital Transformation on Supply Chain Resilience. *Finance Research Letters*, *76*, 106993. DOI: 10.1016/j.frl.2025.106993

Zhao, N., Hong, J., & Lau, K. H. (2023). Impact of Supply Chain Digitalization on Supply Chain Resilience and performance: a multi-mediation Model. *International Journal of Production Economics, 259*, 108817. Sciencedirect. DOI: 10.1016/j.ijpe.2023.108817

Zheng, L., Song, G., Song, S., Huang, N., & Cheng, T. C. E. (2025). How do talent and technology factors affect supply chain robustness and resilience? Evidence from Chinese manufacturers. *Industrial Management & Data Systems*, *125*(3), 899–920. DOI: 10.1108/IMDS-07-2024-0676

Zhou, K., Liu, T., & Liang, L. (2016). From cyber-physical systems to Industry 4.0: Make future manufacturing become possible. *International Journal of Manufacturing Research*, *11*(2), 167–188. DOI: 10.1504/IJMR.2016.078251

Zimbalist, A. (2015). *Circus Maximus: The Economic Gamble Behind Hosting the Olympics and the World Cup*. Brookings Press. DOI: 10.5040/9780815751694

Zoghlami, N., Taghipour, A., Merlo, C., & Abed, M. (2016). Management of divergent production network using decentralised multi-level capacitated lot-sizing models. *International Journal of Shipping and Transport Logistics*, *8*(5), 590–604. DOI: 10.1504/IJSTL.2016.078686

Zouari, D., Ruel, S., & Viale, L. (2020). Does digitalising the supply chain contribute to its resilience? *International Journal of Physical Distribution & Logistics Management*, *51*(2), 149–180. DOI: 10.1108/IJPDLM-01-2020-0038

About the Contributors

Atour Taghipour is a professor in Supply Chain Management and Operations at the Conservatoire National des Arts et Métiers (CNAM) in Paris, France. He holds a PhD in Industrial Engineering and is affiliated with the LIRSA research laboratory (EA 4603), where his work focuses on sustainable supply chain design, digital transformation in logistics, and production systems optimization. Dr. Taghipour has published numerous articles in peer-reviewed journals and contributes actively to interdisciplinary projects at the intersection of data science, resilience, and responsible management. He regularly supervises doctoral research in the areas of supply chain resilience, circular economy, and AI applications in operations. He is also involved in international teaching and research collaborations, particularly in Europe and Asia.

***

Lamia Ben Fredj-Ben Alaya is an Assistant Professor of Production and Operations Management at IHEC - University of Carthage, Tunisia. She obtained her PhD in Management from Pierre Mendès France University in Grenoble, France, after completing her academic background in Production Management in Tunisia. Lamia has supervised many Master's theses on various topics related to Industrial and Logistics Management. Her teaching and research interests focus on Production/Quality Management, SCM, Lean Manufacturing, and Performance Measurement Systems. She has extensive experience as a Senior Consultant, leading or coordinating industrial reorganisation projects for many national and multinational companies in Tunisia.

Othman Boulitama, who holds a PhD in Management Sciences, has received advanced academic training and built a distinguished career marked by successful teaching experience at different educational levels. His expertise notably encompasses the teaching of finance and logistics, fields in which he has consistently combined scientific rigor with an innovative pedagogical approach. He also serves as a reviewer for the Journal of Information and Knowledge Management (JIKM) as well as for books and journals published by IGI Global, while concurrently holding the position of Associate Editor of the International Journal of Innovation, Digital Economy and Management Sciences (IJIDEMS). Recognized for his ability to adopt and integrate new teaching methods, he is committed to creating a stimulating learning environment that fosters both knowledge acquisition and the personal development of students. His patience, rigor, and strong organizational skills constitute the foundations of his professional commitment. Driven by a sustained passion for education and research, he continues his academic work with the aim of exploring new perspectives and actively contributing to the advancement of pedagogical and scientific practices in the field of management sciences.

Swapna Choudhary obtained her Bachelor's degree in Electronics Engineering from RTM University, Nagpur in 2003, her Master's degree in VLSI in 2010, and her Ph.D. in Electronics from the same university in 2022. She has published more than 35 papers in reputed journals and conferences. Her research interests include Networking, Communication, and VLSI.

Alaa Eddine El Moussaoui, Ph.D., is a Professor of Logistics affiliated with the EMIO, LIREEM Laboratory, Higher School of Technology – Nador, Mohammed First University, Oujda, Morocco. He received his Ph.D. in Urban Logistics in 2023 from the National School of Business and Management of Tangier (ENCG Tangier), Abdelmalek Essaâdi University, with co-supervision from KEDGE Business School, Paris, France. His research interests include logistics and supply chain management, urban logistics, e-commerce, transportation, artificial intelligence, machine learning, sustainability, and operations management. He has authored numerous publications in internationally indexed journals, focusing on last-mile logistics, digital transformation, consumer behavior, and AI-driven decision-making in logistics and supply chain management.

Taoufiq El Moussaoui is a Professor of Computer Science at the Polydisciplinary Faculty of Sidi Bennour, Chouaib Doukkali University, El Jadida, Morocco. His research interests include artificial intelligence, text mining, pattern recognition, supply chain management, transport, and smart cities.

Rajiv Ghai is an active academian working in Department of Computer Science and Engineering, Surajmal University, Kichha, U.K, India.

Pushpa Kataria is working as an professsor in Doon Business School, DBS Global University Dehradun, U.K, India

Mohammed Irfan Khan is working as Assistant Professor in Mechanical Engineering Department since 2012. He has done his B.E in Mechanical Engineering and M.E in Industrial Engineering and Management. He completed his PhD in the area of Composite Material and Design. He is currently pursuing M.Tech. in Artificial Intelligence

Geetha MN completed her B.E. Degree in Instrumentation technology from Mysore University in the year 1994, MTech in VLSI Design and Embedded Systems from VTU in 2011 and PhD in 2023 from VTU under the guidance of Dr. U.B. Mahadevaswamy. She is presently working as an Assistant Professor in the Department of Electronics and Communication, VVCE, Mysore, Karnataka, India

Rajlaxmi Pujar is Associate Professor at Indira University, School of Business, Pune. She is a Marketing Faculty with total 26 years' experience, 10yrs in industry and 16yrs in academics. She has presented and published 29 research papers in various National and International Journals including 4 Scopus indexed papers and 3 ABDC. Her interest lies in marketing subjects like Sales and channel management, Integrated marketing communication, Tourism and hospitality marketing, Consumer Behaviour etc.

Priyanka Rana is an academician with over 22 Years of rich experience in teaching, research, and publications. She worked as an Assistant Professor and Head at Lucknow Institute of Technology. She also worked as an Associate Professor and Head at ICRI Bangalore. She has delivered her services in various other colleges. Dr. Rana has several patents published under her name. she is a keen learner and dedicated to imparting value and quality education to students. She has published several research papers on various topics benefitting different lines of society. Also, she has presented various papers in International, National and State level Seminars and Workshops. She is LL.M. and Ph.D. Economics. Her areas of interest revolve around the upliftment of society and women's empowerment.

Amrita Sekhon (MCA, M.Phil-CS, M.Tech-IT, UGC-NET, Ph.D.) Dr. Amrita Sekhon is an accomplished academician and researcher in the field of Computer Science with over two decades of teaching and administrative experience. She completed her Ph.D. in Computer Science from Punjabi University, Patiala in July 2025 on the topic "Design of a Unified Smart Identity based Online Single Window System for E-Governance – Towards Digital Punjab." Currently serving as Assistant Professor of Computer Science at Bibi Sharan Kaur Khalsa College, Sri Chamkaur

Sahib since 2016, she also holds additional roles as Nodal Officer for NEP-2020 Implementation, Coordinator of NPTEL-SPOC, Coordinator of Learning Support Centre- JGND PSOU, Patiala and Co-Coordinator of NIOS Study Centre. Her research contributions span AI in education, predictive analytics, e-governance, digital literacy, and high-performance computing. She has authored numerous research papers in Scopus-indexed and peer-reviewed journals, contributed book chapters, co-authored a book on Fundamentals of Information Technology, and presented papers at national and international conferences, including in Japan, Hong Kong, and India. She has also been honored with Best Paper Awards for her scholarly contributions. Dr. Sekhon is actively engaged in capacity building and training initiatives, having organized national seminars, workshops, and training programs, and has participated in several FDPs, refresher courses, and international conferences. She has also been part of prestigious academic bodies such as the Senate and Faculty of Physical Sciences at Punjabi University, Patiala.

Mohd Asif Shah is the Dean of Economics at Kardan University (ACBSP/IACBE/AACSB Accredited), Kabul, Afghanistan. He has previously served as an Associate Professor at Kebri Dehar University, Ethiopia, and Bakhtar University, Afghanistan, and as an Assistant Professor at FBS Business School, Bangalore, and Lovely Professional University (AACSB Accredited), Punjab, India. He holds a PhD, M.A., and B.A. in Economics, with over ten years of teaching and research experience across India, Afghanistan, and Ethiopia. He also serves as an Adjunct Professor at leading universities in India and Afghanistan. Dr. Shah has published 300+ research papers in SCI/SCIE/Scopus/WoS-indexed journals, holds 100+ patents, and has received 5000+ citations. He has participated in 30+ faculty development programs sponsored by the Government of India and is a frequent keynote speaker at international conferences and seminars.

Vikas Sharma is an active academician and researcher in the field of computer science with 8 years of experience. He earned M. Tech degree specialized in Computer Science. He is involved in academic development and scholarly activities. He is member of International Association of Engineers, The Society of Digital Information and Wireless Communications, Global Professors Welfare Association, International Association of Academic plus Corporate (IAAC), Computer Science Teachers Association and Internet Society. His research interest includes Cloud Computing, Artificial Intelligence, Machine Learning; published more than 60 research articles with 4 books and 95 book chapters in edited books. He is contributing as member of editorial and reviewers' boards in conferences and various computer journals and edited books published by Elsevier, CRC Press,

Taylor and Francis, Springer, IGI global, Wiley Publication, IET Publication, De Gruyter, River Publication etc.

M. Srinu received the B.Tech. degree in Electronics and Communication Engineering from, JNTU Hyderabad, India, in2007, and the M.Tech. degree from NIT, Calicut India, in 2011. He is currently working towards the Ph.D. degree from the OSMANIA University, Hyderabad, India. His-current research interests Low power memory circuits

Shashiraj Teotia is working as Associate Professor in the Department of Computer Application, Swami Vivekanand Subharti university Meerut. He has total 18 years of experience in teaching and research. He is an active member of IAENG AND IJMRA. He has published about 40 publications in various national and international journals. Four various books.

Varadharajan Bhoopathy is a Professor at Sree Rama Engineering College. He holds a Ph.D. in Information and Communication Engineering from Anna University and has over 16 years of academic experience. Specializing in wireless sensor networks and IoT, he has published numerous research papers and holds several international patents. Dr. Bhoopathy is a recipient of prestigious awards for his contributions to education and research. His commitment to academia continues to drive innovation and excellence in the field of computer science.

Tarun Kumar Vashishth is an active academician and researcher in the field of Computer Science with 22 years of experience. He earned Ph.D. Mathematics degree specialized in Operations Research; served several academic positions such as Dy. Director, HoD, NAAC Coordinator, Academic Coordinator, Member Secretary of Department Research Committee, Assistant Center Superintendent and Head Examiner in University Examinations. He is involved in academic development and scholarly activities. He is member of International Association of Engineers, The Society of Digital Information and Wireless Communications, Global Professors Welfare Association, International Association of Academic plus Corporate (IAAC), Computer Science Teachers Association and Internet Society . His research interest includes Cloud Computing, Artificial Intelligence, Machine Learning and Operations Research; published more than 50 research articles & conference papers with 2 book and 80 book chapters. He is contributing as member of editorial and reviewer's boards in conferences and various computer journals and edited books published by Elsevier, CRC Press, Taylor and Francis, Springer, IGI global, Wiley Publication, IET Publication, De Gruyter, River Publication etc.

Pushpendra Kumar Verma is an Associate Professor at IIMT University, Meerut, India, holding degrees in MCA, MTech-CSE, MPhil (CS), and a Doctorate in Computer Science. His research expertise lies in Cryptography, Network Security, and Cyber Security, with additional specialization in AI, Deep Learning, and Machine Learning. With 19+ years of teaching and research experience, he has participated in high-profile conferences, published research papers in international journals and Scopus Indexed Journals, reviewed reputed international journal papers, and held memberships in Vidwan, Springer, IAENG, SDIWC, IEEE, and more.

Index

A

B

C

D

E

T

www.ingramcontent.com/pod-product-compliance
Lightning Source LLC
LaVergne TN
LVHW081534300926
849161LV00006B/1428